VOLUME THREE

BURMA'S VOICES
of FREEDOM

―――――

In Conversation with Alan Clements
AN ONGOING STRUGGLE *for* DEMOCRACY

By **ALAN CLEMENTS**
and **FERGUS HARLOW**

WORLD DHARMA PUBLICATIONS
©2020

VOLUME THREE

BURMA'S VOICES *of* FREEDOM

In Conversation with Alan Clements
AN ONGOING STRUGGLE *for* DEMOCRACY

"By dedicating her life to the fight for human rights and Democracy in Burma, Aung San Suu Kyi is not only speaking out for justice in her own country, but also for all those who want to be free to choose their own destiny. As long as the struggle for freedom needs to be fought throughout the world, voices such as Aung San Suu Kyi's will summon others to the cause. Whether the cry for freedom comes from central Europe, Russia, Africa, or Asia, it has a common sound: all people must be treated with dignity; all people need to hope."

~ **VACLAV HAVEL**, FORMER PRESIDENT OF
THE CZECH REPUBLIC

WORLD DHARMA PUBLICATIONS

Published in 2020 by WORLD DHARMA PUBLICATIONS
Copyright © Alan Clements 1997, 2008, 2012, 2020

Alan Clements has asserted his right to be identified as the author of this
Work in accordance with the Copyright, Designs and Patents Act 1988.
All rights reserved. No part of this publication may be reproduced, stored
in a retrieval system, or transmitted in any form or by any means, electronic,
mechanical, photocopying, recording or otherwise, without the prior permission
of the copyright owner/author.

Cover design by World Dharma Publications
Typography by World Dharma Publications

Library of Congress Cataloging-in-Publication Data

Clements, Alan 1951 —
Burma's Voices of freedom:
An Ongoing Struggle for Democracy
p. cm.
ISBN 978-1-953508-06-5
1. Biography 2. International Relations. 3. Political. 4. Liberty — freedom — Buddhism 5. Spiritual life — Buddhism— non-sectarian 6. Human rights — all aspects 7. Social, Political and Environmental justice — all 8. Activism — all 9. Consciousness — all 10. Politics — global 11. Body, Mind & Spirit

First printing, September 1, 2020

World Dharma Publications

www.WorldDharma.com

TABLE OF CONTENTS

Chapter 26: Conversations with Aung San Suu Kyi 5
Chapter 27: Conversations with Kyaw Zwa Moe 51
Chapter 28: Conversation with Nilar Thein 91
Chapter 29: Conversations with Moe Thway 101
Chapter 30: Conversations with The Moustache Brothers 133
Chapter 31: Conversation with Bo Kyi 149
Chapter 32: Conversation with Phyu Phyu Kyaw Thein 173
Chapter 33: Conversations with Ma Thida Sanchuang 189
Chapter 34: Conversations with Mon Mon Myat 211
Chapter 35: Conversations with Tim Aye-Hardy 243
Chapter 36: Conversation with an Anonymous Activist 299
Chapter 37: Conversation with an Anonymous Pro-Democracy
              Activist 317
Chapter 38: Conversation with Ko Ye Wai Phyo 331
Chapter 39: Conversations with Daw Than Than Nu 351
Photographic Section 395
Author Profiles 457

INDEX OF FURTHER CHAPTERS IN THE SERIES

Volume 1

Introduction
Chapter 1: Conversations with Aung San Suu Kyi
Chapter 2: Excerpts from Selected Interviews with Aung San Suu Kyi
Chapter 3: Excerpts from Key Speeches by Aung San Suu Kyi
Chapter 4: Aung San Suu Kyi Quotes
Chapter 5: Aung San Suu Kyi Timeline
Chapter 6: Conversations with U Tin Oo
Chapter 7: Conversations with U Win Tin
Chapter 8: Conversations with U Win Htein
Photographic Section
Author Profiles

Volume 2

Chapter 9: Conversations with Aung San Suu Kyi
Chapter 10: Conversation with U Kyi Maung
Chapter 11: Conversation with Nine NLD MPs
Chapter 12: Conversation with U Aye Win
Chapter 13: Conversation with Zeya Thaw
Chapter 14: Conversation with Zin Mar Aung
Chapter 15: Conversation with Nay Phone Latt
Chapter 16: Conversation with U Nyan Win
Chapter 17: Conversation with NLD Chairman
Chapter 18: Conversations with Ko Ko Gyi
Chapter 19: Conversation with Min Ko Naing
Chapter 20: Conversations with Sayadaw U Pandita
Chapter 21: Conversation with Sittigu Sayadaw
Chapter 22: Conversation with Cardinal Charles Bo
Chapter 23: Conversations with Al Hajj Nyunt Maung Shein
Chapter 24: Preface to Burma's Saffron Revolution
Chapter 25: Conversations with U Gambira
Photographic Section
Author Profiles

Volume 4

Chapter 40: Conversations with Aung San Suu Kyi
Appendix 1: Introduction to Burma's Revolution of the Spirit
Appendix 2: A Journey into the Heart of Burma
Appendix 3: A Chronology of Key Events in Myanmar
Appendix 4: Selected Articles and Speeches about Democracy and Reconciliation
Appendix 5: Selected Interviews with Alan Clements, 1988 – Present
Photographic Section
Author Profiles

CHAPTER 26

CONVERSATIONS *with* AUNG SAN SUU KYI

1996

> *"The admission of injustice, to a certain extent,*
> *will prevent it from happening again."*

ALAN CLEMENTS: I think it was His Holiness the Dalai Lama who said that we should "foster an appreciation—a real love for our shared human status." There is something beautiful and appealing about the notion. And yet it seems foreign.... When I conjure up ghastly images of Auschwitz and death camps, the sea of cracked skulls from Pol Pot's killing fields, hacked-up bodies of Rwandan Hutus, or women screaming in Serbian rape camps, my heart closes. I wonder if the perpetrators of such atrocities can even be considered as human beings. Quite frankly, they seem sub-human. And Daw Suu, you seem to live and breathe your country's suffering. How do you manage to keep your heart open to the pain?

AUNG SAN SUU KYI: It depends on the circles in which you move. I think I'm very fortunate that the people around me have such open hearts. Because we can afford to be loving with each other, the habit of opening our hearts is always there. Also, if you know that there are people in the world who are worthy of love, and whom you could open up to without danger, I think you are more ready to accept that there are others too who could be lovable.

AC: I'll be specific. How do you look into the eyes of SLORC without feeling a sense of outrage, really?

ASSK: People often come to me and ask the same question: "Why don't you feel any sense of vindictiveness?" I think some of the people who ask this question don't believe that we are actually free from such feelings. It's very difficult to explain. The other day Uncle U Kyi Maung, Uncle U Tin Oo and I were talking with a group of our NLD delegates and we were laughing over this. Apparently, you had asked Uncle U Kyi Maung how he felt the day he heard I was going to be placed under arrest. And he replied that he didn't feel anything at all. And you were surprised by that...

AC: Not only surprised, but I was shocked. Because what he said was that despite the fact that armed soldiers had surrounded your house, and it was likely that you would be taken to Insein Prison, you all just laughed about the crisis and started cracking jokes.

ASSK: Yes, and we didn't feel anything at all. So many journalists have asked me; "How did you feel when you were released?" I have said, "I felt nothing at all." (*laughing*) I had a vague idea that I should feel something, but my real concern was what should I do now? Then a journalist asked if I were elated or felt happy. I said, "No...none of these things. I always knew that I was going to be free one day. The point was, well, what do I do now?" But a lot of people don't believe me.

AC: They assume that it's some form of denial or repression in you?

ASSK: Exactly. (*laughing*) It's very strange.

AC: When you speak of "feeling nothing at all" after your release from detention, are you saying that the past is simply irrelevant?

ASSK: I don't think you can just forget the past but one should use experiences of the past to build up a better present and future.

AC: What about the victims who don't have the resiliency or the depth of spirit that you and your colleagues have, and do feel violated and made resentful by the atrocities committed towards them?

ASSK: Of course. Of course. This is why we are talking about the connection of truth and reconciliation. I think that first of all, their sufferings have to be acknowledged. You can't just wipe away the past. If you try, there will always be this ocean of festering resentment within those who have truly suffered. They will feel that their sufferings have been pushed aside, as though they've suffered for nothing; as though they've undergone torture for nothing; as though their sons and fathers had died for nothing. Those people must have the satisfaction of knowing that their sufferings have not been in vain, and this very fact, that there's an admission of the injustice done, will take away a lot of the resentment. Mind you, people are different. Some will always want vengeance and will keep on thirsting for it even if everyone says: "Yes, we know how you've suffered; we acknowledge the wrong that has been done to you or your father, or your son or daughter." There will always be people who can never forgive. But we must always try to. In Chile they had a Council for Truth and Reconciliation and there's one now in South Africa, under Archbishop Desmond Tutu. I very much believe in it. The admission of injustice, to a certain extent, will prevent it from happening again. People will realize that if you do such things, they get known. You can't hide them.

AC: Do you think it's essentially a human right that some form of justice is still required, beyond just an acknowledgment of the anguish and suffering a family or an individual has been forced to bear?

ASSK: Let's consider it as satisfaction rather than as a need for justice. If you talk about justice as a "human right" it could be misinterpreted as something done under the law. In many countries where dictatorships have fallen and democracies have arisen, you will find that it's not always possible to take full legal action against those who have perpetrated injustices. For various reasons there have had to be compromises. So if one talks about "justice," it might give the wrong impression that everything that has happened must be tried in a court, and that justice must be done in the legal sense. I would rather say that something must be done to satisfy the victims and the families of those victims.

AC: I was speaking to a Burmese friend of mine the other day and he gave an impassioned appeal on behalf of what he called the "88 generation," those university students who spearheaded the mass demonstrations. He said, "We feel hopeless, despairing and aimless. SLORC crushed our hopes of freedom." I would like to take the issue beyond Burma. What advice might you offer to such people living in such psychological pain?

ASSK: The only cure is work. I think that those who are really doing everything they can, whatever it is, do not feel either despair or hopelessness, because they're involved in the doing. To those who say that they are in such states of mind, one must ask: "Are you doing everything you can?" And I think, if the answer is truly "Yes," then you feel neither hopeless nor despairing.

AC: Experience shows that there is often a lag period between the trauma and the action to overcome it. It's a temporary paralysis of the spirit, so to speak. How can one breathe positive significance into despair and hopelessness? How might one give it spiritual meaning and value and turn it around to make it work in his favor?

ASSK: Let me try to explain this with a very down-to-earth example. I have often noticed this: when there is a simple household crisis, such as for example, the pressure-cooker bursting and throwing soup all over the kitchen ceiling, my first reaction is: "All right, calm down." Just tackle it. Because if you just stand there saying, "The pressure-cooker has burst and it's spurting all over the place," you can get into an absolute tizz. But my reaction is to say, "Well, there's no point getting into a tizz. I can't wish the soup back into the pressure-cooker simmering away in safety. I've just got to get on with cleaning it up." So I turn off the gas, and then I get a rag to clean up the mess. That in itself calms you down. You've got to work. If you're apathetic or filled with hopelessness and despair you've got to do what you can. I can't do anything about the fact that I have lost half the soup. But I can certainly clean up all traces of the disaster. Then I can start thinking, "Now, should I cook a bit more soup? Or should I supplement it with something else?" You get down to work and don't just stand there despairing. That's what I would say to people who feel hopeless and despairing: "Don't just sit there. Do something."

AC: So, in other words, the positive action itself is the healing?

ASSK: Yes. There's always something you can do if you really put your mind to it. I do believe that.

AC: Do you feel that there is ever a need for intimate discussion about the often traumatizing emotions of despair and grief without being indulgent?

ASSK: Of course there is. After all, the bursting of a pressure-cooker is a very minor crisis. But with big crises, for example the loss of a loved one, I believe that people must be allowed to talk about it and work through their feelings. But at the same time, you must encourage these people to get on with life; not to just sit and grieve over the person they have lost. So you have got to give them all the emotional support you can, but also try to find something practical for them to do. Such as, to think of those who are still alive and to do something for them.

AC: On the opposite side of things, with your enormous regard and compassion for the victims of suffering, are you also considering how to create safe conditions for the authorities when the struggle for democracy is successfully achieved? Because in a sense, they too are victims, so to speak, of their own fear and self-deception.

ASSK: It is too premature to talk about these things. Such matters should only be discussed when one enters into dialogue. But we do not want to penalize anyone, as such. We want a society where the healing process can take place quickly and that process must involve the satisfaction, to some extent, of the victims.

AC: Healing implies the perception of wound—a psychological trauma or series of them that occurred in the past. But the Buddha insisted that he could not see a first beginning to suffering nor a first cause for the arising of afflictive emotions. Therefore, he encouraged his followers to seek liberation only in the present and not by delving into the past. To explain this point, he used the simile of a man shot with a poisoned arrow. You might know it...

ASSK: That's right...

AC: So. This man is lying on the ground wounded and dying. As the Buddha attempts to save the man's life by pulling out the arrow, the man stops him and says: "Before you remove the arrow I want to know who shot me? Why did he shoot me? From what tree was the shaft of the arrow carved?" And so on and so forth, until the man dies. So my question is, how do the Buddha's teachings of "non-postponement" to the release of suffering fit into your idea of the healing process?

ASSK: There are some things that have to be done immediately and there are other things that have to be done later. Take something similar to the story of the arrow; if somebody is brought in as an emergency case—you immediately give him emergency treatment. But later, it may be necessary to go into the origin of whatever it is he's suffering from, in order for the healing process to be more effective. Now using the simile of the poisoned arrow, the first things to be done would be to pull it out, clean the wound, and dress it. Of course, that's not the moment to be inquiring into what kind of poison it was. But afterwards, it will be necessary to find out what sort of poison was on the arrow in order to give it the right antidote. So everything at the right time.

AC: In your "Freedom from Fear" essay [first published in July 1991, reprinted in *Freedom from Fear* published by Penguin Books, revised edition 1995] you quoted somebody, I'm not sure who it was, who said, "Saints are sinners who go on trying..."

ASSK: Yes. I can't remember who said or wrote it but I came across it a long time ago and I've always liked it very much.

AC: I like it too. Which brings me to the question. Prior to becoming a disciple, Saint Paul, known then as Saul of Tarsus, killed many people, including children, who espoused Christianity. Within the Buddhist tradition we also have examples of archetypal redemption, such as Angulimala—the mass murderer who changed and became a monk, and later achieved enlightenment...

ASSK: I wonder how old they were when they were converted? Do you know how old Angulimala was when he was changed by the Buddha?

AC: Well, from some of the temple paintings I've seen of him he's depicted as rather young...

ASSK: I think he was supposed to be quite young. Because he had started on his finger-collecting business quite early, hadn't he?

AC: To have cut a finger off every victim and to have reached 999 murders he must have started early. But such dramatic spiritual conversions...

ASSK: You mean the blinding flash of light kind of conversion?

AC: No...how should I say it? It's so easy to segregate life into neat little ethical compartments of right and wrong, good and bad, moral and immoral, as if someone really had a hold on omnipotence. And if we don't open to a bigger picture, say as in these examples of redemption, the power of this quote is drastically reduced, if not lost altogether. I would like to understand how to feel more compassion for those who are considered as a menace to society? At times I have considered that capital punishment would be a good thing...

ASSK: Do you really think so?

AC: Would I want, on a personal level, someone to die for his crime? The closest I can get to that issue in truth, is no, I don't think so. However, I do know that if a killer hacked up my loved ones I'd be pressed to the edge and might seek revenge...

ASSK: But if you're a good Buddhist, shouldn't you be trying to change yourself rather than wishing that capital punishment would get rid of them?

AC: Well, all I'm saying is that some people do seem irredeemable. They're "natural born killers" who seem to have a perverse pleasure in making others suffer.

ASSK: How do you know they are irredeemable?

AC: I don't. It just seems rather likely from their behavior.... What do you think?

ASSK: I'm not in a position to decide who is redeemable and who's not. Just because I'm not able to redeem people doesn't mean that they are irredeemable. There are others who may be able to.

AC: Violence is just about everywhere we turn today. Many of our inner cities are war zones. Crime is the number one fear among most Americans. And in Burma today, the repression is escalating all the time. What is the driving force that allows one to keep on going when faced with cruel repression?

ASSK: My colleagues and I have been discussing this issue quite a lot lately. I think it's difficult to find an answer, but there is something innate in every human being. Although this is something that can be adapted, or changed, or made to take a more positive direction, some by nature are more inclined than others to taking a strong position. Of course, the social and political climate has a lot to do with it too. It is amazing to me how so many people simply do what they're told by the authorities. They've been conditioned to obey without questioning the situation. Which is why I always tell them to keep a questing mind. A questing mind is a great help towards withstanding violence or oppression, or any trend that is contrary to what you believe is right and just.

AC: What about the issue of turning away in the face of suffering, especially for those who're responding to their instinct to serve? Is it self-deception, yet another face of fear that masquerades as legitimate avoidance whereby one is paralyzed in spirit and soul from actually doing something to help? I know good people who want to serve, to give back to life, to support the oppressed, but the discussion often ends with who gets what, where, when and how?

ASSK: Well, if you have a mind that is always "questing" you'll find the answers; if you're always thinking of the ways and means of doing something to serve, you will. The "seeker" has the kind of mind that is not just questioning, but actually seeking answers. That is why I say a "questing mind" rather than a questioning mind.

AC: I've seen that many people pressure themselves when the "questing mind" turns rancid, into guilt or fear. Then one hurts to serve, so to speak, and loses the love of service. So is it fair to say that people should not pressure themselves into service but just keep an active inquiry?

ASSK: It's a beginning. Action comes out of thought. It should not be the kind of impulsive action that has no principle behind it. So I think, a first step is the questing process of looking for answers and searching for a way out of any problem. The second step is to put the answers into action.

AC: Going back to 1988. From what I understand, when the National League for Democracy was founded there were three factions that joined into one, and the group that you headed represented Burma's intellectuals—the artists, musicians, lawyers...

ASSK: Yes.

AC: I brought with me a quote from Václav Havel in which he explains the role of the intellectual within society. When I first read it, I instantly thought of you. He writes: "The intellectual should constantly disturb, should bear witness to the misery of the world, should be provocative by being independent, should rebel against all hidden and open pressures and manipulations, should be the chief doubter of systems...and for this reason, an intellectual cannot fit into any role that might be assigned to him...and essentially doesn't belong anywhere: he stands out as an irritant wherever he is."

ASSK: I would agree with everything that Václav Havel says. I would say that basically, in order to become an intellectual you've got to have a questioning mind. I think everybody is capable of having a questioning mind, but not everybody who has one can be described as an intellectual. To be an intellectual also requires some kind of scholastic discipline—that's essential. Intellectuals are very important in any society. Because they are the ones who, like in the quotation, are provoking people, opening them to new ideas, pushing them along to new heights. This is one of the tragedies of Burma—the intellectual is not allowed any place within society. And the real intellectual, of the kind described by Václav Havel, would not be allowed to survive in Burma.

AC: Why?

ASSK: He would either have to repress his instincts as an intellectual, or he would have to leave Burma, or he would have to go and sit in prison. He's got to choose between those three.

AC: So by function, a totalitarian regime attempts to create a mindless, featureless society by crushing the intellectual?

ASSK: The intellectual with his questioning mind threatens the totalitarian mind which expects orders to be carried out and decrees to be accepted without question. There will always be clashes between the authoritarian mind and the questioning mind. They just cannot go together.

AC: But of course, that's the very task you're confronted with in seeking genuine dialogue and potential reconciliation with SLORC.

ASSK: It doesn't mean that because you are part of an authoritarian regime, you don't have a spark of questioning in your mind.

AC: What is the chief factor that promotes the questioning mind?

ASSK: To begin with, you must have an interest in the world around you. If you're deaf and blind to it you won't question what is going on.

AC: Is the non-questioning mind an issue of unrecognized fright?

ASSK: No, I don't think it's just fright. Obviously, we're all born different and upbringing comes into it as well. One may be born with a questioning mind, but it may not have been encouraged, so it could get blunted. If you're bludgeoned every time you raise a question then you learn not to raise questions. And in time, you probably forget how to question. Even if you're not born with a questioning mind, you could be encouraged to acquire the habit. My mother did not encourage me to question, but she certainly never discouraged me either. She didn't say, "Ask questions." But when I asked questions she was always there even if she could not provide the answers.

And then of course, we were brought up on the legend of Pauk Kyine. One of the maxims that we learned from the legend was that if you go on questioning, you receive answers. If you go on traveling, you will reach your goal. If you keep alert and don't sleep much, you will have a long life. This is what we were taught as children. And most Burmese children know this story so well they've learned the maxims by heart. See in that story, the hero saves his life by staying alert throughout the night and by keeping close watch on the world around him.

AC: Perhaps it's impossible to know, but how have you come to have such a love of truth?

ASSK: I was not born with it. It was a matter of training. My mother was insistent on my being honest. In fact, she would get very angry if I didn't tell the truth...

AC: Did she actually explain to you an underlying principle or logic as to why honesty was preferable to deception?

ASSK: She did not always explain why it was necessary to be honest. She just made it very clear that honesty was good and dishonesty was wrong. This was something that I accepted at a very early age. My mother was naturally brave and honest—all those things I had to work to be. That was really good for me because it gives me the confidence that other people too can work towards such qualities.

AC: You seem to keep a relentless pace, meeting hundreds of people weekly. Also, there's a nearly endless line of foreign journalists seeking interviews with you. There are your weekend public talks and then your NLD EC meetings, with decisions that might affect millions of lives. How do you keep up the intensity? Do you ever have to stop and reconnect to that place of inner calm, in order to keep on going?

ASSK: I stop every evening, because in the evening I'm all alone and it's an automatic way of standing back from the action. Of course, there are times when I have to work very late into the night. Then I don't have much time to sit and take stock. The moment I finish work I just go straight to bed. But normally I get a few days a week when everything is quiet by seven o'clock at night and I'm alone in the house. It makes me realize there is always change. Life, in a sense, is lived on two levels, the hurly-burly of the world outside and the quietness of your inner life. And that's brought home to me practically every evening.

AC: When you do have these precious few moments alone at night, what do you normally do?

ASSK: It depends. Sometimes I have to do the most mundane things, like tidying my clothes or my desk. Sometimes I sit and read. I have to say that quite a lot of the time when I finish early, on those two or three days a week, would be taken up with tidying up the mess that has accumulated. But it's quite peaceful. It's manual work. I just put the right things in the right place, that's all. It's almost mechanical.

AC: Are you super-organized?

ASSK: I used to be super-organized. I knew exactly where each book or each magazine was. But I'm afraid I'm not so super-organized since my release. I've just had no time to put everything away in its own place.

AC: Do you ever get to a point and say, the heck with it, I'm exhausted, enough for today?

ASSK: Sometimes I am exhausted. I would like to sleep for about twelve hours at a stretch or just stay in bed for a whole weekend, two days of nothing—except reading for pleasure. That would be my idea of a really good holiday. But, I just don't have the time to do that.

AC: Since the time of your release—do you ever do anything just for the fun of it?

ASSK: There's a lot of fun in my daily life. The people I work with are so nice and they all have such a good sense of humor. Yesterday we had a joint birthday party for two of my cousins, Dr. Sein Win [the Prime Minister of Burma's government-in-exile] and Ko Cho. We had our *lugyi's* come over—our elders as we call them—U Aung Shwe, U Kyi Maung, U Tin Oo, U Lwin [EC members of the NLD] and our aunties—their wives. It was a simple party; not much apart from cake, tea and potato chips. But it was fun. We all had a really nice time. And every day too, there is a lot of joy and happiness—speaking with my colleagues, having lunch together with the office staff—just being with such good people struggling together, is in itself nourishing and replenishing. So I'm lucky to be surrounded by such great people.

AC: Besides being NLD colleagues, who are U Tin Oo and U Kyi Maung to you? Since they are both quite a bit older than you, are they your mentors or father figures as well?

ASSK: I look upon them as my uncles. Uncles are people who stand in for your father. So I do look upon them, in a sense, as father figures. But at the same time, when we work together they are very much my colleagues. On a daily basis they're friends too. Except I don't like to talk to them as friends, because that puts them on the same level as me. I like to think of them as higher, because they're older, and in that sense, I do look up to them. And yet, friends are the most precious things in the world. Friends mean more than anything else to me. So without intending any disrespect perhaps I could say they are two of my best friends—or to use that old phrase, "guide, mentor and friend." They are very different in character but both are equally endearing and equally trustworthy.

*"The greater sacrifice
was giving up my sons."*

ALAN CLEMENTS: Prior to your return to Burma in March 1988, you had been living a classic householder's life in Oxford. That is, until you received word that your mother had suffered a stroke, at which point you flew to Rangoon to be with her. Five months later you were at the center of a nationwide revolution with you as the principal leader. Was it a dramatic transformation for you, or was it a more gradual transition?

AUNG SAN SUU KYI: I was gradually drawn into the movement. To begin with, I was sitting in the hospital looking after my mother and I heard what was going on. Then people would come and talk with me about it, how bad the political and economic situation was. I did not say much, I just listened.

AC: There was no moment of epiphany when you realized that this was the moment for you to enter your people's democracy struggle?

ASSK: No. I don't remember such a moment. It was much more gradual.

AC: So when you came back to Burma to be with your ailing mother, you had no idea whatsoever that you would enter politics?

ASSK: I hadn't even an idea that the democracy struggle was going to take place like that. I don't think anybody did. I did know that things were going to change in Burma because people were extremely unhappy and restless by 1987. They were also more outspoken and openly dissatisfied with the situation. And before I came in at the end of March, the problems with the students had already begun. On 13 March, Maung Phong Maw [a student from the Rangoon Institute of Technology] was killed. So by the time I arrived I knew that things were happening. In that sense, I knew as others did, that Burma was not going to remain quiescent. But I don't think I knew any more than anybody else that there would be such widespread demonstrations for democracy.

AC: During your years abroad, knowing well the conditions your people were living under, did you feel a constant angst, wanting to do something for your people but not knowing how to go about it?

ASSK: No. Of course, I did not like the situation. During my visits to Rangoon I would sometimes spend three or four months with my mother, and always when friends came over, at some time or the other, the conversation would inevitably turn towards the situation of the country.

AC: When you look back to that period, reflecting on the crisis in your country, could you envision the light of political change? It had such a rock-solid dictatorship for over three decades.

ASSK: Always throughout those years I had been very well aware of the fact that the majority of Burmese were growing more and more dissatisfied with the situation. So a lot of us believed that there would have to be a change.

AC: Did you have any idea of how or when that change would occur?

ASSK: No.

AC: Once the demonstrations began, were people prepared for such a violent military response? Did anyone anticipate it? Then again, as I think about it, Ne Win has had a long history of quelling dissent with violence.

ASSK: There had already been a couple of students who had been shot dead. So I don't think it was entirely unexpected.

AC: Did you participate in the demonstrations?

ASSK: No.

AC: Was it a matter of policy?

ASSK: No. It was partly because I was constantly looking after my mother in the hospital when the demonstrations took place. But I don't think I would have taken part in the demonstrations anyway. If you ask why, I'm just the sort of person who generally does not like to take part in demonstrations. Although if I felt that there was a need to do so, I probably would have.

AC: But you obviously expressed your regard for the vision, the courage and the determination of those students who organized and led them.

ASSK: Oh yes. I admired those who did what they did. I was totally behind what they were doing.

AC: Even though you didn't participate in the demonstrations were you in any way involved in their organization?

ASSK: No. I was just one of the large silent majority who were supporting them.

AC: When did your home become the central coordinating headquarters of the struggle?

ASSK: That was much later—only after about mid-August.

AC: You gave your first public speech at the Shwedagon Pagoda in August 1988, in which you announced your entry into politics. It is said that 500,000 people attended. With so many supporters who came out to see you, did you think that a shift from a dictatorship to democracy was near at hand? Or did you predict it would be a long protracted struggle?

ASSK: At the time I don't think anybody knew how long it was going to take. In fact, a lot of people expected it to come sooner than it has and thought that it would just be a matter of months before democracy was established.

AC: Did you have any prior knowledge of SLORC's takeover on 18 September 1988?

ASSK: There were lots of rumors about a projected military coup.

AC: Did that alter your way of thinking about what would be the best way to approach your nonviolent struggle? And were there preparations you made in anticipation of the coup?

ASSK: What preparations could we make? We were just organizing a more cohesive force for democracy, and that is what we continued doing.

AC: On 19 July 1989, you called off a march for the following day, Martyrs' Day, stating: "We do not want to lead our people straight into a killing field." When you think back to that day—the day before your arrest—and the day commemorating the death of your father—what comes to mind? How do you feel, almost seven years later and after several months of freedom?

ASSK: Well, it was not an easy decision to make. I realized that I would not get hurt...others would have. To carry on would have been irresponsible. If others would have got hurt and I had remained unhurt, it would have been a responsibility I could not have lived with.

AC: Did you know at that time that you would be arrested any day?

ASSK: We had heard for some time that I would be arrested after the 19th of July.

AC: How did you hear?

ASSK: Just rumors, lots of rumors.

AC: May I ask you to describe what actually took place on the day of your arrest?

ASSK: Well, I think in the morning...I'm just trying to remember the exact sequence. One of my cousins came in at one point and said that there were soldiers all over the place and something was happening that was not quite right. Then Uncle U Tin Oo's son drove over and said his father had tried to go out for a walk in the morning and had been forbidden to leave his compound. He thought we were all going to be arrested. So we all took it for granted.

AC: How did you feel emotionally in such a difficult moment?

ASSK: I'm not sure that anything was going on emotionally. I just packed a bag with things to take to prison with me. Because we all thought that we would be taken to Insein Jail.

AC: Was your husband with you at the time?

ASSK: No. But Kim and Alexander were.

AC: Was there some degree of shock or panic within your children?

ASSK: No, not at all. I just explained to them—you know, Michael was due to arrive in a few days' time—that if their father did not arrive in a few days because he was not given a visa or something like that, then arrangements would be made for them to be sent back. I told some relatives that if Michael was not allowed to come in, they should just arrange for the children to be sent back. That's all. They understood.

AC: Once it was clear that you would not be taken to Insein Prison and that you were being placed under house arrest, you undertook a hunger strike. Were you prepared to go the distance, if necessary?

ASSK: I never say I'm going to do this or that. That is something I've never done, because I know that in politics one has to be flexible. I'm not one of those people who would ever say, hunger strike until death. I think of that as trying to create a zero-sum solution.

AC: Obviously you did it with a very clear purpose in mind.

ASSK: Well, you do it with a particular end in view.

AC: Was there anyone assisting you? Caring for you?

ASSK: My sons were with me. Then Michael arrived a few days later.

AC: That must be a rather dramatic event to watch your wife or your mother go on a hunger strike...

ASSK: Well, you know, we don't go in for melodrama in our family. We just think of the practical aspect of it. I do not encourage melodrama. I don't like it.

AC: You're extremely rational in that regard...

ASSK: No, I just think that melodrama is very silly. One has to live life on an even keel.

AC: What about the simplicity of pure emotions without melodrama?

ASSK: Well, there is nothing to get emotional about. And how is getting emotional going to help? It just uses up more energy.

AC: How long did your hunger strike continue?

ASSK: Eleven days.

AC: What prompted you to end it?

ASSK: Because I came to an arrangement with the authorities, with regard to the young people [NLD youth workers] who had been taken away from the house.

AC: Did the authorities honor that arrangement?

ASSK: Yes, I must say that they did honor it. They said they would treat these young people well, and they did so. They were not tortured. At least the ones who were taken from here.

AC: Did your house arrest essentially mean the cutting of all outside communication? The cutting of the telephone?

ASSK: We found the cutting of the telephone line funny. Because I always thought that it simply meant they switched it off somewhere at the main exchange. Actually no, they just came and cut off the wires of the telephone with a pair of scissors and carried it away. We found that very funny (*laughing*).

AC: Your house arrest was an archetypal sacrifice, if you will. On the one hand were your family and on the other your principles. The SLORC offered you freedom to leave the country if you wanted on the condition that you remain in exile, but obviously you had a deeper conviction in staying in Burma to further the struggle for freedom.

ASSK: As a mother, the greater sacrifice was giving up my sons, but I was always aware of the fact that others had sacrificed more than me. I never forget that my colleagues who are in prison suffer not only physically, but mentally for their families who have no security outside—in the larger prison of Burma under authoritarian rule. Prisoners know that their families have no security at all. The authorities could take action against their families at any time. Because their sacrifices are so much bigger than mine I cannot think of mine as a sacrifice. I think of it as a choice. Obviously, it is not a choice that I made happily, but one that I made without any reservations or hesitation. But I would much rather not have missed all those years of my children's lives. I would much rather have lived together with them.

AC: Has your family been supportive?

ASSK: Well, my family has been very supportive, which helps a great deal. And also, of course, I have not really been cut off entirely from my family. We don't live together, but it did not happen in one fell swoop. When I first entered politics, my family happened to be here with me tending to my mother. So it was not a case of my suddenly leaving them, or they leaving me. It was a more gradual transition which gave us an opportunity to adjust. Apart from the two years and four months during my house arrest when I had no contact with them, there has not been a sharp break.

AC: Do they have any interest in moving here and living with you?

ASSK: No, not at the moment. Nor do I encourage them, because I don't think the authorities would be particularly keen on making life happy for them.

AC: Are you able to stay in communication with them?

ASSK: Yes, they telephone me once a week and write whenever they can.

AC: Daw Suu, if I may I'd like to ask you a personal question. How has all that you have been through affected your marriage?

ASSK: I won't ever talk about my personal relationship with my family members. I believe in privacy.

AC: I fully respect that, but if I may ask you to clarify what are your basic thoughts behind the need for privacy?

ASSK: I believe in people's right to make their own choices, and people's right to their own privacy. It's for them to decide how much they wish to reveal about their private life. It's freedom of choice. There are some people who like to talk about their private lives—they really love it. I have nothing to say to such people. It's not the way I do things, but of course, that is their choice.

AC: But what distinguishes the separation between that which is for the public and that which is private?

ASSK: That which has no bearing on my political work is private, and I only talk about things that concern the public. As I said, personal privacy has to be respected whether it's mine or that of others. I think my colleagues also believe in this. This is why we've never made personal attacks on anybody or referred to their personal lives, or even their foibles.

AC: As a matter of integrity you avoid speaking negatively about people in general?

ASSK: On a personal basis, yes. Of course, we have had to speak about people when it involves political actions.

AC: You posted excerpts of your father's speeches on the walls of the downstairs foyer. What was the purpose of this?

ASSK: I thought it would be educational for the [SLORC] security men who were here.

AC: Did you ever speak with them? Were they friendly?

ASSK: Of course, I talked to them. They were always very polite and some were very friendly.

AC: In a previous conversation of ours, you said: "I never learned to hate my captors, so I never felt frightened." Was your realization of not learning to hate your captors gained through mental reasoning or was it a sudden insight that developed one day when you looked them in the face?

ASSK: I think it has partly to do with my upbringing again. I may have mentioned to you that my mother never taught me to hate even those who killed my father. I never once heard my mother talk with hatred about the men who assassinated my father.

AC: Never?

ASSK: No...and she certainly never said anything to me that would have even made me feel resentful, let alone filled me with hate. Of course I thought before I entered politics in Burma that I was as capable of hate as anyone. However, later I realized that I did not know the feeling of real hatred, but it was something that I could see in my captors.

AC: You could actually see the hatred in the eyes of your captors?

ASSK: Yes, real hate and malice.

AC: May I ask then, what were your feelings towards your captors?

ASSK: I liked most of them as human beings—I could never help seeing the human side of them, what is likable. This is not to say I liked what they did. There are lots of things that they did and they are doing which I do not like at all. You must not think that I was very angelic and never got angry. Of course I got angry. But I never lost sight of the fact that they were human beings. And like all human beings, there's a side to them which must be likable.

AC: Did you turn your house arrest into a monastic-like life?

ASSK: I started off on the basis that I would have to be very disciplined and keep to a strict timetable. I thought that I must not waste my time and let myself go to seed (*laughing*). In fact, I did not find it at all difficult. I found it very easy to adjust to a regular timetable and I had enough to fill my days.

AC: What was your daily schedule?

ASSK: I would get up at 4.30 and meditate for an hour. Then I would listen to the radio for about an hour and a half. Then came my exercises, followed by a bit of reading before I bathed. After that came the day's program of reading, cleaning, mending or whatever it was I decided would be my chores for the day.

AC: How did you sustain yourself while you were under house arrest?

ASSK: I had a lot of things to do. It's not like sitting in a prison cell. I had a house to look after that had to be kept tidy and clean. I could listen to the radio and read. I could sew. I could do all the normal things that I would have imagined that many people do every day, with the exception of going out and having friends come in.

AC: So your life under incarceration was a huge silence filled with personal interests—household tasks, reading, radio, and sewing?

ASSK: No, I didn't think of it as a huge silence at all. They were just ordinary days. You know, people do like to dramatize things. It's not as dramatic as all that. I'm sure it's much more dramatic for people who are suddenly taken away from their homes and put in a prison cell. But I just continued to live in the house where I was before they put me under house arrest.

AC: Did you have any idea how long the authorities had planned to keep you under detention?

ASSK: The first detention order said one year, but we knew it was renewable.

AC: Did you think that your detention could go on indefinitely, maybe even for life?

ASSK: Yes. After the first extension I had a pretty good idea that this was something they could go on doing indefinitely. Especially after they changed the law.

AC: Did the authorities ever make it perfectly clear that you could be free if you left the country and did any SLORC members ever come to you directly to negotiate a settlement?

ASSK: No, but at one time they did make a suggestion that it might be a good idea. But they never put it to me in quite the way in which they put it to other people: "If she leaves the country...she can be free." But they knew that I knew because it was publicized on the BBC.

AC: You were never tempted by their offer of freedom?

ASSK: No.

AC: What was your reaction to their offer?

ASSK: My main reaction was surprise that they ever thought that I would take up such an offer. And to a certain extent it indicated that they did not know me at all. I don't think this applies only to me. They do not really get to know people in general. I think it's very difficult for those who work by intimidating and using their power to repress others, to ever have the opportunity to get to know people really well. They have not learned the technique, so to speak, of getting to know people. Perhaps they have gotten into the habit of thinking that all people can be either intimidated or bought.

AC: We all have our dark moments where we have to wrestle with our demons. Did you ever get so frustrated that you just wanted to bang the wall with your fist?

ASSK: I did bang the keys of my piano the day I heard that Uncle U Tin Oo had been condemned to four years' hard labor. That put me in a bad temper. I thought that was highly unjust. It was sheer anger.

AC: Was there any period during your detention that you went into a more intensive period of meditation practice? Say for a few weeks or months, perhaps longer?

ASSK: No. But there were times when I did more meditation because I was getting better at it. I think this is the same with all those who meditate. Once you have discovered the joys of meditation as it were, you do tend to spend longer periods at it.

AC: May I ask what were the joys that you discovered?

ASSK: The stages I went through are the ones that Sayadaw U Pandita described in his book, *In This Very Life*. I'm just like any other meditator—nothing out of the ordinary.

AC: Your radio was your link to the world. What did you listen to?

ASSK: The news. I listened primarily to the BBC World Service, BBC and VOA Burmese programs and The Democratic Voice of Burma. I also listened to the French radio but this was more to keep up my French than for any other reason. Sometimes I listened to the Japanese radio but I couldn't always fit it in; there were other things I wanted to listen to on the BBC World Service. So after some time I stopped listening to the Japanese radio. It just came on at the wrong time.

AC: Your period of incarceration obviously coincided with numerous and dramatic world changes, events that changed the political face of the world. Of course, these are too numerous to mention them all, but what were the ones that sparked the most interest in you?

ASSK: Anything that had to do with a democratic movement interested me tremendously. Everything that happened in Eastern Europe, in the Soviet Union, in South Africa, the Philippines, in Bangladesh, in Pakistan, in Latin America—anywhere and anything that had to do with the development of a democratic system of government or a more democratic way of life interested me very much.

AC: Did you have a television?

ASSK: I had a television which I had actually borrowed with a video deck to show some of the students an English Language program. That stayed with me throughout the six years (*laughing*).

AC: Were you allowed correspondence in and out?

ASSK: I carried on correspondence with my family for about the first year. But not after May of 1990. But that was more my choice.

AC: Based on?

ASSK: Two things. One was that they [SLORC] seemed to think they were doing me a tremendous favor by letting me communicate with my family. It was in fact my right. I've never accepted anything as a favor. So I would not accept any favors from them. Also, I did not think that they had a right to keep me under house arrest for longer than a year. In fact, they had no right to arrest all those NLD who had been successful in the elections. So it was a form of protest against injustices they were perpetrating as well as an indication that I would accept no favors from them.

AC: So you accepted nothing from the authorities, not even a penny?

ASSK: No.

AC: How did you survive?

ASSK: I sold some of my furniture.

AC: How did you manage to sell it?

ASSK: The security people sold it for me. Well, not that they sold it, they kept it in the warehouse. They paid me for it and the day of my release they brought back the whole lot. They were going to return it to me, but I said I couldn't accept it until I had paid for it. So I asked them to take it away until I gathered enough money.

AC: And how did you eat? Who did your shopping?

ASSK: I had a girl who'd come in during the week, every morning, and she did my shopping. She arranged all my food and everything.

AC: I've learned that your funds were so scarce that you had barely enough to eat and that your hair began falling out, and there were times you were too weak even to get out of bed.

ASSK: Yes, there were periods.

AC: How desperate did it get? Were you concerned with starvation?

ASSK: My theory was that if I died of anything it would probably be of heart failure from weakness, rather than from starvation.

AC: You had heart problems?

ASSK: No, but it's always a probability if you're undernourished.

AC: How would you say your incarceration has changed you? Do you feel it has matured you in some ways?

ASSK: One could say it matured me, but on the other hand I might have matured in any case. One gets more mature as one gets older, whether or not one is under house arrest.

AC: Where there any favorite books that you read?

ASSK: There were a number of books I liked quite a lot. I enjoyed Nehru's autobiography. I had an old copy of *Pride and Prejudice*, which I enjoyed reading again, but that was just for the enjoyment of the language more than for anything else. But a lot of the books were purely in the line of work, as it were—politics, philosophy, etcetera.

AC: Did you write during your incarceration?

ASSK: No. I didn't see the point in writing unless I could get my writing out to be published.

AC: Obviously some things did get out—your *Towards a True Refuge* essay [composed in the fourth year of her house arrest, as the Eighth Joyce Pearce Memorial Lecture, delivered on her behalf by Dr. Michael Aris on 19 May 1993 at Oxford University. Published in pamphlet form, Oxford 1993: reprinted in Freedom from Fear, Penguin Books 1995].

ASSK: Yes. I wrote when Michael came and when I wanted to send out speeches or when arrangements were made for me to send out speeches through the authorities, which happened twice. The other speeches I just sent out through Michael.

AC: How were you informed of your release?

ASSK: The Head of Police and two other security personnel came at about four o'clock in the afternoon and told me about it.

AC: Were you given any prior notice?

ASSK: Well, I was told about one o'clock that they would be coming at about four o'clock.

AC: What was your first reaction when you were told?

ASSK: Well, my first reaction, I suppose, was that they're coming about my release. Then I thought, what should be my first move...

AC: What did you decide?

ASSK: I decided that I would ask Uncle U Kyi Maung and Auntie Kyi Kyi to come and see me because I have very good friendly relations with both of them. And of course, Uncle U Kyi Maung was the leader of the NLD who led our party through the elections.

AC: Did you immediately recommit yourself to a unified NLD and the continuation of the struggle?

ASSK: Of course. I asked Uncle U Kyi Maung to come over because I had every intention of continuing with it.

AC: How soon after your release did you begin your public talks?

ASSK: The very next day. But I just went out to say hello, as it were, a few words of greeting.

AC: Are there any positive effects that have come from your period of incarceration?

ASSK: Well, I think if the SLORC had not put me under house arrest, our movement would not have attracted so much interest. It's always wrong to repress somebody whom you see as an enemy and who is without weapons. And SLORC, by being so harsh and oppressive in the way they have handled the opposition, has brought us a lot of sympathy in the country as well as throughout the rest of the world.

> *"We have chosen the way of nonviolence*
> *simply because we think it's politically better*
> *for the country in the long run."*

ALAN CLEMENTS: I'm struck by a major distinction among leaders of nonviolent political movements. There appear to be two basic paradigms of nonviolence. One version is rooted in the belief in God; meaning that its power and inspiration come from a theistic or monotheistic understanding of the universe, life and humankind, as seen in the movements led by Martin Luther King, Mahatma Gandhi, Václav Havel and Nelson Mandela prior to his formation of Umkhonto [the military wing of the ANC's struggle in South Africa]. Each of these leaders, to a greater or lesser extent, had conviction in either a Christian or a Hindu conception of existence. Whereas the second version is rooted in the belief in *anatta*—the Buddhist concept of emptiness, or interrelatedness, without any permanent god, entity, or "thing-figure" behind the veil. His Holiness the Dalai Lama of Tibet is one example. Another one is the Vietnamese Buddhist monk, Thich Nhat Hahn who, as you may know, led a nonviolent peace movement during the Vietnam war and was nominated for the Nobel Peace Prize by Martin Luther King in 1968. And of course there's you, Aung San Suu Kyi, a dedicated Buddhist.

When you look at these examples, all the theistic expressions of nonviolence have been successful in their struggles, whereas the Buddhists have not been successful in bringing about political change—Thich Nhat Hahn admits this in his writings and the Dalai Lama states that "time is quickly running out in Tibet." While in your own struggle here in Burma, the results remain uncertain as SLORC repression tightens daily. May I ask you for your impressions on this distinction that I've raised?

AUNG SAN SUU KYI: But in Vietnam, especially in South Vietnam, there are so many Christians, and so many of them were in key positions during the war. Ngo Dinh Diem was a Catholic. I think that's one of the reasons for the failure of the Buddhist movement, because there were so many non-Buddhists holding power. The Buddhist movement could not activate those who were crucial to the situation.

AC: Well, coming back to the question, is there anything to be said about the conviction of those who have God in their souls *vis à vis* those who see *anatta* as their abiding truth?

ASSK: I wonder whether it isn't something more practical than that. Organized movements are essential to the way in which Christianity works. Their churches are organized that way, whereas Buddhists are not really organized around their monasteries. Although one might go to the local monastery, or have one's favorite monastery in which to worship, one does not necessarily stay confined to that one monastery only. It's not like Christians who go to the same church for years and years, and in so doing develop congregational relationships. Perhaps your parents too went to the same church and you know a lot of people through your ongoing association with them. You also know what their parents were like and what affiliations they had. I think this is the way the base for organized movement is formed.

I have often thought that this is probably one of the reasons why Christian-based political movements tend to take off quickly and efficiently. The organization is already there. Look at Latin America, you'll find that a lot of their political movements against the dictatorships, although they were not nonviolent, were church-based, which made them take off rather quickly. Even in Islamic countries they have the mosque, which is formally organized, with regular mosque meetings taking place weekly. This sort of formal organization does not exist in Buddhist countries.

AC: So obviously you don't think that the success of these movements had anything to do with their convictions in God.

ASSK: I think that it's just the fact that they can meet regularly. Even in India the government cannot say that Muslims must not go to the Mosque. It would create such a reaction. They must allow them to go to the Mosque, so they can always meet regularly a minimum of once a week. Whereas, where can Buddhists meet? If the Buddhists started meeting once a week at a particular monastery, the MI [Military Intelligence] would be on to them immediately to find out what the meeting was about. But you can't stop people from going to church. In the Eastern European countries they tried this but once the focus of Western countries was on them and they needed Western loans, they could not tell people anymore: "Don't go to church." It was so in Poland. There was a great deal of church-based political activity.

Now take an example in Burma. Last June Uncle U Kyi Maung started meeting a few elderly friends every Thursday for tea and a good discussion. What happened? They were hauled off by the MI and detained and interrogated for a few days. And if anybody thought of meeting regularly at a monastery in numbers of a hundred or two, there would be serious consequences. Whereas in Christian countries, the government may infiltrate the church with informers, but they would still have to allow these congregations to meet regularly. That's a great plus in favor of any popular movement.

AC: President Nelson Mandela writes in his autobiography, *Long Walk to Freedom* that in 1961 "the days of nonviolent struggle were over.... We had no choice but to turn to violence." To substantiate his turn away from nonviolence to violence he cited an old African expression: "The attacks of the wild beast cannot be averted only with bare hands." Nevertheless, there were some within the ANC who argued that nonviolence was an inviolate principle, not a tactic that should be abandoned when it no longer worked.

To this Mr. Mandela countered: "[I] believed exactly the opposite...nonviolence was a tactic that should be abandoned when it no longer worked.... And it was wrong and immoral to subject our people to armed attacks by the state without offering them some kind of alternative." But if I am correct, you see nonviolent political activism as a moral and spiritual principle and not merely as a political tactic?

ASSK: No, not exactly. It's also a political tactic. Military coups, which have happened enough in Burma, are violent ways of changing situations and I do not want to encourage and to perpetuate this tradition of bringing about change through violence. Because I'm afraid that if we achieve democracy in this way we will never be able to get rid of the idea that you bring about necessary changes through violence. The very method would be threatening us all the time. Because there are always people who do not agree with democracy. And if we achieve it through violent means, there will be the hard core of those who have always been against the democracy movement who will think, "It was through violence that they changed the system and if we can develop our own methods of violence which are superior to theirs, we can get back the power." And we'll go on in this vicious cycle. For me it is as much a political tactic as a spiritual belief, that violence is not the right way. It would simply not assist us in building up a strong democracy.

AC: But when you perceive that nonviolent methods are no longer effective, do you as a leader have a duty to shift your nonviolent tactic to sharpen the point so to speak, of your struggle, or do you adopt the attitude, come what may, to maintain nonviolence, because of a moral affinity?

ASSK: You know we always take collective decisions...

AC: Yes, I know that...

ASSK: And as long as I'm part of a democratic organization I will have to abide by collective decisions.

AC: Then let me ask the question in another way. Daw Suu, I would like to understand you. Is nonviolence an immutable ethical and spiritual principle that will never alter in your approach to the struggle?

ASSK: We have always said that we will never disown those students and others who have taken up violence. We know that their aim is the same as ours. They want democracy and they think the best way to go about it is through armed struggle. And we do not say that we have the monopoly on the right methods of achieving what we want. Also, we cannot guarantee their security. We can't say, "Follow us in the way of nonviolence and you'll be protected," or that we'll get there without any casualties. That's a promise we can't make. We have chosen the way of nonviolence simply because we think it's politically better for the country in the long run to establish that you can bring about change without the use of arms. This has been a clear NLD policy from the beginning. Here, we're not thinking about spiritual matters at all. Perhaps in that sense, we're not the same as Mahatma Gandhi, who would have probably condemned all movements that were not nonviolent. I'm not sure. But he did say at one time that if he had to choose between violence and cowardice, he would choose violence. So, even Gandhi, who was supposed to be the great exponent of nonviolence, was not somebody who did not make any exceptions...

AC: But what about choosing violence out of compassion, if it's the right word, rather than using it as an option instead of cowardice? Nelson Mandela writes: "Leadership commits a crime against its own people if it hesitates to sharpen its political weapons where they have become less effective." Isn't he saying that one's attachment to nonviolence becomes in fact an act of violence towards one's own people, when the nonviolent approach is no longer effective?

ASSK: It depends on the situation and I think that in the context of Burma today, nonviolent means are the best way to achieve our goal. But I certainly do not condemn those who fight the "just fight," as it were. My father did, and I admire him greatly for it.

AC: So it's accurate to say that you're keeping your options open and that you're not confining yourself to one particular approach?

ASSK: We keep all our options open. It is very important that one should be flexible. We've chosen nonviolence because it is the best way to protect the people, and in the long term assure the future stability of democracy. This is why my father changed from violence to nonviolence. He knew that it was far better for the future of the country to achieve a democratic state through political means and negotiation, rather than through military means. It's the same with Nelson Mandela. He changed back to nonviolence when this was possible. Of course, before then he used violence because the nonviolent way was not paying off and it was seen as a weakness rather than a strength. But in those days things were different. When Nelson Mandela and the other South Africans were first trying out the nonviolent approach, the world was so busily engaged in the ideological battle between the East and West, they were not that interested in human rights. In a brutal world, Nelson Mandela and other South Africans felt that they had to choose means that would make an impact and that would move their position forward. In this day and age we can use nonviolent political means to achieve our ends. But if you have a choice and feel that you have an equal chance of succeeding, I think you certainly ought to choose the nonviolent way, because it means that fewer people will be hurt.

AC: I don't think that violence and nonviolence are such clearly separate domains, really. Of course, people often compartmentalize them into black and white categories, but is it possible to have an armed force motivated by the philosophy of nonviolence, or is it completely a contradiction in terms? Can you philosophically foster the mind state of a nonviolent activist even though you may be a combatant and use violence when called upon to do so?

ASSK: You have to define what you mean by violence. If we define violence as any action that gives pain to others, this broadens the definition so much that none of us is capable of real nonviolence. Even if your intention is to help somebody, you may cause pain to that person by telling him a painful truth. So in those terms, it's very difficult to talk of pure nonviolence.

In general what we mean by violence these days is physical violence. As long as your thoughts, emotions and words are not translated into physical action, people will more or less accept that your methods are nonviolent. That, I think, can be put into practice. You can actually keep from performing acts that give physical pain to others. Then of course, there are those who will argue that mental pain is worse than physical pain...

AC: Yes, the Buddha has said this...

ASSK: So then you get into this argument about whether a physical act that inflicts pain on somebody is actually worse than some word or action that gives mental pain.

AC: I know that in Western countries it's been very easy for a lot of us to see the military machine as a body for violent aggression. In so doing we often polarize them from ourselves, judging them as the antithesis of *ahimsa* or nonviolence. But I wonder if there is a way not to divide so sharply those who use weapons "justly" from those who would never use violent means under any circumstance?

ASSK: Take Burma for an example, during the time of the resistance against the Japanese. The Burmese Army was born out of the people and was part of it. And certainly, during the time of the Japanese resistance, the people did not think of the army as "them" and of themselves as "us." We were all one. Even after independence, as long as Burma was a democratic country, there was not this division between the military and the civilians.

This "them and us" syndrome came in after the military took over power and became an elite. The privileged and the unprivileged. That's what it all amounts to. Privilege because they've got guns, money or power and the others don't have any of those.

AC: To continue with Nelson Mandela, I was particularly interested in his recounting of an ordeal with the American journalists from the *Washington Post* who went to interview him at Robben Island Prison. Apparently they tried to label him as a Communist and terrorist, as well as a non-Christian. They asserted that Martin Luther King never resorted to violence. He retorted that he was a Christian and even Christ who was a peacemaker, when left with no alternative used force to expel the moneylenders from the temple.

ASSK: Yes. He took out his whip, didn't he? I don't think one can afford to be dogmatic in politics. Dogmatism is one of the greatest dangers in politics.

AC: Another element of his book that impressed me was the power of the song, his stirring images when he was on trial with a courtroom packed with his ANC supporters singing and chanting. And the same when they were jailed in the earlier days of the movement. He explains how they all sang and chanted hymns throughout the night.

ASSK: That's very African though, isn't it?

AC: It is. But could you imagine hearing the thousands of people gathered at your weekend talks singing songs of freedom? Is there such a tradition of song and dance within the movement, as a means to nurture the unifying forces of love and determination?

ASSK: Actually, we don't have a tradition of community singing or dancing. It's not quite the same...

AC: Even during the marches led by Martin Luther King, song was a vital unifying aspect for the people in the movement. And in Hanoi, during America's bombing of the city, the tens of thousands of men, women and children sang as they hid in shelters deep in the earth. My point is that music and song ground the movement, take it out of the head, and place it in the soul.

ASSK: Well... during 1988 and 1989, some of the young people would sing democracy songs and this would be a great source of inspiration. Also, before the war, during the independence movement, our people would sing inspirational patriotic songs. But I don't think that it is the same as the

African tradition where you just join hands and sing. Singing together as a form of community expression, even if it isn't a political song, is not a tradition among the Burmese. It may be different with some of the other ethnic groups in Burma. I know that we've always looked upon the Karens as particularly good singers. And I wonder if there isn't more of this kind of community singing and dancing among them.

AC: In watching you and your colleagues speak to the crowds on weekends I was thinking that a comparable expression to singing would be your use of humor. The people are constantly laughing...

ASSK: Yes, that might be particularly Burmese. They do have a sense of humor, and they're quick on the uptake. Like the jokes those comedians who were arrested soon after their performance in my compound last month told. Their jokes didn't really attack SLORC as such. But everybody knew exactly what they meant.

AC: I generally see you laughing with your colleagues and they've all told me how funny you are...

ASSK: Well, I have to admit that I have always had a sense of humor. I can always see the ridiculous side of things and this helps me a lot, because I can laugh at my own situation. You know, I've found myself in situations some people have thought rather unpleasant. Of course, if you were really going to get uppity—they could be seen as unpleasant. But often, I've just seen them as rather funny. And I think I told you before, I don't think we've ever had a single meeting [with the NLD EC members] where there haven't been at least some laughs. Obviously, it's not a happy situation we're in, but the seriousness of the situation is something we can all joke about. In fact, lots of Burmese people joke about it; there are jokes about forced labor, about prison. This is very much part of our Burmese culture.

AC: Yes, I've come to see that. Just the other day several of us were listening to U Win Htein [Aung San Suu Kyi's assistant] describe his recent interrogation when the MI drilled him for twenty-seven hours non-stop. As he was unraveling his story everyone started laughing at the absurdity of SLORC's behavior, to the point of tears. He wasn't at all concerned with his own suffering. I think he did say that "it was rather unpleasant," but that's all...

ASSK: Actually, yes, it was the way they talked to him, their questions and views are quite absurd to us. Because they are so way out, really. They're not at all in touch with reality. What they think is so different from what is actually happening that it becomes absurd.

AC: Someone asked Václav Havel about the relationship of suffering and absurdity and he said that, "If one were required to increase the dramatic seriousness of his face in relation to the seriousness of the problems he had to confront, he would quickly petrify and become his own statue..."

ASSK: Yes, I think a sense of humor requires a certain amount of objectivity in the situation, which is why it's so healthy. If you see things as a whole, you can always see a humorous side of it. Which is why we laugh at situations which to some seem so serious. I mean, when U Win Htein and others were laughing at his account of the interrogation, if you see it as a whole it's quite ridiculous. But if you see it from just one angle it could be infuriating, humiliating, or even frightening for some people.

AC: Daw Suu, a simple question: what does love mean to you?

ASSK: I don't really think of love in an abstract way. When I first think of *mettā*, I feel it within our movement, especially between my colleagues and myself. We work like a family—we are not just colleagues. We have a real concern and affection for each other, which is the basis of our relationships. I think this may have a lot to do with the fact that we have to work under such difficult conditions. It's only *mettā* that is strong enough to keep together people who face such repression and who are in danger of being dragged away to prison at any moment. And the longer we work together the greater our bond of *mettā* grows. From there these ties of friendship and affection have spread outward to include the families of colleagues. From there it spreads further, and with it the feeling of family grows. A family with a love of justice, a love of freedom, a love of peace and equality.

But let's go back to the more down-to-earth question of humor. If you're used to laughing at things, you start laughing at your own problems. You get used to seeing the absurd and funny side of things and you don't take your troubles that seriously any more. In the same way, if you are used to giving friendship and affection it's much easier to give it even to people who may think of themselves as your enemies.

AC: How are you able to feel affection towards tyrants?

ASSK: It just happens. I never imagine scenes where I'm oppressing them or getting my own back, or giving them a nasty time and making them miserable. Such thoughts give me no satisfaction, nor are they images that I see as particularly pleasant and desirable. What I do imagine is a time when all this animosity has been washed away and we can be friends.

AC: We discussed in an earlier conversation how insecurity was the root psychology of authoritarian regimes—a mistrust of one's own dignity, one's self-worth, and therefore a mistrust of others. In relationship to this I would like to ask you about finding power in vulnerability, rather than seeing it as a weakness. Indeed, many millions of women in the world today, after so many centuries of male repression, are calling out for us to wake up and see vulnerability as a virtue and a strength, a way into one's power and not a barrier to it. What do you think of this issue, and more specifically, from where does true power originate?

ASSK: The "power of the powerless" as Václav Havel said. I think power comes from within. If you have confidence in what you are doing and you are shored up by the belief that what you are doing is right, that in itself constitutes power, and this power is very important when you are trying to achieve something. If you don't believe in what you are doing your actions will lack credibility. However hard you try, inconsistencies will appear.

AC: And in regard to the issue of women I raised?

ASSK: Of course, women are consciously and unconsciously discriminated against. You'll find very few women in higher levels of administration, and obviously, it's not because they are less able than men.

AC: What about women's rights in Burma?

ASSK: People have often asked me about women's rights in Burma and I have always said very frankly, "Men do not have rights in Burma either." I do know that men are the privileged gender in Burma, as well as in many other parts of the world, but at the moment men are just as vulnerable to injustice and oppression. So first, let's give everybody their fundamental rights. Let's just try to stop men from being thrown into prison. This is not to say women are not thrown into prison too. But there are probably a hundred or even a thousand times more men political prisoners than women. So at this moment I find it very difficult to think of women in Burma as apart from the same movement in which men are involved. But I'm sure that the issue of women's rights will come out once we have democracy and everybody is enjoying their basic political rights.

AC: If I may, I'd like to return to the women's movement on a more global level. Would you speak of the positive signs of the women's movement?

ASSK: There's no doubt that thanks to the women's movement women have achieved greater equality in the realm of jobs and are being given more responsible positions. And there is also a lot more focus on their problems. Even in developing countries where women's issues are not given that much importance, people are beginning to be aware of the fact that they have got to do something to help their women. At the very least, make their lives easier physically. It should not be taken for granted that women must slave away just because they're women. In many rural communities they have to work physically harder than men. The men are there supposedly to protect them in case a lion or tiger comes or an invasion takes place, although such occurrences are becoming increasingly rare.

AC: It is time that men got over the belief that women want or even need men to protect them.

ASSK: Yes. I think it just gives men a chance, in some communities, to chat while they polish their bows and arrows.

AC: Do you see yourself as a feminist?

ASSK: No, I don't.

AC: You've written: "It is not enough merely to provide the poor with material assistance. They have to be sufficiently empowered to change their perception of themselves as helpless and ineffectual in an uncaring world." Fundamentally, what does empowerment mean to you?

ASSK: I think people must be given a reasonable control over their own destiny. They have to feel that they have some power over what happens to them. That is empowerment. But none of us can ultimately decide what will happen to us. There are too many factors involved.

AC: Nelson Mandela mentions in his memoirs that one of the things that he and his ANC colleagues talked a lot about during their many years in prison was how to sustain the awareness of the struggle in the minds of the people. I'd like to ask, how are you and your NLD colleagues attempting to ignite the people's desire for freedom to that level of momentum, as in South Africa, where it became an electrified movement that could not be stopped...

ASSK: What we have to make them understand is that the struggle is about them. That is what we always explain to the people. Democracy is about your job and your children's education; it's about the house you live in and the food you eat; it's about whether or not you have to get permission from somebody before you visit your relatives in the next village; it's about whether or not you can reap your own harvest and sell it to the person you want to sell it to. The struggle is about their everyday life. It's no use saying to a farmer that democracy is about better investment rules: that makes no sense to him at all. But democracy is about securing him the right to sow what he wants to, and to reap at the time he thinks the harvest is ready, and then to sell it to whomsoever he thinks will give him the best price. That's democracy. For a businessman, democracy is a system where there are sound commercial laws which are upheld by the institutions of the state, so he knows his rights and what he is allowed to do or not. He knows how to protect himself if anybody infringes those rights. For a student, democracy is the right to be able to study in good schools and in peace, and not to be dragged away to prison because you happen to be *laughing* with your friends over some funny characteristic of a minister. Democracy is the right to discuss your political views with your friends and to have the right to sit down at the tea shop on the campus and talk about whatever you want to, without wondering whether the MI are listening.

When Uncle U Kyi Maung was under detention, one of the Military Intelligence officers interrogating him asked, "Why did you decide to become a member of the National League for Democracy?" And he answered, "For your sake." That's what our struggle is about: everybody's everyday lives, including those of the MI.

"What we want to do is to free people from feeling complacent."

ALAN CLEMENTS: Daw Suu, what moves you to struggle for your people?

AUNG SAN SUU KYI: When I first decided to take part in the movement for democracy, it was more out of a sense of duty than anything else. On the other hand, my sense of duty was very closely linked to my love for my father. I could not separate it from the love for my country, and therefore, from the sense of responsibility towards my people. But as time went on, like a lot of others who've been incarcerated, we have discovered the value of loving-kindness. We've found that it's one's own feelings of hostility that generate fear. As I've explained before, I never felt frightened when I was surrounded by all those hostile troops. That is because I never felt hostility towards them. This made me realize that there are a number of fundamental principles common to many religions. As Burmese Buddhists, we put a great emphasis on *mettā*. It is the same idea as in the biblical quotation: "Perfect love casts out fear." While I cannot claim to have discovered "perfect love," I think it's a fact that you are not frightened of people whom you do not hate. Of course, I did get angry occasionally with some of the things they did, but anger as a passing emotion is quite different from the feeling of sustained hatred or hostility.

AC: Of course, the potential for hatred to arise dramatically increases as violence is directed personally at someone, both psychologically and physically. Your country's prisons are filled with political prisoners; some, as I have learned, are routinely tortured by the military authorities.

ASSK: I'm not claiming any tremendous virtue for myself when I say that I feel no hostility towards soldiers. This is again a part of my heritage because I was brought up to think of soldiers as part of the family—as my father's sons. Because this kind of feeling was instilled into me from a young age, it's not something one can get rid of easily. But I easily understand why others who have been so ill-treated would not be able to develop a non-hostile attitude.

AC: Clearly, your vision of a democratic Burma includes a genuine reconciliation with your oppressors—SLORC. What do you think is required of the individual to confront his adversary and possibly win his friendship and understanding—not seeking to defeat him?

ASSK: Well, it has to begin with one's self, doesn't it? You have to develop inner spiritual strength, and those who have it do not feel hatred or hostility because they do not easily feel fear. It's all connected. If you can look upon someone with serenity you are able to cope with the feelings of hatred. But there cannot be serenity if there is fear. However, let me say, ordinary people like us, within the NLD, are nowhere near that level where we can look upon everybody with perfect love and serenity. But I think a lot of us within the organization have been given the opportunity to develop spiritual strength because we have been forced to spend long years by ourselves under detention and in prison. In a way, we owe it to those people who put us there.

AC: What is the core quality at the center of your movement?

ASSK: Inner strength. It's the spiritual steadiness that comes from the belief that what you are doing is right, even if it doesn't bring you immediate concrete benefits. It's the fact that you are doing something that helps to shore up your spiritual powers. It's very powerful.

AC: Martin Luther King used the phrase "divine dissatisfaction." He encouraged his people to grow weary and tired of injustice, to become "maladjusted," as he said it, to the racist system by which they were being oppressed. Now, on one level, you speak of genuine reconciliation, but at the same time, are you also speaking to the need of the population to grow uncomfortable and to steadily increase their dissatisfaction towards SLORC?

ASSK: It's not really the need to grow "uncomfortable." Nor are we trying to make the people become more dissatisfied. Our principal task is to encourage the need in people to question the situation and not just accept everything. Now, acceptance is not the same as serenity. Some people seem to think they go together. Not at all. Sometimes, the very fact that you accept what you do not want to accept and know that you should not accept, destroys the sense of serenity and inner peace, because you're in conflict with yourself.

AC: So the overcoming of complacency is the principal focus?

ASSK: Yes, complacency is very dangerous. What we want to do is to free people from feeling complacent. Actually, with a lot of people it's not a sense of complacency either. I think that many people just accept things out of either fear or inertia. This readiness to accept without question has to be removed. And it's very un-Buddhist. After all, the Buddha did not accept the status quo without questioning it.

AC: Yes, he radically questioned. It's the basis of his teachings.

ASSK: Yes, absolutely. In Buddhism, you know the four ingredients of success or victory: *chanda*—desire or will; *citta*—the right attitude; *vīriya* or perseverance; and *paññā*—wisdom. We feel that you have got to cultivate these four qualities in order to succeed. And the step prior even to these four steps, is questioning. From that you discover your real desires. Then you have got to develop *chanda*. *Chanda* is not really desire. How would you describe it?

AC: *Chanda* is normally translated as the "wish to do" or intention. Every action begins with it. Where there is a will there is a way.

ASSK: Yes. You must develop the intention to do something about the situation. From there you've got to develop the right attitude and then persevere with wisdom. Only then will there be success in your endeavor. Of course, the five basic moral precepts are essential, to keep you from straying as it were. With these we will get where we want to. We don't need anything else.

AC: So what you're doing is fostering a sense of individual courage to question, to analyze...

ASSK: And to act. I remind the people that *karma* is actually doing. It's not just sitting back. Some people think of *karma* as destiny or fate and that there's nothing they can do about it. It's simply what is going to happen because of their past deeds. This is the way in which *karma* is often interpreted in Burma. But *karma* is not that at all. It's doing, it's action. So you are creating your own *karma* all the time. Buddhism is a very dynamic philosophy and it's a great pity that some people forget that aspect of our religion.

AC: I've often noticed in Burmese Buddhist culture how people speak of the suffering they face in their present circumstances as simply the bitter fruit of past unwholesome *karmas* or actions. Such people will say: "I brought this suffering on myself through my own past ignorance and therefore I must bear it in the present."

ASSK: I think it's an excuse for doing nothing and it's completely contrary to our Buddhist views. If what is happening now is a result of what happened before, all the more reason why you should work harder now to change the situation...

AC: And, please correct me if I'm wrong, but such people often consider that the best way to change their unfavorable present circumstances is by performing *kusala* [wholesome deeds], such as giving donations to the monasteries, or making offerings to a pagoda or the building of a shrine and so on. This with the intention of generating wholesome *karma* that will hopefully improve their positions in a future life. Which obviously does nothing to change the more immediate source of their suffering, which is the SLORC.

ASSK: This is very much a common attitude. If something goes wrong, people tend to do something just for themselves, as it were. But I think you can also carry on working for others. Perhaps we should encourage this more; the idea that you can gain a lot of merit by working for others, as much as by working for yourself. In fact, I would like more of our Burmese Buddhists to understand this point.

AC: How much of your struggle is in fact, both about self-reliance and the fact that our liberation is inextricably interwoven with that of other human beings?

ASSK: In our movement I use a very practical, simple argument. I always say, "I can't do it alone. If you want democracy, it is no use depending on either me or the NLD alone. What democracy means is government of the people, by the people, and for the people. If you want democracy, you'll have to work for it. You've got to join in. The more people are involved the quicker we'll reach our goal."

AC: You so frequently speak of the power of unity and the need for it. But the SLORC has you so hemmed in. Do you find it frustrating that you cannot yet really organize and unify the people?

ASSK: It's not frustrating because we do unite people. It's not at an obvious rate. But we do unify people, quite a lot. And we manage to sort out problems within our organization. The fact is that at the core of the NLD, we are very united. That is strengthening. We never have problems between us. The fact that A Aung Shwe and U Lwin were out [not imprisoned], and that U Tin Oo, U Win Htein, U Kyi Maung and I were in, hasn't affected our unity in any way. This is something that the authorities find very hard to believe. I do not think SLORC actually believes that we have absolute unity and make collective decisions. They think that one of us is dominating the other. Either I'm dominating them, or U Kyi Maung or U Tin Oo is influencing me, something like that. But in fact, it's nothing like that at all. I suppose they're looking at it from a military point of view, where the commander sends down orders and everybody else says, "Yes, yes, yes." Perhaps they find it unthinkable that there is such a thing as a collective decision.

AC: You said in an earlier interview that "everyone must stand up against the cruel injustices" of SLORC. This reminds me of Martin Luther King's words: "For every Negro that is violated, we have 1,000 more Negroes, who are willing to be violated. For every schoolteacher that is fired from his job, we have 4,000 more schoolteachers waiting to apply for that job. For every Negro's home that is bombed, we have 50,000 more homes that are willing to be bombed, for the vision and the future that we want." Are your people ready to stand up and say, we'll fill the prisons full in order to achieve our goal of justice and freedom?

ASSK: I don't think our movement is at quite that level. One of the reasons why the movement of black people in America was like that was because they visibly belonged to one side; whereas we are not marked out as belonging to one side or the other. I think it's always more difficult when the struggle is between people of one race and one religion. There is nothing that sets you apart except your principles and your goals.

AC: The apartheid of principles...

ASSK: What I mean is this: when Martin Luther King says that, "for every Negro's home that is bombed we have 50,000 more homes willing to be bombed," I don't know whether willingness comes into it. It's probably more the fact that there are 50,000 more black homes who know that they are just as vulnerable as the one that has been bombed.

AC: But, Daw Suu, I think the "willingness" was there. And that was the power of the struggle—dynamic unity. How much are you really willing to arouse that same spirit of dynamic unity that King did with the blacks, in your own people? The willingness to rise up against the injustices.

ASSK: Of course, one wants them to be united. But it's something that we have to work towards, steadily. It's not a job that will ever be finished. I don't think unity is ever complete—at least not in the human world. And although I realize and accept that our unity is not complete, that does not drive me to despair. You just have to keep working towards it all the time.

AC: One of the powers of King's movement was that he felt, as many blacks did, that no matter how cruel and violent the white people were to them in their nonviolent marches, demonstrations, sit-ins and boycotts, ultimately, justice and goodness were on their side. "Cosmic companions" as King put it, or inherent qualities of the universe born from their conviction in the Christian religion. He said that this "knowing" presence of God as they faced brutality was a main factor in keeping the people unified. So no matter how dark it became they always knew that they had cosmic companionship. But this isn't true in Buddhism, is it? The universe doesn't take sides, but is always right because of the law of cause and effect?

ASSK: Yes. In Buddhism, as you know, we believe that you will pay for all the bad things that you have done, and that you will reap the rewards of all the good that you've done. And I think because of that, a lot of Buddhists think that because the authorities are cruel and unjust, you don't have to do anything at all, they will get their own desserts. I don't accept that. I don't think that one should just sit back and expect *karma* to catch up with everybody else. But I do think there is this underlying belief, not just among Christians or Buddhists, but among peoples all over the world, that in the end, right will prevail—the light will have to come. When I say this, I don't mean that everybody holds it, but that the majority of people do.

AC: I know it's a nice belief to hold, that "in the end, right will prevail." What evidence do you have to say, "The light will have to come"? It seems like just the opposite is closer to reality, for so many millions of people around the world.

ASSK: Whatever you may say, the world is better. Because in this day and age you can't just drag someone to a public place, chop off his head, and not have anyone say a word about it. Which government today would hang, draw and quarter somebody, in full view of the public, and think that he'd get away with it? We are less barbaric, people as a whole are more civilized. This is not to say that horrible tortures do not go on. They go on behind the scenes but at least people are beginning to learn that this is not acceptable. Take a place like England, which is supposed to be the mother of democracy. I'm sure there are lots of criticisms that you can make about England but if they had caught the Soviet spy, Kim Philby, and they had hung, drawn and quartered him in public, do you think the English people would have stood for it? Even though he was a traitor, those days are long gone. So people have progressed and not just in democratic countries but even in the old Soviet Union. Of course, they executed traitors but they certainly would not have taken them out into Red Square and chopped their heads off in full view of the public. So that's progress. It shows that people are beginning to understand that barbarism is not acceptable, that it's something to be ashamed of, something we must try to eliminate. You can't deny that there has been an increasing movement to control the savage instincts of man.

AC: I would like to immediately jump in there on the issue...

ASSK: Oh, go on!

AC: There have been more wars and murders in the twentieth century than all previous centuries combined. And Ken Saro-Wiwa, the Nigerian writer and environmental activist, was just hung in full public view of the entire world. Furthermore, CNN and the BBC covered the Bosnian nightmare, twenty-four hours a day, for forty-three months of "ethnic cleansing," in full view of the public. I need more evidence of how you determine your views.

ASSK: Let's put it this way. The values of civilization have become more dominant.

AC: As I said in one of our previous conversations, when European civilization spread, in most places it did so based on a policy of extermination of the indigenous populations. Perhaps from that perspective, there might be more dominant values of civilization today than before. But, I'm not sure at all that I'm convinced.

ASSK: Take Burma under the Burmese kings: those who were out of favor with the king were executed in very cruel ways. Now, Burma has been accused of many, many human rights violations. But do the authorities ever admit them? They do not. They will say, "No, we have not perpetrated these deeds." Whereas in the days of the old Burmese kings, there was no question of denying it. They would just do it. It was their prerogative and nobody would dare to question them. And they would not think there was any need for them to even pretend that they had not done these things. So that's progress.

AC: So are you saying that your country has become more civilized?

ASSK: Yes. It has become more civilized. As I said, think of the days of the Burmese kings when they really had power of life and death over the people. I'm not saying that an authoritarian government does not have power of life or death over the people, but at least they know that it's not right to admit this. That's progress.

AC: That's calculated duplicity...

ASSK: That's progress. They're ashamed to admit atrocities, even though they commit them. At least they know that basically it's unacceptable to torture and to kill people wantonly. And they always deny that they do so. So that's a first step; a realization that what they do is not acceptable. The second step is to know that it's wrong.

AC: You're really cutting them a lot of slack...

ASSK: No. I'm not saying that their instincts are any better or worse than the old kings. But the kings did not feel the need to temper their feelings of vengeance or cruelty. They felt that they had a perfect right to indulge in these feelings. At least the authorities here do not really think it is their right to torture and to kill. They can do it, and they do it. But they will not admit to it. If they are not ashamed of it and they think it's perfectly all right, then why don't they just say, "Yes, we torture. So what?" Now, has anybody in SLORC ever admitted to torture? They always deny it. They say, "No, torture doesn't exist in Burma." They go on denying it to a ridiculous extent. Recently the [SLORC's] representative to the General Assembly said, "There are no human rights violations in Burma." Why do they say that? If they think that it is all right to do the things that they do, they should just say: "Yes, we do that. So what? What's wrong with it?" Why won't they say it?

AC: Well, it's either sheer cowardice, pathological deceit, or the most breath-taking display of self-deception ever known. Or maybe they do recognize it is wrong and as you said, they do not admit it. Yesterday, in SLORC's newspaper, the Trade Minister was quoted as saying in a public speech: "As for the accusations on human rights violations, forced labor and so on in Myanmar, [let it be known that] Myanmar is firmly committed [to] and respectful of the United Nations Universal Declaration of Human Rights. And we, the government, are totally against human rights abuses."

ASSK: Why, this is what I mean...

AC: He goes on to say, "But, here I would like to state that the Eastern concept of human rights is not the same as the Western concept."

ASSK: Yes, but he's contradicting himself because he says that he respects fully the United Nations Convention on Human Rights. But of course, the authorities always contradict themselves and tie themselves up in knots.

AC: What is behind this belief that the Eastern concept of human rights is not the same as the Western concept?

ASSK: There's nothing in it. It's just because they know that they are violating human rights, and so it's self-defense. That's all.

AC: A mindless argument?

ASSK: Totally mindless! I remember at one time, during the early days, that one of the members of SLORC said, "Oh, those people who demand human rights, are they going to demand nudist camps next?" It's quite obvious that he had no idea what "human rights" means.

AC: So you really think they are that out of touch with reality?

ASSK: It's a very interesting question. We've often wondered about that ourselves. A while back, I mentioned Karl Popper's quotation: "There is no evil...only stupidity." And one really appreciates that remark very much.

AC: The SLORC Trade Minister ends his speech by saying: "And the people of Myanmar are living happily under freedom, human rights and democracy...free from any suppression of any kind." Daw Suu, you won, Burma is more civilized today than in times of old.

ASSK: Just look at that, it's just blatant. I don't know what to call it! Well, one's imagination boggles.

AC: Why do they spend the money to print this in English no less? Who's crazy enough to read it besides me?

ASSK: Perhaps they think we need a bit of laughter from time to time.

AC: But on the contrary, last week they stated quite boldly in their paper that they were in fact a "dictatorship." They don't seem to have any shame about that fact.

ASSK: Yes, they are one of the very few governments in the world that ever admitted officially that they were not a *de jure* government at all.

AC: In reflecting upon the issue of reconciliation between the NLD and SLORC, I was thinking today that it's going to require the authorities to reach deep into themselves for the courage to challenge their fear and admit their mistakes. Because, if there's going to be genuine dialogue and reconciliation, obviously they cannot just pull it out of their hats. They'll need a genuine change of heart. And for the first time, I actually feel some compassion for them. That's going to be a colossal challenge...

ASSK: Yes. I read somewhere that it is always more difficult for the perpetrator of a cruel deed to forgive the victim, than for the victim to forgive his tormentor. I found that very strange when I first read it, but I think it's true. The victim can forgive because he has the moral high ground as it were. He has nothing to be ashamed of. Of course he may be ashamed if he had behaved in a very bad way, or if he had groveled. Then he may acquire a hatred towards his tormentor, based not really on what the tormentor had done to him, but on what he had done to himself.

I think it was Shcharansky who said that when he was in prison he had to keep reminding himself, "Nobody can humiliate me but myself, nobody can humiliate me but myself." I think if you haven't done anything that is shameful then you can forgive your tormentor. But the tormentor finds it difficult to forgive the victim because he knows that he has committed an act of shame. And every time he sees his victim he is reminded of his shame. That makes it hard for him to forgive. I think it is the same with the victim who finds it difficult to forgive the tormentor. But the victim who has behaved well finds it quite easy to forgive the tormentor. Because every time he sees the tormentor, I'm sure he is empowered by the reminder of his own noble behavior—his courage. He might say: "I stood up against that man's tortures with dignity." And in a way, it makes it very easy for him to forgive his tormentor.

AC: You could actually see SLORC in this house, sitting down with you and saying, "Daw Suu, we're going to work this out together"?

ASSK: *(smiling)* Oh, very much so. I have no trouble envisaging such a thing. That might just be wishful thinking, in some people's interpretation, but it will have to happen someday. I don't know who will be involved, but it will happen...

AC: Are you confident about that?

ASSK: Oh, yes. That is the only way that countries do go. Mind you, the sooner they go, the less *dukkha* [suffering] there is for all the people concerned. Look at the former Yugoslavia. In the end, they had to talk about it. But look at the numbers of people who have suffered. That is why we say that "It all ends up at the table." But the sensible ones run to the table first, whereas the ones who are not sensible run to the guns.

AC: In your essay *In Quest of Democracy* [written for a projected volume of essays on democracy and human rights and later published in *Freedom from Fear*, published by Penguin 1995] you've written: "Kindness is in a sense the courage to care." Would you say more about that?

ASSK: It's not really my own idea as such. I was discussing this with a doctor friend of mine a long time ago. I was saying that I had a rather idealistic view of doctors and nurses, because my mother was a very dedicated and compassionate nurse. All of her patients loved her, because she was so good at her work, and at the same time she was very gentle and caring. And this doctor said, "Well, doctors and nurses in general are not like that, because not too many of them have the courage to care deeply for all their patients. They have to take a rather unfeeling attitude, otherwise they couldn't cope with those who are suffering." He also said, "There are some, of course, who are truly compassionate and do everything they can for their patients. But those are in the minority, because not too many people have the courage to let themselves feel for their patients. It's too wearing, unless you are very strong and brave."

AC: The courage to let yourself feel?

ASSK: Yes, and to care. You have to have tremendous resources of compassion and strength, because you're giving it out all the time. And unless you have a lot of it, you run out of it all too quickly. You can't cope.

AC: Daw Suu, when it really comes right down to it, how do you cope?

ASSK: I think what really sustains us, is the sense that we are on the side of right, as it were, to use a very old-fashioned phrase. And the *mettā* between us keeps us going.

AC: Are you old-fashioned?

ASSK: Well, talking about morality, right and wrong, love and kindness, is considered rather old-fashioned these days, isn't it? But after all, the world is spherical. Perhaps the whole thing will come around again, and maybe I'm ahead of the times.

CHAPTER 27

CONVERSATIONS *with* KYAW ZWA MOE

2012 & 2020

- "I felt ready to expose any kind of inequality and injustice, even though we were in front of machine guns."
- "Maybe this is something chronic for them, like a disease that they're not aware of."
- "When I was put in jail, I tried not to say the word "*dukkha*.""
- "Without integrity, any kind of authority is not effective."
- "If I have to name the current political landscape of Burma, I would call it "re-civilianizing the militarized nation."

Conversations with Kyaw Zwa Moe, editor of Burma's most well-known and well-established independent newspaper, the English Edition of *The Irrawaddy*, which his elder brother founded in Thailand in 1992. The newspaper relied on undercover reporting to counterbalance the military's draconian censorship laws. Truly a voice of freedom, Kyaw Zwa Moe has dedicated his life to freedom of expression and demonstrated time and again the virtues of hope, empowerment and courage. In this interview, he talks about his student activism [starting at 16 as a high school student] and how he kept himself sane as a 19-year old [arrested], while those around him broke down in jail. Readers will learn how he drew on adversity in prison to inspire him to make a difference, to improve himself and to offer something meaningful to the world after his release. He draws on his own experiences as an educated youth, describing how his upbringing in a freethinking intellectual environment made Burma's injustices unconscionable, obvious and intolerable.

*"I felt ready to expose any kind of inequality and injustice,
even though we were in front of the machine guns."*

ALAN CLEMENTS: You, my dear man, are the person most responsible for my education about Burma, about forming the right opinion on complex issues. Editor of the English editions of the *Irrawaddy* magazine, you're a leading journalist here in Burma. It is an honor to speak with you.

KYAW ZWA MOE: Thank you, nice to meet you.

AC: Most every morning the first thing I do is open the *Irrawaddy*. I've done this for years. In addition, I cannot tell you how many people ask how best to understand the truth of Burma's struggle for freedom, and I tell them: go to the *Irrawaddy* online, and seek no other source.

How to describe you? A risk taker—

KZM: A risk taker; that's a good word.

AC: May I ask, how long were you in prison?

KZM: For eight years, in two notorious prisons: Insein Prison, one of the biggest prisons in Burma, and Tharawaddy Prison, which developed notoriety since the British colony era, when many patriots and freedom fighters, including peasant rebellion leader Saya San, were detained and executed there.

AC: You have... what's the word? 'Sacrificed' so much ...

KZM: That's a big word.

AC: How to describe you—revolutionary activist? A democracy rebel? Dissident journalist? A freedom fighter? All of them, and more. You've taken risks. You've paid a large price for those risks—eight years in two notorious prisons. And, I dare ask about torture; the conditions alone I hear are torturous. My question: People worldwide are asking how a political prisoner in Burma copes with so much *dukkha* (suffering). What were your methods? How did you talk to yourself? And how did you get through the really tough times?

KZM: I'm asked this question quite often, whenever I'm with journalists or foreign friends or diplomats. It looks like a good question, and people want to know the answer, but it's difficult to answer in a sentence or two. Essentially, it's the combination of your attitude and your personality, your positive thinking and your resilience, and your courage and your belief in what you were doing. That mixture of mind states will determine how well you cope with any difficulties and obstacles in prison. Otherwise you will die there. One's mentality is everything.

AC: Mindful intelligence – control your mind or die?

KZM: Yes. Some of my cellmates went crazy after spending three or four years in prison, and a number of political prisoners died in prison due to its harsh conditions. I was just 19 when I was imprisoned, so it was difficult for me to cope with my emotions. I had just passed my matriculation when I was arrested in 1991, when Daw Aung San Suu Kyi won the Nobel Peace Prize. See, our group was called *10D*—10D stands for December 10th, the date Daw Suu was awarded the Prize. That year, hundreds of university students took to the streets in the university campus and most got arrested. I was arrested in connection with that protest. Some were sentenced to 10-15 years, including Ko Ko Gyi, one of the prominent student leaders at the time.

AC: What were you charged with?

KZM: 5(J), the Emergency Provision Act, which was originally enacted in 1950, and used to suppress dissidents.

AC: What does it state?

KZM: Essentially, it imposes death penalties and life prison sentences for treason or sabotage against military organizations, as well as up to seven years in prison for a range of other offenses against the state.

AC: Life under Big Brother.

KZM: Yes. I was charged with organizing political activities together with my colleagues. Another charge was for publishing a political journal, known as *"Oway,"* the same name as the historic student publication that Aung San, the father of Daw Aung San Suu Kyi, edited during the independent struggle in the 1930s. Clandestinely, we published that journal and distributed it. Because of those two things I was sentenced to 10 years by a military tribunal of the regime. I wasn't a journalist at the time, but I'd published, with my colleagues, a political journal in secret. That was one of the main charges against me.

AC: How did you first get involved in your country's struggle for freedom?

KZM: I think the fundamental element in me is just "truth." You know, we tend to be more courageous when young. When I was 15, like other young people in Burma, I felt ready to expose any kind of inequality and injustice, even though we were in front of machine guns.

AC: Talk about rising to the challenge. Peacefully facing machine guns as a teenager?

KZM: Yes, of course. We started our political activities before 8.8.88.

AC: Can you say more about that?

KZM: I think you are aware that, in 1987, Ne Win's socialist government demonetized the currency. Overnight the equivalent of the $100 bill became worthless. Just taken off the market. Instantly, those who had money in cash lost their life savings. And, of course, our families and our parents were affected badly by that, and in the schools, young people, including me, were very upset. We suffered, and we knew our parents were suffering. My father was a lecturer at the engineering university and the public university, and my mother was a businesswoman, so of course, they were affected. That affected the children too. From then on, we were motivated. Another thing was that even before then, I liked reading, so I read a lot of books on politics and on the history of our country. I think that maybe I already had political thoughts in my mind before then. At the time, in 1987, I was 16 years old.

AC: So young to be politically active.

KZM: Yes. Because I've absorbed my political interest from two big bookshelves we had in our house. I think there were over 2,000 books, both Burmese and English language books. Most of the Burmese books were historical literature, about Bogyoke Aung San (Aung San Suu Kyi's father) and other leading members of our anti-colonial struggle under British rule and how they struggled during the independence era. Those books really made me interested in politics before 1988. And one more source would be the environment we lived in and my own family. Every day I heard their views and perspectives.

AC: In '88, in August, where were you?

KZM: In August '88 I was in school, but before then, as I said earlier, one or two months before, at the Yangon University Campus, some students had already staged a protest. I tried to convince some of my friends to join me, to come to the university campus and to support them. We were wearing white and green, the high school uniform, and we went to the university and the students were very happy to see younger students joining them. I organized that kind of small thing in my school, for five people, and then the next day maybe ten people and so on.

AC: You were an activist from the beginning, an organizer, but did you know that your activism wouldn't be tolerated? We all know what happened in '88—diplomats say, as you know, that between 1,000 and 5,000 people were mercilessly killed. Some with bayonets and others at point blank range. Did you have any idea that what you were doing could result in death, or torture, or prison?

KZM: Definitely. I think every young person was aware of this. When we read the history books, for example, in 1962, Ne Win's government and his deputy, Sein Lwin, tried to kill many young people and blew up the student union building. We learned a lot about those kinds of dangers and risks—killing, torture, and so on—from books about our own country and its authoritarian government. At the same time, we knew that our government was that same government. So, we expected those kinds of terrible things might happen to us if we continued our activism. Ne Win's government was especially oppressive. They always responded brutally to any peace movement. Even though we knew that, we just continued doing what we believed in.

AC: And what is motivating you, at the heart of it all? A change in the government? Freedom for your people? What were your ideals?

KZM: I think as a young person you don't really know or realize what a democracy is, or what freedom is, though you enjoy it from when you are born. You get it from books, from TV sometimes, from movies, and we also learned from acquaintances that it was much better than this government's restrictive policy. What we clearly knew, however, was that the socialist government was very oppressive, because some of our older relatives and acquaintances were put in jail quite often, even though they didn't get involved in serious political issues. Also, some of my grandparents and relatives got involved in politics from 1962 or before then, so they retold their stories—very thrilling stories and very interesting stories, even from the jungles. I was brought up through those written histories and their stories. I learned a lot from those people as well as from the books.

AC: You grew up in an atmosphere of deep respect for your conscience and the ability to express your dissent. In other words, you were an activist by growing up in this remarkable family of intellectuals, political activists and so on. However, you're a young man. You're 16 years old in '88. What were your mother and father saying to you? Were they proud of you, were they frightened for you, or both?

KZM: Yes or no. I mean, of course, all our parents were afraid that their children would be killed or put in prison. So of course they tried to stop me, especially my mother. Actually, however, she was also very supportive, and she was against the socialist regime too. But the thing was she also knew, and I knew, that I might end up in jail. Maybe I'd even be killed on the street by the soldiers. That's why she kept trying to stop me, but she couldn't. I think she gave up, especially when in '88 everyone took to the streets and she was kind of encouraging me at the time. That means she was against the dictatorship like her son but just didn't want her son to be killed or arrested. But after the military staged a coup, she tried again to talk me out of it, because some of my friends were arrested before me. So, from 1988 to 1991, I secretly continued with my political activism as well as publishing the *Oway* political journal. In English, it translates as the voice of the peacock. As you know, the fighting peacock is our symbol of revolution.

AC: You set out to deliberately challenge the mindset of dictatorship?

KZM: Definitely. I and other young protesters knowingly or unknowingly were disgusted by all types of injustice. That's why they were really angry when they found out about our activities three years later. So, I didn't take part in the 1991 protest in the university campus, but when I was interrogated in the military intelligence unit, MI7 and MI6, they found out what I'd been doing since 1988. Especially the political journal, run by 10 of us. That's why, even though I hadn't taken part in the recent protest, they didn't release me.

AC: How did they come to find you? Can you take us back there?

KZM: I was at my home, on the night of December 14th. I'd just come back from Mandalay where my relatives live, and I was arrested that night. That means they were watching my house for a long time. They knew the instant I'd arrived back and ordered the military intelligence units to arrest me.

AC: Your mother and father were there?

KZM: My father was away at the time, but my mother was with me. They knocked on the door just after midnight and asked if I lived there, even though they already knew me, already had my pictures. They searched the whole house, especially my room and especially the books and my cabinet, for an hour or two. After that, the captain, who was wearing civilian clothes, said to my mother, "I want to take Kyaw Zaw Moe for a moment." That's all they said. For a moment, because they had questions to ask.

My mother knew what it meant, but she didn't say anything. Only nodded. She told me to wear a jacket because it's winter, so I put on a jacket and went out with them. They handcuffed me, put me in a truck and hooked the handcuffs above my head.

They took me to MI6. Ten days in two interrogation centers. Both of them are notorious—MI6 and MI7. MI6 is responsible for any kind of underground movement. MI7 is responsible for student activities, student protests, so I was put in two interrogation centers. Eight days in MI6, two days in MI7. That means two units wanted to ask a lot of questions of me, because of the journal as well as my activities since 1988.

AC: Day one, what did they do?

KZM: Well, of course, as they did with other political activists, they tortured me, beat me, physically and mentally tortured me. I wasn't allowed to sleep at night. The whole night they kept interrogating me, until maybe 4 or 5am. Only then was I allowed to go back to my small cell. Then they came back in the afternoon and took me for another interrogation into the night or early morning.

AC: Unimaginable. What is going through their minds?

KZM: It's torture. That's why I always say, whenever I'm interviewed about that moment, that those 10 days in the MI were *hell*. Really Hell. Intolerable. After, when you're sent to the prison, you're relieved, happy because the interrogation period is over. Sometimes people are interrogated again, even in prison, but it's different from the cells in the interrogation center, which were really terrible. They always put you on a hook or put a blindfold over your eyes. You can't see anything for three or four days. Sometimes you get just one meal, and no water sometimes.

AC: What did they want to know? They already know everything, right?

KZM: Well, they didn't know everything. We couldn't tell them about all of our activities, because if we told them everything, all the people we'd done things with, our colleagues, our friends outside, would be arrested. We tried to give only a very small amount of information to them in the beginning. That was our strategy. Even though we didn't have any experience in interrogation, we'd heard lots of stories from former political prisoners and politicians. They always told us not to give all the information in the beginning. But definitely tell them later, because if they start torturing you, you can't stand it. If they torture you a lot, if they beat you a lot, you'll spit it out. But maybe after two or three days. You should try to lie, to give misinformation to them, so that during that time our colleagues could run away. That was our strategy. That meant they wouldn't get more people from our network.

AC: Talk about mind control. When you think back to that time, to those men, what have you done with your bitterness, your anger, your hatred, if you even have any? Where is it today?

KZM: I don't know how it is for other people, but for me I wasn't angry. Of course, I didn't like the military government and Khin Nyunt, the spy chief at the time, and its entire system. I don't like those dictators, but I don't have any feeling for revenge.

AC: What feelings did you have?

KZM: When I was put in jail, we all shared our feelings with our cellmates. Luckily, I was put in a cell where there were only political prisoners. I was the youngest in my cell, and there were five of us. Of course, none of us wanted to be in jail, behind bars. I'd just passed my matriculation and I was waiting to attend university. All of the universities and colleges were shut down because of the 1988 protest and 1991 protest, so I was just waiting to attend university. I was keen to study further but I was put in jail. So, I should have been angry, but I managed to cope with my desire. That's why I tried to get books in prison even though reading and writing were illegal at the time, were not allowed for political prisoners.

AC: No books, no paper, no pens?

KZM: No books, no paper, no pens at all. All stationary was illegal at the time, but I was keen to learn something, and, as I said, I also had English language books on my bookshelf, that I started reading some English books as well. So, in prison, I tried to get the English books, to learn the language. It was a long process.

AC: So, you're saying that you were blessed, really, in a horrendous situation, to have your friends and colleagues there, other political prisoners? Talking with them was a way to process and come to terms with the trauma of torture and imprisonment? You would openly talk together?

KZM: Yes, that's right. Talking was accepted. In a small cell, it was ok because the guards couldn't hear what we were talking about. Sometimes a guard might try to listen to what we were saying. It was usually the prison guards—not really the MI guards—who were not really politically aware of what we were talking about, so it was ok. Officially we weren't allowed to talk about politics in prison, especially when you shout it to other cells. But sometimes we broke the rules and regulations. Sometimes we even sang songs in the cell.

AC: You kept your revolutionary spirits high in every way you could?

KZM: We did. On another note, what I want to say is that three or four years later, in 1994, my mother died in a car accident. She was quite young at that time, maybe 49 years old, and she was the only person who supported me, who came to visit me in prison. Every two weeks she bought food and anything I needed in prison, even for my cellmates. Then she died, in a car accident. It was shock. Some even said that it was an assassination, but that wasn't true. I knew it wasn't because the military ferry collected her tricycle (she was on a tricycle). But some people, especially some of my friends, thought that it was deliberate. It wasn't. If I had believed it was intentional, I might have had hatred for the military regime, but it wasn't true. Anyway, my point is that I passed through a lot of difficulties in prison and in the interrogation center without hatred.

> *"Maybe this is something chronic for them,*
> *like a disease that they're not aware of."*

ALAN CLEMENTS: Almost all human rights organizations worldwide have documented in detail, in Burma, the various forms of torture, the number of political prisoners, and all forms of human rights atrocities from forced labor to the systematic raping of women to ethnic cleansing. You are, from a young age, in 'hell,' as you said; a country described as a prison within prisons. My question: Why do people commit human rights atrocities?

KYAW ZWA MOE: Well, that's a very good question. The first thing is, I think, that they have fear. Those people, especially those in power and who have been in power for a long time, they simply don't want to give it up. They want to keep that life for a long time, even maybe for their next generation, their relatives and cronies and subordinates. That's one thing. We can call it "power greediness." The power, the lifestyle. I think sometimes even policies are made up to keep their lifestyle. So they misused power.

AC: To enshrine their authority?

KZM: Yes. Like the Constitution. And look at other countries, like North Korea and other dictatorial countries, where they've been doing the same thing. If you look at those dictators, from one country to another, even though they have different backgrounds, different color and different history, sometimes they look like they were born from the same mother! They have the same attitude. So maybe this is something chronic for them, like a disease of which they're not aware. Psychologically they really believe in what they're doing. The previous military government kept saying, 'This is for the country, for the people.' Every government says so, but I think they also believe in what they say, after repeating it again and again for years, for decades. I think people can easily start to believe their own propaganda, their own lies.

AC: The Khmer Rouge said they didn't know that what they were doing was wrong. In the Nuremberg trials with the Nazi hierarchy, they felt that it was a moral imperative to continue the holocaust. There are so many examples of wrongful wars started by lies and propaganda. Do you think Than Shwe and the previous regimes, whether Saw Maung or Ne Win, believe that it's morally right to kill, torture and oppress the people?

KZM: I think all dictators have that kind of belief. I think Than Shwe or maybe Ne Win might have thought that sometimes they had to oppress the people. But for what? They always said their actions were for the sake of the people and the whole of society. So sometimes I think they didn't mind killing 3,000 or 4,000 people, like in 1988. They might have believed that it was for the benefit of the other 40 million people. Maybe they thought that it was the right decision, because "this small group has the wrong perception and wrong direction just for their willingness to keep power and to continue to enjoy their wealth and privileges."

AC: Many people have asked me, while travelling in Western countries, "Why does Burma oppress its own people?" As an American, many people think that America's free and that we're a great country. Of course, there are great things about America. But the truth is that we are often a violent and aggressive nation. Our governments have repeatedly played out their megalomania and wrongfully invaded other countries—Vietnam, South American countries, Afghanistan. How many people have died in Iraq? They're not only wrongful wars, they're savage acts of aggression—acts of cruelty based upon some perversity, some ideology called "regime change" or "spreading democracy" and or the need to "secure oil." And so, the clique of men up in Naypyidaw and here in Yangon, Than Shwe, Ne Win, Khin Nyunt, and everyone else, it's a case of 'protect the fatherland.' And is that rooted to some extent in a fear and loathing of Western countries? Is it the hypocrisy of Western countries that repels them, that justifies the killing of the few to save the many? What did they tell the public about why they were killing monks in 2007? In other words, how do they justify killing unarmed people?

KZM: Well, since 1962, when Ne Win staged a coup, killing some young students and blowing up the student union building, what they said is that they're trying to rescue the country to rebuild the nation. The main reason was the ethnic rebels and communist rebels at the time. They always used the phrase 'the multi-colored rebels around the country--'

AC: Are a threat...?

KZM: Are a threat. They were a threat, that's why they tried to modernize the military in their own way and build up the military.

AC: The whole notion of the Kachin problem, the Rakhine problem, the Karen, the Shan war—all of these, from the Burman's point of view, are threats to the sovereignty of the whole, thus they must kill anyone who protests anywhere?

KZM: Of course, for the unity and the sovereignty of the country.

AC: So, they're protecting you from the possibility of a Kachin overthrow, a Karen overthrow?

KZM: Right, and of course look at Yugoslavia at the time, especially in 1962 before Yugoslavia collapsed. I think they shared that kind of fear, and Ne Win and other leading members of the socialist regime had that same fear. I think even U Nu's government, from 1948 to 1958, had that same fear. That they're trying to keep the whole country in sovereignty and as a union, because when they struggled for independence, before 1948, some of the ethnic groups didn't join the struggle for independence. Since Bogyoke Aung San's era, the Burman politicians and the other ethnic people, I think, had a problem. Some of the ethnic groups were loyal to the British Army, so that meant Burman and other ethnic people—not all, some—didn't trust each other. They didn't have trust, because, like Bogyoke Aung San and other leaders, they might feel that the British had colonized the country, but some of the ethnic people were loyal to the British. They might feel that they were not really unified, not really united at the time. They tried to keep it united with arms after that, U Nu and especially Ne Win, after 1962. Even during U Nu's era, they couldn't manage to hold peace talks with all of the ethnic people. That's why Ne Win staged a coup, with arms and the military. That's why Burma had a military regime from 1962.

AC: Your country, from what I know, has been brutalized from the outside. The British came, and it wasn't pretty. They oppressed the people, and in many ways created a slave state.

KZM: The Japanese came.

AC: In World War II. And their bombing obliterated much of Mandalay and Rangoon, correct?

KZM: Right.

AC: The fiercest fighting from the Japanese Army towards the Allied soldiers took place on this soil. I remember Sayadaw U Pandita telling me that when he was a young monk it wasn't uncommon to see Buddhist nuns raped by soldiers. And I was also told that by the Mahasi Yeiktha, before it was built, there was a Japanese torture center nearby. I heard some grizzly details of that era. In other words, Burma has been brutalized. And then from within you've had this succession of heroic men—Bogyoke Aung San, your first Prime Minister, U Nu, who of course, was ousted by Ne Win. The great Secretary General of the UN, U Thant. But more to the point, you can almost understand the mind of Ne Win after what you've seen here in Burma for 150 years, the wars and the British invasion, the unthinkable hypocrisies and brutalities of the Japanese. Look at Britain—wherever Britain went they sent a wave of exploitation that essentially committed ethnic cleansing in every country they went to, and if it wasn't a physical death it was a mental death. In Australia they killed almost every aboriginal. In other words, you have been dealt the worst blows, and so this aggressive xenophobia by dictators here is palpable.

KZM: True, and though I don't have any experience of when the British or the Japanese invaded, I think I could understand after reading a lot of books. These days foreign journalists are saying this government is xenophobic, Ne Win's government especially, but I think I can understand a bit about the mindset of those leaders at the time, even Ne Win. As you said, they had had that experience, from the British and from the Japanese. That was a relevant reason for them to say publicly that we needed to be united, otherwise foreign invaders would come. Than Shwe was the same. They had that kind of fear and attitude and responded out of that fear.

For us, for other people, for outsiders, especially these days in the 21st century, people believe that it was just an excuse. Of course, it became an excuse with time and policy changes, but they still have that kind of mindset, it's how they grew up. It's kind of understandable how they became dictators.

AC: They've taken it to the extreme.

KZM: Yes, of course. Look at the name 'Naypyidaw.' It means the 'Abode of Kings.'

AC: I assume all dictators have grandiose images of themselves. After all, stating the obvious here, they control and kill with impunity with their massive military forces stocked with tanks, jets, and rockets, along with a police force following their every command. Setting aside the person here, the dictators, the problem is this psychology. The mindset of dictatorship is what we need to study. The psychology of tyranny, domination, and corruption. My question: You've been invited to address Parliament; you have 10 minutes. What would you say?

KZM: *(Laughs)* Very good question! Well, we have a lot of things to be resolved in this era. The first thing is that they must change their mindset. We were talking about their mindset, their attitude and where they came from, from a historical point of view, but if they really want radical change, revolutionary change, I think they have to change their mindset first.

Let me explain. Since coming back last year, I've found all of the people—not only the authorities but everyone, from clerks and low-ranking officials and drivers and street vendors—are used to this oppressive society. They were born here. There are a lot of flaws that they don't see or know need to be fixed. So, especially with the leadership, the ministries, and the president, some of the leaders in Naypyidaw, might want to keep this reform process going as much as they can. But the problem is that they don't know how to do it. They're not sure whether they've changed their mindset. That is the first thing for everyone—the mindset. They have to change it. This is a quite broad issue. To be specific is more difficult.

AC: I think it was Daw Suu that said, in addressing those who've been imprisoned—prisoners of conscience—that in this country where there is no freedom, freedom is found only in conscience. And even so, they imprison those with a free conscience, like yourself. Eight years. She went on to say that 'although they imprison your body, they cannot imprison your mind,' unless you let them.

KZM: True.

AC: Take that thought process to the authorities, the government, retired or not-so-retired, the people at large, even leaders around the world, they're in mindsets, as you said. They believe that what they think is true and right, even at the expense of others. And I've often thought to myself, 'I'm a president, I'm going to have a glass of wine tonight, and I know that my orders have killed innocent boys and girls in another country.' How do they do that? I don't want to become accustomed to that, so my question: mindsets need to change; your mind is remarkably refined but for Than Shwe and dictators and presidents and prime ministers, even priests who are committing paedophilia, how do they change their mindsets? How do they free themselves from those delusional mind-structures?

KZM: That's the work of democracy. That's why when you tell anyone else to change their mindset or attitude it's a big challenge. They first have to understand that they need to change, right? Which means they first have to understand that what they are doing is wrong, and then they have to have the willingness and moral courage to correct themselves. Otherwise they won't change. They have to realize what you've said is right. It's really difficult.

AC: Maybe this is where anti-torture torture comes in?

KZM: *(Laughs)* Yeah, maybe, maybe.

AC: *Dhamma* torture or wisdom torture—the overhauling of a corrupt mindset with mindful intelligence.

KZM: Sure. And discipline. In prison, we were in a special jail attached to Insein Prison, a small prison. I think there were about 400 political prisoners in two buildings, maybe a little less. In our building there were about 23 cells downstairs and I was put in cell number 13. All of us were political prisoners, from 19 years old up to 60 or 70 years old, seasoned politicians as well as senior journalists. I met a lot of people there. I was fortunate to meet a diverse group that were educated and experienced, as well as young students who were courageous. But the thing is that they were habituated to what they had done in the past. Even if you're young, sometimes you don't know what you are doing even in the morning. You wake up, you go to the bathroom automatically, and you might wash your face and brush your teeth. Are you thinking while doing it? Generally, you don't think. You just take it for granted. This is the attitude. This is just what you're supposed to do in the morning. Who told you? Your parents, right, when you were young? Just, "go to the bathroom and wash your face and clean your hands." That's what you do but you never question if it's true or if that's the right moment to do it. This is a good example—no one is thinking about what they're doing. Maybe 70 percent of what you do every day, you do without thought.

Take smokers, for example. Sometimes they don't know what they're doing, they're just smoking. After they finish a meal, they take out a cigarette and light it, but sometimes they have no idea what they're doing. My point is that in prison, young people like me sometimes got some freedom; sometimes you could visit other cells and talk to the other political prisoners. That was a really good opportunity for us. But most political prisoners—I won't say all, but most—just killed their time. Killed their time talking to each other, repeating the same old stories. I mean, if someone in my cell started talking, I knew what he was going to say. It's always the same story. We didn't have any new stories in prison.

My point is that some of those political prisoners didn't want to learn anything new in prison. I have to include a little self-criticism, and maybe my question at the time was, "Why did they put me in prison?" That was a big question for me, "Why? Why ten years?" I was 19 years old when I was put in jail. Quite young. I had no weapons, nothing. I was nobody. Why did they put me in prison for 10 years? This question I think I answered for myself. I believed that the military regime wanted our group, and all the political activists against the regime, to be dead in prison.

AC: What do you mean?

KZM: In 10 years, after you're released, you're finished. Dead. You don't even know what's going on outside prison. You can't follow anything that's going on outside the prison. That's what they wanted. They tried to kill our mentality, our brain capacity, everything, our thinking, our philosophy. Kill it. That's their main thing. That's why, in prison, my idea was to learn anything I could, anything I could get hold of.

AC: Learning was your resistance?

KZM: It was my resistance, a power that kept me alive in prison.

> *"When I was put in jail, I tried not to say the word "dukkha"—suffering."*

ALAN CLEMENTS: How did you keep your learning alive in prison? What did you do?

KYAW ZWA MOE: I tried to smuggle books into prison, although illegal. I tried to learn something every day, language as well. I tried to convince some of the wardens and guards who were sympathetic to the pro-democracy movement, as well as to young student activists like me, to smuggle in small pieces of paper. And they did, some of them. Just a single piece of paper. Street vendors wrapped betel nuts with a piece of newspaper or a piece of magazine. The people who eat betel nuts brought the betel nut packet to the prison. They are allowed—everyone chews betel nuts. The prison guards could bring it in, so I told one person specifically to please wrap the betel nuts in paper which is written in English—"Don't bring it in a newspaper in the Burmese language." We asked for the newspaper to get information, but I always asked them to wrap the betel nuts in an English language paper. I wanted to learn the language. Even just half a page was enough.

AC: And you would read this, and study whatever was on that paper?

KZM: That's right, because if you start learning a language you need to have a word or two at least. If you don't know that, you had to ask some other experienced and older politicians who knew some English what the words were, and they explained it to me a little bit. Later I tried to get Newsweek and Time magazine. I got a lot of books in prison during those eight years. I was released in 1999, and I think that same year the ICRC came in, and after I was released, some of the prisons started allowing political prisoners to read books *(laughs)*.

AC: Just as you're leaving?

KZM: Yeah, bad timing for me! From 1991–1999: no books. But I still got several books, including a dictionary, and especially old issues of Newsweek and Time magazine. I even got some Bertrand Russell essays, and some essays of Martin Luther King. That's why I never had regrets. I always kept my mind active.

When I heard from inmates that my mother had passed away, it took only two or three days to restart my study [learning] again. I tried to focus on my study [reading in my strict timetable]. I wanted to forget or overcome the saddest news, you know? Otherwise you cannot do anything—you cannot think, you cannot learn, you can't study anything with that kind of bad memory creeping into your mind all the time. That's why I tried to transform those bad and sad news and incidents into energy for me. So, for eight years that's what I did in prison—learning, improving my knowledge. That, to me, is political resistance against the military regime or the dictatorship. That was my philosophy. Maybe other people can't understand it. Some political prisoners might want to have a meeting amongst themselves, talking about political issues and policies, but what I was thinking was 'what are we talking about without new information in our brain or learning something new?' It's nothing to me. That, for me, is just killing time.

AC: Inspiring. And after your mom passed away, who came to see you?

KZM: My grandmother. My mom's mother. She's still alive [she passed away two years ago].

AC: You've dealt with much suffering, so much *dukkha*.

KZM: *Dukkha*, yes, but if you don't think they're *dukkha* it's better for you. If you think 'that is a *dukkha*' then that is a problem, for me.

AC: So that's another form of resistance, not to think of *dukkha* as *dukkha*? How do you do that? What is your method of not experiencing *dukkha* as *dukkha*? Interesting to hear that.

KZM: I think that the combination of your attitude, your personality, positive thinking and also your ideology, and what you want to do, determines the way you live. In prison, it's very easy to say the word "*dukkha*." Everyone is saying it in Burma. This is Buddhism. Buddhists like to say "*dukkha*." When you go to the monastery the monks will talk to you and say, "this is a *dukkha*, this is another *dukkha*," things like that, but people just end up saying "*dukkha, dukkha, dukkha*" all day. Of course, they have a lot of *dukkha* here, when they take the bus, when they walk in the streets, everywhere, everything is *dukkha*. It's a really poor country so it's a real *dukkha*. But if you keep saying *dukkha*, and you would feel that all of those things are *dukkha*, real *dukkha*—then you live a life of *dukkha*.

AC: If you label it as *dukkha*, interpret it mentally as *dukkha*, it really becomes *dukkha*?

KZM: Yes, and if you keep saying it then it becomes an attitude, and that attitude I think goes into your blood, seeps into your veins. You're now in the cycle of *dukkha* as a traditional Buddhist way, you know? That's why when I was put in prison, I tried not to say the word "*dukkha*." The point is that if you face "*dukkha*," you have to overcome it. But not to say it without solving it.

AC: The transformation of language itself as *Dhamma* practice.

KZM: Yes. Of course, I'm a human being and sometimes I happen to say it, but I'm trying to say it less and less and less. I don't like saying and reciting *"dukkha" (laughs)*.

AC: *(Laughs)* What would you say instead? Did you call it '*sukkha*'—happiness?

KZM: *(Laughs)* No, you can't say that! That is different, it's not true so you can't say so.

AC: You practice *sati*? [mindfulness].

KZM: I am not quite sure. I never meditated in prison.

AC: Not at all?

KZM: Nobody taught it to me. Some people said that meditation will keep you alive in prison, whenever you face *dukkha*, but I never did. But that doesn't mean that I wasn't in some way meditating—meditation is just a process in your mind, right? Simply a process to check your desire. For example, in prison, if you want to eat something sweet, like chocolate, or in Burma we have *htan lyat*, jaggery or traditional Burmese delicacy, but you don't get it, then what will you do? I'm asking myself, can I say aloud, "Oh, I want some jaggery, something sweet!" Of course, sometimes we say so, but I don't want to repeat it again and again, especially with my friends in the cell who were older than me, senior students. Sometimes some of them would say, "Oh, I want to eat this and that," and I listened and thought, 'Ok, I also want to eat, but, you know…' If they say it repeatedly, I told them in a friendly way, like a brother, 'don't say this, just try to forget it, forget what you think because you cannot get it in the cell at the moment.' In that way you can cope with your desire. If that desire accumulates in your mind you might go crazy! I'm not talking about the desire to eat jaggery or something sweet, but…

AC: The desire to be free of the prison?

KZM: Yes. For example, my house was not far from the prison where I was kept—only three or four miles. Sitting in my cell on a quiet night, 8pm or 9pm, when it's quiet in prison, you can hear voices outside, buses going in the direction of my house, sometimes the bells of trishaws. You can hear all that, and at times, I immediately felt desirous of returning home on that passing trishaw. If you followed that desire all the time that would become a major problem for you. Of course, wanting jaggery is nothing, in comparison.

Sometimes when my mother came to visit me, I couldn't physically touch her—there were three layers of iron bars between us—but a visitation every two weeks became a routine to me. And inevitably, with unrecognized desire, grasping and attachment builds, and sometimes I really felt that I wanted to return home with her. As I saw this, I learned to keep it in perspective. But if one isn't, as you might say, mindfully intelligent, that kind of desire and feeling can build and make someone go crazy in prison. So, it was essential to cope with your desire, in any way you deemed right and beneficial.

For me, I did not have any formal meditation method, but I think I was meditating in my mind, having a mindful or conscious eye, so to speak, on that kind of wanting and getting rid of that unrealistic desire, at that time, as quickly as possible to its first arising. But at the same time, if you don't have any desire, you won't have anything. That is another problem. So, you have to use the middle way, I think.

AC: Interesting. Please say more.

KZM: For example, I really wanted books to improve for my knowledge in prison. For that I had to take repeated risks. But, if you have a desire for books and equally knowing how difficult it is to get them in prison, and if you don't try to get them, then you will not fulfil your desire for learning. You are compelled to think differently about the things that you want—you ask yourself, 'what is it that I really, really want or need? Jaggery? Just for the taste? For vitamins? For health? Is that needed more than books?' Books are really important for me, for my future, for the time when I'll be released. You have to weigh desires with the risks, consequences, and value involved in acting on them. So, in my case, I became determined to try, come what may, to get as many books as I could, even though it was really risky. In other words, learning in prison through books far outweighed the danger in not getting them and or being caught with them.

AC: What might happen?

KZM: When you were found with a piece of paper or a pencil, or especially a book, you were put in solitary confinement, your legs shackled with iron chains and you were not allowed to meet family members for three months. Which meant that you didn't get food or anything else from them. You had to eat only lousy prison food. A lot of things might happen, and then if you're found with a political paper your actual prison sentence might be extended by 7 year to 10 years. That's what happened to U Win Tin.

AC: U Win Tin, the NLD co-founder and journalist?

KZM: Yes. A group of political prisoners in 1995 or '96, in Insein Prison, were found with many books, even with secret reports to the UN human rights rapporteur at that time. Someone would have smuggled these in and, of course, they're also trying to smuggle them out, to send reports to the UN. That's why they got an extended prison term.

AC: I know this is probably not a necessary question, but for those people around the world who have never heard a prisoner of conscience speak from Burma, what was the day-to-day life of a political prisoner during your years of imprisonment? What time do you get up, what do you do, what do you eat, what do you say, what do you sleep on, what does the air smell like? Anything you wish to share, please.

KZM: Well, our cell was smaller than normal ones which are about 8 x 12 feet. The British built Insein Prison in 1887. For the cells in our prison, we had smaller ones. I think it was 8' x 8' and we had five people in it. We had to sleep side by side. And then, in two of the corners of the entrance door, we put food and some plastic plates to eat in one corner, and the other side was our toilet. Our cell was our living room, our washing room, our dining room, our bedroom, our meeting room and our study room, if you studied. That's where we lived for eight years. When you wake up, sometimes you would wash your face with a plastic cup of water, or maybe we would wait until the doors were opened. Sometimes we didn't have space to throw the water in our cell. And we just had only two earthen bowls for excrement. That was the toilet. Two earthen bowls, for five people.

AC: May I ask a very basic question: how did you clean yourself?

KZM: Ah, ha, sometimes we... well, some people used water, but we didn't have enough at that time. The problem is there are only two earthen bowls, and you were locked up for maybe 23 hours a day. Five men in an 8' x 8' cell and only a little bit of water. No running water. Just drinking water in an earthen pot. They put that pot outside our cell. That was the only water we had to drink, but sometimes we could ask people outside—the criminals, who sometimes had to clean the compound—if they would fill one bottle with water from the tank.

AC: And they did?

KZM: Yes, they did, sometimes, but we couldn't rely on it. Most prisoners used clothes to clean themselves, tearing up small clothes, especially longyi. When the longyi's got old we kept them and tore them up. Overall, as you can imagine, it was a challenging reality.

AC: And what about medicines, if you're sick?

KZM: We had to ask our families to send in medicine, like paracetamol and some other medicines.

AC: What about a mosquito net, no such thing?

KZM: No, not at all.

AC: And there are mosquitos in there?

KZM: Of course, a lot.

AC: And bedding, you had a blanket?

KZM: Yeah, we were allowed to have one blanket.

AC: A pillow?

KZM: No pillow. A blanket was ok, and sometimes we could have more than one, but no pillow at all. Never a pillow, and the blankets, we asked family members to bring three or four blankets, which you could fold into something like a bed, with two or three, so it's good to sleep. Otherwise the floor is very rough, very cold concrete, and the concrete is not smooth, not even on the surface, so we needed blankets. The people who could afford it had blankets brought by their families, but some people could not afford them. Some political prisoners, their families could not even meet them, so sometimes we helped. We made a point of sharing our food together in the cell.

AC: Are there lights?

KZM: Yes, one small bulb.

AC: Off and on?

KZM: Mostly on, because it's prison.

AC: They kept it on?

KZM: Not in the daytime, but at night they kept it on all night. You couldn't turn it off.

AC: So, the prison by function is torturous.

KZM: Oh, it is. You could easily get any kind of disease there—no hygiene at all. None. You have to keep yourself healthy; to be very careful when you eat.

AC: All five of you: did you talk about what was going to happen at 10 o'clock, or 11 o'clock? Who decides what? When did you exercise, when did you sleep, when did you get up?

KZM: Well, living there, together for all those years—even couples, even husband and wife, would never stay like that, 24 hours a day in one cell. They couldn't! They would start fighting. It's really difficult to stay with the people in a cell for 23 or 24 hours of the day. They become more than family. They know everything. We know everything about each other. Their attitude, even their smell, everything. In that situation, compromise and negotiation are important. Otherwise you fight with each other, even physically. The basic thing which made us cohesive, not fighting against each other, was our shared interest in politics.

AC: Politics were the binding force of your discussions?

KZM: Political integrity was. There was no class—like A or B class for political prisoners, for instance—in Burma's prisons. So, the system leads us to be seen as criminals, by the authorities and wardens, and other criminal prisoners. But in truth, we hadn't committed a crime. We were arrested and put in jail because of our beliefs. That was our integrity. We always reminded ourselves and each other that we are political prisoners. That meant that we could not be degraded, as with other criminals. Even in our attitude we should be very careful when we act and when we speak with criminals or with the wardens. We tried to be careful when we dealt with them. A fight or a brawl between one political prisoner and another would create a bad image for the community of political prisoners in the prison.

AC: You were guided by conscience for the greater good of the community of other political prisoners?

KZM: We were respectful, even though we didn't like each other sometimes. Of course, we're human beings, we're under a lot of pressure. Sometimes we argued a lot, we fought verbally, but we tried to calm down and reconcile our differences. But some people couldn't. It happened; fights occurred sometimes. But in our cell, it was rare.

AC: You learned democracy in an 8' x 8' cell, the hard way?

KZM: Yes, to some extent. I would say that I not only learned democracy inside the prison I also practiced it there. I believed in using the experience and activities to learn and grow; what you're thinking, processing, dealing and compromising with. That is important. Sometimes when people asked about my ideology it's difficult to say because it doesn't come from books. But I did go to Berkeley University to learn journalism at the graduate school of journalism and other subjects like Southeast Asian Studies six years after I was released.

AC: The full spectrum of study from prisoner of conscience to elite academic training.

KZM: Yes. This is another example of how I learned in prison and how I learned outside prison at a prestigious university. Before I received a scholarship to join the visiting scholar program at UC Berkeley in 2005, I became a reporter at the *Irrawaddy*, but before then, as I told you, I read a lot of books in prison. I didn't know about journalism at all, I didn't have any journalism books, how to write the news or how to write a lead—I never learned that in prison but I read a lot of stories and articles in Time and Newsweek and other magazines. I think that through those books and magazines I absorbed a lot of writing skills, as well as story structures, writing styles and quotes. I tried to remember good quotes, sentences and phrases in those magazines, and I created interviews by playing dual roles as interviewer and interviewee, especially at night when my cell was quiet. Actually, it was for language as well as for knowledge, trying to memorize some of the things going on outside the prison and outside the ward. Many things happened when I was in prison, like with South Africa and with Yugoslavia, and Russia. So, sometimes I wrote down questions for Nelson Mandela or Daw Aung San Suu Kyi and I myself answered thinking myself to be in their shoes.

AC: Nelson Mandela's release, the Yugoslavian horrors...

KZM: Yes, and Croatia and the Serbs...

AC: Yes, I was a year in Zagreb during the war, and later in Sarajevo, and then we had Rwanda...

KZM: Rwanda, of course... I learned a lot about them through those books and news magazines I managed to smuggle into prison. If I hadn't managed to read those stories, I'd know nothing after I was released.

AC: Where were you when Daw Aung San Suu Kyi was released in 1995?

KZM: I was in Insein's annex prison. From 1991 to September 1999.

AC: How did you come to hear of her release? I was in Burma at that time, for six months; that's when I reconnected with U Tin Oo and met U Kyi Maung and so many other great minds for the first time.

KZM: That's when you did the interviews with Daw Suu for *The Voice of Hope*?

AC: That's right; U Tin Oo, U Kyi Maung, U Win Htein, and U Aye Maung, we all became a close circle of friends and family at that time. You were in prison and heard of Daw Suu's release? Did you think you were going to be released as well?

KZM: *(Laughs)* Every prisoner thinks they're going to be released every day! Either the next day, the next day, the next day (tomorrow, tomorrow, and tomorrow), because they have that desire all the time. They don't want to spend even one minute in prison! Even though they pretend it's ok to think like this, practically it's better not to expect release, depending upon the political landscape. As I said, every prisoner wants to be released as soon as possible, and I was among them. But sitting and just hoping for that is a waste of time. It's better to live in the present spending our dark time valuably. That's why I said earlier that prisoners shouldn't expect release the whole time. If they are obsessed with that, they could go crazy.

AC: I think it was Nelson Mandela who once said something similar: 'There wasn't a day that went by for 27 years in prison that I didn't think of being freed.' So, despite your spiritual freedom and your meditation and your conviction in your beliefs, how do you cope, way deep down inside? Is one always thinking of their release?

KZM: Definitely. It's always there. But with regard to your question, in 1991 I was put in jail and four months later I was given a 10-year sentence by the military court, on March 23rd, 1992. One month later, Saw Maung was ousted, then Than Shwe stepped in, and announced they were holding a national convention in early January of 1993. I think they announced four statements at the time. We couldn't listen to the radio, but we heard from the wardens and from our meetings with family members, so we knew. The last one was that the government were considering releasing some prisoners—they didn't say 'political prisoners,' just 'prisoners,' some prisoners who are not supposed to be dangerous for the government. That's what they said. So, of course, we were young students, and we thought, 'Ok, this time we might be released!' *(Laughs)* But it didn't happen. They didn't release me, but out of about 140 people in my group, over 90 people were released.

AC: Anyone from your cell?

KZM: Yes, two guys from my cell were released. I wasn't one of them *(laughs)*.

AC: Did you ever give up hope in prison?

KZM: I don't think I ever gave up hope, because if you give up hope it's easy to get some kind of mental illness, that will lead to physical illness. If you do, you cannot eat, you cannot sleep, you will get other weaknesses and diseases. And depression. That is the main thing you have to get rid of, all the time.

AC: So many people in the world today are depressed, so it seems…

KZM: Definitely! *(Laughs).*

AC: My country eats antidepressants, Valium and other pharmaceuticals, as if they're candy. It's so common, even among children. And frankly, it's a depressing situation when you pay attention: wrongful wars, slaves to a consumer-driven economy and deadening jobs, the prospect of environmental collapse and some are even talking about near term extinction. As you described earlier, we often don't question things; we get up in the morning and turn on the computer, eat, and then start the car or make the commute to work out of habit. But when you start to question, there is very little support for following your heart and taking risks for passion. I hear the same thing from many people: how deadening and depressing my life is inside the economic cage. But then what? How to break free? So often they choose depression as a way to stay imprisoned, so to speak. In your case, how did you in fact ward off depression in prison?

KZM: Well, it's the same thing we were talking about earlier, '*dukkha,*' right? Depression—*dukkha* is the same category. *Dukkha*, when you keep saying that— *dukkha, dukkha, dukkha*—you believe you are in *dukkha* all the time.

AC: *Dukkha* validates *dukkha* and if not resolved, it becomes chronic *dukkha* or depression?

KZM: Yes. If you feel depressed, I think that first of all what you have to do is get rid of it as soon as possible, especially in the cell.

AC: You have to get rid of the label of it as 'depression'? You can't call it depression? You can't call it '*dukkha, dukkha*'?

KZM: That's right, but it's up to each individual person how they deal with that kind of word. For me, I don't even want to say the word. *(Laughs).*

AC: Which word?

KZM: *Dukkha.*

AC: *(Laughs)* I am a convert! Mindfulness of language *Dhamma.* Henceforth, I'm going to eliminate it from my vocabulary! No more use of the D word *(laughs).* And that means I am no longer a Buddhist, right? *(Laughs).*

KZM: *(Laughs)* Of course, I have to admit that sometimes I just spat out that word, if I really felt depressed. Sometimes it automatically comes out of your mouth, you can't control it. But what I'm saying is try and control that kind of feeling, *dukkha* and depression, as much as you can. Otherwise it will creep into the whole of your body. As you said, exercise your mindful intelligence. But don't use the D word! *(Laughs)*.

AC: You have to be disciplined with your thinking about yourself, right? You must be self-responsible, meaning that you must be conscious of how you relate to yourself, and some things you must encourage and some things you must resist.

KZM: True, that's right.

AC: This is the survival code for political prisoners?

KZM: Not only a survival code but also as a way of getting something out of that *dukkha*. *(Laughs)*.

AC: That's another major point, how to make 'prison *dukkha*' a positive experience?

KZM: It's not difficult to survive in prison, you just have to know the way and the methods. What's difficult is to learn something, to educate yourself, to be mindful of what you're doing in prison. For that you need a daily roadmap. That's what people have outside prison. If you want something in your career or calling, you need a roadmap, and for that you need to be disciplined. Again, that's why I never regret my imprisonment. It was a sad story but it's a long time ago. I wasn't really happy, but I wasn't sad. Because I gained something out of prison.

AC: So, what you're saying, in this moment now, taking your wisdom teachings from prison into life and going beyond Buddhism; what you're saying is that if we can make this moment now something that speaks to our heart about learning something that's important to us, that's what keeps you free? Is that what you're saying? How to bring importance and meaning to this moment?

KZM: Definitely; how to make your life meaningful is important. To me, something meaningful is to do something good for your people, your community, your country or your world. Let's call it pluralism. Our lifespan is not that long—maybe less than 100 years, for everyone, you and me and everyone else—but before you die, what you've done is important. I may die tomorrow, but what I have done so far is crucial. It's difficult to measure, but what you've done, especially for people and society, is very important. Wherever you are, if you can make that moment meaningful to you and or to anyone else, it's very, very good. That is the meaning of life.

That's why I really wanted to learn something in prison. The main reason is to continue to effectively contribute to my society after my release.

AC: That's how you kept your sanity?

KZM: Yes. I tried to define that attitude of mind, by learning. This was political resistance. Learning in prison, just reading something in my tiny cell, was political resistance against the dictators, against any dictator in the world. Even if I'm reading a novel, even if I'm reading *Wuthering Heights* by Emile Bronte, or *Great Expectations* by Charles Dickens, no problem—you are learning something there. Some people might think I'm exaggerating: "this is not political resistance against the dictators, you are just reading." But to me, it is resistance against the dictators' wish to kill my knowledge and wisdom in order not to continue fighting them. And with that, I become resilient. I believe that without learning something, without reading a lot in my cell, I wouldn't have been able to contribute to the *Irrawaddy* when I was released. And then, I wouldn't have been able to write the stories you've read over the past years. That's my contribution to my country with what I've learned in my cell.

"Without integrity, any kind of authority is not really effective."

ALAN CLEMENTS: People the world over are looking at your country with a controlled or cautious optimism, as it's been termed by Daw Aung San Suu Kyi. We want to believe in this flicker of democracy. There are about 55 million people in Burma. What do you think is most urgently needed among the people to move democracy forward? How would you advise your country men and women to practice freedom today, to keep the revolution of the spirit alive and forward moving?

KYAW ZWA MOE: They have to speak up, and they have to tell the truth. Not only ordinary people but also the leaders, on both sides, the leaders in Naypyidaw and Daw Aung San Suu Kyi, and also the ethnic leaders. If they're still pretending in the reform process, what can they do realistically? That is very important as a first step. People, especially the politicians and even political activists, sometimes cannot speak their minds. They have to look at the political landscape first. For example, look at the Rohingya issue, look at the Kachin issue, look at the copper mine issue in Letpadaung, where Daw Aung San Suu is the chairman of the committee, and with the Rakhine issue, where Ko Ko Gyi is part of the committee. They have to speak up and tell the truth. They shouldn't be talking out of fear that this reform process will reverse because of their words. That is very important for both sides, the opposition as well as the government. The government is also important. What are they doing—are they pretending? Or are they really trying to reform, genuinely, through this political transformation?

AC: You know, this brings up a very troublesome and crucial issue, which is the question of healing for the country. How do you propose your country deal with the crimes against humanity committed by the dictator and the generals?

KZM: Well, that is our history. That really happened in our past, but the question that both sides have to consider is when it's the right time to deal with it. I don't think we can eliminate the effects of those atrocities, because even me and my family were affected by them. It's an issue for the politicians, especially Daw Aung San Suu Kyi and other political activists, to decide what they should do.

Why am I putting that issue on the leaders? Look at Burmese society—on one hand they are peaceful, and they are patient, and they are reluctant to disclose their own desire. But at the same time, on the other hand, many people were killed. Many were tortured, brutally, by this military mechanism. This is the complexity in our society. It's in a fragile state, at the moment. That's why I think that some of the political leaders, including Daw Aung San Suu Kyi, were criticized by other groups, about why she and some other political leaders were quiet on some human rights abuses. That's why they were being asked that question.

AC: Can you see a truth and reconciliation council forming in Burma?

KZM: Yes, it should be formed.

AC: Would you be in favor of amnesty for those who committed atrocities?

KZM: I don't think I can decide that; the people, the committee that is to be formed for that issue, should decide. But to me, to many Burmese people, even though they suffered a lot in prison, even though their families suffered because of political persecution, we do not have feelings for revenge.

AC: You have none?

KZM: No.

AC: I ask you to take Burma into a global context: millions of people are coming to Myanmar; billions of dollars are being invested in the country, but only by a few people; a handful of foreign billionaires are doing business with a handful of billionaire cronies. In other words, Burma is no longer one of the most isolated countries in the world. What do you want us, the world community, to know about Burma so that we know what we can do, before we come, before we invest, so that we can know right from wrong, and know how best to support your transition to democracy?

KZM: Very good question, and a very complex issue. When I was in Naypyidaw, I raised that question with Daw Aung San Suu Kyi's aide. You know, now we're looking at Cambodia; twenty years ago, Cambodia had an election organized by the United Nations, and where is Cambodia now? Many people, foreign committees as well as an international non-government organization came to Cambodia, tried to build up the country politically and economically, but over twenty years. The problem for me, the question, my main concern, in terms of the world coming to Burma, is a gold rush. Everyone is coming, as you said, with billions of dollars and with their own agenda, not only businessmen but also the governments as well as the non-governmental organizations and foundations. I doubt that all of them have a sincere agenda to help us. They have their own agenda.

For businessmen, they definitely come here to make a profit out of our businesses, and probably other countries might also have that kind of agenda. I mean, don't look only at Western countries but also try to look at Asian countries, China, India, right? They have their own agenda in coming to do business. We have to protect ourselves. We cannot tell them, but Daw Aung San Suu Kyi has definitely told the leaders of other countries, 'please, you can make a profit here but please also take care of the people,' try to share the benefit with local people and take care of environmental issues as well. We have to protect ourselves. Of course, we can tell them, but whether they follow our instructions is another matter.

So, we have to come up with our own policies, especially from the government and political parties, if they can establish a good government. What I believe in is ourselves, in what we can do and should be doing. That is most important. Out of it, we can come up with a good policy for our own people. Definitely, without opening our gates they won't be able to come in, so that is the basic and most fundamental thing, to open up.

I mean, look at the situation before 2010 and after 2010. This government, the leaders, changed their costume and changed their policy a bit, and then people came in. That is my positive point of view for the government, for what they did. We have to create that kind of political environment. Of course, the authorities, those in power, have to create that kind of environment where healthy competition might happen. So, they can come in first, and after that I think the policies and guidelines have to be drawn by the political leaders and government. Only after that can we tell anyone, 'you shouldn't do this and that, we have these rules and regulations.' I think they will listen to us if we have that kind of integrity. Authority will follow integrity, I think. Without integrity, any kind of authority is not really effective. This is the nonviolent way. If we want to get real authority, we should have integrity. We've lost many things in the past five decades. We have to build it up again, to rebuild the country. We must rebuild our integrity. That is crucial for the future well-being of the country.

AC: Yes, you have lost so much.

KZM: We've also lost the younger generation. We lost our education. We lost their health. We lost pretty much everything. So we have to rebuild. In that sense, we are the only ones to reconstruct this country. And it must be emphasized again, that there needs to be a change in mindset: freeing the mind is a future of freedom.

AC: Well, you know, from my perspective, as I mentioned the other day, I would like to officially say it again to you, because you're a remarkable inspiration, and your respect for people, for colleagues, your country, filters through everything you share. In the spirit of South Africa; Desmond Tutu was here, I have a remarkable respect for him; his book, *No Future Without Forgiveness*, is very powerful, being the head of the Truth Council for years. You speak about the power of truth; symbolically, for a lot of us around the world, we fear the idea of imprisonment. And you describe not just physical incarceration, but lying next to your friends for eight years, and I want to let that in, deeply.

Daw Suu, the previous time I saw her, one of the first questions I asked for *The Voice of Hope* was, 'How should we know Burma today?' and she said, "Let the world know we are still prisoners in our own country."

You were in prison at that time and, although she was released, the country was a prison camp. So, my way of saying, in the spirit of South Africa—I don't know how long it was after Mandela's release, and other members of the ANC before Robben Island Prison was closed and made a world heritage site—I think Insein Prison should be closed, the prisoners released, criminals relocated. The British built it, who needs it—dictators have used it to try to kill the spirit, to kill the mind, in your words, of your people. Close it. Close it and let investors and tourists come to a museum of conscience that's constructed on your terms, as a former political prisoner. You let us see what you want us to see there. Make it a world heritage site as a testament to the revolution of the spirit and your country's success in forging democracy out of dictatorship.

So, on that note, thank you for taking the time to share your life. And I hope the whole world will come to support your country, meet you, support the *Irrawaddy* and, most of all, support global human rights and freedom of press. Thank you for your courage, especially your bravery in having books brought in underground to prison. May this book with your words be smuggled into prisons and serve as a light of hope dispelling the darkness of despair.

KZM: Thank you.

AC: And I love the fact that you're a non-meditator.

KZM: *(Laughs)* A meditator in spirit or a meditator without a method. Just do what's right, that's all.

AC: *(Laughs)* You've taken it to a new dimension. It's brilliant. Language Dhamma.

Conversation with Kyaw Zwa Moe

January 2020

> *"If I have to name the current political landscape of Burma, I would call it 're-civilianizing the militarized nation.'"*

ALAN CLEMENTS: It's been a long time since we last spoke and so many significant events have occurred here in Burma over those years. As editor of perhaps the world's leading magazine offering in depth coverage of your country's most important news, may I invite you to provide an overview or a synopsis of the most critical issues your country is facing today in moving away from military rule and forward towards democracy?

KYAW ZWA MOE: We are still at the state of the unfinished story of our democratic movement. We are halfway from military rule to genuine democracy. We could say that we have democracy because the government we have now was elected by the majority of the people in 2015. It's a kind of a democracy, right? Basically, democracy means that you get the government that you voted for.

Now we've learned in reality that democracy alone is not enough. If a democracy is controlled by an undemocratic constitution, it is almost meaningless. Now our country is facing that problem, but we sensed it a long time ago, when the previous military regime got their drafted constitution approved in 2008.

In fact, democracy doesn't come with civil rights, equality, autonomy, prosperity and so on. Democracy doesn't automatically give such values; it's just the right to vote for a political party you like. So, democracy must come with constitutional liberalism, which is even more important. Constitutional liberalism is to get civil rights, to get your individual right and to get the rule of law implemented. Now we are facing the constitutional crisis drafted by the ex-junta. I believe that's one of the main missions the elected government has been struggling with. On the other hand, the powerful military has been safeguarding it.

Today, the country is darkened by clouds both old and new: the undemocratic, military-drafted Constitution and the military's continued important role in the political arena; the unfinished 70-year-old ethnic conflicts; the rise of ultra-nationalist groups; new but incapable ministers and high-ranking officials; and seemingly intractable problems like slowing economic growth, a conservative mindset and old-fashioned bureaucratic attitudes.

So, our struggle for democracy is unfinished. The process is to gradually reduce the power of the military from the political arena. If I have to name the current political landscape of Burma, I would call it "re-civilianizing the militarized nation."

AC: I read in a recent article you published in the Irrawaddy the statement by Mon Mon Myat, Daw Aung Suu Kyi's biographer: "It is now part of the world's politically correct orthodoxy to blame (Nobel Peace Laureate) Daw Aung San Suu Kyi for the Rohingya refugee crisis and to condemn her for defending Myanmar against the genocide case brought by The Gambia before the International Court of Justice (ICJ)."

A complex issue, no doubt.

May I ask for your most candid thoughts on Mon Mon Myat's comment as well as your personal analysis of Daw Aung San Suu Kyi's presence and her statements at the ICJ?

KZM: These days, I have seen all objective assessments and nuances lost in regard to the Myanmar issue, including the role of Daw Aung San Suu Kyi and herself. It's disturbing to see the pure and massive character assassination beyond criticism against her. As an independent media, we've criticized her and her government too. But what we have been seeing these days in the media is far beyond criticism. I think only time will tell.

Since I heard of the decision by Daw Aung San Suu Kyi to go to The Hague, I believe that she made that decision because she felt that she should go there as a leader of this country. Not more than that, and not less than that. But some people thought that she intended to go for her political benefit in the upcoming election in 2020. And some people, especially in the international community, thought that she went there to defend the military. Both are not more than assumptions.

In reality, what she did there was a public disclosure of human rights violations committed by the military and security forces in 2017. Actually, that must be news for the international media too as it's really new. But all focused on her denial of genocide charged by The Gambia. For now, I think we just have to wait and see what kind of decision will be made by the ICJ in the future.

If I read Daw Aung San Suu Kyi after her return from The Hague, I think she would feel that she's done her duty on that matter and she will continue to carry out what she has believed. You know what kind of person she is. She might not be affected much if the result comes out against her will or defense at the ICJ.

AC: Yes, she's remarkably resilient. Another question: Overall, how should we understand the crisis in Rakhine, with nearly 750,000 Rohingyas currently subsisting in refugee camps on the Bangladesh border? You are a highly respected investigative journalist, what should we know that we may not know, or know as clearly as you do, to bring greater clarity and fairness to the situation in Rakhine? And, may I add, in all fairness to Daw Aung San Suu Kyi, are criticisms towards her simply playing into the hands of the military? Who may well have orchestrated this tragedy? Regardless, do you see any missteps on Daw Aung San Suu Kyi's part, and if so, what are they, please?

KZM: The Rakhine issue is complex. It is not that simple to say it's a citizenship issue, it's an immigrant issue, etc. And, we can't also rule out that it is a legacy of the Western imperialism in the 19th and 20th centuries across the world. But we can't accept any human rights violations against anyone. If the military and security forces committed extrajudicial killings or war crimes or any crimes, the generals have to take responsibility.

For Daw Aung San Suu Kyi in that particular issue, I don't see any different options in terms of dealing with the military she couldn't really control personally or constitutionally. In the wake of Rohingya crisis in August 2017, she was criticized that she was silent to criticize the military for their disproportionate military clearance. We knew the situation in Naypyidaw was quite tense at that time and everyone there lived under fear without knowing what would happen between the military and the government. The impression was that anything bad could happen. I think such an impression was haunting the entire country. But the international community might not be aware of that. But such an oversight is understandable.

AC: I was deeply impressed by your previous award-winning book, *They Must Apologize to the People*. Here we are many years after that book was published and still no apology from any of the principle people who either ordered or carried out the orders to imprison, torture, rape and or murder innocent peaceful monks, students, laywomen and laymen over the past 32 years from the time of the uprising in 1988.

May I invite you to speak openly here: If you were allowed on Myanmar national television and invited by those very people who committed those atrocities to explain why you think it is important for them to confess their wrong doing and seek forgiveness from the people, what would you say to them?

KZM: Imagine that you were abused and attacked physically and violated officially and publicly. All of your rights were taken away by those who committed those violations. You were punished in prison and so on. After you completed your sentence, you were released and you live now in the same society or country where your violators are still in power or still enjoying their political and economic privileges, let alone any punishment for their public violations. Under that situation, will you feel safe? That's just a basic need for a person whose rights were violated. In that case, you will need an official apology or confession, at least, from those violators that what they did to you was wrong. If you got such an apology, you would feel safe, at least.

I don't think that the people of Burma, generally speaking, are revenge-seekers. They are forgivers. Regardless of their ethnicities or religions, they tend to forgive. But no matter what they are forgiving, those who committed atrocities are responsible to apologize. To apologize for a committed person needs a process in which the person understands what he did was wrong ethically or morally, and that what he did affected other people's lives terribly. Only from that point can we move towards the genuine national reconciliation that our country desperately needs. Sadly, we are not close to that situation yet in our country. It's an inconvenient truth in our society.

AC: As I have walked the streets of Yangon over the past days I have become painfully aware of the massive move this country is making towards development, with hundreds of 10 to 20 story condominiums being built, a city that is in grid lock most of the day with over 300, 000 cars, trucks and buses, and more taxis than New York City, and with an infra-structure from the 1950s. The air is so toxic it's nearly unbreathable and the electrification of the country is moving as fast as money will buy.

In addition, we are in a severe drought here, the likes of which have never before been known. Here we are in the dead of winter and the temperatures are summer-like.

I am also told that a quarter of all farming land in the country will go vacant this season from not having water.

The dams have never been this low.

And I am also told that many thousands of farmers and villagers are fleeing to neighboring countries to work as migrants to send money home to their families to avoid hunger and possible starvation.

Meanwhile, the developed world, and Myanmar too, to some extent, are struggling to come to terms with the catastrophe of capitalism and the perception of unlimited growth in a world of finite resources.

Worse still is the climate emergency we are in and how many are speaking not only of the certainty of the sixth great extinction, but that we're entering near term extinction. As Greta Thunberg, the young Swedish climate emergency activist, nominated for the Nobel Peace Prize, in her impassioned speech at the United Nations some months back she blasted world leaders saying: "You have stolen my dreams and my childhood with your empty words. And yet I'm one of the lucky ones. People are suffering. People are dying; entire ecosystems are collapsing. We are in the beginning of a mass extinction and all you can talk about is money and fairy tales of eternal economic growth. How dare you!" She is calling for worldwide civil disobedience. I call it a global revolution of the spirit.

Meanwhile, as Myanmar is trying to discover democracy and a regard for human rights, after decades of violent dictatorship, the world is in utter collapse from the greed of unlimited growth and consumerism.

There may not be life in this world as we know it, and soon.

May I ask, what are your thoughts on the environmental catastrophe we are in and how would you encourage stakeholders in your country to come to terms with this reality?

KZM: The question you've just raised here is globally alarming. The first thing to tackle this unprecedented issue is for leaders of all countries—both developing and developed ones—to be knowledgeable of the severity of this issue. Only then can the entire world come together globally on how to hopefully solve this problem for new generations. Top leaders of a country like ours—a poor, politically fragile, and conflict-bounded one—must understand how they or we as a whole country must start planning to prevent this matter from getting worse. The Myanmar Sustainable Development Plan introduced by the government in 2018 seems pretty good. I think the MSDP has the holistic vision for a peaceful, prosperous and democratic country. When I read MSDP, I noted that it admitted our country is vulnerable to the risks of climate change, suffering widespread natural disasters such as coastal storms, floods and droughts. It also said that the country's development strategy "must be sensitive to those climatic vulnerabilities so that our social, economic and cultural lives are as resilient and safeguarded as possible from a changing climate." Such a holistic strategy is good but the question is how the government can really make it happen in terms of implementing such a big mission.

AC: I would so like to dive into this issue further with you, but I realize time is of essence. The issue of defamation. You recently reported that over the past four years, "the military has sued 96 critics, according to Athan, a group advocating freedom of expression." In addition, "since the National League for Democracy (NLD) government took office in April 2016, the military has opened 47 lawsuits against 96 people, including 51 activists, 19 individual citizens, 14 journalists, five religious representatives, four artists and three members of political parties."

You went onto say that "the military used the Telecommunications Law, penal code, laws protecting privacy and security and the Unlawful Association Act."

You concluded by saying, "Apparently, most military lawsuits were in response to criticism about human rights violations by the armed forces and demands for amendments to the military-drafted 2008 Constitution."

Two notable cases struck me deeply, and they were against the spoken word artists in the Peacock Generation performance troupe who were sentenced to six months of hard labor in prison for satirizing the military in their performances. And filmmaker U Min Htin Ko Ko Gyi—co-founder of the human rights and human dignity international film festival—was sentenced to one-year imprisonment with hard labor for criticizing the military in a series of Facebook posts.

My question: Without seeking shared incarceration here, can you shed light on what these nonviolent artists and activists actually said and posted, and why is a country proclaiming its commitment for global human rights, peaceful democracy and a desire for national reconciliation behaving in the opposite way? Can you shed light on their thinking, and their hypocrisy?

Furthermore, is there a de-facto official guide here in Myanmar of the 'dos and don'ts' of what you can and cannot say to cross the line with the military between freedom of expression and defamation? Why is criticizing the military so wrong, set aside it being done with humor and satire? I mean, The Gambia just recently paraded the military in front of the world at The Hague with a long list of accusations describing how the military generals perpetrated mass atrocities against Myanmar's minority Rohingya Muslims. And they imprison artists and filmmakers?

My late teacher, Sayadaw U Pandita, called it the lack of *hiri* and *ottappa*, the lack of moral shame and moral dread. In other words, the absence of conscience.

How more politely can you call a spade a spade?

Am I crossing the line here? Is this defamation?

My two-part question: What are your thoughts on any part or parts of what I just said, and how best to ignite the conscience of an oppressor?

KZM: In terms of your question, you might be crossing the line and in terms of an answer I am about to tell you here, I might be crossing the line too. Who knows? Only the generals would know. Regarding the freedom of expression or press freedom, I wrote a commentary a couple of years ago when some journalists were charged by the military for their reporting. I called it "Press Freedom and the Invisible Line." For everyone, a journalist or a person who expresses his or her feeling or criticism on social media, that invisible line exists. So we all have to be mindful when it comes to doing this professionally or personally. Yes, the most sensitive authorities are from the military, because most charges came from the military and almost all of those who are being charged are human right defenders, journalists, critics, artists and so on. But please note that there are also cases charged by authorities of the government or the ruling National League for Democracy or any other organizations or individuals and businesspeople.

As you know, calling a spade a spade has been a big issue in our country. The worst time was under the previous military regime. But it has yet to vanish. Again, I think it is totally related to political mindset and attitude. One leader or one person's understanding or knowledge as to how important and valuable freedom of expression and the press freedom are for providing information, floating thought-provoking ideas, creating public discussion to accept more liberal ideas and so on. Of course, they must be used but not abused for personal or political benefit. But I don't think all leaders or people in developed and democratic countries can really cherish them. There is no shortage of such people, even among leaders. The good example is Donald Trump. So, in that case, I think mechanisms or rules and regulations are more important to stop those who are sensitive or tend to use our outdated existing laws to charge anyone who criticizes them. One good example is the removal of the censorship board by ex-president U Thein Sein's administration in 2012, which opened a new chapter for press freedom to some extent, though it couldn't create an atmosphere for a totally free press.

I think it's quite difficult to ignite the conscience of an oppressor. We have been trying to do it over many decades but have failed, to be honest. Some of them have changed not because their consciences were ignited but because they were forced to change by circumstances. So, we need to enact new laws to safeguard press freedom or eradicate outdated laws which are being used to abuse it, and to create an environment in which no one with or without power can misuse any laws such as defamation.

AC: On a final note, your recent book, *The Cell, Exile, and the New Burma*—a collection of essays on your country's political transformation from military rule to democratically elected government—recently won the National Literature Award, the most prestigious literary award in Myanmar. Rather than asking further questions, may I invite you to please share a few of your most cherished excerpts from your book that you feel are perhaps your most favorite and or reflect the essence of your values, your learning, your life's work?

KZM: Regarding my book, I just want to share the remarks by the Committee of the Literary Award for the book. It says, "As there is a book entitled "The 1988 Uprising in Burma" about the 8888 Uprising written in English from the perspectives of authorities by President Maung Maung (1925-1994) and published in 1999, there should be books written in English from the perspectives of Myanmar citizens who took part in the 8888 Uprising. It can be said that "The Cell, Exile and the New Burma" book has filled the gap in that regard."

"It is a great work that gives the readers both knowledge and aesthetic pleasure. Though it cannot be called a historical treatise or a reference book, it does reflect the dawn of pro-democracy uprising in Myanmar. The author depicts how he struggled behind bars and in exile with unwavering commitment and untiring perseverance; and how he strived to learn journalism."

It's nice to read the remarks. But my main intention in publishing that book is how Burmese people have struggled to achieve their aspirations of democracy, freedom and justice over the past three decades. As the struggle is not finished yet, I want my own people and people around the world to understand our country's struggle, how we have been determined since the beginning and how complicated and difficult our life has been, and what the challenges are that we will be facing by learning from the past that we experienced. Otherwise, we won't be able to solve these problems. Nor will the world understand our country.

As you know, our entire society was crushed under the boots of the consecutive regimes in much of the past six decades. On September 7th last year, exactly twenty years after I was released from prison, I wrote a story, named, *Recalling the Day When I Was Reborn*.

I wrote, "It was an institution that named itself the State Law and Order Restoration Council (SLORC) that "killed" me, along with all of those who tried to remove it in order to restore a government elected by the people.

"What I meant was that the intention of SLORC's leaders was clear: to kill our spirit, our passion, our commitment, our conviction, our courage, our wisdom, our integrity and the like. Those are values, but I would call them the "weapons" with which we waged combat against the country's most powerful institution. Thus, they needed to "kill" those who wielded such weapons.

"But when I was released after almost 8 years in prison, I didn't feel like a warrior who had been stripped of his weapons. I even felt stronger than before. Not only had I escaped being killed, but I had also acquired stronger weapons during my eight years in the "tomb."

"These weapons are part of our essence; they flow in our veins. But we also drew inspiration from figures like South African anti-apartheid leader Nelson Mandela, Czechoslovakian dissident leader Vaclav Havel and American civil rights leader Martin Luther King Jr. In prison, we overcame physical and mental difficulties without despairing, as Mandela did during his 27-year imprisonment.

"So, as I walked out of the prison, I felt as if I were walking out of university after having completed a post-graduate degree. That's the joke I tend to tell my friends and others who ask me what eight years of imprisonment feels like.

"But I really believe it's true. In fact, that description doesn't fully capture the very rare opportunity imprisonment gave me; one that few people in the world ever receive.

"Life in prison, with its ruthlessness and inhumanity, is beyond the experiences of dissident life. As I endured and tried to cope with those difficulties, which simply don't exist in everyday life, I felt I was taking an examination—not simply to pass a class, but to survive, to preserve the life my mother had given me. These kinds of tests truly develop a person—both in terms of IQ and EQ.

"On that morning as I walked out of the prison, I couldn't fully enjoy my freedom knowing that thousands of my fellow political prisoners were still behind bars. Besides which, I wasn't free politically; the country was still under the rule of the same institution, which had renamed itself the State Peace and Development Council and was regarded one of the world's most oppressive military regimes.

"Which is to say, I didn't walk out of the prison feeling I had won. No, not at all. But nor did I feel that I had lost the battle. I felt like I had undergone a long, intensive period of special training, not only to continue our unending struggle, but also to cope with an uncertain and unexpected world. I felt I had been reborn to continue the struggle we began before I was arrested—to free our country from any form of authoritarian or military rule.

"It's been for 20 years since I was released. And we have already struggled for democracy for more than 30 years. Our mission is not accomplished. If I have to analyze based on the current political landscape where we've seen the military having strongly resisted to let the 2008 Constitution be amended, I think our democratic struggle might take another 30 years to get a pure elected government which might be called a genuine democracy. But since we know that democracy is far from perfect, we can't say there will be no more problems even at that time. But at least, we can then say we are free from the military-dominated era."

AC: Thank you for your time and your insights. An honor, as always, to speak with you.

KZM: Thank you and thank you for you long and deeply valued support of our ongoing struggle for freedom and democracy.

CHAPTER 28

A CONVERSATION *with*
NILAR THEIN

March 2013

- "None of the students were scared."
- "Even though they forbid me from speaking with other prisoners, I tried to help them."
- "Everyone knew I wasn't doing this for my popularity."

Interview with Ma Nilar Thein, a member of the All Burma Federation Students Union. Ma Nilar Thein joined the student movement when she was still in high school. People in Need awarded her the Homo Homini prize for her promotion of democracy and human rights. Today she is secretary of women's affairs at the 88 Generation Peace & Open Society. Like many other political prisoners and activists, her life has been one of personal sacrifice for a greater calling, requiring her to entrust the care of her daughter to family members when she went into hiding, and again during her 13-year prison sentence. In this candid interview, she shares the lessons learned from her prison experience, offering readers a detailed account of her early activism and what compelled her to continue as an outspoken advocate of democracy and human rights. Nilar Thein was rearrested in 2016 for supporting student protests.

> *"None of the students were scared,*
> *they just put their heads on the desk—*
> *it's called a 'silent strike.'"*

ALAN CLEMENTS: Greetings. Thank you for taking the time to speak with me and to the people of the world through our set of books, *Burma's Voices of Freedom*. Of course, as a freedom fighter, please say whatever you wish, as your words will stand alongside Daw Aung San Suu Kyi, U Win Tin, U Tin Oo, Min Ko Naing, Ko Ko Gyi, U Win Htein and many other courageous voices of freedom from your country.

How long were you in prison and what were you charged with?

NILAR THEIN: In total, for 13 years. The first time was for one month. The second time for eight years and seven months. The third was for three years and seven months. I was 16 years old when first arrested. In 1987, after the government demonetized our national currency, I was involved in a high school organization and we published a paper about the situation. I was arrested because of that paper. I was in 10th Standard at the time. The authorities came and took me from my home. They arrested four of my school mates as well.

What happened was, and I am sure you know this, the government devalued our money, as I said, and overnight a number of denominations where worthless and equally, many of our people were impoverished. They lost their savings. I thought this was an outrage and grossly unfair. Everyone was in a panic, everywhere. The hardship for the people was overwhelming. I couldn't stand people starving.

AC: Where were you in 1988, during the uprising?

NT: I was in school. And participated.

AC: Did you think you would go to jail?

NT: The military were after those who were striking and then guards came into our school. We all knew we would likely be jailed one day. This is Burma. Dissent is not tolerated.

AC: Freedom loving people around the world look upon Burma as an activist country throwing off the shackles of dictatorship. No easy task. How have you and your family suffered under totalitarianism?

NT: When the government devalued the currency, we were angry and sad, and there were so many difficulties. Houses were destroyed. Some people destroyed everything they saw. Even when they saw military cars, rage would come up. I thought how unfair this was. I didn't even know what the politics were. All I knew was the feeling of anger.

AC: And from this, at 16, your activism was born?

NT: On the board in my classroom I taped a 25 kyat and 75 kyat note. None of the students were scared, they just put their heads on the desk—it's called a 'silent strike.'

AC: What did the teacher do?

NT: The teachers were also suffering, and when we put our heads down the teachers didn't know what to do. Then the military guards came, and the teachers tried to protect us. Then, when the military cars were outside the school, everyone converged, and they noticed me.

AC: And then what?

NT: After that the '88 uprising began. At that time, I participated in the Student Union with Min Ko Naing, Ko Ko Gyi and others.

AC: And the second time you went to prison for eight years?

NT: Yes, eight years at the time of '96 RIT student uprising. I wasn't an IT student, but I wanted to support them. I went there, into the crowd, every day, to support them. One day, the sixth day, some of the military people stopped me when I went to the crowd. They arrested me for fighting with the military.

AC: You got into a fight?

NT: Yes, at first verbally, but then I fought with my hands, with everything. I was arrested and taken to Insein Prison for 10 months, then transferred to a prison in Ayeyarwaddy.

> *"Even though they forbid me from speaking with other prisoners, I tried to help them."*

ALAN CLEMENTS: What was the day-to-day life like in prison?

NILAR THEIN: Although I had many difficulties, I had something I trusted in. That's what I fought for and it was worth it. I knew I had to hang on to that truth.

AC: What did you fight for? What did you have to hold on to?

NT: What I held on to was that what the government was doing was not fair, and I didn't like the way the government was acting.

AC: Aung San Suu Kyi has said that they can imprison your body, but they can't imprison your mind, unless you let them. Therefore, we must always remember this, we must always keep our mind free. In prison, how did you keep your mind free?

NT: I just put my mind on to other things, like reading, planting, playing with animals, talking with other prisoners, things like that. You're right, they can't imprison your mind, so I refused to let my brain die—just learn, learn, and keep learning.

Even though it was forbidden to read, I snuck in things to read. Even though they forbid me from speaking with other prisoners, I tried to help them. I helped them with their health, in teaching them things, and in every other way I could. Whatever they needed I tried my best to provide.

AC: How were you treated by the prison guards?

NT: At first the guards had forbidden me from helping other prisoners, but I tried. I tried to sneak in things to give them before the guards could see. After that the guards knew that I was helping them, so I was a little more free to donate time in the medical section of the prison.

AC: May I ask, were you tortured?

NT: I wasn't physically tortured, but they tortured me mentally. In prison the food is not good, so we did a hunger strike to have them give us better food.

AC: Were you successful?

NT: The hunger strike included five people, for 72 hours. After that, the SP negotiated with me, and gave us what we wanted.

AC: You're courageous.

NT: It felt more like I was doing the right thing. Another time, I wanted to know in which prison they had put my husband. But the government would not say which one. So, I did a hunger strike for seven days and then they said 'no.'

AC: You stopped?

NT: Yes, because of my health. It wasn't that I wanted an agreement. I just wanted a 'yes' or 'no,' because I'd been waiting for that for so long. I wanted them just to give me an answer. And they wouldn't give any answer. That's why I went on hunger strike for seven days and the answer they gave was 'no.' They would tell me which prison he was in.

AC: Yes, mental torture. How long had you been married?

NT: We were married in 2006 and imprisoned in 2007 at the time of the Saffron Revolution. My husband was also imprisoned at that time.

AC: Do you have children?

NT: I was imprisoned when my daughter was four months old.

AC: And your husband, where was he?

NT: My husband was captured first. After that I was captured.

AC: And what about your baby?

NT: When I was running from the military my child was with me. But after one week I gave my baby to my mother.

AC: You're hiding and running from the police in the Saffron Revolution?

NT: Yes. I was hiding for over a year.

AC: And your baby was with your mother? Your husband was in prison? And you're running house to house, hiding from the authorities in Burma?

NT: Yes.

AC: Terrible. Are you seeing your baby?

NT: No, nothing.

AC: This is unthinkable *dukkha*, unthinkable suffering. And after one year on the run, then what?

NT: On September 11, 2008, I was captured, arrested and taken to prison.

AC: Any word about your baby?

NT: When I was running, I was in contact with my house by phone from time to time, so I knew everything was okay with my baby. And when I was in prison, when my mother came to see me, my baby was with her.

AC: Born in 2007, so she's six years old? A daughter?

NT: Yes, a daughter.

AC: I have a six-year-old daughter. Her name is Bella. Your daughter lives with you?

NT: When I was in prison the baby was with my sister-in-law, in her house, and now they can't be separated. They live together.

AC: What is your relationship to your daughter now?

NT: She accepts me as her mother, but still, after all this time, they can't be separated.

AC: Unthinkable. You know; everyone in the world knows that torture exists in Burma. I didn't personally know how hard your life has been. My question: how to get someone who tortures others to understand a new type of thinking, so they stop harming and torturing others? How to have the torturer change their ways?

NT: Take for example Khin Nyunt (former chief of military intelligence). Even though he thinks he's the brains behind everything, when we look at his situation through the perspective of our Buddhism, when people do bad things they end up in a bad way. So, they know themselves that if they do bad things they will end in a bad way.

AC: They know this?

NT: Yeah, they know that.

AC: So why do they do it?

NT: Because the government forced them to do it. They know it's wrong, but the government forced him to torture and be cruel to our people.

AC: Are you saying that someone forced Khin Nyunt to torture dissidents?

NT: Yes, because if he didn't torture, his own family would be in great danger.

AC: What you're saying is that everyone fears the dictator? Khin Nyunt was afraid of Than Shwe?

NT: Yes.

AC: And Khin Nyunt knew he was doing wrong, for sure?

NT: Yes.

AC: How then to make someone like him understand that it's wrong to torture and wrong to follow orders to torture? How?

NT: Most people have kindness inside of them, so we have to show them this kindness in us when inside the prisons. For example, guards are torturing prisoners, and when those guards have children and they're disabled, they feel pain. Such torturers need to see the universality of suffering and reverse their attitude to compassion. We must show that reversal of attitude by example.

AC: What would you have done if Khin Nyunt or Than Shwe came to your cell? What would you have said?

NT: I would treat them as normal men, not with hatred or a desire for revenge. I'd put myself in a good mind.

AC: Before you said you're willing to fight?

NT: That guy that arrested me was ordering the others to hit me, but they didn't. He ordered them, but they didn't. He fought me because he ordered someone to fight me who didn't want to fight me. Otherwise, I always put myself in a good mind. Always.

> *"Everyone knew I wasn't doing this for my popularity, that I have a really kind heart."*

ALAN CLEMENTS: When looking back over 13 years of prison, what was the most important lesson learned?

NILAR THEIN: I learned one thing in my last time in prison, and that was I helped everyone in the prison, even the criminals, including the staff of the prison, the guards, everyone. I helped them. With meditation and cleaning; I helped them. I volunteered. Did everything I could. Cleaning their clothes, everything. When I was dying inside the prison because of my health, I donated meditation. Everyone knew I wasn't doing this for popularity. They knew I had a kind heart. So, when I was dying in prison everyone cared for me. I meditated as they cared for me, and in that space, we cared for each other. I know that if I can put my mind towards kindness for everyone, at least there is this little something I can do to give back.

AC: There are many young activists around the world who look to you and to your people for inspiration, on how to challenge tyranny, challenge injustice, challenge totalitarian structures. But some of them, in stepping up, they have fear, and if they had a little bit of encouragement, they would get strong and act. What advice would you give to the boys and girls around the world who want to do the right thing and become activists?

NT: Everyone has their fears, but if you think about what you're challenging, and ask yourselves what you really want, and you know that you're challenging something because of what you want dearly, if you *know* that and think that it's worth it, and you trust your worth and the truth, that it's really true, the fear will automatically disappear.

AC: Your daughter is blessed to have you as her mother.

NT: Thank you.

AC: How do you feel that the people of Burma can achieve national reconciliation and heal this wound of horror?

NT: Everyone can put their feelings in front, lead with their feelings, because our country is now changing. The transition has started. So, everyone can put their feelings in front. Feelings are very important, because I too have suffered so much from them. Now I will tell the story how I feel it, but if we think that it is for our country, it is for our nation and for the public, to improve the situation, if we think that way, then everyone has to negotiate with each other, not fight.

AC: You believe this will happen?

NT: We have to try. We've been trying for 20 years and even now it's not completely changed. But we must keep trying. It's just the first step of our transition to democracy, just one step forward. But we must keep trying. It's not the whole light, just a little light. We see a flicker of light. And we must keep brightening the light, so to speak.

AC: What does freedom mean to you?

NT: When they captured me, when they put me in prison, I wrote down all the truths and all the feelings I had inside of my heart. I wrote them all down, one by one. This is an act of freedom. It is a freedom they cannot stop.

AC: When you look back at your life as an activist, would you do anything differently?

NT: I have no regrets for what I've done. None. But I think that I have to try even harder now. I have to put in more effort.

AC: Have you met Daw Suu?

NT: Yes, I have.

AC: Under what circumstances?

NT: I wanted to meet her, so Daw Suu had a meeting with other political families at my house. My daughter drew a picture of Daw Suu and we gave it to her. She was really happy.

AC: What do you see for your future?

NT: I like social work, I like volunteering and donating to the poor.

AC: Last question: millions of tourists are coming to Burma. What do you want them to know about your people, before they come?

NT: Our country has many lovely traditions and sights to see, and we are all trying our best to improve our country. On the other hand, there are difficulties—so many poor people. We just want everyone who visits our country to help us as much as they can.

AC: I don't know anyone like you. To be one year without your daughter, on the run—how did you feel? How did you keep going?

NT: There was a day when I cried the whole day. But when I saw a video with the faces of the child refugees in our Kachin State, where they are having a horrible war, when I saw their faces, I was relieved that my baby was in a safe place. Better off. I was relieved. I also felt a renewed sense of conviction after seeing those child refugees that it was crucial to remain an activist to help my people achieve a better life.

AC: Your story is epic. You're a woman; you're strong; you're a mother and married. Your little girl is living with someone else; you're humble. You're an inspiration. Thank you for keeping moral courage and conscience and universal human rights active in our world.

NT: Thank you. And thank you for supporting the same in Burma and worldwide.

CHAPTER 29

CONVERSATIONS *with* MOE THWAY

March 2013 & January 2020

- Introductions
- "Even if we could defeat this army through arms, they also have families."
- "Freedom also carries responsibility."
- "I honestly don't feel hatred."
- "I was afraid of being arrested, [but] I'm more afraid of being controlled."
- 'The only people who can make these deals are cronies.'
- 'The best way to help the people is to directly fund small, local NGOs'
- "We have gone from a uniformed military dictatorship to a weak civilian dictatorship with no power."

Conversations with Moe Thway, co-founder of the band and movement Generation Wave. A tireless activist and cultural provocateur who riled the country's military regime with pamphlets and sticker campaigns, releasing 'the black album' as a protest in 2009 and leaving copies in Burmese teashops. Both he and Zeya Thaw became figures in the pro-democracy movement for their outspoken and daring criticisms of the military regime and trace a direct line of development to the Generation 88 protests and campaigns proceeding them. Moe Thway established the Generation Wave Institute as the changing political landscape allowed them to move more above ground, with aims of creating a support structure that would enable Burma's youth to find proactive ways of challenging repressive regimes. In this interview, he shares his insights into Burma's current political landscape and how it shaped his youth, activism and political and moral philosophy as the impetus behind the Generation Wave. He talks about the ongoing dangers and the subterfuge of a corrupt civilian dictatorship.

Introductions

ALAN CLEMENTS: My name is Alan Clements. Just recently, President Thein Sein un-blacklisted me after 17 years for a book of conversations I did in 1995 and 1996 with Daw Aung San San Suu Kyi titled, *The Voice of Hope*. This was just after her first release from six years of detention. I am back in Burma to start a new set of books titled, *Burma's Voices of Freedom*. At the time of my previous visit, I don't think Generation Wave existed, yet I've heard so much about it. So I'm curious about what you've done, why you went to prison; your thinking about your country's transition to democracy, about the nature of freedom, about the religious and ethnic conflicts, and especially, what you've learned growing up under military dictatorship. And of course, anything you wish to speak about.

MOE THWAY: Welcome to my country. My name is Moe Thway. I was one of the co-founders of Generation Wave, but now, after the change to becoming an institute, I work with another organization, the National Youth Congress. I'm also involved in the Peace Network.

AC: Let's start here: Who and what is Generation Wave? And why was it formed?

MT: Originally, there were four founders in Generation Wave when it started. And all four of us founders have been close friends since we were in kindergarten. We also went to the same high school. Our first involvement in politics was together in 1996, when there was a student protest in Yangon. We joined them, and we also did some political activities in our high school. We made poster campaigns and demonstrated with the university students. That was our very first political involvement.

In 2007, at the time of the Saffron Revolution, we each became involved in the uprising, as individuals. After the crackdown by the government, we called each other and met in a friend's house. Then, the four of us decided to found an organization.

At the time, we believed that the fight against the military dictatorship was our responsibility. And we decided to take down the dictatorship through the power of the youth and the power of the people. We also decided to use nonviolent ways to take down the military dictators. So we called a few old friends who were also prominent leaders of the 88 Generation and we discussed our ideas with them. In thinking about the name of our organization, one friend from the 88 Generation suggested that we should include the word 'Generation.' It's meaningful, he insisted. Another guy said that we should include 'Wave,' because it too was meaningful. At that time, we discussed this among the four of us and agreed to use that name, Generation Wave. Our name was not given by them as a pair of words—one gave one word, and another gave the other word, and after thinking it through, we combined them and came up with Generation Wave.

There have been 50 years of military dictatorship in our country. So, all those who were fighting—all the revolutions and movements by students in all those years, fighting against the dictators—made it an ongoing revolution carried forward generation by generation. In the same way, we used 'Wave' as the image of that struggle. We're carrying this nonviolent revolution as a wave, generation by generation.

AC: People who don't grow up under dictatorship, who don't grow up under the threat of violence and imprisonment and torture, obviously, don't know what that's like. What is it like to grow up under dictatorship, under the threat of violence and torture and imprisonment everyday of your life? What does it feel like inside? How do you cope, emotionally, psychologically and spiritually? What goes through your mind, day to day?

MT: I was born in 1981 under a single party dictatorship. Until 2012, for my whole youth, I lived under dictatorship. Frankly speaking, from birth, until I learned about human rights and democracy in 2007, I didn't notice the repression. Honestly, I didn't notice anything. The only thing we knew was there were many things we could not do.

AC: Essentially, you normalized the oppression?

MT: Yeah, it felt normal because I was born into oppression. From birth, there were so many restrictions imposed upon the people.

AC: What can't you do as a young man under dictatorship?

MT: Under dictatorship we could go to school and study only what the school teaches us and then—you know; our dreams and our ideas were limited. There were many things you couldn't do. For example, if you wanted to make a solo performance, even if it wasn't political, it wasn't allowed. If you wanted to write a poem about your philosophy, about freedom, or if you wanted to write about existential thoughts, it wasn't allowed. There were many restrictions, but we were used to them. We honestly didn't think it was a problem.

Only after we knew about the world outside of our country, that there were a lot of things that people *could* do, did we realize the injustice of these restrictions. For example, in Europe and America, they don't censor their artists. They can sing, or they can write poems, or they can publish books without censorship. Only after we learned of the freedoms of the outside world could we compare our situation. From this comparison, we learned more and more how repressed life was in Burma. Then, I felt like we were prisoners in our own country.

Now, it's different from before. Making individual statements like I'm doing now was dangerous and you could be sentenced to decades in prison, maybe 20 or 30 years. But after 2012, things changed a bit, both in the media and in some political activities. I don't mean that the country has changed to a democratic society, but it is changing, I think.

AC: You were eight years old during the 8.8.88 nationwide uprising. You were aware enough to know that thousands of your people were being killed, and perhaps many older brothers and sisters had to flee the country.

Then, in 2007 at the time of the Saffron Revolution, you're 26 years old and there's another massacre, of Buddhist monks and others. You've seen merciless brutality. How has state-sponsored violence impacted you?

MT: The uprising inspired us. Even in 1988, when I was only eight, there was a period under President U Maung Maung when he didn't take any action against demonstrators. At that time, people felt free and could demonstrate in the streets. So, for me and friends, it was like playing. We didn't really demonstrate but we played during the demonstrations in the streets, we held flags and shouted "democracy." It did inspire us to see our peoples' solidarity and their demands for freedom and equality. It entered our hearts. It moved through our veins.

Also, as a child of only eight years old, I heard many gunshots around my area and then I heard the news that many students had been killed. As I moved closer to the situation, I saw these horrors with my own eyes. I also saw many students arrested and thrown into jail cars. After I went home, I saw these prison vans drive by my own house, and I'll never forget seeing and hearing the students shouting for help from those vans. Of course, we knew something terribly was happening. It was hard to face.

Moreover, the people doing these horrible things to the students were in uniform. They were riot police and soldiers. We felt disgusted. It embedded in our minds that soldiers and police were really bad people. They were not good. We hated them.

We also experienced this in 1996, when we were around 15 years old. Then in 2007 I became active in the demonstrations and was lucky to escape from being beaten or shot. Again, at a demonstration near the Shwedagon Pagoda, I saw many people shot and beaten. The murdering of my people—innocent, freedom-loving people—changed my life.

AC: On whom did you place responsibility when witnessing your own military kill unarmed Buddhist monks, students, and friends? Did you ever think that they were simply following orders, and direct your outrage towards the dictator, General Than Shwe? Did you end up hating dictatorship, or hating the man, or condemning the police or all of the above?

MT: My immediate response was to blame the military government, and also blame the soldiers and the police. Even though we knew that they did these things under orders, we also felt that maybe they could have avoided doing that, according to their own free will. But after thinking about my country, again and again, I realized one thing: it's all about fear. Fear is everywhere in Burma. And the dictator also has fear. He has fear of losing power. And in the military and police, they don't avoid commands from officers because they fear losing their position and rank and the security of their lives and those of their families. So, they shoot the demonstrators because they're afraid of losing their position and security for their families.

Fear is deeply rooted in our country. It's so rooted in our culture that it masquerades as right action, even wisdom. And clearly, we are not yet mature enough nor wise enough to build a free-thinking democratic country. Maybe some people will disagree with me, but we must essentially stop being afraid. As Aung San Suu Kyi said, "fear is a habit and I'm not afraid." We all must make this our motto. Cease listening to the habit of fear and align with the voice of your freedom.

> *"Even if we could defeat this army through arms, they also have families."*

ALAN CLEMENTS: So, your experience of violence contrasted to the courage and solidarity of your people was your awakening to the power of universal human rights? Before you answer, let me say, I've asked a lot of questions to a lot people, and very few are as politicized as you, and it's so understandable because you have come of age under violent dictatorship. You're also among the first I've heard use the word "overthrow." And you would think it would be a natural word to use, considering the decades of horror of this military regime. Of course, you know this as well as anyone, having seen two major massacres of peaceful demonstrators as a young man.

MOE THWAY: Yes, it's trauma.

AC: I'm right there with you. You are brave even to be sharing this with me now. By way of saying, I so honor your courage. Shall we cease the conversation or continue another time?

MT: No, please let's carry on.

AC: As an American, I grew up in culture where I thought we were free, and there is a fair degree of freedom, but there's also a high degree of coercion and propaganda. Noam Chomsky has used the term 'manufacturing consent'; there's a belief that you're free but the powers that be clandestinely engineer your support for oppression. And we export our violence in America. We attack other countries. In Burma, the military attacks its own people. They make this very clear. And you, essentially, have seen this from your earliest days. So, you're a rare person in the world who knows the consequences of not living in a free country. So my question: What does it mean to have a free mind? Or to desire freedom when you know that if you speak up for it you might be killed or imprisoned? What does it mean to confront that fear? What does it feel like to start saying, 'I refuse to live under the obedience of a lie and I'm willing to die, if need be,' for freedom?

MT: I think it's based on morals. The reason I became involved in the 2007 revolution is that I heard about fuel prices being raised ten-fold by the government. So, at that time, many people were walking on the streets because they didn't have enough money for bus fare, and the bus service stopped because it wasn't viable for them to run. It was better for them to cease their services than lose money to keep running. That's why many people were walking.

Then a few activists demonstrated against the rise in fuel prices. At the time, I didn't feel concerned about that, I just listened to the news and watched and waited, to see how the situation developed. But after a while, in Upper Burma, some monks meditated and prayed for the people to have peace, because, you know, living with very high accommodation and fuel prices does not lead to peace. That's why they meditated for peace.

After hearing the news about the soldiers beating the monks in Upper Burma, I got very angry. Beating monks was unacceptable. And when I heard the call for demonstrations in Yangon, the first day I saw them downtown, and then the second day I joined them. From that day onward, I demonstrated with the monks and the people until the government crackdown. My feeling was that the raising of the fuel price ten-fold was not only inappropriate, it was a type of violence. Nor did they consult the people. So I didn't feel it was right to violate the people in this way, and so I joined the demonstrations to express my conscience.

The only thing we demanded was respect for the will of the people. But instead, they declared code 1.4(4) and started shooting people. I was outraged. It's absolutely wrong to kill people who are peacefully demanding respect for their wishes to be respected.

At that time, I hated the government. I was also thinking, 'How can we resolve this problem?' I found only one answer: we needed to take down the dictatorship. At the time, I didn't understand much about democracy and how we have to structure the Constitution or what the main tenets of democratic society are. I didn't know any of this. I only knew we had to take down the dictatorship.

Another thing I knew was that to fight dictators, who have a fully functioning well-organized army, it's not possible to fight them with weapons. At the time we were reading many books and also watching movies, like bringing down the dictator in Serbia, and we also watched movies about Gandhi's independence movement in India. So we chose to use nonviolent tactics.

We also heard about our older generation, and the student army in the jungle, and how they fought for freedom for more than 20 years and nothing came of it. It's difficult to confront a well-organized army with several hundred thousand soldiers. It's impossible, really. They're organized, paid, and have support of their families and relatives. They have houses given to them by the government. So it's not possible to fight such armies with only a few students who've held guns for only a few months. It's impossible. Even if we could defeat this army through arms, they also have families. They have many relatives in the country, and they're also our people. Even if we could defeat them, it would create more hatred in the country. More and more trauma in the country. Using violent means is not a good way to take down a military dictatorship. That's why we decided to use only nonviolent methods. Then, we learned how to make nonviolent campaigns and organize nonviolent demonstrations.

AC: Generation Wave formed based on a dedication to the philosophy of nonviolence?

MT: Yes, that's true.

AC: That was the defining youth movement at that time?

MT: Yes, it was.

AC: What is Generation Wave today, six years later?

MT: We started our first activities by distributing leaflets, and also a postal campaign, and at times we used letter campaigns. We'd find addresses and send people letters. Just random people. We'd send statements with motivational words. We used many ways to motivate the people, but if you just throw out leaflets into a market, only a few people will get them. And after a while the police will come and gather them up. So people can't get the information. But even if you're a colonel in the military or a police officer, and one of these envelopes comes to you, sent from someone anonymous, and in this letter it's saying that we need to take down the military dictatorship, you won't be afraid. It's safe for you to read it in private. Nobody knows you've read it. And we stamped our organization name on the letter, so they'd know the youth are still fighting against the dictatorship. We believed we could encourage our people in this way, telling them 'You don't need to be depressed, the youth are fighting for freedom, for you, in every possible way.'

"Freedom also carries responsibility: If you want to be free, you need to take the responsibility for it yourself."

ALAN CLEMENTS: How do you pursue freedom under such harsh conditions as military dictatorship? How do you keep your mind free and not succumb to fear?

MOE THWAY: Keeping one's morality is essential. Under dictatorship everything is corrupted, so for instance, if you go to the township administration house or your village administration office and you ask for some form of permission, they will abuse their power. Abuse happens everywhere under dictatorship. Compare this situation with your moral standards.

When we were in school, sometimes we needed to pay bribes to our teachers to get good marks. If you didn't pay, you couldn't get a good position, even if you were a good student. In this way, people are corrupted, and also the society becomes corrupt. But I never encouraged those things and my parents also never encouraged those things with me. In this refusal, we can start using our freedom, and don't care if we don't get good marks. Also, not caring if I don't get a good position. We can be satisfied with the purity of our effort in school and let that be enough. As it's been said, freedom is its own reward.

AC: So, you refused to participate in corruption. That was one of the main ways you kept your mind and conscience free? And when did you first become an activist?

MT: Only after the Saffron Revolution when we founded Generation Wave.

AC: Did you think you could be killed?

MT: Yes, of course. We knew that very clearly. As I said, we've witnessed many people being killed, and many people being beaten, and many people being arrested, right in front of our eyes. We knew that we could be killed or arrested, or tortured, at any time. That was clear.

Also, our older generation have many sad stories about student activists and political activists. In prison they're tortured; we knew that. Actually, to be honest, we were also afraid of being beaten or tortured, or shot in the street. But, we needed to make the decision. We needed to make a choice, whether we would live under military dictatorship with fear, or whether we would overthrow it with moral courage, and take that risk. So, for me, my morality didn't allow me to obey their injustices, their restrictions and oppression. My morality was the most important thing which inspired me to do these things.

One more thing was seeing people getting arrested and being shot and beaten and killed in the street. It made me feel guilty, you know? I felt I was also responsible for that. I felt I should do something because of that. I should stand up and speak out against that injustice. We should overthrow the dictatorship.

Also, there was one particular event that happened in my life, also in 2007, on my street. I saw from my window that some people caught a thief. He had snuck into a house and tried to take things, and many people caught him. Then, some of the guys, beat him with chairs and sticks. So I shouted from my room, "Hey! Why are you doing this? Even though he's a thief the only thing you must do is send him to the police station—you have no right to torture him!"

They were surprised and looked at me with anger. It was dangerous for me. They could make problems for me. But I felt I shouldn't let them do this injustice. I mean, it's somehow related to the country's situation in September. So I shouldn't allow these dictators to kill our people. I have the responsibility to stop that. That's why I found a way to stop it and became involved in politics.

AC: You've been an activist for most of your adult life. You've grown up, as we've spoken about, under the harshest conditions. These regimes, here in Burma, are notorious as some of the most militant of all dictatorships in the modern era. Around the world we see revolutions starting, coming, fading, new ones beginning; by and large, people don't want to live in fear. If you were to pass on a single lesson to a younger generation, on what it means to stand up for your rights, what would that lesson be in waging nonviolent revolution?

MT: What I want to pass on is that freedom is in every aspect of our lives. We should never ignore that. We are, I feel, born free, which is why we have a responsibility to keep our freedom, as long as we are alive.

Freedom also carries responsibility: If you want to be free, you need to take the responsibility for it yourself. If you don't take responsibility for yourself, other people will take it. Since others take responsibility for you, then you've lost your freedom, little by little, until you are totally without freedom.

For the next generation, we need to depend upon ourselves. We need to dare to take on the responsibility ourselves, and also take responsibility for the people around us. Because, according to existentialism and according to the Buddha, our people, humans, have a responsibility for everything relating to themselves. I believe that.

I've posted on Facebook about North Korea—with North Korea and South Korea, the tension is really high, and it looks like it may erupt in war.

I'm not sure if that's true or not, but I worry about that. I'm also worried about the things happening in Syria. Because war is collective, you see. If North Korea and South Korea go to war, America will become involved and then China too, and soon it will affect us all. So, I'm also somehow responsible for preventing a new world war in this way. Sometimes people just forget how interrelated everything is.

I've also heard that many of the youth in developed countries forget to become involved in politics and social things, because they think that they're already free, that they don't need to do anything because they have rule of law already and many other things. But I don't feel that way. Freedom is something we always need to care for. As soon as we forget to take care of it, we will lose our freedom. So I say to the new generation in Burma, now that we're working for the freedom of our country—maybe in the next 30 or 40 or 50 years, we believe, this country will be really free, a just and peaceful country—that I'm also worried that the next generation will forget to keep that freedom.

AC: Speaking of freedom in the future: People in your country acknowledge there's a reformation going on, a transition from dictatorship to democracy. What do you think is required here, of all your people, to not lose hope or this freedom? I know you've just answered it in one way, but what is required today to put revolution into everyday action? What are a few daily duties everyone can do to safeguard your country's best future?

MT: Everyone can do their part in moving our country forward. This is important. Whatever one feels is morally right, let it contribute to building the foundation for a new democratic society. Let us all contribute to strengthening the pillars of freedom—freedom of speech, freedom of expression, freedom of thought, and especially freedom of press.

The good news is that many of our journals can easily get news freely and release that news freely, and equally, our people have the right to interview and give news to the media without fear of being arrested. This is a big. This is hugely important.

In addition, there is political freedom. We have an upcoming by-election, and people should know that they have the right to organize political campaigns. That's also very important.

Practice freedom every day and in every way you can. Participate in politics. Participate in the transition. Creatively cultivate our democratic culture, because democracy means governing the country according to the creative and conscientious will of the people. If you don't speak out with your most creative and caring will or desire, leaders won't know what you need; they won't know what you want and how you feel.

They will just take you for granted and do what they want. Be heard. Participate. Give back. Take risks. Stand out. It's that simple. That's why we need to let our voices of freedom be heard. Tell the leaders our needs and equally our dreams.

For example, if we do not want this education system, say it, and explain the type of education system you want. Or maybe we don't want to see that much money spent on the military and we would rather see that money go to help the poor. Let that truth be known. Again, speak your mind. And when you do, be prepared to face obstacles. Sometimes you will have to confront the government. You need to take risks. You need to accept challenges. Otherwise the government will take the lead and will inevitably pull the country towards their own goals.

So in my opinion, active participation by the people—voicing their views, making their truths known, using the power of their own voices, their own conscience, and to speak out—this is active democracy, this is participation in the transition to a democratic society. This is the most important thing we can do at this time to put this dictatorship behind us once and for all.

> *"I honestly don't feel hatred. My opinion is that Than Shwe did those things because he was in fear."*

ALAN CLEMENTS: If I may, what future is there in Burma without addressing the atrocities committed by those men who ordered them? And how would you like to see those decades of atrocities dealt with? And before you answer, please allow me to provide clear context: most of the world knows what those violations were committed by the dictatorship—mass confiscation of land, businesses, bank accounts, and homes; rape; mass rape and torture, systematic horrific torture; terror, imprisonment, and murder. Men with known names, addresses, phone numbers and families, ordered those violations of human life and human dignity.

My question: Should those men be tried and imprisoned in the same way they did to you and many tens of thousands of others in Burma? If agreed by the courts, should they be imprisoned or executed? What should be done with these men in order to restore decency and justice and rule of law?

And if I may, before you answer, what *is* justice here? What *is* reconciliation as it relates to accountability and justice? Years of people's lives have been taken. Many others who were not killed lost their minds, traumatized into the abyss. Others lost their wives, their children, their mothers, their fathers. Again, men known by name ordered this, people who are free and alive today in Burma, with lots of power, with lots of money, luxuriating in their private villas and massive pools, with dozens of slave-attendants looking after their every need, flying in their jets, motoring in their limousines, etc., etc. What should be done with these men to restore trust and for the betterment of your beloved country? And I am not asking this to incite revenge. I'm asking you for your most heartfelt and honest response to an archetypal dilemma.

MT: It's really difficult, but morally speaking, they should be taken to court, tried, and sentenced according to law. This would be the most moral approach. But in the current situation and in accord with the political 'games' being played, it's extremely controversial to implement such justice. That is, because of the 25 percent of the military in Parliament, and also those in the government.

See, I think these men are very much afraid of being taken to court for their crimes against our people. That's why they inserted that 25 percent military presence into Parliament, and also into the 2008 Constitution, where they inserted clauses that give the military the responsibility for protecting the Constitution.

Also, in the Constitution, one article means that their actions prior to the 2008 Constitution cannot be punished by the law after 2008. It's really controversial to implement a moral idea of justice. So, to be honest, take them to court and sentence them according to law. But I'm afraid that if we try to do that—and they are also afraid—they will try to get power back, and they will commit yet another round of more killings and violations.

AC: This is the way they are thinking: they're fearful? Than Shwe is frightened? He really believes he might go to court and be tried for his crimes against humanity and sentenced?

MT: Yes. I think they are very much afraid of that.

AC: He's married. He has children and grandchildren. Many of these other senior generals, and many of the Parliament members who've now become civilians, who were former military generals, have huge networks of cronies. Do any of them show signs of being frightened, and if so, how do you see it? Are they secretly buying land in New Zealand? In China? In South America? Do you hear of offshore accounts? Are they buying vast amounts of Bitcoin? What do you hear?

MT: My opinion is this: It's essential to keep the transition moving forward towards a new more open democratic society. And, at this time, we shouldn't demand justice for the past. That is, until we've built the foundations of democracy, rule of law, and respect for basic human rights. We should not do anything until we're rooted in the new system and that freedom from fear has genuinely taken root in Burma.

Only after many years of a new society should we take legal action, and by that time it'll probably long after they've passed away. But history has a way of being remembered. Last year many of the former generals in Turkey were taken to court for the military coup in 1980. The only thing we want is to reveal justice, to show what really happened in our country, and to make a lesson for our next generation.

AC: Do you feel hate?

MT: To be honest, I don't feel hatred.

AC: May I ask, what are your true feelings towards U Than Shwe? He ordered you and your family and friends to be interrogated, tortured and imprisoned. He's now in Naypyidaw in his newly created kingdom, living a royal family like life in his mega-mansion, not far from Parliament, with his 25 percent military appointed members for constitutional protection. It couldn't be more brilliantly designed, even by the best thinktanks in Beijing, Moscow, or Washington, D.C. He's out navigated international law and created his own domestic protection along with a personal army of 400,000 soldiers programmed to do what they're told, even if it requires ethnic cleansing. There's something not right about that.

MT: Than Shwe did those things because he was in fear, and merely a slave to his fear. That's all.

AC: What is the most important feature of the *Dhamma*, the Buddhist teachings, that supports your political attitudes, and your understanding of democracy? In other words, how do democracy and *Dhamma*, or Buddhism and universal human rights, connect or intersect? And where do Buddhism and nonviolent revolution connect?

MT: I'm a Buddhist. I meditate. Buddhism influences everything in my life. Buddhism, to me, is about freedom. The ultimate goal of Buddhism is *Nibbana*, freedom from all cravings and fears, all hatreds and attachments. To abandon these sufferings, you need to be courageous, and dare to mindfully control your mind.

Also, according to Buddhism, emotions are conditioned and impermanent, and therefore, a source of suffering. Mind states incessantly give us trouble. So, to relieve ourselves from these sufferings, we need to know the truth of change, there is no solid existence, no constant unchanging self in this universe. Only change. New things come into being and pass away. They happen and then disappear. In theory, if we knew the truth of 'Only Change' we won't be intoxicated and wicked according to illusion. According to the Buddha's *Dhamma,* everything is illusion, like a dream. So, in that sense, Buddha never encouraged hatred or revenge. Hate is the issue, not what you hate. In that sense, he always encouraged *mettā* or loving kindness even towards the enemy, even towards people who may kill you. He always encouraged us to use *mettā*. This has deeply influenced me. For instance, even though I'm shouting at times in protests, I'm aware of not doing it with ill will or violence in my voice.

AC: Beautiful. Thank you for that. It's possible that U Than Shwe and others in high power will hear you through the words of this book. If you were to speak with him, or he came to you and, hypothetically, wanted your advice on how to move from this place of fear, fear for himself, fear for his family, saying, "I'm 80 years old. I will die soon, but my children will live on, and they'll live with great fear if I don't change the course of the future," what advice might you offer him in achieving genuine national reconciliation in your country, as well as safeguarding the freedom of all those people he loves?

MT: My advice is this: Even if you did all those things with a good mind, one thing that's sure is that many bad things happened. With that in mind, please apologize to the people for those bad outcomes. And, if you did those things with a bad mind, please apologize to the people as well, and do so before you die. If you apologize to the people, you could go forward into your next life without worrying about all those mistakes.

AC: Just an apology? No court, no long prison sentence, no loss of wealth? Just a sincere apology to the people?

MT: Yes. And I mean apologizing in a truly meaningful way. An apology is a confession, an admission of your responsibility and your guilt. According to our culture, our Buddhist culture, if someone apologizes to you, you need to forgive them. That's all I ask of him, please apologize to our people. Set a noble example for the next generation.

AC: How would you like him to apologize? On national television? Addressing Parliament and having it broadcast both in Myanmar and around the world?

MT: The best way would be to apologize on Myanmar television, openly. It would be a profound moment, because he would be publicly taking responsibility for his mistakes. Personally, I think most everyone in our country would celebrate and honor him. If he found the wisdom and courage to actually apologize to the people, that confession would make him a very impressive man. It would help him to be a true gentleman. It would also be the single most important event in inspiring national reconciliation.

AC: We all have fear. We all want, I think, to do the right thing. What encouragement would you give him on how to overcome his fear and offer a heartfelt apology?

MT: If he doesn't find the moral courage to apologize on national television, he will have to keep living with that worry and fear that is inside of him until he becomes self-honest. And that worry and fear is, no doubt, a source of great shame and anxiety.

Even though he's not in an actual prison, he's in his own solitary confinement—the inner prison of his fear. He's committed so many mistakes, killed so many people, repeatedly abused his power and violated the rights of so many millions of our people. He will be in his own inner prison forever, that is, until such time as he reveals those bad things to the people, to everyone in our country, even to the people he ordered to do the killing. He must apologize to everyone and forgive himself as well. His *kilesas*, his destructive forces, took him over. They overpowered his goodness. He must make his *Dhamma* right again. And the way to overcome his inner prison—to free himself—is by apologizing to the people. And on television. We are waiting, U Than Shwe, for you to make history. Please come forward, now.

AC: You're a brave man. And a wise man. Thank you. Very inspiring. And may it be so.

Conversations with Moe Thway and Alan Clements

At his home, Yangon, March 2013

> *"The reason I continued my activities is that I'm more afraid of being controlled by someone else."*

ALAN CLEMENTS: Going a bit deeper and more personal, what do you think about in your private time? How do you speak with yourself when alone? What are your hopes and dreams? And what do you respect the most about yourself?

MOE THWAY: My answer to how I think when I'm alone; as a youth,

I experienced restrictions—ridiculous restrictions. Because 20 years ago many things were stopped; many things could not be expressed, especially in politics and the arts. In that sense, I hated someone trying to control me, without good reason. Under the military dictatorship we were not even allowed to sing songs we wanted to sing. We were not allowed to write the poems we wanted. We were not allowed to engage in the businesses we wanted. So in that sense, they tried to frighten us: 'If you do this, you can be imprisoned. If you say that, we will arrest you, and imprison you. If you are involved in politics, we will jail you and torture you as well.' And they could imprison you for a very long time. And they did. This was the culture I came of age in. Prisons within prisons along with the fear of torture at any time.

If we have to *choose* to obey them and stay in an unfree situation, or if we chose our freedom and deal with the consequences, the choice is *always* ours. So, I decided to choose freedom and not being controlled. That's why, in 2007, I joined the Saffron Revolution and became involved in politics. I believe that we are responsible for our country's future and participating in our escape from dictatorship. That's why we did what we did. This is what I think of myself when I'm alone—I want to be free. I want to be free and responsible. So I chose freedom. And I also take responsibility for my freedom, in that I carry out my moral and political duties and, in so doing, I care for the freedom of others.

AC: Thank you keeping freedom alive...

MT: I would like to add something. Many people asked if I was afraid when I decided to become involved in politics, when I became involved in underground revolutionary activities. I reflected upon this many times and found that I'm human: I have fear. To be honest, when I was doing revolutionary things under the military regime, we stayed underground. At the time, I was afraid of being arrested. But the reason I continued my activities was that I was more afraid of being controlled by someone else. That's why I overcame this fear. I decided to choose freedom, to face the challenges, and risks.

AC: It's six years after you decided to enter revolution. Who are you today?

MT: We cannot obtain our freedom alone. If we want to be free, our neighbor should be free. If they are not free, we are not free. Their situation can affect us. So we are in this together. That's why, now, in this situation, we have more freedom than before. But among the people, there's fear, and many still don't realize that they have to take responsibility for the country to obtain their freedom. So many people remain afraid of the government. That's not good. If we don't use our freedom, if we don't practice it, after some point another dictatorship will occupy our freedom. That's why we have more freedom today, but we must expand that freedom in every way possible. We need to practice that freedom and educate our people about the nature of freedom as well. We need to share our philosophy of freedom with everyone. This is what I'm doing now—the day-to-day spread of freedom, sharing freedom in every way possible.

AC: Human rights in action?

MT: Yes. In that regard, I'm interested in sharing more about our co-founders of Generation Wave. So, we have four co-founders and one has moved on and is focused on his own business now. Three are still in politics. So, among those three, we are in three different roles, or three different channels. Our friend Zeya Thaw is now in Parliament as a politician. In my opinion, he might be thinking that he needs to take part in policy making to create a new future. Because policy making is important to make the foundations for a future society. Me and another co-founder, Min Yan Naing, are outside of Parliament. We did some activities together last year. But this year we had two ideas. My friend, he wanted to train the youth to be politicians, like Zeya Thaw, especially to be members of Parliament and leaders in government. He chose that and decided to start an institute focused on capacity building.

As for me, I'm focused on the grassroots and the youth. Actually, as we've got more free speech in the country, unless we speak out with our voices for our rights, those rights could be lost. That's why we need to raise the participation of the people, and raise awareness about politics and democracy, and human rights. But to raise that awareness, I don't believe that we can only make workshops and trainings and seminars, these indoor things. We need to practice it practically.

If some people, or the government, commit an injustice against a village or community, the youth must practice their freedom. They need to speak out in the street or in other ways of protesting or through demonstrations. In this way of awareness raising, we build practical applications. By sharing this, I hope that people will know clearly what the three of us are doing now; three very close friends in very different positions and places, but all practicing and sharing freedom.

Also, the central reason of the organization was to overthrow dictatorship in our country. It was not only us, of course. All opposition and pro-democracy activists, before 2010, had the same idea: to bring down the dictator. That was our objective.

Now, the dictator has retreated, and we believe he did that because of our activities and also international pressure. We are transitioning to a new government and new system. In this situation it's like we've demolished the old building and now we need to build a new one.

In this period there are many different ideas. Because we believe in democracy, we want to build a solid and creative democratic society. According to democratic principles, we also need to accept different ideas and diverse thinking. We must include all ideas and exclude nothing. We want a robust, safe and creative society.

> *"The only people, the only businessmen who can make these deals and partner with international corporations, are cronies."*

ALAN CLEMENTS: With the military-drafted Constitution enshrined in law and with the military's veto power in Parliament, along with ownership of the most important ministries, the old guard is firmly in control. When you consider that their cronies own the banks, the money supply and big businesses, we have in Burma a reconstituted, somewhat-civilianized dictatorship. And, I might add, it seems that they are enslaving the lower class in mega-garment factories with goods destined for the West. Is this description inaccurate and dictatorship has, in fact, retired? Or are we experiencing just another face of dictatorship with greed driven, crony totalitarianism at the top?

MOE THWAY: Yes, dictatorship has retired. But it is far from dead. We must be vigilant. We must remember that the current president, Thein Sein, was one of the generals under the dictatorship. He was the prime minister during the Saffron Revolution massacre. We should never forget that. That means that dictatorship is still alive in our country, even though it's not in control like before. And yes, cronyism is alive and thriving. I'm saying this to my friends as much as I can, reminding them of that.

You know; the 25 percent military presence in Parliament is not there to control the country or control our freedom anymore. It's there to protect the retreat of the military dictatorship. They ensure a secure retreat for the former dictators. Once they have successfully retreated, that will disappear. Because, in Parliament, they just sit and do nothing. They don't support new laws nor reject them. They don't disturb Parliament. They just sit waiting, and if a new law comes up that threatens the ex-dictators, then they immediately protect their old leaders. In my way of thinking, that's all they do. And at the same time, there are many new laws developing in the country to prepare for a new society and a new economy.

As you pointed out, one of the biggest problems is that ordinary people are slaving away and have almost no money. Also, almost all of our country's resources have been stolen by ex-generals and their cronies. So now, when foreign investment comes in, the only people, the only businessmen who can make deals and partner with international corporations are cronies. That's a massive problem. It's similar to what you said, we have a greed driven totalitarian capitalist culture owned and controlled by those cronies loyal to ex-generals and former dictators. It's a dangerous situation.

Before 2008 there was no constitution, and before 2010 there was no official government. And the Constitution is a sham—a fake one—and we didn't vote for that. In the 2010 elections, many people didn't vote. And now, according to the situation, Aung San Suu Kyi and pro-democracy politicians and activists are forced to accept their legitimacy because the international community also accepts them. That's why, in this situation, the biggest benefit goes to the dictatorship and the cronies: they get legitimacy. All the money and resources they've stolen, and all the mistakes and murder they've done, is now legal. It's really dangerous for us.

In the hands of those cronies, all that dirty money has now been washed. To be honest they've washed their money with international approval and international acceptance. That's why I said recently in an interview with a reporter (it may have been the BBC when Obama visited) that I warned the American government that the cronies and the ex-military are willing to wash their dirty money in an American washing machine. This is their greatest chance to bleach their blood money.

Before 2010, some of Burma's most notorious businessmen, like Tay Za and Zaw Zaw, and many others, were on the EU blacklist. They could not make deals with international corporations. Now, they've been un-blacklisted and allowed to do anything they want. The international community has accepted them. Now they can do anything they want anywhere in the world, with their dirty money. The new economic playground is soaked in our blood. It's horrible.

For future politics, in a democratic country with an open-market economy, the people who have the most money control the market. In America, corporations control politics. It's so obvious in the international policies of the US. Let me say it this way: They may give us more freedom here in my country, more freedom of speech, more freedom of expression, more freedom of association—all of those freedoms they may give us, but simultaneously, they continue to loot the future and develop a new economy on the old model. The former generals and dictators and our cronies own everything. A reconstituted Big Brother. This is way I say the situation is dangerous.

AC: What is the value of the present government? Could it be as simple as a cosmetic change from dictatorial imprisonment to economic slave state?

For instance: the cost of real estate in Yangon, as you know, is now on par with some of the largest cities in the world. Condominiums I've visited and luxury villas being built by the Shangri-La group, 10 million dollars US for a large suite; six- to fifteen-thousand dollars a month to rent two, three, and four-bedroom flats in these new developments. I interviewed dozens of workers on these sites coming in by the truckload, hundreds of teenage boys working for $3.00 a day. It's slavery. And the money is going into the hands of a few people in a country of 55 million people. Has the dictatorship become a "ghost slave" factory for the West? For China? Japan? Has Burma become a semi-disguised totalitarian slave state?

MT: I think this is true. International businesses and conglomerates are capitalizing on our country. They invest and run their businesses with our cheap labor. We know that. But the problem is, we don't have money or infrastructure to build a new society. We must find money from outside. We must find infrastructure from the international community. If we want technology, we have to pay for it.

Now, some people are petty. Many others don't know anything. They read in the news that the Japanese government helped us settle our debt to the World Bank. So naturally, people are happy. What they don't know is what we must give back. Nobody gives anything to us without taking something back.

Again, the problem is that in order to get infrastructure and technology, and the money to modernize our country, we need to give something back. We have natural resources and human resources. So that is what we give, cheap as the labor is.

We've lived under the horrors of dictatorship for more than 50 years, and in those years, we lost all opportunities to build our own businesses. Now, we don't have anything. We don't have infrastructure, nor do we have education and health systems. The only thing we have are natural resources and human labor. These are what internationals will pay for. And we cannot avoid this deal.

Regardless, we still have a chance to choose what kind of development or what kind of investment to accept. It's like, for Coca Cola and for Microsoft, what will we chose? If we have Microsoft in our country, we can learn new technology and we can also earn money with our labor. After 20 years, we will have earned money and also technology from Microsoft. But from Coca-Cola, they come in with their recipe and grow their trees on our land and make their Coca-Cola with our workers. Then they sell it to our people. And they put our money in their pocket and take it out of the country. So there's nothing we get, except Coca-Cola, with cane sugar, cavities, and caffeine. Thank you, Coca-Cola *(laughs)*. Thank you, cronies.

AC: Burma's already has one of the biggest methamphetamine problems in the world?

MT: It does. And heroin and opium too. Our leaders should be smart. They should know what to do. Also, if we accept Seagate or Intel or some other industry that will affect the environment, or if we invite in people who run agriculture or forestry, what kind of business will we choose—will it be sustainable for both our environment and the global ecosystem? We need to think. But we have only a small window of opportunity here. And the imbalance against us massive. The dictatorship not only kept us in the dark ages and darkened the darkness, so to speak, with their fatalistic oppression, they kept us in 4th world status, denying us decades of growth with so many great opportunities to prosper. And now, we have only a very small chance, and equally, it's the greatest chance we have to decide our future.

Another thing, for example: the old government made a contract with China for mining projects and the Mison Dam. It's like we're hanging ourselves. It's suicide, really. Without the Ayeyarwady River how can we keep our environment, keep our weather and climate and our social and cultural things? We should be aware of this blindness.

In addition, if there's no Ayeyarwady, there's no tourists—who will be interested in our country? And if we can be smart and steadfast in keeping our country green, we can prosper in tourism. People all over the world can see our great country and be inspired by our ancient history, our ethnicities, our diversity, our moral courage, our commitment to nonviolence, and our *mettā* and our *Dhamma*—our love of mindfulness and freedom.

But we do not want to hire out our magnificent forests to other countries. We don't need to cut down trees. We must keep our forests. Let us not do what much of the rest of the world has done; let us save our forests and do our part in saving the world from environmental collapse. People are taking about this more and more. We must be smart to confront our ignorance and greed. You can't breathe money. Save our trees.

This is the time for great leadership. And I'm just sharing ideas to help our leaders be more aware of what's best for our country and our people. We still have the chance to choose. As we develop our country, we must ask whether we will invite those corporations that will destroy our country or hurt our country's sustainability, or will we work with those companies that truly care for our people and the future of life.

We are a new generation. We are young. After decades of having our lives stolen from us, we want a different today and a different tomorrow. We no longer want to deal with violence and oppression. Please stop this madness. I am asking our leaders to be smart. I am asking them to bring foresight and compassion to their decisions. Could there be anything more important? It's really a decision between freedom or slavery. Between life and death. Please think carefully.

> *"The best way to help the people in Burma is to directly fund the small, local NGOs and the civil society organizations."*

ALAN CLEMENTS: The president's spokesperson made the comment yesterday—paraphrasing him—that 'we didn't expect with the reforms going on, that with freedom of expression, it would reveal so much hate in society, so much mistrust among people, and that we, as a government, can't do it alone.' He went on to say, 'People must learn to trust each other.' No easy task after five decades of top down corruption and totalitarian terror, and it continues today in many areas of the country. May I get your thoughts on this?

MOE THWAY: I don't think there is hate among the people, but there is certainly mistrust among them. But this mistrust arose for a reason: the dictators intentionally grew mistrust among the people. Because, under those 50 plus years of dictatorship, they ruled with extreme greed, cruelty, and authoritarian narcissism. They did not consider the will of the people. They forced and frightened government officials, civil servants, ministers to township and village administrations; they forced and frightened them all, and this split the people. Why? Because the dictators wanted as much information as possible to control our revolutionary impulses, to control freedom fighters, and maintain power at all costs. So they split the people, continually sowing seeds of fear and discord that led to a near perpetual tsunami of societal mistrust. That is one thing.

Another thing—and it's a new idea I got last week after speaking with you—that in those 50 plus years of dictatorship, the biggest impact they made is that they demoralized the people. They committed so many injustices. They killed so many people. Anyone who criticized their actions was either imprisoned, tortured or killed. In this way, they destroyed justice. They killed the truth. And they tried to kill our spirit.

People who simply wanted to live life needed to support the dictatorship either directly or indirectly. The indirect way was to accept them. In this complacent acceptance, the military demoralized those people and they became sheep. Even when we saw so many of our Buddhist monks beaten and killed in the streets, we didn't dare to do or say anything. People saw high school students, and even younger, killed in front of their eyes. They didn't dare do anything. They were cowards. Only very, very few did anything. In this way the dictatorship demoralized the people. And that demoralization produced great mistrust among the people.

For example, if you're a director or a clerk or a supervisor in a government office, maybe a township administration office or maybe a ministerial office, and you want to keep your job because of your family's survival, in this way, they forced all of those people to participate in the military-backed political party. And they forcibly prevented you from being involved in politics. You cannot say political things. It's not about only one person—he also has his family. He's afraid for his family. He's said to his family, 'Hey, don't become involved in politics.' It not only affected him, it affected his family, and also their relatives. So, in their community, other people who are not related to government jobs, don't trust them, because he's working with Home Affairs or some government office. The people are thinking they could cause trouble for us. Or if we talk about politics, maybe they'll give information to the police. In this way, the dictatorship aggressively cultivated mistrust among the people, to control them, of course.

In addition, they propped themselves up further by their calculated use of propaganda, saying things like 'they are fighting in the ethnic areas because those ethnic people want to liberate their area from our country.' Because we were without freedom of press, there was no alternative narrative to the party line. So, more or less, the people gradually believed the propaganda, little by little. In this way, they split and destroyed the unity of the country, and in so doing, killed the will of the people. In this way we lost our trust among our people, and among our ethnicities. This is the biggest impact of the military dictators. Because of this, I'm worried. I'm worried about the Meiktila violence, and I'm also worried about the violence erupting in other areas of the country.

You know, many people today are talking about 'Buddhist Burmese,' so it's like a great nationalization that is growing. When we're talking about 'Buddhist Burmese,' what are the Kachin going to think of us? Because they're not Burmese, they're Kachin, and they're not Buddhist either. Many of them are Christian. And also in Shan State, and in Chin and Karen and Mon and Rakhine State. I'm worried about this. They are restarting Burmese nationalism. It's not good. That also arises because of the mistrust and the demoralization sown by the dictators beforehand. So it's really dangerous for us.

Look at the violence last month in Upper Burma. In that violence there were many police with weapons—they had M16s. They had submachine guns. But they were not ordered to control the situation. What does this mean? So many people mistrust them. People don't trust the police, at all. They're watching the violence, and the police did nothing to stop it.

Only after someone in the government gave the emergency order for the region were the military were sent to the area. And then only the military controlled the situation. So I want to ask this government: Do you want to send this message to the people? That only the military can build peace? Only the military can control violence? Is that the message they want to give to the people? If so, for what purpose?

Then, after some days, on March 27th, Senior General Min Aung Hlaing, the chief of the military, got a promotion. For what reason? I didn't see any reason. And then they show up with all those advanced weapons, and we never knew when they even bought them or who they acquired them from. When did the military buy advanced rocket systems and tanks? We had never seen them before.

Then in his speech, Senior General Min Aung Hlaing said the military still needed to take the lead in politics even after 2015. He said that. I mean, all these things are connected. I'm not accusing them that all these things are connected but it sure seems so. So what message does the current government want to give us? Who are the people responsible for that violence? I mean, it's certain that the police could have easily controlled the situation. Not one of the people who were violent had a gun. The only weapons they had were makeshift swords. Only the police had guns. They could have easily controlled the situation. But they didn't. So it's really confusing. Brings us right back to the issue of mistrust.

AC: A final question, and please take your time. We have elections coming up. There's a lot of conversation about the *faux*-constitution, and there's even a committee to investigate possible reforms to it. There's speculation on Daw Aung San Suu Kyi, if it's changed, becoming president. The question: What to do at this point in Burma's transition to democracy? What should the world and the people of Burma do at this point with what we know?

MT: It's clear for me. I have a plan for myself and also for my group. I'm not interested in the upcoming elections. I mean, as we talked about before, we've lost our morality and our trust among the people. Without this morality and without this trust, we can never make a new society. We can never approach peace. We can never become developed, without that trust and morality. And the morality is connected with freedom, also. If there is no freedom, if there is no justice, you can't keep your morals. So my plan and my vision is clear: I'm not concerned about political things. Only a little bit. What I'm doing now and what I'm going to do in the future is to reconstruct morality, and to practice how to value freedom. This is what our people could consider doing as well. We can practice freedom, and there are so many ways to practice freedom and democracy.

We can become involved in social organizations and movements to help the people. And vote. And read the newspapers and have active discussions about everything important to the betterment of our country—on the nature of morality, tolerance, diversity, compassion, mindfulness, freedom, *Dhamma,* everything meaningful—especially with friends, maybe three, four, five people in your home, with green tea; our people should discuss our country's situation.

Now we are getting this chance. Now we can read political books. There are many great books being published every day, so we should read more, gather more, discuss more, and participate in politics more. If we see injustice, support protests and demonstrations, and participate in campaigns, with signatures and stickers or t-shirts, or demonstrating, whatever supports increasing our acceptance of universal human rights. In this way we expand our freedom, day by day, little by little. In this way, we can push the government to be accountable and responsible, and simultaneously distance the dictators.

If we ignore these things, leaders will become unaccountable. For example, last week we did a protest near Sule Pagoda about the mining project. We protested and demanded that action be taken for the crackdown on the mining project demonstration. That means that we were just helping, pushing the government to be accountable; saying that the government cannot treat the people like this in a democratic system. We want to leave such violent treatment to the past. That is what military dictatorship and fascists do, not a democratic government. So if they want to be a real democratic government, they should control themselves, be accountable, and take responsibility. In this way we are supporting the government to be more democratic. This is what we can do to further our freedoms.

The international community—now they are helping our country. We are seeing many international donors and international embassies donating millions of dollars to Burma. Whether this continues, I do not know. But my question to the international community is this: who are you donating to? If you are donating to the government or government related agency or pure civil society or NGOs—to which group is the international community donating? That's really important. The best way to help the people in Burma today is to directly fund the small local NGOs and also the civil society organizations. In addition, the international community can educate them, provide training for them in organizational development and financial management and how to help the community.

Frankly, at times it seems that some countries and donors are just giving funny money to the government and or government-related agencies. As if they just want to be able to say, 'Oh, we helped Burma to the tune of 150 million dollars.' But they don't really care how that money is spent. So I want to recommend to those internationals take more responsibility for your money and secure a clear plan in how it will be spent.

AC: Is there a final statement that you'd like to make? Anything at all, please.

MT: I'd like to continue briefly with my last comment, about money, but not only money—we also need technical and capacity building in our country. The international community can help us in that way, for the short-term, like giving short trainings, in our education and healthcare systems. If our people are sick, we can't work together with the international community. And if we don't have education, we cannot help the world, nor can we help ourselves. So, my recommendation is that if the international community wants to help Burma, it's better to have education and a healthcare system. This is the best way.

But one last thing I would like to say: things may get worse here in Myanmar. Or, they may get better. We cannot see the future easily or clearly, or say for certain what will happen or what won't happen. But for me, I've decided that I will carry on. I will walk on. And I will also encourage our people to walk on, because this is our best option. It is our only option, really. Whatever happens to us, we need to walk on. We need to face the future, however it comes. This is my last comment. Walk on with *Dhamma* in your heart.

Thank you so much.

AC: Thank you.

Conversation with Moe Thway

January 2020 in Yangon

"We have gone from a uniformed military dictatorship to a weak civilian dictatorship with no power."

ALAN CLEMENTS: Many people are saying that post elections (in 2015), Myanmar has blazed a path to democracy without rights. Your thoughts?

MOE THWAY: Myanmar's so-called democratic transition slowed down since the NLD (National League for Democracy) government took power after its victory. Aung San Suu Kyi asked people not to celebrate the result of the 2015 General Election, as she worried it might be seen as a threat to the USDP (Union Solidarity and Development Party) and the military.

She also asked her MPs not to speak with the media and take interviews regarding their victory. I see in those cases that she used excessive and unnecessary power over the people and the elected MPs that limited their freedom of expression.

A few months later, the NLD party amended both the peaceful demonstration law and the telecommunication 66(D) law, but those laws are still highly repressive and there is no real change, and as a result our freedom expression is severely handicapped.

In addition, Muslim candidates were excluded in the 2015 elections. A bridge in Mon state was forcibly named the "Aung San Bridge" by the NLD Union Parliament, despite the Mon local parliament and the people's opinion. Nearly 750,000 Rohingya people were force out of the country and more than 10,000 killed, with hundreds of villages set on fire and the land bulldozed in an attempt to hide the evidence.

Two of our journalists wrote about a massacre of 10 Rohingya by the Burma army and were charged and imprisoned for 500 days by NLD government order. More than a hundred of our civil rights defenders and activists were charged and imprisoned for protests. The list could go on.

Clearly, Aung San Suu Kyi's government has no respect for universal human rights, especially minority's rights. And human rights and freedom from fear are what she built her entire reputation on. I do not know how else to say it, but to me, this is a major lapse of conscience. I think you call it hypocrisy. Or fraudulence, or both. Among my peer group we say, 'The Lady's not walking her talk.'

AC: Where is Burma today in its so-called transition to democracy? And what are the obstacles the country is facing in its attempt to make dictatorship history?

MT: Myanmar's so-called transition to democracy is dead. It's turning into yet another authoritarian, semi-civilian dictatorship from a military led one. The main obstacle is the lack of true democratically intelligent leaders, with true leadership qualities. As I said, these so-called democracy leaders are not genuine. They are hypocrites.

AC: Much of the world has been focused on Daw Aung San Suu Kyi's address at the ICJ at The Hague in refuting The Gambia's accusation of genocide against the Myanmar's military of Rohingya in Rakhine state. In addition, you may have read that Bob Geldof called Daw Suu a "handmaiden of genocide" and his friend Bono of U2, in a Rolling Stone interview, called on Daw Suu to resign.

A two-part question: May I ask for your own most candid views on Daw Suu's presence in The Hague, and her overall handling of the

Rohingya crisis, as well as Bob Geldof and Bono's statements? Further, what could she have done differently in your opinion?

MT: She did not need to go and defend the perpetrators of genocide. The government could have easily sent other relevant officials instead of Aung San Suu Kyi herself. But, clearly, she chose to do it herself because she wants to show the Myanmar people that she's the guardian or the defender of the country's dignity, but in reality she became the one who destroyed it and disgraced our Myanmar's history.

On the other hand, the people who didn't really have access to the true information about the genocide and other atrocities believe her and showed more support. And at the same time the majority of the population believe that the entire world is threatening Myanmar and see Rohingya as troublemakers and intruders.

In her efforts to support the country, she actually destroyed the morality of the people, instead of showing them the good practices of democracy and helping the people in rebuilding true timeless values within society. Basic values, such as transparency, honesty, compassion, kindness, forgiveness, and most of all, accountability, the very basis of rule of law. She failed the country.

AC: I will leave my response to your views in the Chronology Section of this book. My next question: Daw Aung San Suu Kyi has made peace and national reconciliation the priority of her government's vision. What are the main obstacles for peace and reconciliation to be realized? Among the stakeholders, who must do what, how and when to realize this essential goal?

MT: I don't think she is paving the way for true reconciliation. In this country, reconciliation is needed not only between the people and the army but also among the different ethnic groups, and also among each other. What she's doing is trying get some kind of elite political agreement between herself and the military. This is not true national reconciliation. Again, she's thinking of herself and not the whole of the population.

AC: Again, I will leave my response to your views in the Chronology Section of this book. If I may, another question: People the world over criticize the despicable nature of totalitarian dictatorship. You've lived most of your life under one of the world's most brutal dictatorships in modern times. Can you illuminate what are the main signposts to look for to see the emergence of dictatorship? Also, can you shed light on how the very psychological mindset of dictatorship can easily be adopted, often unknowingly within the collective, even by those who once opposed it, that is, if one is not vigilant and mindful? And if you will, what is the allure of dictatorship by those who espouse, protect and propagate it?

MT: You can't stop a war by another war, in the same you can't eliminate dictatorship by forming another dictatorship under the guise of democracy. Myanmar's pro-democracy movement failed to empower and build a peoples' collective leadership. Rather it built a personal leadership. We built someone's power to be enormously strong to fight against our opponent the army, instead of building a genuine people's power to change the system. So when the leader became corrupted the entire movement collapsed.

We have gone from a uniformed military dictatorship to a weak civilian dictatorship with no power, that for some reason supports the reconstituted uniformed dictatorship. As they say, power corrupts, absolutely. Our government is a perfect example of that statement.

AC: You are a founder of Generation Wave and a long-time activist for human rights, democracy and freedom of expression. My question: You have an open channel to Daw Aung San Suu Kyi. She in fact, wants to hear your views, openly. What would you share with her in the spirit of compassion, caring and frankness, to further the democratic aspirations of your people?

MT: Very simply, I suggest that she re-read all of her books and act as she said, then Myanmar will overcome from all those challenges.

AC: I ask you the very same question but addressed to former General Than Shwe, including his wife, friends, family and cronies associated with them. U Than Shwe wants to know why you may think it is wise for him to confess his transgressions to the people over the decades on Myanmar National Television and furthermore, apologize to the people. He also wants to know if there is anything else you want him to know, since you are a major voice of young people in Burma today, the vast majority of voters in the upcoming elections. Please, may I invite you to speak openly, for the future of freedom in Burma.

MT: If Than Shwe confessed his mistakes and wrong doings against the people, then it will be a great lesson for his followers and the next generations that abusing power is wrong. And the most important thing is that even though you were bad, if you knew your mistakes and take accountability for them, it's the right thing and you can correct your horrid history and give a precious legacy and a safe world for our next generations. In our history, U Saw, the man who assassinated Aung San, wrote his confession, apology, and remorse in a letter to his daughter before he was hanged. Now, today, no one in Myanmar hates his descendants. Why? Because their Grandfather was a very bad person but he finally regretted his mistake and corrected himself, to save dignity for his family. Than Shwe, may you do the same.

AC: A final question: Hypothetically, you have been invited to speak to all members of Parliament, including the unelected 25 percent appointed by the military. What are the most essential points you would share with them?

MT: Democracy, human rights and peace will bring a better future and society for all of us including the families of the military. In democracy, the peoples' choice is the epicenter of power and not the army. Civilians must rule the country, not the military. I call upon the army to go back to their barracks and perform their original duty, which is to protect the people and let the people (including themselves) decide who to lead them and how, by free and fair multi-party democratic elections.

AC: Thank you for taking the time to speak with me. An honor to connect with you again after all these years. May peace come to all people in Burma. May peace come to our troubled world.

MT: Thank you very much for giving me the opportunity to express my opinions. And thank you for your long time *Dhamma* support of our peoples' aspirations for true freedom.

CHAPTER 30

CONVERSATIONS *with* THE MOUSTACHE BROTHERS

February 2013

- "For the election in 1990, my brother organized, supported, everywhere."
- "Don't stop the pressure. There must be more and more pressure."
- "They can raise my hand to break the stone, but they cannot close my mouth!"
- "Par Par Lay helped them forget their suffering."
- "The sons and daughters of dictatorship, they grow up without any real sense of initiation, of ceremony—the teachings are lacking."
- "Tomorrow what happens? Everyone is worried."
- "Everybody must make real peace. Real peace. Because we're family."

Interview with U Par Lay and the Moustache Brothers, a famed comedy trio whose biting satire saw the authorities ban them from performing anywhere outside of their home. Two of their members were sentenced to 13 years' hard labor after performing at Daw Aung San Suu Kyi's house in 1996. Their much sought-after act led to world renown among the tourist community and earned them a listing in the *Lonely Planet* guidebook. Their activism was a beacon for the oppressed, their courage and conviction only sharpened by their prison experiences, where they kept up the act solely for the comfort of other prisoners. With vibrant humor and deep compassion, in this interview they share their inspirations, their experiences of confronting injustice, their love for Daw Aung San Suu Kyi, the need for openness and dialogue, and the spiritual strength needed to overcome oppression. Ultimately, they provide a shining example of the valuable role comedians, performers and artists play in a climate of oppression.

At their home and theater, Mandalay, February 18th 2013

"For the election in 1990,
my brother organized, supported, everywhere."

ALAN CLEMENTS: An honor to be speaking with you for our books, *Burma's Voices of Freedom*. These books will become internationally famous now, because of you—the dictatorship-fighting, revolutionary nonviolent spoken word mavericks that you are—the Moustache Brothers of Mandalay. What an honor to see you again.

LU MAW: Yes, we remember meeting you—me and my older brother, U Par Lay, and my young brother Lu Zaw, at Daw Aung San Suu Kyi's house back in January 1996. The Independence Day performance.

AC: Yes, an unforgettable day that was. And now 17 years later. I'm so very happy to see you all again

LM: Great to see you too.

AC: People the world over are talking about Burma. Is your country moving towards a true democracy or is it still a dictatorship, partially disguised?

LM: Well, from the coup d'état in 1962, when General New Win seized power up until now, there is only a small change. A very tiny opening, that's all. After Ne Win was gone, another general came along, Thein Sein. And now this general is president, only without a military uniform. They took off their uniforms. That's why the high officials of every town are the same generals but without their uniform. They haven't thrown them away; they keep their old skins next to them. That's why in Burma today the only thing that changed, really, is the name: Myanmar. Inside it's the same old liquid. That's why we say, 'new bottle, same liquid.' There is only a minuscule change but with the same people, the same mentality, the same way of thinking. These former military people are all the same—the prime minister, the chairman, the president; their names are different, their uniforms are gone, but it's the same people and the same way of thinking inside their minds. But there is some opening withing the media, with slightly less censorship.

AC: Can you freely travel to perform your shows?

LM: No. We are banned from performing outside of the house. The reason for the ban is because in 1996 U Par Par Lay was arrested and sentenced to seven years hard labor for performing at the Independence Day celebration you attended at Daw Aung San Suu Kyi's house.

AC: For satirizing Burma's Big Brother for 90 minutes, seven years' imprisonment with hard labor?

LM: Yes, pounding stones every day. See, he got seven years on top of his two previous arrests that he had already served. But in 1996 he was not in the Mandalay Prison, nor was he in Yangon's Insein Prison—he was sent to the Kachin State hard labor camp, the worst prison camp in the country, in a country filled with many hellholes.

AC: Hard labor for satirizing dictatorship in your comedy show?

LM: Yes, he was forced to hard labor—'break the stone, break the stone,' 20 hours a day, 'break the stone, break the stone, or we will break you.' At the time, many tourists were already coming before 1996. *The Lonely Planet* tourist guidebook wrote about us in their guidebook, so many international tourists were coming to Burma, before my brother was arrested. That's why I performed for the tourists even after his arrest. I would tell the tourists my brother's story, and I would also tell his story to the many magazines and newspapers around the world that come and visit. They even made a movie about my brother.

AC: Three times in prison. How many years in total?

LM: Too many to count, because one day of hard labor is a lifetime, he said. But many years in prison, seven or eight or so, for my brother, U Par Par Lay. The last time he was imprisoned was during the Saffron Revolution, in 2007. All we did was show our support for the Buddhist monks peacefully walking in processions on the streets in Yangon and Mandalay. At that time, there were so many peaceful processions by Buddhist monks. They were praying and giving *Dhamma* sermons and chanting the *Mettā Sutta* (on loving kindness) all along the way. We followed and made donations and showed our solidarity.

AC: Why are you so 'dangerous' to the military, to the dictator?

U PAR LAY: We aren't dangerous. We're funny. The situation is dangerous. Everyday life in Burma is dangerous; the government doesn't like us nonviolent peace-loving spoken word activists. They especially don't like ones that make others laugh and think about freedom.

AC: Who is the government, really? Is the former general Than Shwe the government behind the government?

LM: It's the same old people—the names have changed but dictatorship is the same.

AC: Back in 1996, across the lake from Daw Aung San Suu Kyi's home, there was Ne Win's home, the former dictator. Everyone use to joke that 'the old man' was listening in no matter where you were. Is Ne Win's appointed heir, Than Shwe, listening in?

LM: Ne Win was very lucky, he had seven wives! That's why he left his role as national dictator in order to isolate his dictatorship on his wives. No pun intended *(laughs)*. But maybe Than Shwe is watching, who knows? Who cares, really? My brother is a perpetual political prisoner. I only support my brother in making sure he goes back to prison by writing very funny jokes about how dumb it is to put funny people in prison, especially, when it makes a dictator laugh too *(laughs)*.

AC: Would you ask U Par Lay why he was arrested the first time?

UPL: [He shows a photo of himself with Daw Aung San Suu Kyi] In

1990, Aung San Suu Kyi and I were very young. It was 23 years ago. At that time, I supported Daw Aung Suu Kyi everywhere. She was under detention then. One joke in particular the government didn't like. And so, I was arrested and sentenced to six months.

AC: What did they do to you in prison?

UPL: I was in Mandalay prison, and every political prisoner was chained with iron bars and spent the day cleaning the prison. A good period for me to write many new jokes in my mind.

LM: And when released after six months, we started travelling again from village to village to do our performances.

AC: In 1995, before your performance at Daw Aung San Suu Kyi's house—he was in prison, right? And on Independence Day in 1996 he'd just been released from prison, his second term?

LM: Yes, that's right. When you saw us on 4th January 1996 in Yangon, we performed our best jokes. When we returned to Mandalay on 7th January, my brother was arrested, and sentenced to seven years hard labor. He was released July 2001. And then again, he was arrested a third time in 2007.

AC: Pray not a fourth time.

LM: It may be coming! *(Laughs)* But maybe now they won't touch us because they have become so fond of our jokes on the benefits of dictatorship as the best way to inspire the people *(laughs)*.

UPL: Dictatorship is also good for your children. Ivy League colleges won't let them in *(laughs)*.

AC: What is your core message, the soul of your comedy, so to speak?

LM: Let me speak for my brother, Par Par Lay. See, he's famous and respected and so he is invited to many different wards and areas to give impassioned speeches, encouraging the people, saying, "You must be brave, you must choose freedom. Be true to your conscience. Be brave." That kind of thing. "The 10 commandments of an activist." But he refuses to take money and offers everything at no charge—freely.

See, my brother is fearless. His speeches and performance are fearless. When the people hear him, they also feel fearless. That's another of his messages, "Do not live in fear." As Daw Suu said, "Learn to act despite the fear." That's what we do in our shows, make comedy that makes you quiver with freedom. And you taught me the meaning of quiver, so thank you.

AC: You are most welcome. As Daw Suu said, something along the lines, that we should never let our fears prevent us from doing what we know is right.

LM: Yes. We must shake off our fear and act despite the fear, until fearlessness becomes natural. Like in the case of my brother. He's fearless, that I know.

AC: Do you have fears?

LM: Aging, that's all *(laughs)*. And you?

AC: All the usual suspects—disease, death, not getting what I want when I want it—all those classical Buddhist forms of suffering *(laughs)*. And how young are you?

LM: *(laughs)* I sometimes act like a child, and cry too, especially seeing my brother go to prison yet again. But I'm 65 and feel 35. But every night I tell tourists I'm 62! Last year 62, this year 62, never goes up. Never will go up, unless my wife leaves me, and then I'll get old and probably die on the spot! *(Laughs)*.

AC: So, every night, what do you do here in your home theatre?

LM: Tourists come; we perform, we dance, we sing, we laugh and joke and have fun. Simple, we point out the virtues of dictatorship and how peaceful life is without rule of law *(laughs)*.

*"Don't stop the pressure.
There must be more and more pressure."*

ALAN CLEMENTS: What is required of your people to safeguard the transition to democracy and avoid backsliding into dictatorship?

LU MAW: See, now, many of our people are no longer silent—they're talking openly in tea shops, at the market, in the monasteries, everywhere. They are no longer quiet. They are talking, feeling, and expressing with each other, and this is a very good thing to continue. In this way, we can evolve our freedom of speech and freedom of thought.

AC: What are the primary subjects of conversation?

LM: They're talking about just that—freedom; freedom of expression and the overall importance of human rights, and especially rule of law, and about the mistakes made by the government. There is also talk about how some companies have way too much power and control and exploit the people.

Since many people have TV, and they read the journals and magazines, we are seeing more freedom in the media. From this the people are also talking at a national level.

Little by little, the people are become braver, and as they feel their freedom more, they have less fear. But this is Burma, remember, where anything could happen, and it does. But we must all try to do what we can to move this freedom process forward.

AC: So, the people are seeing that by exercising their freedom of speech it protects and promotes human rights?

LM: Yes, they are beginning to know this. We must all be bold and speak openly.

Also, as I said, my brother is touring many villages and performs, expressing his devotion to freedom and fearlessness on his terms, and encouraging others to do the same. People are responding. They have been oppressed for so long they do not want to turn back.

AC: How did Burma become so repressive?

LM: I think you know that Burma has had a long succession of military dictatorships. How did it become like this? Mental corruption. Lack of *Dhamma*. No meditation. Bad parents *(laughs)*. Not easy to know the 'why?' But what we do know is that many people paid with their lives. Many schoolboys and schoolgirls, Buddhist monks and nuns, paid with their lives. And so many others paid the price of prison. My brother, U Par Lay, was imprisoned three time. And three times he kept his mind active and his comedy alive even while in prison.

But many other schoolboys and schoolgirls in '88—the generals arrested so many of them and gave them five years', 25 years', 50-year long prison sentences. Also, the same among our ethnic brothers and sisters—Shan leaders and Kachin leaders and other ethnic groups too—so many were arrested. These courageous people are our country's greatest wealth, and our greatest investments to change a repressive system.

Now, after international pressure, some of our most famous political prisoners have been released. But still, we must keep active and use our minds and voices to change the system for good. We cannot turn back.

And we Moustache Brothers will keep telling the people the importance of maintaining dictatorship and the joy of oppression *(laughs)*. I can't stop myself. Blame it on my brother, U Par Par Lay—he's fearless. I am just copying him. His satire makes me laugh *(laughs)*.

AC: For your brother, please. You make people laugh, you make them cry, you inspire them to stand up, to feel free. On the other hand, dictatorship wants to crush the people. A challenging question: How did the dictators—Ne Win, Saw Maung, and Than Shwe—get this way? Is there something about Myanmar culture that gives rise to dictatorship? Was it the dark underbelly of 150 years of British colonialism, three wars and their form of apartheid? Is it a traumatic reaction to the Japan's tortuous invasion in World War II? Or is it just human nature, with the seed of dictatorship in all of us? Can you offer some insight into this?

LM: My brother says, dictatorship is in all of us according to our Buddha's teaching. We are all stupid to some extent and we can all do very stupid things. We are all prone to anger and greed and pride. Some of us more so than others. And that is precisely why we perform, to tell audiences jokes and stories that inspire their love of freedom, their love of dignity, their love of integrity, while increasing their revulsion of dictatorship.

As for me, all the mess started in 1962 with General Ne Win forcibly taking over the government from Prime Minister U Nu. Later, he appointed dictator #2, Saw Maung. Then dictator #3, Than Shwe, and now, almost-dictator #4, Thein Sein—but Thein Sein is really General Thein Sein, only without a uniform. It's a little change. One dictator finished, that's another dictator finished, and yet another, and now this 'almost-dictator guy'—but we hope he really is a man of integrity.

Now, with Aung San Suu Kyi... We *love* her. The Moustache Brothers love her so much. Now The Lady is inside Parliament. She can speak. It's more open. We hope and pray and meditate and encourage the devas to protect her and we also send her loving thoughts that she rises to the very top, and dictators are no more—gone for good. And I do not want to see my brother in chains again. Let them pound rocks in chains for a day and see what it feels like. It is not right to torture anyone. That is why each of us must remove stupidity from our own minds. We tell jokes to help our audiences to do just that.

AC: Challenging our own stupidity. Love it. Regarding Daw Aung San Suu Kyi, why is she so special to you?

LM: First, Daw Suu is General Aung San's daughter. We love General Aung San. He brought independence to our country. She followed in her father's footsteps. We also love her education, and we especially love her ability to speak the truth. She speaks openly and directly. She never hides from the truth. And she's also like our sister.

AC: Why is truth so threatening to some people?

LM: *(Laughs)* Because Ne Win, despite being a general, was a small man and was afraid, and because of that had a closed-door, closed-mind policy.

And he wanted all the people to be afraid and closed-minded, just as he was. So General Ne Win instituted a closed mind, closed eyes and closed mouths policy. He was the only one who wanted to talk. What do you say in America? He was a "control freak," and paranoid.

On the other hand, Daw Suu is open minded and supports the open-mindedness of our people. My brother, U Par Par Lay, does that too. He opens minds! Why is openness so threatening to people? They are afraid to laugh at themselves. Laugh at their own stupidity. We Moustache Brothers are only comedians, so you may want to ask a dictator why truth is threatening. Then you will know the truth! *(Laughs)*. Although it will probably be a lie! *(Laughs)*.

AC: Lots of people in the world today are struggling with repressive governments and standing up for freedom and rights. You are respected activists, freedom fighters, satirists, comedians—you use your mind to confront injustice. There are lots of young boys and girls looking for inspiration to confront their own Big Brother, their own Big Sister. If you were to talk to the world and give them one piece of advice on how to challenge an unjust system, what advice would you give?

LM: Nonviolence is the way. Create change without blood. Be steadfast in this approach.

AC: Tourists are coming back to Burma. What should they know about your country?

LM: Yes, Burma has opened its doors. Thein Sein even let you back in after 17 years. This is a good sign. As you know, before it was a closed-door country, and we couldn't talk. Ne Win, as I said, was paranoid, a control freak, xenophobic—except towards his partially Italian wife! *(Laughs)*—and closed Burma's doors to the world. The media was not let in. No foreign press were allowed. But now the BBC, VOA, and RFA are all coming; it's a tiny bit open. Before it was hard to speak and work. What happened in Burma only happened with bribery and corruption. Money, money, money. Corruption in education; corruption in healthcare; corrupt government officials; everything was corrupt; everything happened through bribery. Money. Money. Money.

Now back to the tourists. For me, I take 'what's wrong with dictatorship' and share it with tourists. And they take this learning home with them, to their countries, and in that way, freedom from dictatorship spreads. We work secretly at home performing, talking and telling the truth to tourists. Now it's a little easier than before and so we keep on talking and performing on the value of freedom. So, my feeling is to not stop the pressure. No matter what, keep the pressure on. Keep spreading the message of freedom and integrity. The tourists should help us spread the message of freedom worldwide. There must be more and more of it, until all of the people in the world speak up freely and openly and live freely and openly.

We also give tourists other important information. For instance, we tell them, "Don't visit Yangon only or Mandalay only, it's not enough." We encourage tourists to travel—go everywhere in our country, from the deep jungle to the tea shop, to the ocean side to the mountains, to the poorest villages in Yangon to the mansions of Naypyidaw, meet and speak with the people; ask them questions; in this way our tourists will learn about our peoples day to day lives and their feelings, their sorrows and their joys. In this way, the tourists can get the real truth of our country. But I must emphasize, they must go to Shan State, Kachin State, Mon State, Rakhine State, Karen State—they must go everywhere. Not only to jewellery shops, souvenir shops, or fancy pagodas, or fine dining in five-star hotels. Don't spend all their time there. Go off the beaten track. Go to places few people go and most of all, as I said, speak with the people. Learn about our people by asking them questions. As Daw Suu has said so much, "We must learn to ask questions."

AC: What does freedom mean to you?

LM: Freedom means saying, feeling, and expressing the truth of the situation and not pretending it is different. Tourists come and we tell them the truth. For example, my brother recently joked: "One month ago I could not sleep, I could not drink, I could not eat, because I has a tooth ache and I needed a dentist. So I went to the outside toilet and I found a dentist inside. I said 'Dentist, please check my teeth, I have a bad tooth ache.' The dentist asked me, 'Where have you come from?' and I say, 'I come from Burma,' and he says, 'No, why have you come to the outside toilet?' and I said, 'Because I have a toothache but I'm not allowed to open my mouth!' We are tired of our country being closed. Closed minds. Closed mouths. Enough.

AC: The power of the open mind; thank you. Good to see you all. It's been 17 long years. May tourists the world over come and visit you.

LM: Our entertainment is not just for tourists, the media are welcome too—we keep an open house for everyone, even those who don't laugh at our jokes. We do satire. We do not mean any harm. We are nonviolent comedians. My brother has been thrown three times in the slammer; three times in the clink; three times up the river, where he was a rock pounding chained workhorse.

UPL: My name Moustache Number 1, Par Par Lay.

LZ: My name is comedian Lu Zaw.

LM: Our father was a comedian, and our grandfather was also a comedian—the Moustache Brother comedians are three generations. We are chips off the old block. We serve village to village, travelling and performing. Before 1996, we travelled everywhere—Shan State, Kachin State—everywhere. We do one-hour shows, and our drama play is just over two hours. We also do all night shows. We joke. We are comedians for the people, not for the government.

AC: Thank you very much.

LM: Thank you.

Conversations with The Moustache Brothers and Alan Clements

At their home and theater, Mandalay, February 18th 2013

"They can raise my hand [to break the stone], but they cannot close my mouth!"

[Lu Maw translates as U Par Lay speaks enthusiastically throughout]

ALAN CLEMENTS: I'm here with Burma's preeminent spoken word artist, U Par Lay and his esteemed Moustache Brothers in their home theater in the west end of Mandalay, the vaudeville section of the city--

LU MAW: No. This is Mandalay's Broadway! *(Laughs).*

AC: Speaking of Broadway, your story should be turned into a Broadway musical. And I'm here to watch your performance tonight. But before you take the stage, I'd like to have a few words with this gentleman, U Par Lay, who I first met in 1996 at Daw Aung San Suu Kyi's home, on your Independence Day performance. Now, these gentlemen have a special place in my heart. I remember U Par Lay—his first act upon release from prison back in 1996 was coming to Daw Suu's house to perform on Independence Day, when everyone gathered and risked arrest and imprisonment. Would you take up back to that time?

LM: So, at the Independence Day performance in 1996, at Daw Aung San Suu Kyi's house, there was a big gathering, as you know, a big celebration, despite the fact that we were under the shackles of military dictatorship at the time. What happened that day was that U Par Par Lay made a *lot* of jokes. I mean a lot; not one, not two, not three, over three-hundred jokes. At that time, the dictatorship was strong and mean—hardliners. And U Par Par Lay made fun of them, satirized them. Why not? The military are always chasing power, but their lights are off and on, not 24-hour's steady! They've got faulty electricity upstairs. Downstairs is good, where the family lives. Upstairs has a short circuit or something! *(Laughs)*. U Par Par Lay made jokes and they got angry.

So, at midnight on the 7th January, after we returned to Mandalay, there's a loud knocking on the door—*knock, knock, knock*. The 'KGB' had come and dragged him away. He was charged under Section Number 5, for saying political jokes. Us Burmese can be so hot-headed! Some find it so hard to laugh and prefer to get angry.

My brother was sentenced to seven years' hard labor. He was first taken to Mandalay prison, then hooded and shackled and secretly taken to the Mandalay railway station, and from there to the notorious Kachin State hard labor camp. There he was forced to "break the stone, break the stone," all day long, "break the stone!" The Burmese named the prison "one long iron bar."

Now, I only learned of where my brother had been taken through the radio, through the BBC or VOA or RFA. And it was only later, when some prisoners from the hard labor camp were released, did those prisoners tell me my brother's situation: chained and shackled pounding rocks all day long. All for what? Inspiring people to laugh? Inspiring people to love freedom?

U Par Par Lay was released in July 2001, and we immediately joined together for a performance. Directly afterwards, the very same senior military official in Mandalay, who arrested my brother years before, called him to his office and demanded, "Don't perform to tourists, ever! You must stop performing now!"

But because of my brother's fearless spirit, we disregarded the officer and carried on performing, not only once, but every night! We couldn't care less about his order—it went in one ear and out the other, or how do you say, like water off a duck's back! *(Laughs)*. In other words, we didn't give a rat's ass! *(Laughs)*.

AC: *(Laughs)* U Par Lay was pounding rocks all day long with chains on his arms and legs—what was he feeling inside? How did he manage to make it through?

LM: Listen, in that hellhole, there was no running water, never a shower, and the food—like dog food. And no medicines whatsoever. The weather was also horrible. Many people in his hard labor camp died from disease and malaria. But my brother's heart, he says, was very good, very strong. As I said, he's brave and fearless.

AC: Did he ever have thoughts of revenge?

LM: No, not at all. During that term, the other political prisoners (there were only two at the hard labor camp) were constantly entertained by U Par Par Lay. My brother was always telling them jokes, especially before they slept. They knew very well that he was a political comedian, and they demanded! "Oh, Par Par Lay, tell us jokes!" He was their entertainment, every night! U Par Par Lay would tell them over and again, "The government can make me raise my hand to break the stones, but they cannot close my mouth!"

AC: Epic courage.

> *"They were shackled with iron, wounded, bleeding; some even died by morning. Par Par Lay helped them forget their suffering."*

ALAN CLEMENTS: Why is the nonviolent way better than using violence to overcome dictatorship?

LU MAW: Although they have hundreds of thousands of armed soldiers, jets, rockets, tanks, and billions of dollars to keep themselves and their soldiers happy, we three comedians are unafraid, and we fight without violence, by using our brains, our mouths, our voices, our conscience, and by the power of laughter. We tell jokes, that's all. Simply said, laughing together is far better than knocking someone over the head with a club. Further, although we are only three, we make the oppressors shake. We bring their behavior out into the open. We expose their way of thinking to the public and satirize it and make jokes. That's why we are artists. We are comedians. And we do our comedy work to change government policy. That's all. We are spoken word freedom fighters. This is a far better way to create change than fighting. All we do is open up the space to *share* in an open conversation, mind to mind, mouth to mouth. This is the better way. Kiss or kill? We are comedians, on the stage of our own home performing, just talking. No hitting. No violence. Only theater. We tell jokes. Just laughter. We are comedians.

AC: What is most important for the people of your country to understand today?

LM: Freedom. The value of freedom. Breathe it. Live it. And it is not about money, money, money. It's about peace, not fighting. It's about love, not hating. It's about laughing, not hurting. It's about democracy, not dictatorship. Let us all contribute to making our country peaceful and prosperous. Let everyone put down the weapons, please. As John Lennon sang, "all we are saying is give peace a chance."

AC: People look to the three of you as revolutionary heroes.

LM: *(Laughs)* You think we are heroes!

AC: Indeed. I asked this question before but allow me to ask it again: What would U Par Lay say to the nonviolent activists around the world who want to challenge their own fear and change the system they are a part of? What advice would he give to the young peace-loving revolutionaries worldwide?

LM: Whether artist or writer or teacher or preacher or intellectual or farmer or builder or even a soldier, organize only through truthful speech and only in peace. My brother has given political speeches in so many villages. He could be arrested at any second. Taken right off the stage and back into chains pounding rocks. He's brave. I'm brave just thinking about the bravery he has to confront that situation. You too must be brave. When you're right, and you have the right, and the chance to say what's right, why be afraid? Speak up. Stand up. You must be open; you must talk. You must gain strength from your actions. Gain strength from the rightness of your speech and actions.

AC: How did he cope with his pain? What did he *do* with it?

UPL: I am a comedian. I do my best to make people happy. Although the people are suffering, they love our jokes, they love laughter. When they hear our jokes, they forget their pain. This is what I did to cope: tell jokes to others.

AC: They forget their suffering; beautiful. Amazing.

LM: After international pressure, Par Par Lay and Lu Zaw, who was also imprisoned, were released in July 2001, after serving five years and seven months. During their time in the hard labor camp, there were many prisoners, and at night after pounding rocks all day, there was great suffering. They were in chains and shackled with an iron rod. They were wounded and bleeding, and some even died by the morning. They were all very sad. And before the other prisoners would sleep, they requested, 'Please, we want to hear your jokes.' Everyone encouraged Par Par Lay to joke and sing. Everyone would often clap and chant and encourage him. See, my Par Par Lay helped them forget their *dukkha*, their suffering. During the day they are shackled and breaking stones, all day long. They are exhausted and very sore, but they would forget they were tired, and they sang his songs with him until the pain went away, and remember, some died by the morning, died while trying to sing.

UPL: [Sings beautifully in Burmese]

LM: Human being—man; woman; human being, we are all human beings.

AC: You guys are truly amazing. You're democracy heroes! May your spoken word tradition of revolutionary activism spread worldwide.

LM: Please let me explain again. My brother was arrested three times. The first time was over 20 years ago, on the 1st of June, near the first election in 1990. He was sentenced to six months. In 1996, when you were there, in Yangon, he was arrested for a second time and sentenced to 7 years, and released July 2001. And then again in 2007, he was sentenced to two months for organizing donations for the Buddhist monks during the Saffron Revolution. Altogether, three times in the slammer. Me, I was never arrested. I pushed my brother to—'go, go, go'—that's the reason I'm so brave—fear always pushing fearlessness forward! *(Laughs)*.

AC: Thank you. A final question: What's the most important aspect of the Buddha's teaching for a comedian?

UPL: Learning to laugh at your own suffering. And cry if you are creating suffering for others.

LM: Otherwise, create peace wherever you go. And at times, of course, some will get angry at your words. That's okay. Know that you are doing your job. That's satire. That's comedy.

UPL: That was the life of the Buddha. Most loved him, some criticized him, and one person in particular even tried to kill him. That's life.

LM: But keep doing your job, keep doing your *Dhamma*, keep living your freedom.

AC: *Sadhu, sadhu, sadhu.*

CHAPTER 31

A CONVERSATION *with* BO KYI

March 2013

- "So long as there are political prisoners in Burma, there will be no national reconciliation."
- 'We need to educate the soldiers and army officers, the guards and police.'
- "I already knew the risks, before I was arrested, and so I prepared myself."
- "Now we're sitting together at a table with those who tortured us… solving the problems together."
- "Without responsibility, you cannot have freedom."
- "We still face a lot of challenges."

Interview with Bo Kyi, winner of the 2009 Human Rights Watch Alison Des Forges Award for Extraordinary Activism and founder of the Assistance Association of Political Prisoners (Burma) or (AAPP-B), which provides support and services to political prisoners and their families. Himself a former political prisoner, Bo Kyi refused to be cowed by his ordeal, teaching himself to read and write English in jail, where he spent eight years before immigrating to Thailand to campaign for the release of his fellow political prisoners. In this exclusive interview, he talks in detail about the work of the AAPP-B, the challenges it faces, and how he overcame his own challenges as a political prisoner. He demonstrates the revolutionary spirit of his activism and the turmoil of his country, describing how he went from working underground to becoming a leading member of the government-recognized political prisoners review committee.

"So long as there are political prisoners in Burma, there will be no national reconciliation."

ALAN CLEMENTS: An honor to meet you, Bo Kyi. Your life and work are an inspiration. You were imprisoned as a prisoner of conscience a few times. How long were you imprisoned for, and where?

BO KYI: I served seven years and three months, for two arrests. I was in Maing-Sat Prison for thirteen years, from 1999 to 2013, and I was just recently released. This is my second visit to Burma since my release, primarily to meet with government officials because I was included in the Prisoners of Conscience Affairs Committee as a representative of the AAPP-B. I've returned to Burma to meet with that committee, and to work for Myanmar's political prisoners and to help the families of political prisoners as well.

AC: You've been interviewed many times since you were released. Is there something specific or of essence that reflects where you are today in your activist work?

BK: When I returned to Burma, I had the good chance to meet with many former political prisoners, and most of them had just recently been released. After meeting with hundreds of them, I began to understand just how deeply they have suffered and I also realized that most of them had nothing—no belongings, no money, no home—to go back to. They had nothing other than their conscience and their memories of horror and resilience.

In addition, sadly, many of them faced grave health issues. Some needed to be hospitalized. Others suffered from the trauma of torture and extreme isolation and had the worst mental health challenges. Almost all had their educations ripped away from them, jailed while in school or college. Without education few could find work, and without work, no income.

That they were imprisoned at all was tragic enough but to see the ongoing tragedy in their lives made me feel a deep personal pain. I realized that although our political prisoners had been released many remained imprisoned by circumstances—financial, social, emotional and psychological. They needed help. They needed rehabilitation. They needed assistance. There was none.

AC: What does your association do for former political prisoners and their families?

BK: We have two main activities. One is Inside-Burma. When we look at Inside-Burma activities, we monitor the day-to-day circumstances of political prisoners and the political activists. Another thing is the Assistance Program, which provides assistance to political prisoners who remain in prison, through their family, or directly through the prison itself. We are trying to remain as active as possible in our assistance. We would work around the clock if we could.

AC: There are still prisoners of conscience in Burma's prisons?

BK: Oh yes. And arrests continue to this day. We are far from free. Also, along the border areas, because of the civil wars, say in Kachin State, many villagers have been detained. Even though they were not convicted, they were placed in detention. There are around 100 of them jailed in Kachin, as far as we know, and also in Rangoon, Mandalay, and other cities. They're facing trial under Section 18, for demonstration without permission. There are other political prisoners, already convicted—at least 240. In total, more than 400 political prisoners remain in prisons today.

AC: And what is being done for those political prisoners, specifically?

BK: They're asking for their rights; many of them belong to ethnic armed forces. Because there are multiple civil wars in Burma, there are many armies in Burma. Ethnic armies are fighting for their rights, because they think they do not have equal rights and therefore are fighting the Burmese government. So, some of their members have been arrested. We feel that, as long as there are political prisoners in Burma, there will be no national reconciliation. That's why we are advocating with the government to release the remaining political prisoners, unconditionally.

AC: What are they waiting for?

BK: Well, we're working with the government for the release of the remaining political prisoners—I hope. In the meantime, we need to put more pressure on the government, not only from the domestic side but also through the international community. Without pressure they will not release the remaining political prisoners.

AC: There's bargaining going on?

BK: Yes, the government uses political prisoners as bargaining chips and our people will not be released unless we apply consistent pressure.

AC: How are you applying pressure at the moment?

BK: By elevating the importance of respecting universal human rights. Since the Burmese agenda is at an international level with the United Nations General Assembly, the government's image is at stake. So, every policy maker and national leader talks about Burma's human rights violations and determines whether the United Nations should investigate Burma's situation or not. So conforming to international standards of rule of law is really important.

Up to now, we have seen the complete absence of rule of law in Burma. One could easily say Burma is lawless. Dictator law. Military law. Outlaw law *(laughs)*. Of course, without rule of law, how can we protect human rights for our people? And that includes rule of law in the ethnic areas as well. The rights of our ethnic brothers and sisters must equally be protected.

We do not even have at this time any reliable mechanism in place to take action against those who have tortured others. In other words, without rule of law we have state sanctioned torture in place. We cannot go on like this. It must stop and stop now. That's way we need such mechanisms in place: to safeguard the sanctity of human rights.

In order to create that kind of mechanism via the government, the international community—all world leaders—should put more and more pressure on the Burmese government. So that's what we do—we advocate for that pressure, and therefore we engage with the government. I'm not blaming them. What I'm saying is that we need to correct this problem and improve the quality of the lives of our people. This is one of the main roads to peace, as I see it. Make torture illegal and a punishable crime.

AC: Make Burma a safe haven by respecting rule of law and global human rights?

BK: Exactly. The sooner the better and everyone will benefit. See, now that we have the government showing some sense of friendly cooperation in working with Daw Aung San Suu Kyi and in working with '88 Generation students, the country is receiving more benefits, and as a result, the government is receiving more legitimacy. And so more foreigners are investing in Burma, and our people are beginning to benefit. But reforms should reach to the ground level and touch the lives of the poor. We need to protect and promote global human rights for everyone, especially the poor. Otherwise, it's pointless.

*"We need to educate the soldiers and army officers,
we need to give education to the prison guards, and the police."*

ALAN CLEMENTS: You have courageously and compassionately stood in solidarity with your brother and sister political prisoners. You've consistently advocated for their welfare and voiced their cries when they were being tortured and could not speak. And may I ask, if you are willing to share, how have you personally suffered under this regime, under the many years of military dictatorship?

BO KYI: I've had a hard life over the years. The worst part was that I did not have the opportunity for a better future, not for myself alone, but for my son and daughter. They have suffered. They are stateless. Although both parents are Burmese, they are not considered Burmese citizens. Nor are they regarded as Thai citizens. They did nothing wrong. They only suffered because of me. I took action, and they suffered the consequences. I have no regret for what I did. I made my choices because they were right. But there were consequences, especially for my children. Frankly, I feel sorry for the new generation, all the young people, including my son and daughter. But we must move on. Taking positive actions for a better future is the best remedy for suffering. That is what I believe.

AC: What was it like in prison?

BK: Prison is hell. I was brutally beaten for two weeks by the prison guards because I was wrongly accused of trying to start a demonstration in prison. I was not trying to start a demonstration. But they had their mind set on torture and that is what they did—for two weeks, with my legs shackled with iron chains and bars, they beat me constantly. I couldn't move and was forced to endure their violence. After a day of being beaten, trying to break me, I could not sleep, the pain was too great. This went on for two weeks. That was the worst of prison.

AC: And you were placed in a cell with other political prisoners?

BK: Yes, but sometimes I was alone. I was in solitary for nearly a year. After that I was placed in with two other political prisoners. In the beginning, I was not allowed to go outside other than 20 minutes a day. The rest of the time was inside my cell.

Another thing was that we were not allowed to read, write, or study anything. Nothing. No books, no pen. Reading and writing materials are the enemy of the prison. But even though they did not allow me to study, I practiced English while I was there.

AC: The mind of a torturer? The mind of a dictator? Why?

BK: Yes, we asked ourselves that all the time. Why are they this way? How did they get this way? How could they stop this mindset? But for me, I always came back to the present moment and the practical. "Learn English," is what I told myself. See, before I was arrested, I could not speak, or read, or write English at all. By the time I was released from prison, I could work as a private English teacher for high school students. It meant I did not lose it when I was in prison. I won. I kept my learning alive. I kept my freedom of choice and freedom of thought active.

AC: Brave man, wise heart. Brilliant.

BK: Dictatorship wanted me to be useless by my release. They want to steal your mind. They want to break your mind. They want to shape it into their own nothingness. Therefore, they placed me in isolation, and did not allow me to read, write, or study anything. Although, they did not kill my physical body, they tried hard to kill my mind—my intellect, and my spirit. But I built up my intellectual thinking—reading, writing, and studying.

AC: But I thought you were not allowed books, paper and pens. How did you study?

BK: Yes. Because in prison we read many books without words. This meant weaving together an education in different ways. For example, even though we could not see each other in our cells, if the prison guards were away, we could speak out to the other prisoners. We could share. That's the way we could read and study. His spoken experiences for my spoken experiences. This way I could read, I could share my experiences verbally. That's the way we studied—sharing our experiences. In this way, we also kept our dignity and resistance active. Most of all we kept our freedom alive. In other words, I read a lot of books without words when I was in prison *(laughs)*.

AC: *(Laughing)* Interesting, and beautiful. You know, I think it was Daw Aung San Suu Kyi that said that they can imprison your body, but they can't imprison your mind, unless you let them. Therefore, we must always remember to keep our mind free.

How else did you keep your mind free in prison?

BK: It wasn't always possible, but mostly I tried my best to keep my mind in the present, in the now, to live and think and be in the present, not the past or the future or just letting my mind wander. The best freedom in prison is a well-controlled mind. And then I always tried to do something good or beneficial. Of course, a lot of the time I had nothing to do. Your whole life is in a small cell for 23 hours and 40 minutes of each day. That is a lot of time to be present *(laughs)*. So a lot of the time I walked in my cell. And you try to think good thoughts, beneficial thoughts in the present. And not just any thoughts. Sometimes, I would write on the concrete, creating something. Sometimes, certain thoughts appeared in my mind, so I wrote them on the concrete. Then I tried to memorize what I could memorize. Somethings I couldn't memorize, but no problem. In this way, I stayed busy. The most important thing is to be healthy, not only physically but also in an intellectual way, and also in a disciplined way by controlling your thinking and being present.

AC: Are you Buddhist?

BK: Yes, I am a Buddhist.

AC: How did you bring the teachings of the Buddha into your life as a political prisoner?

BK: I am only a traditional Buddhist by birth. So, I don't know that much about Buddhism, but I try to study it and ask others. What I do know is that Buddhism is practical—it applies to every circumstance in one's life, improves your way of being and doing. For example, before I was arrested, I was rude. The way I spoke to people was often quite aggressive. In prison I got the chance to listen to one of the Buddhist monks who was arrested. He taught me, "You must learn to control yourself first. You must learn to control your speech and not to say rude words." That is the first thing. You need to control yourself.

After that, the second thing he told me, "You must train yourself not to think of such rude things in the first place. You must learn to control your mind." I practiced that. Then, finally, I could control my speech, not to speak rudely.

After that he told me, "Contribute something beneficial to your neighbors—this is both good and important to do." That is the third thing.

He didn't teach me about future lives, he only taught me about present moment wisdom. "Live in the present. Do the best you can now. Control your mind. Help others." I liked that. And even now, I practice that *Dhamma* as much as I can, right up to now, with you *(laughs)*.

AC: Thank you for gifting me with your presence and your insights. You have documented the human rights atrocities in Burma in tremendous detail. The world knows them now. In trying to understand the mind of the torturer, specifically the man who tortured you; I have two questions. One: when you were being tortured, what was your experience? What were you thinking? Did you disassociate? Feel rage? What did you feel, in yourself, towards him and the world? Would you be willing to bring us back to that experience, and share your learning?

BK: Yes, of course. Actually, the prison guards who beat me, I knew them well, because the prison compound is small. I knew them. Two or three weeks later, it was their duty to take care of us again. When I saw him, I didn't feel any hatred for him. Rather, my hatred was towards the political system, to the chain of command, to the dictator. Let me say it this way, most of the prison guards are uneducated. They do not think of right or wrong, good, and bad; they are uneducated human beings and sometimes they feel anger towards me or others and sometimes they don't. They are not concerned with the 'why' they feel or the 'why' the do what they do, and they certainly don't ask their superiors 'why' we should torture prisoners of conscience. They just do what they are told. That is uneducated human nature. But now, what we are doing is trying to change the political system, by re-educating those in the system. And in so doing, we do not want to do to them what they did to us. We do not want to take revenge against those who tortured us. In the meantime, it's difficult to forgive without an apology or compensation.

Another thing is that we were tortured intentionally, not by the group, not by the institution, so it's likely that we cannot forgive without getting something. We don't have any problem with them individually. Maybe if you beat me, I have a right to complain to the police, but if you do not apologize to me, there's no way to forgive you. But if you apologize to me, I can forgive you easily. It's the institution—we need to change the institution so that it doesn't happen again.

AC: What specially must change within the institution?

BK: Army commanders need to change their mindset, need to change their institutional 'do as you are told' thinking so these atrocities cease within society. Soldiers and army officers need to be re-educated. As do prison guards and police. We want them to know that torture is absolutely wrong. We want them to know that if they do torture anyone, they'll be imprisoned. That's the new mechanism we must create. Before we create that mechanism, all soldiers, army officers, prison guards and police need to re-educated. We want them to understand right from wrong, good from bad, freedom of mind from blind allegiance. They need a psychological and emotional re-education to know the difference between cruelty and compassion and military dictatorship from a democracy that honors rule of law and universal human rights.

AC: Where did this culture of torture come from, here in Burma?

BK: It came from a totalitarian system of authoritarian-minded individuals from the top down. From a leader that says, "Do it," all the way done to those who 'do what they are told.' In order to establish democratic institutions, it's one thing to challenge one's own fear and hatred, but then we must overcome the very conditions that we're born into, so that the mind of the torturer, the mind of the dictator, is prevented from arising in the first place. We must identify the psychology of oppression and learn how to remove it from society, remove it from one's own mind. And that means everyone.

> *"I already knew the risks, before I was arrested,*
> *and so I prepared myself, in my mind,*
> *for how I should respond in prison"*

ALAN CLEMENTS: Burma is transitioning to democracy and you're respected as a revolutionary, a person of conscience, a former political prisoner committed to freedom. There are many young revolutionaries worldwide who are looking for role models and guidance, and some of them are even in prison right now. If you could give a couple of lessons that you've learned in keeping freedom alive to those activists and political prisoners, what would you say to them? What would you say to those girls and boys?

BO KYI: The first thing is to believe in yourself. I believed that I did nothing wrong. What I have done was right: I was arrested because I organized a demonstration calling for the release of student detainees, to recognize our Student Union as a legal organization, and to end oppressive authoritarian rule. I believed in myself; it was *right*. And I was arrested wrongfully by the Burmese regime. Why? Because they live in fear. They are afraid of losing power. Because of their fear, I was sent to prison. But despite being locked up I did not feel I was in prison. To the contrary, I felt that it was the university of life.

AC: But you were beaten, Bo Kyi. You were tortured. You spent most of your adult life in prison. What a price to pay.

BK: Yes, it was a huge price. But I knew, before I was imprisoned, that I would be in prison sooner or later, if I was lucky. If I was not lucky, I would die during the demonstration. Some of the students died during the demonstration; I was only arrested. I knew the risks, before I was arrested, and so I prepared myself, in my mind, for how I should respond in prison, what I would do to survive. I had thought about it before I came to prison. We all knew that if we took to the streets and demonstrated that we had to be prepared to face the consequences. And if I were to go to prison rather than being shot and killed, I knew, in order to survive I would have to physically and psychologically strong. You need to act knowing both the bad and good consequences, fully. The good consequences were that the military regime knew we meant business and they had to take us seriously. And, if I went to prison, it would be a continuation of university life—a chance to keep learning alive. Ultimately, we felt it was better to die with integrity than to be a slave to fear.

AC: Think carefully before one acts? And prepare yourself for the worst outcome?

BK: Yes, because our situation was like this: I knew I had to prepare for two things. Firstly, that demonstrating in Burma might mean death. As I said, you could be shot and killed during a demonstration. Many were. Very recently, you will have seen, I was told you were there just after the Letpadaung Copper Mine crack down; when the government used extreme violence to crackdown on peaceful demonstrators. Even though we see some positive movement towards a democratic society, we still see violent crackdowns by the government. It's shameful. So, we cannot guarantee that it will be safe in taking peaceful actions in Burma. Therefore, we must take risks. We must change the entire system; we must change all oppressive institutions and re-educate those in power to live by peace not violence. They must join us in creating a democratic system and put dictatorship behind us, for good.

AC: But dictators are dictators because they're dictators. That's what they do. They don't dialogue. They thrive on violent control. They terrorize you, torture you, break you, try to wash your mind of yourself, your freedom, your uniqueness and even kill you if need be. You know this. In other words, it's not easy for a tiger to become vegetarian. Dictators may be dictators because that is who they are. It's their animal nature. Let me ask: How do you feel about those who have committed these atrocities? You know their names; you know their family members' names; you know their home addresses, and the names of their children; and it seems to me—logically speaking, here—that they don't want to suffer what they have meted out to others. My question: How do you feel about these men who've committed crimes against humanity, gross atrocities against their own people, against you, and your own children? How do you wish to deal with them in this transition from dictatorship to a democratic nation?

BK: I want truth and justice. I want truth and reconciliation. That is important: we want the truth, we want to know who did these things, and who ordered them. In the meantime, I do not have any intention or any wishes for them to be imprisoned.

AC: You're advocating truth equals amnesty?

BK: Not complete amnesty. I first want them to openly confess what they've done wrong to the country and to the people. That is what we really need.

AC: A public televised confessional?

BK: Yes, exactly. A public televised confession to the nation that is honest and sincere. That will be the most helpful for national reconciliation.

AC: Well, can I ask you a very personal question? These books will be read, if Than Shwe remains alive, by the former general and dictator. His wife will also likely read them, as will his children and grandchildren. In addition, General Min Aung Hlaing and his wife will read them. Perhaps all regional commanders and their wives will read them as well. I also pray that they are translated into all languages in Burma so all ethnic groups can read them. I would like to see the whole country, and all leaders in world, also read them. Can I ask you, imagine Than Shwe is here with us.

He is saying, 'I don't want to go to prison. I don't want to put you back in prison. We both want peace, security and freedom. I want my wife not to fear persecution. I want your children to be recognized as Burmese citizens. I want to do what's right for all political prisoners. Help me understand what is right. What do you want me to know for the betterment of our country?'

BK: We need to negotiate. For example, you're one of the richest men in Burma now; how do you use your money for the betterment of the people? We don't want all your wealth, but some of it should be immediately used for the benefit of the people of our country. You acquired most of it on the backs of the people, now show your goodwill and return it for their upliftment. That would go a long way to restore goodwill and trust and moreover, reconciliation. So, with your confessional we want you to give some of your wealth to benefit the people. That's one thing.

Nor can we give you blanket amnesty. We need to negotiate that point as well. For example, many of your officers stole land from our farmers. *That* is a problem. Up to this point, the farmers have suffered a lot. And we ask you, how do you wish to resolve that problem as well?

Now, Than Shwe and others are saying, 'We have already left power, it's not our concern.' But actually those problems have been created by generations of military leaders, including you. They have a responsibility for solving these problems. I want to see them commit to solving these problems together with the new generation. Let's start there and see how the reconciliation process evolves. Let's see how sincere they are. Let us see concrete actions that benefit the victims of their decades of criminality.

AC: You want their active involvement? You want a redistribution of their wealth? And would you say more about how you want the former dictator to confess publicly?

BK: Yes, because their wealth has not been earned in an honest way. They stole a lot of land from our farmers and created unthinkable suffering for them. Imagine someone coming along and arbitrary stealing your land and for our farmers, it was their livelihoods as well. And Than Shwe and Thein Sein and so many other senior officers became richer and richer from that land that they stole. The Buddha didn't teach us to steal as one of the five precepts. He didn't encourage us to kill or violate others as a guiding principle. He didn't say that cruelty was the best form of compassion. The military leaders got it all wrong and I'd like to see them explain that to the public—to openly confess on national television what they've done wrong, why they did it and how they would like to make amends and move forward. After that, they need to share their wealth with the poor and the farmers, as well as give the land back to the people they stole it from.

AC: So, 'let bygones be bygones' isn't your idea of reconciliation?

BK: Let bygones be bygones after they give the land back, redistribute their wealth and apologize to the people on national television. Let me supplement that with a personal story. For instance, the intelligence officers who arrested me—after I was released from prison the first time, that very morning I arrived in Rangoon and met the intelligence officer who arrested me. When he saw me he literally ran away. He was obviously scared and ashamed. So I followed and caught up with him and said, "There is nothing to be afraid of. I want you to visit my home, please. We can sit together, have tea, and talk with each other, get to know each other. And please don't fear or worry for arresting me. You're an intelligence officer. You received orders to imprison me. But those senior soldiers—the generals—who ordered you should be held accountable." I went onto tell him, "The guilt and shame that you have is from your interrogation of me. You had no right to torture me, and yet you tortured me. That is against the law. We need to analyse things like this. Maybe if you're a soldier and you receive an order to arrest me, you must arrest me. But according to international law, it doesn't allow you to torture me. But yet you tortured me. And now you have fear and shame. If we had rule of law in our country, you should be tried and imprisoned because of this. But I do not have any hatred towards you." That is what I explained to him.

AC: And what did he say?

BK: He listened, because I forced him to listen. He couldn't run away! I treated him very well as I said those words to him very calmly. Two weeks of tortuous beatings from this man while in chains and iron bars. But I did not feel hatred towards him. He was in pain and I was free.

AC: Oh my... And his response?

BK: He couldn't speak. He was shocked by my words. But maybe other intelligence officers will begin to monitor me now, for their idea of state security.

AC: You're being monitored now?

BK: Yeah. That's ok, but another thing is that we need to create a balance between state security and individual freedom. In the past, we did not have individual freedoms under the name of state security. For the time being, it's somewhat curbed compared to the past. So, we need balance in that area, with state security and individual freedom. That's important for a democratic society.

> *"Now we're sitting together at a table
> with those who tortured us...
> solving the problems together."*

ALAN CLEMENTS: Let's go into some of the primary issues that you're facing with former prisoners of conscience. You mentioned earlier that some of your comrades have mental disorders. What are some of the symptoms that see?

BO KYI: Because they were imprisoned for such a long time, and tortured both during interrogations and during their years in prison, they still suffer, and suffer a lot. Prison doesn't just stop because you're released. Torture doesn't just disappear. Isolation and despair don't just evaporate. Many of these former political prisoners live with extreme trauma. Many of them suffer from acute depression; some are easily angered; others feel they have nothing to give or nothing to offer and others feel they have nothing that is their own. Sometimes they even find it difficult to request anything of others. They suffer from so many emotional issues. Since they were cut out from society for such a long time, and repeatedly tortured, after release, they find it almost impossible to reintegrate into society. Meanwhile, the government doesn't take any responsibility for their rehabilitation. None. The present government doesn't even recognize the existence of political prisoners in Burma. They are less than ghosts.

AC: Even the MPs?

BK: Even the MPs. Therefore, we put a lot of pressure on them, for the government to recognize them. As a result, just recently, they announced that there are political prisoners in Burma. They even set up a political prisoner's review committee, to develop the determent of political prisoners. They invited me to be part of the review committee. Now we're sitting together at a table with those who tortured us.

AC: Face to face?

BK: Yes, face to face. We are sitting together trying to solve problems with those who ordered our arrest. This includes President Thein Sein, who also used to be the prime minister of Burma in previous governments, and also deputy Home Affairs minister. It was usually the Home Affairs minister who ordered his followers to arrest us. But now, as I said, we're sitting together trying to solve the problems.

AC: What do you see when you sit with these folks? Are they squirming? Are they nervous? Are they condescending? What are the range of emotions that you see in them?

BK: Mostly they're reluctant to discuss openly and freely, likely because they are trained to always listen to their superiors. Take, for example, the chairperson U Soe Thein, who is the minister from the president's office. Everyone needs to listen to what he says, and they have no right to speak freely. They're government lackeys. They're obedient. And they control themselves to stay quiet and not speak up. Whereas on our side, we have much more freedom and we use it.

AC: This is military culture in Burma? This is totalitarianism?

BK: Yes, this is their military culture. Although many top civilian officials are still from the military. That is also something we need to change.

AC: How many political prisoners were there over the years?

BK: Within the past two years, nearly 1,000 were released and since '88 there were around 10,000 in total.

AC: How many prisoners died in prison?

BK: From 1988 until now, 154 political prisoners died, both in prison and outside after release.

AC: Ideally, what would you like to see for your former political prisoners? What would you like to see the government do, Daw Suu, the president, all the MPs, if they say, 'Ok, what would you like us to do?'—how would you advise them?

BK: I want them to establish a rehabilitation program for released political prisoners. Not only for the political prisoners but also for common prisoners. We need to change the prison conditions. We need prison reform; we also need other judiciary reforms. All are related. We cannot think in an isolated way. All are related. The judiciary—they levied wrongful charges against the people. Many people in Burma didn't receive a fair trial; that is the first thing.

AC: No trials—military tribunals?

BK: There is a court, there is a judge, there is a trial, but it is not a fair trial. The judiciary is not independent. Another thing is that they changed the name 'Prison' to 'Correctional Department.' Actually, they only changed the name; the conditions remained the same. There is no preventative measure in prison, so torture is pervasive.

AC: Torture continues to this day as routine throughout Burma's prisons?

BK: Yes, for sure. Also, the prison population should be treated as human beings and not as livestock. Whether it be the President or Daw Aung San Suu Kyi or Than Shwe, they might end up in prison, you never know, but they must be treated as human beings.

AC: Do you fear being re-imprisoned?

BK: Yes. I don't fear it, but I know it's a possibility. This is Burma.

AC: Is there a risk of us talking?

BK: Yes, of course. Journalists are under fire in Burma and so are activists. But if I want to get something—give an interview on the truth of our situation—I need to give something back, accept the consequences, whatever they may be. As do you, as you know. So yes, there's a risk, but it's a risk we need to take. Without taking risks we cannot do anything. Because of taking risks I've been imprisoned twice. Another thing is that to make the decision to flee from a country is not an easy way.

AC: I can't imagine. What's it like to flee one's home? And where are your children?

BK: My children are living in Mae Sot, on the Thailand-Burma border. They will come back to Burma with me next month. Although they do not have passports, luckily my wife has a Burmese identity card, so they can come. Otherwise, they could not come as they are not regarded as Burmese citizens.

AC: Successive waves of suffering, and so many obstacles...

BK: That's life. So we need to go forward. Maybe one day we can solve all the problems.

AC: Soon after Nelson Mandela was released in South Africa, they soon closed Robben Island prison and made it a world heritage site. What do you think about doing that same thing for Insein Prison—closing it and making it a world heritage site?

BK: We want to create a torture museum.

AC: As a way of never forgetting?

BK: Yes, precisely. A museum of torture so that no one forgets what the people endured to bring freedom and democracy. In Mae Sot we created a photo exhibition which focused on the lives of political prisoners in Burma. Many people visited it.

AC: The one you hope for in Burma, where would you hope for it to be?

BK: To start, I want to move the museum in Thailand to Burma. We don't have plans to do that at this time. We need to wait for the right time to move it Burma. They did something similar in Saigon, Vietnam—the American war atrocities museum. We could do one in Burma called the British war atrocities museum, but it would be far better to do a torture museum. It is our people who need to never forget, not only our independence but the right not to be tortured.

AC: As an American, I have visited that museum. It's repulsive what my country did to the Vietnamese people, all in the name of a lie. May I ask: What specifically does your "torture museum" reveal?

BK: There's a model of a prison cell block, like the cell block we stayed in prison. Also, there are chains—we were forced to wear chains for punishment. One time I was in chains for 45 days. They said it was for security, so they kept my legs in chains for 45 days. The other things in the museum are photos, faces of the individual political prisoners. We also have a model of Insein Prison in Rangoon, built by the British. Also, we display the international awards given to political prisoners. In Burma, there are 42 prisons and over 100 labor camps. Because there is such a vast network of prisons and a long culture of torture, we cannot monitor them all.

AC: Is there still forced labor in Burma?

BK: Yes, of course, there's still forced labor in Burma. And sometimes prisoners are sent to the frontlines as human minesweepers. Although, one of the common prisoners, who was arrested because of murder, was given 10 years' imprisonment, and after that he was sent to the frontlines as a porter, in 2008. He's still in the military hospital. He wasn't released. He lost a leg. How much money did he get in compensation? Six dollars. Losing one leg is worth six dollars in Burma. We have to think carefully of what kind of government we really want; I want a government that truly values human life, and a president who truly values human rights. We need these kinds of people. And we need them now.

"Without responsibility,
you cannot have freedom."

ALAN CLEMENTS: Many of us in the world, Bo Kyi, are trying to understand the meaning of reconciliation on a personal level. Each of us have our falling outs. There are betrayals that seem beyond forgiveness. One day great friends and the next they become rivals, even enemies. Reconciliation obviously implies courage, in that we must challenge our righteousness of being wronged and or fear and shame of having done wrong, and come together, talk things through, and, hopefully, reconcile. For some people the challenge is epic, like your torturer, who has to reconcile that he tortured you. It would be unimaginable to face the challenge of a senior officer who ordered mass murder or ethnic cleansing, to come to terms with the wrongness of that behavior. They must come to terms with their own ignorance. As we know, it is not easy to see what we don't know. My question is two-fold: How do you personally practice reconciliation as an individual? And how do you foresee your country achieving national reconciliation as a whole?

BO KYI: Even though we want reconciliation, to get it will be a great challenge. To start, every side should have discussions freely and openly. We need to take our time. We need to sit together. We need to be patient and courageous. We must be skilled in the art of listening which means being skilled in empathy, truly listening to the other's views without the need to make them wrong or right, just listening as free of judgment as possible. That's the way, and if we need to argue round the table, so be it. If that's the way we need to reduce our tension, little by little, so be it. But most of all we need to listen, be patient and honest. We must also move forward without violence. That is essential. To me, that is the best way. Overall, we need to stop the wars in the ethnic areas, we need to stop hurting one another. We all need to sit at a table, and talk, and listen and argue around that table, and in that way, we have the best chance of reconciling among ourselves.

Also, I need to reconcile within myself. Sometimes I have thoughts that are good, and sometimes I have thoughts that are bad. I need to negotiate within myself. I need to analyse myself. Self-analysis is important. In the end, we need to forgive. With forgiveness will come peace, I hope.

AC: The world over, take away someone's freedom and they often suffer the greatest pain. Give them that freedom back and they often celebrate with the greatest joy. Freedom is everything. It the oxygen of civilized existence. The Universal Declaration of Human Rights enshrines the most essential freedoms to safeguard in this world; freedom of thought, freedom of expression, freedom of assembly and so on. May I ask, what is the most precious aspect of freedom to you?

BK: It's simple: freedom and self-responsibility must go hand in hand. For example, even though you have your freedom, you cannot act without considering your neighbors, or your society. Therefore, freedom also means responsibility. If you do something that you call exercising your freedom, how does it affect others, how does it impact others. Responsibility is important. Without it, you cannot have freedom. Because it may just be that your freedom is an annoyance to others. In other words, my torturer's freedom to torture me was not freedom at all. It was blind adherence to an ignorant state of mind. It was stupidity. So, we need to understand the difference between freedom of thought and thoughts conditioned by propaganda and indoctrination.

AC: Can you say more, please?

BK: We need to understand the wisdom of freedom and not to immediately assume that what I am thinking or saying or doing is actually a good thing. As I said, we need to assess the impact of our so-called freedom on others. Freedom means that we at times look out for the individual and at other times we look out for the collective, because people cannot live alone. Therefore, we should also focus on the collective, on collective freedom.

Maybe sometimes we need to control ourselves. For example, now we have neighbors, in the night time, if we play music and they cannot sleep, that is not freedom. That is annoying to others. If you believe that is freedom you have mistaken freedom for callousness, entitlement, or pride. Like my torturer—he was an uneducated human bring without ethical training as well. He was blind to his *Dhamma*, to use a Buddhist word. He was unaware of the harm he was creating. All of the world, every minute of every day, people are doing things that annoy and or harm other people. Therefore, you need to examine your speech and behavior and take responsibility not to harm others.

AC: When in prison, what freedom did you miss the most?

BK: I wanted to go outside. I wanted to study. I wanted to be with my girlfriend.

AC: Did you think of freedom every day?

BK: No. Because I did not want to think about my release date. And I did not want to think of my release date, because in Burma, even if we've completed your term, we cannot have expectations of release. They can re-arrest us even when we are in prions under the State Protection Act. Therefore, we cannot have expectations of even our release dates. Freedom and release dates are different.

AC: What makes you happy?

BK: Burmese people love joking, they love humor, so we try our best to be happy in Burma, even in prison. Sometimes we had nothing to eat, only the lowest quality rice with maybe some grains. The three of us together in our cell, we'd look at the rice and then we could laugh and say, "Let's think that we are now in a great hotel, and here is a really great meal," and then we'd eat one grain, and then say, "Let's think we are now in another great hotel," and do the same. Making a mockery of the prison food through humor was a simple form of happiness.

AC: Mindful eating in prison?

BK: Yes, transform everything into the joy of freedom. In that way, we encouraged ourselves to eat the lowest quality food, even though we didn't want to. Meanwhile we knew that we needed to eat it to be healthy, or something closer to being less ill *(laughs)*. There is nothing that you cannot endure if you can satirize it or find humor in it. That's another way we managed in prison: laugh at the absurdity of it.

AC: Do you have any regrets?

BK: None. Not one. In the meanwhile, you know, prisoners now—not only political prisoners, but also common prisoners—are treated like animals. So I'm really angry when I get information of ill treatment. I get emotional.

AC: What is most urgently needed in your country today?

BK: To create more understanding among the different groups. All the groups, including all ethnicities, including the government, including the opposition—we need to talk together and work together and argue together to build unity and trust and peace.

Actually, the first thing we need is to stop war. Stop the killing. That is crucial. We need to solve the problems in Arakan State. That is also crucial. Then we need to develop the economy. Those are important steps, but in order to do so we need to create rule of law, and we need to stop human rights violations. We cannot say just do one thing only. But, if I had to say one thing beyond ending war and murder, is the problem with the military Constitution, we have a major constitutional crisis. The core problem for our future is resolving a constitution designed by the military that enshrines their control over the country.

AC: If you have a chance to address both Parliament and the whole of your country on how to resolve the constitutional problem, what would you say?

BK: For the time being we need to explain to the chief commander of the army to stay within the law. That is the most important thing. And we need time to actually change the Constitution.

But the problem is that the army doesn't listen. They do not listen to others.

AC: Only their senior general?

BK: Maybe. We don't know. Now we can say, for example, that the president ordered the army not to attack the Kachin, but still they're fighting. This means the president cannot control the chief commander. As for the Constitution, the president cannot remove the chief commander.

AC: So, this is a *faux*-constitution? Or I should say, one that enshrines the military?

BK: That's right, it's not a constitution. It's a fake one. The army needs to reconcile with the Burmese people and the ethnic peoples. We value the role of the army in the country, so therefore people set up an army. The army is for state security. They should not be involved in civilian matters. They should stay under the civilian government; they should abide by the rule of law. The army shouldn't take land from farmers. The army should be upright. Dignified. Just the way that General Aung San intended when he started it.

AC: How best to communicate these important points to the army?

BK: That is based on the chief commander or the military leaders. As I said earlier, there needs to be a re-education—a new spiritual, political, and social education.

> *"We can see that the government is making small, positive steps towards a democratic society, but in the meantime we still face a lot of challenges."*

ALAN CLEMENTS: Millions of people around the world are focused on your country. I'm one of them; I have a tremendous love of Burma; it's my spiritual home; it's given me many gifts, and they continue. What advice do you want to share with the world, for leaders, activists, visitors, and investors? Can you speak to those people—what do you want them to know about how best to support Burma?

BO KYI: Now we see the government making small positive steps towards a democratic society. Meanwhile, we face many challenges. To reach our goal of a true democratic society with regard for rule of law and human rights, we have a long way to go. We need to move gradually, step by step, all the while fighting for our rights. Our leaders should make laws in Parliament to protect our people and create a national independent human rights commission. We need these things as soon as possible to protect and promote human rights. We also need to protect workers' rights and set up labor unions. Not unions just for show, but genuine ones. We also want to support investors in our country, and we want them to invest in the well-being of our people. In addition, the government should cease allotting so much money for the military budget. We should redirect much of that money to help the poor and underprivileged, the majority of our people. Please use the money wisely; that is essentially what I am asking, and make it totally safe in our country to exercise freedom of speech. We have been repressed too long. The time for change is now.

AC: May your country know peace, and may all people thrive in freedom. And I wish, through all of the horror that you've personally dealt with, that the lessons you have shared are ones heard around the world—enabling people from all country's to embrace the nonviolent approach and give peace a chance. And so I thank you from my heart. Really, an honor to meet you, and a tremendous inspiration.

BK: You are most welcome. And an honor to meet you as well. Thank you very much for coming here, and also it is my pleasure to talk with you for your books. I cannot travel across the country, but may the *Voices of Freedom* go everywhere. Thank you very much for that gift of conscience and caring.

Suggestions for those who are in COVID-19 quarantine camps, hospitals or in-home quarantine.

Ko Bo Kyi, March 2020

As an activist under the military government in Myanmar, I spent most of the 1990s in prison, including more than a year in solitary confinement. For 23 hours and 40 minutes each day I was kept in a small, 8-by-12-foot cell with a mat, a bowl for a toilet and food provided by my family. I was not allowed to use a pillow because it was deemed a luxury. I only saw my family for 15 minutes every two weeks. Most days passed slowly without seeing another human being. I was bored. I was lonely. But I survived.

Now, because of the COVID-19 pandemic, many people around the world, even those who have never experienced the iron fist of military rule, are faced with long stretches of time in quarantine, or in self-isolation. More than a third of the world is now under some form of lockdown, while in some places soldiers patrol the streets and curfews are being implemented to enforce social distancing. The coronavirus knows no national borders, no religion, no ideology. It affects us all.

Being told to stay in the comfort of your own home is vastly different than being handcuffed and thrown behind bars. Today, we have smartphones, Facebook, Netflix, podcasts and online grocery deliveries. I had virtually no contact with the outside world. I was not even allowed to read or write.

But there are still many similarities—particularly if you are quarantined or self-isolating alone for an indefinite period—including the anxiety of not knowing how long the situation will last, and the daily dread of wondering whether you will survive the ordeal. When you lose your freedom, you feel fear, hopelessness and an inability to be useful. You feel as if you can't protect your family, your loved ones or even yourself. After that, you may lose your confidence.

Here are some basic tips and advice I can offer based on my experience.

Accept your reality
I didn't want to live in a prison cell alone, but I had no choice. The military regime wanted to break my spirit by keeping me confined and isolated. But they couldn't stop me from coming up with my own projects and activities.

Once I accepted that I was going to be in jail for a long time, I made a decision to study English. The prisoner in the next cell could speak it, so whenever the guards went away, I'd ask him to shout one or two sentences to me. I'd scrawl the words on concrete and memorize them.

Eventually, I approached a sympathetic prison guard and asked him to smuggle in a dictionary one page at a time. He did, but after memorizing the page, I had to eat the paper to avoid detection. Over time, I ate many pages of that dictionary.

Some of my friends composed songs, poems, novels and articles on the concrete floors of their cells before memorizing and then erasing them.

Keep active
When I was in jail, I didn't think about my release date because it was one of many things out of my control. But I could try to be healthy. I walked up and down my cell for many hours a day.

Take it from me: Doing exercise will help your physical and mental health. Exercise! If you can, walk at least 6,000 steps a day. If you aren't able to do that, think of another way to stay active. Practice meditation or try yoga.

Stay positive
Most people are able to use the internet to reach family and friends. But the ease of internet access—which we didn't have in prison—is a double-edged sword because you are bombarded with terrifying news. While staying informed is important, try to read something positive to create more of a balance. Instead of news, try calling a friend. Do something productive, whether it is small or big. Clean your house. Cook a meal.

Maintain perspective
I am sure that even though we find the situation difficult, there are many people around the world whose suffering is much worse than ours: victims of domestic violence, refugees, people displaced from their homes, political prisoners and prisoners of conscience.

This is true in my own country. Even though Myanmar has undergone many positive political changes in the last few years, there is still much pain and suffering. While many countries have released prisoners during the coronavirus crisis, Myanmar has yet to do the same. Instead, the authorities are continuing to arrest and imprison people—human rights defenders, journalists, and activists—simply for speaking out.

We should all use this time to think about what others are going through and try to help raise awareness about their plight.

CHAPTER 32

CONVERSATIONS *with* PHYU PHYU KYAW THEIN

March 2013 & January 2020

- "I have come to understand that I myself am the revolution."
- "Freedom really comes from inside."
- "It's not an ideological error. It is just business."
- "They purposefully lowered our standard of education, health and everything else."

Phyu Phyu Kyaw Thein is a singer and performance artist who is known as "Burma's Lady Gaga" for her stage presence and elaborate costumes. She speaks about what it means to be an artist in a repressive society, of her connection to her fans and to Jesus, and how the two inspired her to live her life as an act of inner revolution.

"I have come to understand that I myself am the revolution."

ALAN CLEMENTS: I'm blessed to be here in your home, Phyu Phyu Kyaw Thein, in Rangoon, Burma. Thank you for speaking with me.

PHYU PHYU KYAW THEIN: It's my pleasure.

AC: I would like to speak with you about your art, your life and your love of music and freedom. Just as a brief introduction: I've come to know of your work—your art, and performances—only in the last month. Everywhere I travelled in the country I saw photographs of you, posters, album covers, concert images. I asked myself, who is the woman dressed in these outrageously exotic costumes and with so many cheering fans. So I did a search and found many of your music videos. I also learned that your fans refer to you as "Burma's Lady Gaga." Is that an accurate label for your art and music?

PPKT: I've heard that people have termed me the "Burmese Lady Gaga," but, to tell the truth, I'm senior. I started my singing career ten years ago. Since 2003 I've been doing these kinds of performances on stage and in this very closed country. It wouldn't seem so strange compared to people around the world, but because I'm in this closed society, because people have never seen very much of the world, I have become one of the strangest things happening here.

AC: *(Laughs)* Well, the people I've asked about you, they refer to you as "high art," and Lady Gaga, of course, is held in high esteem for her talents among millions of people worldwide. She's admired as a boundary-pushing liberated artist. How would you characterize yourself as a singer, a musician, a vocalist, a lyricist—and is it fair to say, an activist as well—using your voice, your freedom of thought and expression, to challenge the norm? Of course, referring to your country as "a closed society" is remarkably restrained, as most refer to it as one of most repressive dictatorships in modern times.

PPKT: I'm not a political activist. I just want to realize my full potential, that's all. I love freedom, I cherish it, and what I believe is that I just want to live as a human in the world in which I'm born. After a few years in my career, I have come to understand that I myself am the revolution.

AC: You're a revolution?

PPKT: Well, millions of my fans might say that it is their revolution too.

AC: What is the spirit of your revolution?

PPKT: What I mean is that I, myself, am the revolution, because when people heard my voice for the very first time, they had never heard that kind of voice before. And then when I perform—I want to be a performer, an entertainer, not just a singer—and when they see me singing, and when they see I sing with my heart and I speak from my heart, then it is freedom of expression. But my expression, and my expressiveness, is quite strange for my people.

AC: How so?

PPKT: Because we never dare speak out about our feelings. Many decades ago, there were some artists like me—our Burmese music history is quite familiar with my kind of artist, but then the power of the dictatorship has been the strongest within the last two or three decades, starting from 1988, with that massacre.

AC: How did the massacre impact you?

PPKT: I was 7 at the time, and I remember seeing many, many terrible things. It was terrible. And I think the most powerful time of dictatorship was around 1999. At that time, when I had started my career in 2003, I had a TV commercial clip. It was my very first TV commercial, where people around the country would see me. It was only a 10 second clip. When people heard my voice, when they saw my mood and my movement, I could see, I could feel, that they embraced me wholeheartedly. But what I faced was strict censorship. In your career as an artist in Burma you have to be aware of that. The authorities from the censorship board banned my TV commercial. They said "We have never seen this kind of thing—it's very different from the usual things that are happening, and she looks too bold, and too strange, and her voice is too weird; she looks so brave and outspoken."

AC: They actually censored your bravery? And had the courage to admit it?

PPKT: Yeah. At first, they didn't admit it, they just banned the clip. Of course, I found out a few months later, because some of the people from that board had become my fans, and those fans started to tell me what had actually happened to my TV commercial.

AC: Converts from the censorship board? Art as revolution at its best.

PPKT: Yes, it was mainly the families of these authorities. Everyone has the freedom to feel the music and be changed by it. It's the most touching thing in the world, to me.

AC: You're an active artist performing in a broader theater of tyranny. You sang from your heart and were cut down; you know what it means to challenge the boundaries of autocratic rule. Let me ask: Why is high art, and why is the power of a liberated woman's voice, so threatening to the male dictators? Why does your love of freedom—to be true your voice and your integrity—scare these men in uniform so much so that they have to silence you by taking this video clip out of the digital world? What are they sacred of?

PPKT: That's the exact question my whole family have asked, many times, for many days, many nights, many months. For many years. At first it was really difficult to understand. I was not doing anything special, for me. For me, it's normal.

[Power Cut] [All laugh]

PPKT: Don't worry, we have a generator.

Sister: You might have thought things were changing! Not yet *(laughs)*.

PPKT: It's a reminder that you're in Burma. I used to say that when I was on stage and it happened. The electricity just disappears.

AC: You always have to prepare for backup?

PPKT: Yeah, yeah. At concerts, the organizers have big generators. When the generators started to work, I used to say, "Hey, it's a reminder that we're in Burma."

Sister: Because her fans start to forget, after seeing her for five minutes, that they're in Burma. They feel transported. They forget.

AC: Beautiful. I've spoken with many political prisoners recently released, in the past few months, and they were not allowed paper, pens, books, never mind music.

PPKT: Yes, their life in prison was unimaginably hard.

AC: It's no wonder that you're a threat to their tyranny, in that you communicate the direct experience of freedom. Fans become fearless, for a moment, feeling relief from their suffering. And from freedom comes unity. Who knows, from a concert, the next thing you know dancing breaks out around the country. That's the power of music, isn't it? Even the power of just one song. But you were saying something quite profound, both of you, about your audiences being transformed and transported...

PPKT: No, please continue.

AC: Well, let me ask you this, from another angle; the human rights abuses in Burma have been well documented, by Amnesty International, Human Rights Watch, the United Nations, and so on. What we don't know is why men and women commit these violations in the first place. In bringing democratic institutions and a higher regard for freedom to society, how to encourage the oppressors to change their ways from censorship and incarceration to a love of freedom? How to make that shift?

For example, you had Than Shwe and military as your audience—how would you perform? There's Than Shwe and there's ten thousand Than Shwe think a-likes. Or there's ten thousand Kim Jon II's. Or ten thousand new dictators to come. Knowing what you know, how to ignite a revolutionary shift in them from the authoritarian mindset that says, "She's wrong and I'm right," to, "Wow, she's amazing, and I can be free too and so can our people. I henceforth will not only cease torturing our boys and girls in prison, I will release all political prisoners, compensate them and give Daw Aung San Suu Kyi and the NLD a chance to run the country"—far-fetched, but why not be revolutionary?

PPKT: *(Laughs)* That's the one thing that I'm not sure I can do, but every day I've been praying for my fans, for my people, and, of course, those people in the dictatorship—praying even for the dictators and the tyrants. I want to see a change in my country. I've been praying this way for more than 20 years.

But there was a time, in 2010 or 2011, when I nearly stopped praying for this. I had lost hope. I had come to think that democracy won't happen in my lifetime. I started to lose hope. But then God showed me that it was a blessing to actually witness just a little change in my lifetime. I'd started to lose hope about that. It's really a bad feeling to lose hope.

Now, I'm hopeful again. And I'm grateful for that.

AC: The transitions we're seeing in Burma today are something to feel hopeful about?

PPKT: Yes, I would say that. But, to tell you the truth, while today is better than previous days, that doesn't mean that there is the promise of something better tomorrow. I can't have 100 percent trust in this change because we were trained to be suspicious about our situation. All of us lived under dictatorship for more than five decades, and we've been tortured. Not just physically—I've never faced physical torture and the terrible things that the political prisoners have faced, but our minds were tortured. Our minds were forced shut. Our behavior and our hope, our trust and our feelings, our future, all of it was tortured. We grew accustomed to torture. So we can't remove that feeling of suspicion from our minds very easily. We were made to be like that, or pay the price of physical torture, or even worse.

AC: Forced to keep your mouth closed when all you want to do is sing?

PPKT: Yes, but to answer your question—you asked what could change the mind of the dictatorship from 'they are right and we are wrong' to them being free also; as a Christian, I pray. I believe in the power of prayer.

But I think education is also needed. The education sector has been terribly weakened in our country. In fact, it has faced systematic destruction. If you want to destroy a country, just destroy the children, and in so doing, you destroy the future. Education, that's the main thing.

"Freedom really comes from inside."

ALAN CLEMENTS: What motivates you?

PHYU PHYU KYAW THEIN: Freedom. I just want to be free. I just want to express myself freely, and I just want to live to the full limits as a human. Not just as a woman. I am not a feminist or an activist for anything, but I just want to feel like a full human being in the world.

AC: Do you feel limits on your freedom? Either inside or self-directed, or exterior?

PPKT: The fears that come from external persecutions, they may have the effect of entering interiorly. But I am sure that I'm free of that insecurity inside of me.

AC: Gone?

PPKT: Yeah. Maybe because I was raised as a Christian in this country, where we are only seven percent of the population. According to my upbringing, we believe that freedom really comes from your mind. True freedom is freedom of mind. But, of course, there are times that I doubt my feeling of freedom. When I started my career, as a celebrity singer, when I faced censorship, and when I faced the many things that I had never before encountered in my personal life at home, I had to adjust. I had to address these insecurities coming from external forces. I had to balance them. Ultimately, I could always conclude that freedom really comes from inside. And I want all my people, all my fans, to understand that. I want all my fans to feel that, to feel the way that I'm feeling. I want my people to understand it in the way I act.

AC: Do you feel that you're actively participating in your country's struggle for democracy?

PPKT: Indirectly, I think.

AC: Do you ever bring the democracy word to stage?

PPKT: In a different way.

AC: What way would that be?

PPKT: As I said earlier, I, myself, am the revolution. And I always speak up for things happening around the country. After this change, it won't be difficult to say the word "democracy," but in previous days, saying that word out loud could make you disappear. And I didn't really need to say that word aloud—like the joke that we told you when the electricity disappeared, that usually happened during the concerts. The organizers, they have their own big generators backstage, but before that we're all in the dark for a few minutes. When the generator works, and when my microphone worked again, I said this joke: "Hey, it's a reminder that you're still in Burma," and my friends are really happy to hear that, and they laugh.

Just saying that joke could put you in prison. But because a lot of people have become my fans, and because those masses are behind me, I have to say that I was lucky, because my fans used to feel like they were transported, or they were transformed in the very limited moment that I was performing to them. They used to feel that they weren't here, and that joke really hit their hearts. Even saying that could take you to prison.

Another example in my life is that I used to wear a beautiful mask on my face when I performed, since my early days. People loved it, but my picture, with the mask on me, it took more than three years for that to appear in the papers. They always banned those kinds of pictures of me. Even wearing that beautiful mask wasn't allowed.

AC: You've taken many risks in being true to yourself. You've stepped out of the totalitarian "beat," so to speak, and you dance your dance, and sing your song. You're keeping alive revolutionary rock?

PPKT: You could say that, but I just love to sing, and I love freedom and I love being true to myself.

AC: Who are your inspirations?

PPKT: Well, there were a lot of artists. I've been watching Elvis Presley, Bon Jovi, Madonna, Michael Jackson, Celine Deon, Shakira, Axel Rose and Aerosmith and a wide variety of artists, because my family loves music too, ever since I was a child. From only two or three years of age, I could recognize the voices of Elvis Presley, Conny Francis, Cliff Richard and Pat Boone. They were my parent's favorites. And then, when I entered kindergarten, five or six years of age, my sister had become a teenager and she started to listen to the local artists.

AC: When did you get your first microphone?

PPKT: My father bought it for me as a young girl. I used to sing at home—karaoke.

AC: You are a megastar here in Burma. Have you travelled abroad to perform?

PPKT: I go around the ASEAN countries, and to Australia, Japan and the United Kingdom. But mostly for the Burmese communities, of course.

AC: Millions of people have listened to your music and love it. I have a young daughter. She loves singing, dancing and performing. And the question is this: people, whether they want to sing or whether they want to be a president or whether they want to be an author; whether they want to be a mother, whatever they want to do, like Martin Luther King said: if you're going to be a street sweeper, sweep the street with dignity and power. You are an empowered person. No doubt you're human. How would you encourage the millions of boys and girls, men, and women, across all religions and cultures around the world, to be true to themselves? To find their voice, regardless of whether they can sing or not; how do you come to terms with your authentic self, your innermost voice and say, "I am going to be me"—and voice your voice—"and to hell with the rest"?

PPKT: I have just one thing to say: be yourself. Just be yourself. Be true to yourself, and you will find yourself. Because no one can lie to themselves. You can lie to other people, but you can't lie to yourself. You can try but you will know that you are lying deep down inside. Best to be true to yourself and face the consequences, I think.

AC: Your country has shown that there's a pack of people that do lie to themselves.

PPKT: *(Laughs).*

AC: Maybe they know what they're doing and they're just too scared of the consequences of facing that truth. Maybe you're right. But what you're saying is: Don't lie to yourself, and if you are, ask your friends or family for help? People so easily put others down; put you down for the color of your skin, put you down for the shape of your body; ageism, racism, shaming, blaming; the world demands that you to conform, tells you to deny your uniqueness, to bury who you are really are, or else. Lie or be judged, scapegoated or jailed.

How would you encourage those folks who don't feel that it's easy to be true to themselves? What do they need to know or do to break out? Do you need a friend to encourage you? A parent? A manager? A major setback? What's required for someone to just say, "Listen, I can do it too. I am going to do it! I'm breaking the chains of self-servitude!"

PPKT: I have only one answer about that, but I'm not sure if I say aloud whether it would be funny or not—some people would think that it's quite odd but it's the truth for me. But, yeah, you have one clue in your question—"a friend," you asked. Yes. A friend. But it's not just a mere human friend. I have Jesus as my friend. I don't have to be scared of who I am or what I'm doing.

AC: May I ask a personal question about your faith? I come from a Christian background. I have a high regard for the Christian faith. I have a high regard for people who care about caring. Who is Jesus to you?

PPKT: He is my savior. And he is my friend.

AC: Is he historical, real, symbolic?

PPKT: He is so real for me. That's all I can say.

AC: You carry that feeling with you on stage?

PPKT: Yes, I always pray before I go on stage. I pray for my fans, and every situation, every little thing. But regarding my fans, I never preach. I never say that you should trust in this religion or that you should change to that religion. It's their freedom. It's their right. Everyone has the right to choose what they want to worship, or who they want to trust. Everyone has that right.

Here we have freedom of worship to a certain extent. You might say that Christians are only seven percent of the population in this country and you may hear news that some Christians are persecuted, but in my own experience, in towns or in cities, I've never witnessed it. I go to church freely, every Sunday. There was no discrimination at school because I'm a Christian, or at work, or anywhere else. So, I never preach or tell my fans what they should do, or that they should believe in Jesus. But my performances are not about religion. It is something bigger than religion. It's about freedom.

AC: Have you met Daw Aung San Suu Kyi, and if so, would you share your impressions?

PPKT: Yes. There were two times. She is so honest, so clear. To see her, she is so transparent. I feel so peaceful when I see her face. Every word she says is very precious. It was at Christmas Eve last year that she invited all of us artists to her home, and that was really great. We were so happy to see her in person. Our family have been praying for her for many years, and that was the time, as I told you, that I almost lost hope that she would ever be out of prison again. To see a person in life, alive, the one that you've been praying for so long, to see her in person, freely, it was really a blessing for me.

AC: You are loved by your people, you have their heart, so to speak. And you are loved beyond your own borders. You've travelled. You're not "just beginning" your career, it's ten years into it, but you're a young woman, and you've got a lot to share on stage and in your personal life.

My question, Phyu Phyu: The whole country is hoping, I would say, for trust in this break in tyranny; they want to believe. Most of them, as we know, and I think you articulated it earlier, they've never known freedom. Five decades is a long time for the majority of people in this country. They've only known the terror of free will landing them in prison, or disappearing, or being killed or tortured. I'm not asking what you would do to encourage your people, but what do you want to say to your people, as a whole?

PPKT: I understand that building trust is really difficult, even in the first instance. But after it has been broken, it is even more difficult to build again. I believe that we will have to take more years to build that trust again. We might be thinking, you might be thinking, people might be thinking, "Will that ever happen again in our lifetime?" As I said, I've questioned this myself. But even if you don't witness it in your lifetime, you should do something, a little something while you can, while you're living, because that will result in a better future in the time of your children. So, it's promising.

AC: I love your country; it's been my spiritual home...

PPKT: I can see that in you.

AC: Your culture and your people have given me so much. And I'm also terrified of the psychology of totalitarianism. I've seen what's happened here. I saw what happened in Yugoslavia during the final year of their war. It's terrible. I don't want to see the full fury of dictatorship resurface ever again, even as an outsider, looking in. That's why I'm here speaking with you and so many other good people of this amazing country—you're not just one of Burma's voices of freedom, you are one of the world's voices of freedom. My question, Phyu Phyu: many millions of foreigners are looking carefully at Myanmar. They want to believe. Billions of dollars are being invested in your country. Several million people will visit Myanmar this year. You're a voice of freedom; what do you want the people of the world to know before they come about your people, that might help them when they do come, whether as a tourist, or a businessperson investing money in the country, or a world leader? What do you want to share with them?

PPKT: I'm glad that everybody is now watching. Our country should be watched. We can't let dictatorship happen again, but we can't protect against that kind of thing on our own. Because we were cut off from the world, we faced many terrible things. There were more terrible things than you have ever known. We don't want to go back to that kind of horror again. No one wants to go back to those days. But we have come to know that there are many needs in this country. The basic needs are education, health, communication and, of course, with business and politics, everything is intertwined. Every sector has an effect on the other sectors, and it's really good that there are a lot of watchers around the country. Without them, without you, without the people around the world, without these inquisitive eyes, we could unfortunately be brought back to that old situation any time. And, money—does it go to help the people or not? Please be sure that it goes to help the people. Our people need all the support they can get. But it must be the right kind of support.

AC: Thank you Phyu Phyu for sharing yourself so openly—your art, your heart, your life—with me and the world. May your revolutionary artist's way inspire generous to come in being true themselves.

PPKT: It's my pleasure. Thank you for listening to my slow words.

AC: You speak like a monastic—slowly, clearly, and poetically, with heartfelt resonance to deep feeling, so you're speaking my language. Thank you so much. You have a beautiful mind.

PPKT: As you do. Thank you. I am very much honored.

Conversation with Phyu Phyu Kyaw Thein
Yangon

January 2020

ALAN CLEMENTS: It has been many years from the time we last connected. So many changes both in Myanmar and worldwide. May I ask, what have been some of the most impactful events both in your country and in your personal life that have fostered in you a deeper commitment freedom, especially freedom of expression?

PHYU PHYU KYAW THEIN: In the 2015 election, what people elected had the chance to become a true civilian government for the first time in decades, even though it still had limited power to rule. That was the biggest turning point in every level of our lives. You must have noticed that freedom of expression is coming alive by our people since then and as never before in the recent history of our country; sometimes to the point of abusing it, as you must have witnessed on Myanmar social media.

AC: Cliched as it sounds, the vast majority of people, both in the world and here in Myanmar, wake up each day to go to work—to provide the most basic necessities for themselves and their families, food, shelter, clothing and medicines.

May I ask, what gets you out of bed in the morning to face another day in the life of Phyu Phyu Kyaw Thein? And beyond that, what stirs your heart, takes you to places that only passionate purpose knows?

PPYT: I am grateful to God that I am alive and see another day to follow my passion which has become my profession, like some other fortunate people. It's more than enough reason to get up, isn't it?

AC: Indeed, blessed are those who have passion. Along those lines, we all have our edges and our personal and professional challenges, especially talented artists like yourself. You once described yourself as having the understanding that "I am my own revolution." My question: What might be the new outer boundaries that you are pressing in yourself, both personally and creatively, your next or new revolutionary edge? Can you take us there? What is it? What does it feel like? Essentially, where do you want to take yourself in your artistic self-expression that you have never gone before? Is there a next incarnation of Phyu Phyu Kyaw Thein?

PPKT: Well, it's totally unexpected that this next incarnation is not in me, but in the crop of young aspiring artists that I have come across in Myanmar Idol season 4. I never imagined that I would have inspired so much in this new generation of artists, to be that outspoken, unapologetic and undaunted! Many finalists have stepped out of their comfort zone by choosing to sing some controversial songs with unusual arrangement (for local audiences, that is) risking losing votes and elimination. It's so fulfilling to see many *Phyuphyukyawtheins* in the sense of artistic freedom sprouting in artists almost two decades younger than me.

As for my personal project, I am now trying my fingers at composing and quite excited to release my compositions in 2020.

Another dream project I am working on is crossing EDM and Opera. These two genres seem opposing, but they complement each other well, so the new genre is named *Optronica*. For me it would be "Poptronica." In fact, both genres are still strange to the majority of our public. Anyway, I can't settle if I can't find a challenge. So be *Phyuphyukyawthein* and there I go!

AC: Touring the country and performing as much as you do, and to such large audiences, has given you rare access to a diverse segment of the population. Further, you are an esteemed judge on your country's most popular TV show, Myanmar Idol. And with it have an even larger access to the population. I don't like to generalize or ask others to do the same, but if I may, what are the hopes and fears that you see in the youth today, in your national audience?

PPKT: Yeah, I am blessed to be able to travel and see my vast and beautiful land and to connect to the diverse groups of people. You must go and see it with your own eyes to know what it is like. Words, photos, and essays are just fragments of the reality. There is nothing as unique as this land. Of course, it's one of the poorest and the least developed countries in the world. But I feel so rich to experience the different foods, cultures, nature, landscape, language, art, attire and so on, just by passing from one region to another.

MMID (Myanmar Idol) this season is the reflection of that diversity in that the eleven finalists come from different ethnic backgrounds. I'm thrilled to see these eleven young artists come together in their love of music and meet in the MMID camp of Yangon where they love each other throughout the contest. It brought me to tears when they covered a legendary song named *There is still a song for unity*. I heard many of the public shared the same feeling. In a country struggling with the longest running civil war and stagnating peace talk, this is epic.

AC: Having travelled and performed in so many countries it has afforded you a unique understanding of the great diversity of cultures on our planet. On the other hand, the vast majority of people here in Myanmar have never travelled outside the country, and likely never will. A two-part question: From your travels, what are some of the lessons you have learned from other cultures that may be beneficial for your people to know about? And secondly, with the vast diversity of ethnicities and languages here in Myanmar, and knowing that most people around the world will never visit here, what are some of the characteristics or qualities of your peoples that most inspire you that you wish to share with the outside world?

PPKT: One, the way people respect each other's freedom in Western culture is very impressive. My Western friends admit that they were not that way since time immemorial and that they progressed in recent history. That's a very encouraging point when I share the story with my fellow public that cultural values evolve with time, based on the political system, social system, technology, education, economy, wars, peace, etc., and so on.

Two, as a result of my travelling I came to realize that there are as many home-bounds in the world as in my poor hidden country. Myanmar is a fascinating array of peoples, of culture, of ideology, of languages, of culinary practices, ancient monuments, kingdoms, and most of all it is changing in every aspect with unprecedented speed. It is probably the fastest changing spot on earth, despite all the setbacks from inside and outside. Just be sure to buckle your seatbelt if you ever plan to visit here.

AC: So many young people worldwide are aspiring artists—performers, singers, musicians, painters, designers, actors, writers and so on—desiring to find their own unique voice and expression in a marketplace that has never been so crowded and equally, so talented. On the other hand, here you are, a young Christian woman in a traditionally conservative Buddhist country and an avant-garde performer, no less, who has cracked the mold, so to speak. And although you have been described as "Burma's Lady Gaga," you were a megastar years before she even started her career, and further, actually dressed and performed in some of the most artistically creative costumes the world has ever seen, from the very start of your career. I visited your Instagram page and was awed by the diversity of your outfits and costumes, as well as the class you have in wearing them. All by way of saying, you are clearly your own unique person.

My two-part question: What's it truly like being Phyu Phyu Kyaw Thein? What are some of your dreams and fears? And secondly, what advice would you offer the many millions of aspiring artists—those boys and girls in every city and every town of the world—that want to "Be True to Themselves" and throw of the shackles of conformity and take that risk to be truly authentic, come what may, and not bend to censorship, cultural pressures, or even commercial success, ie. applause and money?

PPKT: Thank you for your generous compliment. The credits go to my team: my manager/sister, assistants, designers, stylists, makeup artists and hairstylists who also have struggled and improvised (even using chopsticks for a strange hairdo) despite limited access to formal training and materials. They have made my dreams materialize on stage!

One: To be like PPKT? Well, I'm quite a minimalist and down to earth in my personal life despite my complicated stage costumes and dramatic performance. I am blessed with endogenous adrenaline flush and always on the high even without a coffee.

Two: I must admit I am one of the luckiest few to succeed as a stubborn artist. But if an artist works for passion, she will never regret even if she fails to get public appreciation in a given time, place and era. Art has such ecstatic power. After all financial wealth is just a number after a certain amount. I resist and persist and that's all I know how to do as well as singing.

AC: If you had a single wish fulfilling prophecy what would it be?

PPKT: May my poor, unfortunate and belittled country and people see a better, peaceful world for her next generation.

AC: A political question: Much of the world has been focused on Daw Aung San Suu Kyi's address at the ICJ at The Hague in defending The Gambia's accusation of genocide against the Myanmar's military of Rohingya in Rakhine state. In addition, you may have read that fellow artist, Bob Geldof called Daw Suu a "handmaiden of genocide." And Bono of U2, in a Rolling Stone interview, said she should resign.

May I ask for your own most candid views on Daw Suu's presence in The Hague, and her overall handling of the Rohingya crisis, as well as Bod Geldof and Bono's statements?

PPKT: The story of our country is very complicated, subtle, and at the same time intriguing. There are still millions, or even billions, of people who do not even know this country exists! Even those few academicians specializing in the study of our country have a hard time to unpuzzle and to catch up with the velocity, the magnitude, and the meaning of changes occurring in past few years. So it's not surprising to hear different opinions about the country or about Daw Suu from different corners of the earth. But one thing for sure is Daw Suu, as a devout Buddhist, forgives them for she knows that "they know not what they say."

AC: A final question: hypothetically, you have been invited to speak at all members of Parliament, including the unelected 25 percent appointed by the military. What are some of the most essential points you would wish to share with them? And if you had one song you wished to sing to them, would you please share the lyrics?

PPKT: The song named *War* (In Burmese *Sitt*). It's from my solo album titled *Thou Shalt be Remembered*, released in early 2015 (the civilian government won the landslide victory in the election end of 2015). It was the time of quasi-civilian government where there was no more official censorship or dictatorship. But after the release of that album, I received threats carefully passed to me by grapevines that I would be blotted out of the entertainment industry in three years. The song *War* was debuted with Metropole orchestra in the Masterpeace concert held in Ziggo dome Amsterdam in September 2014. The concert organizers in my country were briefed by local authorities to request me not to perform that song if they hired me. It was banned to be performed by contestants in televised singing contests. Apart from *War*, the album contains a song with a covert reference to the Saffron Revolution of 2007, and a total of ten mainly inspirational songs in different style of rock music.

Well, the lyrics talk about the tragedy of wars in general with no references to any particular army, and express the longing for peace. The most touching words for my public are "no country can be built on bullets."

AC: May your song become the global anthem for the United Nations. Thank you once again for taking the time to speak with me and to the people of the world as one of your country's leading voices of freedom.

PPKT: My pleasure to talk to you again after all those years. Best wishes for your books.

CHAPTER 33

CONVERSATIONS *with* MA THIDA SANCHUANG

March 2013 & January 2020

- "When they found out this doctor and writer is only one person, then they thought I was dangerous."
- "We cannot say we've already reached out destination."
- "To practice *Vipassanā* meditation I need nothing more."
- "Whatever you do, please act from your heart."

Conversations with Ma Thida Sanchaung, one of Burma's foremost intellectuals, a journalist, author, human rights activist, surgeon and Harvard graduate. During her time as a political prisoner she won both the Reebok Human Rights Award and the PEN/Barbara Goldsmith Freedom to Write Award, later becoming an International Writers Project Fellow at Brown University. She has written three books about Burma's shifting political landscape, including a memoir of her experiences. In this interview, this accomplished woman talks of the challenges and obstacles facing a free media in Burma, and the challenges the country faces in realizing meaningful democracy, using the title of the last chapter of one of her recent books, *A Fork in the Road*, to describe the current landscape, which is still rife with corruption, censorship and self-censorship. She also talks openly about her time in prison, and how *Vipassana* (insight) meditation helped her navigate past the obstacles of poor treatment and ill health.

"When they found out this doctor and writer is only one person... then they thought I was dangerous."

ALAN CLEMENTS: An honor to meet you, and thank you for taking the time to speak with me as one of your country's voices of freedom, to be included in our forthcoming series of books, *Burma's Voices of Freedom*. I'm speaking with you in the offices of the Myanmar Independent News Journal here in Yangon. How independent is the news in Myanmar today?

MA THIDA SANCHUANG: Actually, it's quite limited. Because of the of the Official Secret Act, civilian civil servants cannot give any information. It's hard to reach any government official for information. So, it's exceptionally difficult to make balanced, independent news.

AC: What happens when you contact the government for information?

MTS: Mostly they deny the information, or say they have no authority to answer our questions. Or some say we have to submit a request form a week ahead, and they accept our application, but never reply. Things like that. It keeps going on and on. Further, it's really hard to find out whom is responsible for giving information, in the first place.

AC: You're an independent news agency, as in independent from a government, but with a government that will not cooperate. You're the editor here at this well-known weekly; are you able to write what you want? Print what you want? Or are you censored?

MTS: In regard to censorship, they just abolished the censorship process, so we can now write whatever we want, but it's a hard to call it 'freedom' because I want to write my news features with a lot of detailed information included, more investigative, in-depth reporting. But it's nearly impossible to get detailed information. So even though we have some freedom, I cannot say it's 'real freedom,' I can only say it's the absence of official censorship. And not only for my journal but for others as well; you have to notice that media ownership plays a crucial role in terms of self-censorship. A lot of the news journals and periodicals are based on permission from the ministry of information. Without license no one can own any form of media. Only those connected to the military—those cronies, or the daughters and sons and relatives of generals, can get that permission. So, you can imagine what news they're publishing, what angles they approach stories from. So, even without official censorship, you cannot call it 'freedom.'

AC: Let's go back in time, if we can. You're a former prisoner of conscience: why were you arrested and imprisoned?

MTS: The regime's accusation was altogether for endangering public serenity, contacting illegal organizations, and publication and distribution of illegal stuff. So altogether four acts: 5(j), 17.1 and publication acts 17 and 20. So, I was sentenced to seven years, three years, five years, and five years—altogether 20 years. With that said, the actual so-called crime I committed was reading a journal and passing it on to others. That's all.

AC: Essentially, they saw you as a public enemy and wanted any excuse to put you away?

MTS: Yes, arbitrary arrest.

AC: Why were you perceived as such a threat?

MTS: I guess they had misinformation—a medical doctor was taking part in an anti-government movement and a writer was taking part against the National Convention, something like that. So probably, at that time, instead of transferring to the elected body in 1990, they invented the National Convention to draft the Constitution. And I was adamantly against it. They had that kind of misinformation, and when they discovered that the doctor and writer were the same person—me—and not two separate people, they deemed me as dangerous. That's all I can imagine.

AC: Where you a member of the NLD (National League for Democracy)?

MTS: No, but I took part in the '88 demonstrations. After that, I joined the NLD to help in any way possible. Mostly I was a reporter and member of the information section, primarily during Daw Aung Suu Kyi's campaign trips throughout the country in 1988/89.

AC: What year did you go to prison and for how long and where?

MTS: At the time of my arrest in 1993, I was working as a surgeon at the Muslim Free Hospital in Kyauktada township. I was sent to Insein Prison and stayed for 5 years, 6 months, and 6 days.

AC: May I ask, what was it like in prison? How did you manage to stay true to yourself?

MTS: Overall, I was terribly ill. I contracted pulmonary tuberculosis, and I already had endometriosis. Nor would the authorities allow proper treatment; my body weight went down to 80lbs. I was skeleton-like. I had six consecutive months of fever, so a lot of people thought I might die in prison.

AC: Oh my... Few of us in the world know of the life of a prisoner of conscience. You've given, I would say, an ultimate act of courage for your country's democracy. May I further inquire, what's it like to live in prison, as a political prisoner? What was your day-to-day ritual? The smells, the sounds, the relationships, the food, the hygiene, one's inner world—do you mind sharing, for us on the outside, a window into those challenging years? And perhaps your experience will support the life of another prisoner of conscience somewhere alone in the world, should this book be smuggled into this person's cell.

MTS: Every day is such a challenge. It would take a long time to explain the incessant challenges and what goes through your mind, so let me take a short-cut: a person's life in prison is like that of an animal. No human rights. No medical treatment. The life of a political prisoner is beyond your imagination. I couldn't even walk to the interview room to meet my parents, and the distance was short, only a two-minute walk. When I suspected I had tuberculosis, I waited three weeks for an x-ray, and another three weeks for the results. When it showed I had TB, my parents got permission to send in medicine. But I waited two more weeks to receive it, and when I finally got it, the authorities took it away and made me wait two more weeks before I was allowed to actually take it. Life in prison is terrible.

AC: Such deliberate cruelty. Unimaginable, what our species is capable of doing.

MTS: Indeed. But after some time, I turned it around. I saw that prison cannot force me to abandon my will for freedom. Let me explain. I was locked up in a small cell, alone in solitary confinement. I was not allowed to read or write. I was not able to contact friends, relatives, or colleagues. My world was this tiny cell. And the many rules and regulations I had in prison made me think a lot about freedom. I kept asking myself, "As a prisoner, can I not do anything anymore?" And my answer was always the same, "No."

AC: As my teacher Sayadaw U Pandita would always say, "To know your mind is the most important task of your life." Prison became your prism to know your own mind?

MTS: Yes, that prison cell began to reflect the power of my own mind. I learned that no one could hurt me without my consent. I reminded myself to keep my authority. I told myself that prison itself is not the real challenge, the true challenge would be the way I face myself in prison. Good and bad is a state of mind and it was my choice of either fighting against or fleeing from any given situation. In other words, freedom was my choice. Freedom is my own right or property. And why should I give up this freedom? And I choose to bring freedom to all my challenges in prison. That is why prison itself didn't ultimately bother me or break me. I made it a practice, a personal challenge every day, to freely choose the way I lived my life in prison.

AC: Imprisoning a surgeon, human rights advocate and writer strikes me as the epitome of totalitarian delusion. What would you say are the roots of authoritarian corruption?

MTS: As I see it, there are four causes for corruption—greed, anger, fear, and ignorance. Among these, the most dangerous is ignorance. Why? The lack of knowledge and awareness are obstacles for anyone to be independent. If someone is weak and dependent, that person will rely on other people's biases or one's own misguided emotions. They would then be easily gripped by greed and anger, forming corruption of their own views. Or they would be fearful of other people's orders or demands, and then become corrupted by trying to accommodate those distortions. Therefore ignorance, lack of knowledge, illiteracy, and unawareness are the most dangerous causes of corruption.

*"We cannot say we've already reached out destination,
we are still at the fork in the road."*

ALAN CLEMENTS: Burma is transitioning from dictatorship to democracy. Where are we now in that transition?

MA THIDA SANCHUANG: I finished writing a book called *The Roadmap* a year before I finished my prison memoir, while at Brown University. I published it under the pseudonym Suragamika. That book is about Burma from 1988 to 2010. In the book are seven chapters. Our roadmap to democracy has seven steps. So, I intentionally made the book into seven chapters. The final chapter is *Fork in the Road*. That's where Burma is today, at a fork in the road. We have not reached our destination, we are still at the fork in the road.

There are several other things that are going to happen. Some people are concerned whether one of the ways of the fork will take us backwards, while others have great concern about not going backwards or going forwards, but being in stasis, or stagnation. There are several other ways Burma can change. That's why I would say the current situation in this so-called transitional stage is a fork in the road.

AC: I hear so much about the cronies in Burma, how corrupt they are and equally, how they own and control everything. Two questions: Would you please explain what 'cronies' refers to? And how best to address the problem of cronyism in Burma?

MTS: What we understand about cronies here in Burma is that they are very close to the generals of both the old and current regime, and they monopolize all business opportunities and they also abuse all the established laws to earn money.

AC: 'Cronies,' by and large, means those with extremely close ties to the friends and families of the dictatorship and the former generals, and current generals? Is that who the cronies are?

MTS: Yes. Both military and civilian.

AC: How many cronies would you say there are?

MTS: Not that many. It's a couple of hundred. And Burma is 55 million people, so it's a small number of people—a tiny fraction really—who control ownership and the flow of money to nearly everything. And under the tip of the iceberg we cannot say how many more families have a major stake in the money. That might be a few thousand.

AC: How rich are some of the cronies?

MTS: It's beyond our logic because we've never been exposed to that kind of wealth. But have you not seen some of their mansions? They live like kings and queens.

AC: Yes, I have seen many of their mansions. I have only seen estates of this size in Palm Beach and Beverly Hills. What do the cronies own to give them this type of wealth?

MTS: They own everything. They control all the resources—gems, oil, gas, land, labor, mining, timber, construction, roads, bridges, electricity, food, imports, hotels, and of course, weapons

AC: The arbitrary confiscation of farmer's land is also crony-based?

MTS: Mostly, and or directly related to the military.

AC: Essentially, anyone doing business in Burma must do business with a crony?

MTS: Not only with cronies but also with the army. For example, the Myanmar Economic Holding Company is owned by the current army. It's very complicated, and highly secretive, but what we can say, as I just said, is that all land confiscation is directly related to the military. That we know for sure.

AC: They take what they want when they want it? They do what they want when they want to? And they conceal it for the most part, other than the stealing of land?

MTS: Yes, that's right. Cronyism and corruption are one and the same.

AC: This is Burma's government?

MTS: Well, it's not completely that way anymore, but still we cannot explain how much these people related to the government have or how they got it. We cannot say or know exactly. Historically speaking, everything operated according to the law of corruption—one's own ignorance, greed and fear.

AC: How does this relate to foreign investment? How can a potential investor feel confident in what he or she is investing in when the country is essentially an economy ruled by corruption and collusion?

MTS: Corruption begets corruption. But it's hard to get factual information. Because some of the names of the authorities of these big companies or projects are not real names.

AC: They mask reality?

MTS: Yes. It's very shadowy. That's why we cannot say, we cannot know, the real truth, so to speak. It's hard to get real information and even when we get it, it's often purposely distorted.

AC: Who owns the banks in Burma?

MTS: That we know. Cronies own the banks. Throughout our history, if you want to run a business you have to deal with the army, and you have to deal with the cronies. That is Burma. That was Burma. Maybe it is changing, slightly. Maybe.

AC: This is a succession of dictatorships that are hyper-capitalistic. They're so materially driven. You spoke about the four causes of corruption. What's underneath this ignorance? Why do they purposely ruin the country, to own everything, so that they die and the country dies as well? Absolute power corrupts absolutely?

MTS: Yes. But you know, most of our issues are beyond logic, because they never learned logic. They have no logic. Nor do they have any understanding of basic human decency. You might say it is the lack of conscience. And within that 'lack' imagine a volcano erupting extreme greed. If you have never had money and someone comes along and says, 'Hey, here's ten million dollars, it's yours, if you do this or don't do that.' But the really sad thing, they never think to promote the development or the welfare of the local people.

AC: Over the past months, I've travelled here in Burma to many places—cities, villages, monasteries and mosques, even a visit to Ne Win's house and to Insein Prison as well, along with a visit to Hlaingthayar. Most people seem to be bearing up, but the poverty in some areas, such as Hlaingthayar, was heart breaking. Frankly, I had never seen conditions like this anywhere in the world; not even the slums of Calcutta.

Now, I have asked this question many times before: many millions of tourists will visit Burma over the coming years. What would you say to them before they arrive to help them better understand the truth of Burma and to make their experience more emotionally and spiritually rewarding?

MTS: I wish they would learn as much about Burma as possible before they come and in so doing, learn about the reality of our peoples' lives at the grassroots level. It's a truth beyond the media. The media cannot reflect the full picture of what's happening in our country. So, please look deeply into the issues, before coming. Don't believe only what you read. Cross check information. There is a lot of propaganda and misinformation both in the country and from outside about our country. I would invite tourists not only to experience the lives of marginalized people, but ordinary people as well—what are their lives? 'What are their struggles? What are their needs? What makes them happy.' So, please learn about all our people. The cronies as well. Try to find out who they are. What makes them tick. Ask questions from your heart. Travel our country from your heart. And most of all, please, give back to the poorest of the poor you meet.

> *"To practice Vipassanā meditation I need nothing more.*
> *All I need is to look at my body and mind.*
> *That was enough in prison."*

ALAN CLEMENTS: A more philosophical, spiritual question, if I can. You've dealt with sufferings that few of us on the outside can truly understand. How do you keep your hope alive under such dire conditions as dictatorship and prison? Where do you find hope and how do you keep your expression of freedom active when you're confined by prison bars and by totalitarianism?

MA THIDA SANCHUANG: Beyond what I expressed earlier, it's simply one answer: *Vipassanā* (insight) meditation. That's my refuge. And as a meditator, I live in the present. I avoid dwelling in the past or imaging the future. So my short answer would be that I always try to live in the present, second by second. Practicing *Vipassanā* meditation gave me a lot of freedom and independence. It was my refuge.

AC: In prison, did you have a sitting meditation practice?

MTS: Not only sitting, I practiced in all postures. I tried to keep my meditation active 20 hours a day.

AC: You were a yogi prisoner of conscience?

MTS: Yes. I told them, 'Thank you for arresting me, thank you for prison, thank you for giving me this chance.'

AC: You did the *Bodhisattva* reversal—turning obstacles into inner states of excellence? My *Dhamma* teacher, Sayadaw U Pandita, would speak to me about the necessity of cultivating this *Dhamma* attitude as a prisoner of *Saṃsāra*.

MTS: Yes, prisons within prisons. And the prison authorities were so annoyed. I thanked not only to the jailers but also the generals, the guards of the country, the guards of the prison of Myanmar.

AC: What was their response?

MTS: Nothing. But I'm not joking—I'm saying this seriously. Otherwise I might not have had a chance. Now, you know, I'm busy, and don't have a chance to practice my *Vipassanā* meditation that much these days. That was my only chance to practice.

AC: What you're saying is that freedom is a state of mind? And if the thought came into your mind—I'm confined, I'm imprisoned, and so on—you let it go? But didn't you want to be out of prison? Free to be free in a bigger field of freedom, so to speak?

MTS: Sure, I wanted to be out of prison, but I used my logic. Based on all my knowledge of when I could be released, since I was sentenced to 20 years' imprisonment, I could be released after 20 years. But still I noticed there are a lot of people being put back in jail under 10(a), 10(d), even though they'd served their prison terms. So, according to my *Dhamma* belief, the theory of cause and effect, if I did something bad the effect will be that I might not be released from *Saṃsāra*, even though I might be released from prison. So where is my real freedom, where is my true freedom? That's the very first thought I had.

So, to have a chance to be released from prison, what do I need? What can I do? I used to say, 'I want to be independent,' I don't want to be dependent on anyone else, so I'm always thinking of how I can be independent. When it came to being released from prison, what could I do? Nothing. I had to rely on a pardon from the government or the prison authority or the judges, etc.

AC: So, you're using the wisdom of *Dhamma* logic or mindfully intelligent reflection?

MTS: Yes, you could say it like that. Sure. I cannot use my own effort to be released, but for release from *Saṃsāra*, who else can I rely on but myself? What else can I depend on? Nothing. I'm the only one who can do this. I have my body and mind. To practice *Vipassanā* meditation I need nothing more. No law enforcement, no physical assistance, nothing. All I need is to look at my body and mind. That was enough for me in prison. It's total independence, you know? Just practice. That's why freedom and independence are always within, not outside.

AC: Did you feel anger or bitterness? Did you feel sorry for yourself, ever? And if so, what did you do with your anger, or your self-pity?

MTS: To be frank, before I practiced *Vipassanā* meditation in prison I primarily survived on pride. Otherwise, I felt I could not survive. It was a frustrating life, so I lived on pride.

The essence of Buddhism is to learn three things: impermanence, suffering, and no-self. After understanding this, that everything is impermanent, what do I worry for? Whatever comes to me, it will change, it is impermanent. So, if good comes, should I be happy? No. It's impermanent. It will vanish. But when bad comes, should I be sad? Not at all. They too are impermanent. Knowing this, I had no worries. I felt indifferent between good and bad things, because of the understanding of impermanence.

And the second thing: suffering. Whatever comes to us, since it's impermanent, it's suffering, in that it cannot provide lasting satisfaction. Since I learned that all is suffering, why worry?

AC: But your life in prison was a succession of sufferings, right? You were treated, as you said, like an animal.

MTS: Yes, it was quite bad.

AC: If I may, I think you agree that it's important to let the world know the true conditions of your life under dictatorship, because it can happen anywhere in the world. Your insights may well help to prevent a dictatorship from arising or a prison guard who is torturing someone to quit and become a human rights activist. Would you share more?

MTS: As I said earlier, prison was terrible, and as soon as I noticed I had an evening rise in temperature and chest pain, I thought it might be the tuberculosis, so I informed the medic in charge, and she denied it. It took three weeks to get a chest x-ray, and two more months to have the anti-TB treatment. At that time, I had endometriosis with agonizing pain; I went down to 80lbs, with months of fever. I couldn't eat or drink, and after anti-TB treatment and hormonal therapy my liver shut down, and I was vomiting all the time. And overall, they couldn't care less that the treatment was ineffective.

AC: Torture upon torture.

MTS: The problem was they never cooperated with me. They wanted me to bribe them and I didn't.

AC: What did they want? You are a prisoner for God's sake.

MTS: They wanted money. They wanted me to ask my parents to send in money, but I refused.

AC: This *Saṃsāra;* what a *Dhamma* challenge it is!

MTS: Yes, the *Dhamma* challenge never ends. Not only that, but because they knew I was so outspoken, I never let go of freedom of expression in prison. Because of this they hated me. They never cooperated with me to get treatment until they thought I might die. Only at that point, they sent me to the outside hospital very late at night. Since it was so late, I couldn't get treatment. In the morning, the medic in charge of the ward—one of the teachers in my medical school—asked me about my history and then, just before she started doing the physical examination, an order came in to discharge me. Without even having an examination, I was sent back to the prison.

To be brief: once back at the prison, in front of the ward there was the medic in charge and the jail authority from Insein Prison, and I warned them: "From this point on, you are responsible for the consequences, not me, nor the hospital." I was instantly sent back to my cell.

At that time, I couldn't walk because of exhaustion, and my situation became critical. Regardless, I was put back in my cell, and then sometime later one of the medical staff came and asked me to give up all the medicines that I kept in my cell.

I said, "Why? Why should I give up my medicines?"

His reason was that that I might commit suicide with them.

AC: Such evil. Such ignorance. Clearly, they wanted you to die.

MTS: My response: I declared a hunger strike. In so doing, my request was two things: to give back my medicines, and secondly, I no longer want to be consulted by the medic in charge. She cannot give proper treatment.

AC: How did this play out?

MTS: My hunger strike took only 30 minutes! As soon as they noticed the high-ranking officers and military intelligence people came to my cell, along with the superintendent of the prison hospital, and we had a conversation.

In brief, they asked me why I asked these questions.

AC: They're a smart bunch.

MTS: I told them and raised the questions with the prison authority. I explained that I had given up on the medic in charge because she's inept and making me die—and my problem is I don't want to die! I want to be alive. That's why I wanted to keep my medicines. And that's why I want nothing more to do with the medic in charge.

But the jail authority couldn't understand—'Oh, no, no, no, she's really taking care of you!'

AC: This is truly Orwellian.

MTS: Then I asked him, 'Ok, if you're told you're going to die in six months by your family doctor, what are you going to do?' He said he might eat whatever he liked, do what he liked, and he might go somewhere nice.

I said, 'No—if I was you, I would change my medical doctor!'

Then, his response—that's what was very interesting. He said, "You're free, we're not. Please understand us."

Here I was locked in this tiny cell 23 hours and 15 minutes a day, because we were allowed to have a walk or shower 30 minutes in the morning and 15 minutes in the evening. Apart from that we were locked in the cell.

I said, "How is it that you say I'm free, although I'm locked behind this door for 23 hours and 15 minutes per day?"

He answered, "No, you are free in your thoughts and words. Since we are government employees, we are not free. We've only learned about freedom right now."

AC: You believed him? He had enough insight to recognize that he was imprisoned?

MTS: Yes. He was imprisoned in his beliefs and I was free in my expression.

AC: If only that feeling could spread like a meme. Is that the nature of this country, all those who work for the military and the cronies, blind obedience?

MTS: Mostly, yes, but not pure obedience—it's related to fear.

AC: Fear; 'If we don't follow orders, what happens?'

MTS: That's right. Fear of the consequences of disobedience They will be dismissed.

AC: How to turn the fear around? What's required to turn back this dictatorship-driven culture of fear? How to stop this blind obedience?

MTS: Education. Because dictatorship is the lack of education, and it's also a lack of wisdom. Because of fear they cannot learn. Because of a poor education they cannot learn. I mean, 'poor education' means they never learn deeply about any subject. What they learn is to fear or be feared.

AC: What do you advocate as the practice of active democracy in Burma today?

MTS: A simple way is to educate people. Schools, workshops, seminars, reading, media, capacity building, and also alleviating the poverty issue. If you're poor you cannot learn, obviously. I think, even if you look at the recent violence, you find three root causes.

AC: The Muslim/Buddhist crisis going on?

MTS: Not only that. I don't want to isolate on that crisis alone. I mean violence—the pure act violence. Violence driven by any violent group. It might be religion-related, or ideological, or cultural. I'm speaking about violence at large. And not only physical violence but so many other kinds of violence as well. Physical, emotional, psychological, financial, social.

The three root causes we have to deal with—one is poverty. The second is poor education, and the third is the attitude towards the law. People's attitude towards the law is confused, because, under the dictatorship the practice of law by people from the judiciary system was corrupted, so people think the law is harmful, the law is unjust. That's why they never think they have to deal with the law or rely on the law to save their lives. That's why, whatever they face, they solve their problems outside of the law. That's why there is no rule of law in the country. It's lawless by and large, except for the law of corruption, so to speak. We must deal with these very deep rooted three problems. Our work is to turn them around.

> *"Whatever you do, please act from your heart,*
> *not for having recognition as someone who does this,*
> *but for doing what you want to do. That's all."*

ALAN CLEMENTS: Speaking of rule of law, what are your thoughts on dealing with the human rights atrocities in Burma, both by those who committed them and those who ordered them? What should be done?

MA THIDA SANCHUANG: When I'm asked if I can forgive them, I say I can forgive them, but I cannot forget. But, with my own logic, with my own knowledge, with my own wisdom, even though I can forgive them, we need two steps: firstly, their acknowledgment. It's like in *Vipassanā* meditation practice, acknowledgment is the very first step. Acknowledgment or awareness. People have to be aware or acknowledge these human rights violations. So, the violators should acknowledge or confess what they did.

AC: Is this happening?

MTS: No, not yet.

AC: So no one in a position of power has confessed to having ordered the torture, rape or killing of a democracy activist or political prisoner?

MTS: No, especially regarding the past.

AC: Is there any conversation such as this going on in Burma today?

MTS: Not really. It's taboo.

AC: Too much fear?

MTS: Way too much fear. So, without any acknowledgment or awareness or apology, how can we forgive? If someone wants to be forgiven, they must do two things—one is acknowledging the reality of what they have done, and the other is apologizing.

AC: Can you envision this happening in Burma?

MTS: It's really hard to imagine.

AC: Do you recommend that the perpetrators of the violence write their admission of wrongdoing in the national newspaper and seek the peoples' forgiveness, indirectly? Or address the nation on national television? What would be the most effective way to move the country forward?

MTS: I'd prefer to get files from the violators documenting what people have suffered.

AC: As in detailed documents?

MTS: That's right, detailed documentation, a filing—not to make any action, just to confess, to document in detail what's happened.

AC: Like a 'special crimes against the people' committee?

MTS: Yes, a special committee like that; acknowledgment, and then, if they don't want to use the word apology, they just have to say they are responsible for such and such wrongdoing. That's enough for them to be forgiven. Otherwise it's hard. Without a confession, how can we forgive?

AC: As for me, I say, why wait for an apology when you can practice active *mettā*. But that's me, and I have not been the victim of torture or rape or having my land stolen from me, and so on.

Would you recommend that Parliament take this up and form a committee?

MTS: Of course, and the sooner the better for the healing to begin.

AC: In order to go forward, in order to heal, in order to reconcile, this is a must?

MTS: Yes. Because, as with a wound, if we have a scab, we cannot see how deep the wound is and what's going on inside the wound. We must take off the layer of scab to see the wound. Otherwise we cannot heal.

AC: So the person who sentenced you to prison, in order to heal, you want that person to admit their wrongdoing?

MTS: Yes. But on a deeper level, for me, because of my Buddhist logic, there are two causes: one cause might be my past wrongdoing, the cause and effect theory. Another cause, the current effect, is not a single person but the system or group of people who have fear. The key reason I went to prison might be my past wrongdoing, in a past life I mean, and obviously it might be fear that put me in prison.

AC: The fear put you in prison?

MTS: Yes.

AC: I'm not sure I know what you mean. But let me say, fear is often deeply embodied in people, way deeper than their consciousness mind. The Khmer Rouge; many of them said they didn't know what they we were doing was wrong. The Nuremberg trials; 'let us finish what is morally right for us to do.' Ignorance runs deep, as we know. Look at corporate America, run primarily by greed. One could easily argue that America itself is a massive terrorist entity, in that my country has historically inflicted murderous anguish on innocent populations. Many of our leaders are textbook war criminals, based on international law. Many of these same global leaders say the same thing about the leaders of Burma, war criminals. And you're asking them to acknowledge their atrocities. And no one really knows where the first order was given to commit an atrocity. Generally speaking, all fingers point back to Than Shwe, the former dictator. May I ask you—not to put you on the spot, and perhaps former General Than Shwe will read this book—what would you say to him? Would you speak directly to him as you did the medic in prison wanting to take your medicines away? Share your truth, please, for the betterment of your people.

MTS: You know, I never believed that only one person can ruin the whole country. If we are to say it is a corrupt system, this system is this way based on a lot of people, not only one person. At every level, horizontally or vertically, there are numerous people responsible for this corruption. So many people cooperated or contributed to this culture of corruption. I cannot say a single person ruined my country. It's the psychology of dictatorship that should be acknowledged as evil and abandoned, not one person alone.

AC: I notice that when I have fear in myself, although my urge is to be more transparent, sometimes fear gets the better of me. How does one who has been held down by fear and delusion, who says to you, 'I want to believe you, that addressing my shortcoming is appropriate, but I'm fearful,' how would you encourage me to overcome my fear and to do what's right by the people?

MTS: You know; it's quite hard if you have no knowledge of Buddhism. If you learn Buddhism, there are many ways to overcome your fear and transcend misdeeds. Mindful effort is required. For example, practice *Vipassanā* meditation and reach the first stage of enlightenment. In this way, it will give you a way beyond your fear.

AC: You're suggesting that Than Shwe do a *Vipassanā* meditation retreat?

MTS: Not only that. There are two ways—one is the *Dhamma* way. If they do believe in Buddhism, they should actually practice it, to ease their psychological fear and so on. The other way is to practice rule of law.

See, you cannot escape the law, *Dhamma* law and rule of law.

Sometimes people might think they will be happy if they can escape from the law. Indeed, you can escape from physical punishment, but self-blaming or knowing yourself that you're doing something wrong, it can ruin your life. So please have the courage to get out of this great psychological fear. Otherwise you cannot escape your fear and there cannot be true healing.

AC: What you're saying is that this is an opportunity for redemption?

MTS: Yes, yes, it's a great opportunity for that. For example, with the former dictator Ne Win, without doing anything he passed away, naturally. But he passed away under house arrest. So, who else will know what he felt? He might have died with great remorse. It may have put him in hell, not only from what he did that was wrong but also the very regret itself may have sent him to one of the hell realms.

If you are a true Buddhist, you have to think two ways—not only of your wrongdoing but also of your regret. Either way you can go to the lower realms. If you really want to get out of negative consequences, here is your opportunity. Take it.

AC: In your book, *Roadmap*, is there a road on your map where those responsible for the atrocities do not acknowledge them?

MTS: That book is a not about them but about the others.

AC: Where will the country go without acknowledgment?

MTS: I cannot find it, that's why I used the example of healing a wound. That's why we have to be daring enough to take off the layer of the scab.

AC: A final question: There are millions of people around the world who want to become activists, who want to stand up and speak their mind, who want to confront injustice. What advice would you give the next generation of activists, those daring few who want to take a nonviolent stand to protect the environment, freedom and human rights?

MTS: Please focus on the issue, not the individual. And most of all, be true to yourself. If you don't really believe in the sanctity of humanity and human rights, in protecting the environment, in the future of life itself, please don't continue. Whatever you do, act from your heart, and not for having recognition as someone who does this, but for doing what you want to do because you love it. Because you know it is right. That's all.

AC: Thank you. A great honor to meet you. And thank you for your bravery to keep alive freedom and universal human rights and under the darkest hours. Your life is a bright shining light of hope and liberty.

MTS: Thank you for caring about my people and your own commitment to speaking the truth and acting in conscience.

AC: Thank you. May our conversion serve to uplift the spirit of those who committed atrocities both in Burma and in my own country. May we all honor each other's best intention to heal, not divide.

MTS: Yes. May we all come together in peace.

Conversation with Ma Thida Sanchuang

January 2020

> *"While the whole world is seeing our conflict*
> *as more or less a religious or racial one…*
> *it is mainly political."*

ALAN CLEMENTS: It's been seven years since we last spoke. May I invite you to offer an overview or a synopsis of the most critical issues you see your country facing today and your thoughts on how to move forward towards true democracy?

MA THIDA SANCHUANG: Well, our country is facing a highly disruptive syndrome of disrespect, distrust and dilemma. After a number of politically driven communal conflicts surfaced in the first new government, social harmony among different communities vanished and people lost their trust in the new political structure; lost their trust in the new civil-military hybrid structure. As a result, they became utterly confused about national reconciliation and future of the country.

For me, in moving forward towards true democracy, we need both belief and commitment on the meaning of true democracy and the value of Human Rights from all five pillars: executive, legislative, judiciary, media and civilians, plus, and most importantly, from state army.

Authoritarian legacies are still going strong in Burma, not only among the army community but also among civilians. Sub-nationalism is also popular among all non-Bamar ethnic communities. So, we truly need education-based awareness promotion about basic human rights and democratic values and practices. However, it will take time.

We also need to have a strong trust and mutual respect for each other, on every level, including our day-to-day, morally inspired interactions with each other. Towards this goal, one of the struggles we are having is the lack of mechanisms for establishing transitional justice. And this also needs a lot of time to overcome. Therefore, we all must embody patience and compassion within society, towards each other, towards our leaders, and towards those who steward our institutions into the future.

AC: I read in a recent article in the Irrawaddy the line, "It is now part of the world's politically correct orthodoxy to blame Daw Aung San Suu Kyi for the Rohingya refugee crisis and to condemn her for defending Myanmar against the genocide case brought by The Gambia before the International Court of Justice (ICJ)."

May I ask for your most candid thoughts on this comment and your thoughts on Aung San Suu Kyi's statements at the ICJ?

Also, how should we understand the crisis in Rakhine. This is your country. Your people. You are a respected investigative journalist. What should we know that we may not know, or know as clearly as you do?

And, I may add, in all fairness to Daw Aung San Suu Kyi, all criticisms towards her seem to play into the hands of the military. Is that true? How could she have done anything differently, please?

MTS: Well, there is an obvious difference between perspectives from the outside and from inside. Though the current 2008 Constitution does not allow the civilian side of government to effectively influence ground military handling, from the eyes of our people and outside, it, of course, should take the lead to defend our country's image and its people. This is the double blade situation for her and her administration.

While the whole world is seeing our conflict as more or less a religious or racial one, on the ground reality, it is mainly political. The timing of the ICJ is indeed matched with the timing of the beginning of campaign for 2020 election. Therefore Aung San Suu Kyi's initiative on defending the ICJ case was interpreted as an election campaign for the NLD by the military and its political party, USDP.

But for the eyes of the general public, Aung San Suu Kyi took the lead to defend our country's image. And for the eyes of activists and other opposition, mainly the non-Bamar ethnic community, she had tried to protect military, although it is the sole responsible institution for a ground operation in Rakhine state.

Then general public's stand with her on the ICJ case was the signal not just to support her and her NLD, but also to show how much they are still against the military and its party. On the other hand, for some people, standing with her was a wrongdoing as it meant her disloyalty to the people by defending military.

The military said it will support Aung San Suu Kyi for her ICJ presentation but soon after she returned home, she attended an official state event on one of the ethnics' national day and military TV channel broadcasted about that event but did so without her image. In this case, we can clearly see that she is still not accepted as a leader of the country by military. On the other hand, she still needs to work hard to be accepted by the military as it is the key and most powerful institution to possibly change the undemocratic 2008 Constitution.

Therefore, most of the actions and reactions by our people and the state military are aimed only at the national level. The international community and the international media might not understand this.

Anyhow, many of us want her to establish much more practical and proactive mechanisms to achieve social harmony among all our different and diverse communities, and to establish transitional justice, and greater respect for the values of democracy.

We also know it will take time as our problems are huge and complicated.

AC: On a final note, you are a prolific author, the writer of many books. Rather than asking further questions, may I invite you to share with the world a few short excerpts from any of your books that you feel reflect not only the essence of your life, values and work, but would be important for the world to know about your country, especially at this critical time before the upcoming elections.

MTS: Well, most of my recent writings are in Burmese. I will choose only few short excerpts from my books in English.

In my memoir, *Prisoner Of Conscience: My Steps through Insein*, I wrote about a short conversation with a military intelligence officer on the day of Aung San Suu Kyi's first release from house arrest in 1995. My answer to him is still my simple goal and value of my life and work. Here it is.

"He asked me abruptly, 'What is your political goal?' I said, 'I just want to be a good citizen—nothing more, nothing less.' He looked puzzled at first, but then he smiled."

Another excerpt is from the last chapter of my prison memoir.

I would always say, "Worry that you might harm somebody, not about others wanting to harm you, because that's their problem."

About my country, I still believe we are still at the fork in the road. Here is what I wrote for the last chapter *Fork in the Road* of my documentary fiction *The Roadmap*. This excerpt is from sub-session 'To Traveler (early 2009).'

"You know you can't change your country by yourself. You are not sure how you can get through the near and distant future. According to the regime's Constitution, even if the 2010 election is fair, it will take at least two decades to make a democratic country. Future parliaments can't easily change the constitution. But what can you do? ...."

As I wrote the above excerpt in 2010, a decade later we are still are at the fork in the road and the challenge of the Constitution is still there. No one from outside would thoroughly understand our complicated context. Our people are already confused about our road to democracy because of our past and present experiences. We know we could follow the steps of an international standard to reach our destination, that of true democracy. We really cannot afford to be stuck somewhere in the middle, as we have gone through very hard times along a very hard road. We want the international community to look beyond the popular media news about our country, and to listen not only from either government or army or activists, but more from the general public's feelings and experiences. We also want you to believe in us and support us for our determination towards our destination—peaceful democracy. Whatever will happen to us, we need to get out of this fork in the road. In so doing, the right and true belief from the world community as well as having their generous and compassionate support will definitely help us to find our own way out.

AC: I thank you with a deep bow of gratitude and may your ongoing wisdom and courage to bring democracy to your people.

MTS: Thank you very much for your long-standing support. It means a lot to me and to the people of my country.

CHAPTER 34

CONVERSATIONS *with*
MON MON MYAT

2018 & 2020

- "When you speak up about wrongdoing in your environment, you're also protecting that environment."
- "I didn't know about democracy before 1988."
- "In this country, there are probably two governments."
- "People should be aware that Daw Suu still doesn't have full power."
- 'The international community, and the international media, don't see clearly.'

A documentary film maker, seasoned journalist and author, Mon Mon Myat co-founded the Human Rights and Human Dignity Film Festival in 2013. Now in its fifth year, the festival tours the country bringing films and documentaries that open a dialogue on freedom in a country denied access to information for decades. Mon Mon Myat has been on the campaign trail with Aung San Suu Kyi since her release in 2010 and is currently working on a documentary about the Burma's human rights icon. Here she talks openly about her life, her work, and Burma's fraught transition, including her analysis of the situation in Rakhine State and the international media's response.

> *"When you speak up about wrongdoing in your environment, you're also protecting that environment."*

ALAN CLEMENTS: You've recently completed a book, *It's A Long Way to Panglong*, and you've also made a documentary film of it with the same title. Let's start there. Would is your book and film about?

MON MON MYAT: The book is a collection of speeches that Daw Aung San Suu Kyi gave during her political campaigns (since the time of her most recent release from house arrest), starting with the 2012 by-election, up to the 2015 national election campaign. The last speech we have is the one she delivered at the opening of the 21st Century Panglong Peace Conference.

AC: You will have all of Daw Aung San Suu Kyi's speeches from that time period in your book?

MMM: Almost all. There's a total of 16 speeches in the book. In many of her speeches she talks about the Panglong spirit and tries to empower that same spirit in the people so that our country can become united.

AC: Would you explain what Panglong means?

MMM: Panglong is the name of a town in Shan State where Daw Suu's father, General Aung San, signed a treaty with ethnic leaders to gain independence for Burma in 1947. As you know, we were under British colonial rule at that time and didn't have our independence. So together, under General Aung San, the country united and signed an agreement to fight for the country's independence. For us, Panglong represents the spirit of union. It communicates unity among all our people.

AC: Through your book and film, it is your hope to keep the spirit of Panglong active in present day Burma?

MMM: Yes, I would very much like to spread this message of unity both through the book and film, especially since I was planning their release at the same time as when the new government, led by Daw Aung San Suu Kyi, was going to organize the 21st Century Panglong Peace Conference.

AC: You are also the co-founder of the International Human Rights and Human Dignity Film Festival here in Burma?

MMM: Yes. This is our fifth year coming up.

AC: What a remarkable achievement. Now you've made Burma—once a prison within prisons—the epicenter of an international film festival highlighting human dignity and universal human rights. What a gift to our world and, of course, to your people. Thank you for your vision. Thank you for bringing it to fruition.

Back to your book. How did you manage to acquire all of Daw Aung San Suu Kyi's public speeches from 2012 to 2016, all the while she was traveling and campaigning the country?

MMM: After her release from house arrest on November 13, 2010, having had the chance to meet her in December for the first time, I interviewed her for the news agency I was working for. In that interview, I asked a question related to her nonviolent approach to our country's struggle for freedom. I asked it because it had already taken 20 years and many people had concerns about whether the nonviolent approach would really work for our country.

AC: How did she respond?

MMM: Her answer was amazing. Using a quote from Mahatma Gandhi, she stated that the nonviolent approach would take longer than the violent approach but that the healing would be far easier than with a violent approach. You can get a result very quickly using violence she said, but it's not easy to heal the wounds caused by its use. She knows that it will take time, but she firmly believes it will succeed one day.

AC: And that initial interview inspired you to follow her on her travels around the country?

MMM: Yes. I'd never witnessed her political campaigns before, so this was a great opportunity to see her nonviolent approach in action.

AC: You literally travelled the country with Daw Suu on successive tours for nearly four years?

MMM: That's right. We went to more 50 places. Sometimes in one day she might go to three places—a village, a town, and a city. Sometimes, she'd even go to six different places, from town to town and village to village. She's dedicated to the well-being of our people.

AC: And there you were, following her with your camera city to village to town, filming and recording?

MMM: Yes, that's right. We transcribed every talk of hers with the help of my colleagues.

AC: What a great *dāna*, as you would say in your country. And a great gift to the world. And you chose 16 of the key speeches for the book?

MMM: Yes, 16 out of the many hundreds. See, I didn't get them all, because I wasn't experienced at the beginning. Year by year I got better at recording her speeches. It was only in the 2012 by-elections that I recorded every speech in its entirety.

AC: You've seen Daw Suu up close and intimate in crowded and often challenging contexts. I'm told there were tens of thousands of people at some of her talks. Could you describe Daw Suu, the Nobel Peace Laureate who spent 17 years under house arrest, and then released to share the wisdom of nonviolence, freedom and democracy with her people? What did you observe? And who was the Daw Suu you came to know?

MMM: I found her to be a person who tirelessly works for our country, who has dedicated her life to our people. This country and its people are her family. She even left her family for this country. She's the most inspiring leader in my life.

You may know this, that Daw Suu expanded her concept of family from her own immediate family—her two sons, and late husband, and others too—to embrace all our people as family, all ethnic minorities, even the oppressors, the former generals. She even embraces the Tatmadaw—the entire military, all soldiers. I think, as you know, as a meditator, that she is full of *mettā*. Her heart if full of loving kindness. It doesn't matter whether you are an enemy or a family member. She has the same loving kindness for every person. I saw this *mettā* radiating from her over the four years I was travelling with her. And it increased over time.

AC: Traveling and giving talks in hundreds of villages and towns, she consistently showed loving kindness and compassion? Did you ever hear her criticize the military, or her captors?

MMM: If needed, she criticized the military sharply, but never did she criticize a single person or one group. She only pointed out the flaws of a system and never judged or vilified a person.

AC: She criticized the system or the mindset of dictatorship?

MMM: Yes. That's right.

AC: How would she criticize dictatorship?

MMM: Because she's moving forward towards building a true democratic country, she wants people to know how dictatorship ruined the country and ruined the country's future. She made sure that people knew the disadvantages of military dictatorship.

AC: Were there key themes that you heard from her during her speeches that you would share? Were there consistent ideas that she tried to communicate to the people to empower them, to help them understand forgiveness, and or to understand the flaws of dictatorship?

MMM: Many things were inspiring, but one thing I like most about her is that she encouraged our people to stand up for their rights. And not to rely only on her, or only on a leader. If I remember correctly, if you rely on a person or a leader then authoritarian rule can arise at any time. But, if you stand up for your own rights, then you are the one who will build this country. These are not her exact words, but this was the meaning I got from her.

AC: To stand up for your rights means having some recognition of what those rights are that one needs to stand up for. As I understand it, after decades of brutal dictatorship, few people, if any, knew what freedom of speech was or freedom of expression. What rights was she most vocal about, that she advocated for people to stand up for?

MMM: To speak up about what's happening around us. To tell the truth about the violence. Not to stay quiet out of fear. When you speak up about wrongdoing in your environment, you're also protecting that environment, because you know the wrongdoing. If you keep quiet, then nobody will know. Once you speak up about this, other people will also know. She spoke in this way. And most of all: we must stand up together.

"I didn't know about democracy before 1988. [Aung San Suu Kyi] created less fear for us"

ALAN CLEMENTS: Take us back to August of 1988, the nationwide nonviolent uprising that was violently crushed. This was a year before China's Tiananmen Square. Where were you in August '88?

MON MON MYAT: I was here in Yangon, studying at the university's Institute of Economics, but my native town is Magway, near Bagan. When the student uprising happened, the government shut down all universities. I had to go back home. I didn't join the uprising in Yangon, but joined the uprising when I got back to my home town, together with the other university students from my home town, so I can say that I was also part of this '88 Generation movement, from my native town.

AC: You were inspired to stand up for freedom and democracy?

MMM: Yes. Which we did in Magway.

AC: Was there opposition to that, like there was in Yangon?

MMM: It was the same everywhere. We were oppressed by the military in most cities where there was an uprising. They shot and killed people everywhere. The whole country was under violent siege. Even in Magway, people were killed on the day of the military coup in September 1988.

AC: How did the violence impact you? And were you with your family?

MMM: I have three brothers. Two of them were also university students and took part in the revolution following the '88 military coup. There were also political parties cropping up at that time, for the 1990 elections, so we were also part of the political activities, people gathering, taking part in campaigns from different political parties. We also took part in the campaign for the NLD party. We knew that the 1990 elections were important, and felt that the NLD must win, because we believed in our leader—Daw Aung San Suu Kyi—and the party.

AC: You're an activist, journalist and filmmaker. You've created, with your partner, an international film festival. You are a vital voice of democracy in your country today. Would you please share the key points in the process of becoming politicized? For example, you grew up under violent dictatorship. What was it like to live under such oppression? And what was your process of awakening from it? Can you help us understand that inner voice that said, "I refuse to live any longer under dictatorship—I've had enough!" How did you emerge and become an active citizen promoting human rights and democracy?

MMM: I didn't know about democracy before 1988. Frankly, I'd never even heard the word. It was like living in a house where all the doors were always closed, and the windows boarded up. You could eat and live in that house but had no knowledge whatsoever of anything outside. We could only read the newspapers that the government provided, so we only had their distorted views and propaganda, and that meant we had no power, so it seemed. But in 1988, after the violence, we realized that a military dictatorship was bad. When we witnessed innocent people being killed, people who were nonviolently participating in the protests, killed for no other reason than to keep power, that negative image of the military sank deep into our hearts. And this grew in power and made us want to stand up—to take part in overthrowing the dictatorship.

AC: It took cold blooded murder to ignite the fire of activism?

MMM: Yes, that's right. Seeing violence set my heart on fire. But also, democracy and human rights were introduced by Aung San Suu Kyi at that time. Then after her first release in 1995, as you know, she gave speeches every weekend at the gate of her house. I would go and listen. That also encouraged us. She created less fear for us, because most of us were quite fearful that someone might come in the middle of the night and arrest us. Or even when we were just sitting in a tea shop, or that someone would be listening to our conversation, and then the next moment, we're handcuffed and taken to prison. Our fear made us insecure. Listening to her speeches empowered us. It lessened the fear and, most of all, we learned that we should speak up.

AC: I remember listening to those speeches with the assistance of a translator and was deeply moved. May I ask, what was the essence of what she saying that inspired you to challenge your fear and risk imprisonment to speak up?

MMM: She's had the same approach from 1990 until now—not only is she a leader but also an educator of human rights, activism, and democracy to the people. She'd use simple words: to lessen fear, speak up, and stand up for our rights. She was always teaching us like that. That was inspiring, because we can't just keep quiet in the face of injustice for the sake of our own well-being. We should speak up for others as well. If we wanted freedom, we had to start acting and speaking freely. And to care for the freedom of others as we would our own. Those simple statements made so much sense to me. To all of us!

AC: So, you gathered on weekends to listen to Daw Suu, U Tin Oo and U Kyi Maung talk on the role of a nonviolent freedom fighter in your country.

May I ask, what did you do with your fear? After all, and I remember this so clearly, all of you on the street were facing imprisonment, even torture. They were putting boys and girls far younger than you in prison at that time. In becoming an activist, how did you learn to manage your fear? How did you speak to yourself?

MMM: Of course, I was afraid. But years before, the very first time that military intelligence came to our house to find my brother, who was involved in political activities as a leader in our town, I was shocked. It was very late at night. I remember the moment so well. My mother was so worried. But my mother was also the one who encouraged us to speak up and stand up. She encouraged our activism. See, she had been a student activist in Ne Win's time. She took part in the U Thant uprising. That was back in '74. And she took part in the uprising of '88 as well.

AC: There you go, it runs in the family. You are in a lineage of activists.

MMM: Yes, and she was also forced to move to another place, very far away from Magway township. This was punishment for her activism. The authorities forced her to move. They gave an order to transfer far away from Magway. This is the behavior of dictatorship. Do as you are told or pay the price.

AC: Unbelievable. These folks need *Dhamma* therapy and a long-term meditation retreat. You mentioned a brother—where was he?

MMM: He wasn't arrested, but he couldn't move freely because he was put under observation by military intelligence. He became depressed. That drove him to using drugs, after the 1990 election. During the elections we expected a lot. That after the elections, if the NLD won, our country would become much better. This was our great expectation.

AC: Of course, the elections resulted in an overwhelming victory for the NLD, under U Kyi Maung—Daw Suu was under arrest, along with U Tin Oo and other leaders—and the military annulled that election and arrested most of the MPs, and other MPs fled.

MMM: Yes. Many people got depressed and lost heart in the system.

AC: Have you also experienced depression?

MMM: Of course. We'd been in an utterly hopeless situation here in Burma in the 1990s. Even when we returned to studying, we felt, if we graduated, so what? What would we do? It was pointless. We were prisoners in our own country. Prisons within prisons.

AC: You've dealt with so many hardships, living all of your life under totalitarian governments where there was no regard for human rights, and then the massacre of your fellow students. Your mother punished. Your brother traumatized and turns to drugs to cope. So much trauma...

MMM: Yes, and some friends fled the country and went into exile. Others disappeared in the jungles.

AC: Yes, I met many of your student friends at that time when I was in Mannerplaw in Karen State. It was deeply troubling to see the plight of so many students. And so many refugees, so many displaced people along the borders. It was apocalyptic.

MMM: A very depressing situation.

*"In this country, there are
probably two governments."*

ALAN CLEMENTS: Inevitably, people around the world will read this book and your words, including my fellow Americans, now living under a new government that could easily turn authoritarian. And in your country, Burma has turned away from dictatorship towards democracy. But, maybe, it is merely an offshoot of its dictatorial roots and may sprout into a new form of totalitarianism. Maybe the few rights that you do have at the moment—pray not—will erode. My question: What advice would you give to your people to avoid backsliding?

MON MON MYAT: The lesson we learned from living under authoritarian rule for such a long time is this: It's easy for those who have power and weapons to make people who do not have power and weapons fearful. It's easy. You just arrest the activists and leaders. That's one thing. And then, create shocking stories and spread them throughout society. In this way, you make people aware that if you act in this way you will be taught the same lesson. Just broadcast the violence to scare them.

For example, ever since the uprising in 1988, they've been arresting hundreds of people. And in so doing, they have created great trouble for their families. And then, those stories of cruelty made people scared. We had already experienced one generation of students oppressed. They had a lesson for us: even if you want to go back to school, you must sign a document saying you will not engage in political activities. They wanted to make the word "politics" scary. So as soon as someone heard the word "politics" it would send a shiver down their spine, so much so that people were scared of participating in politics. That is why most of the world called Burma a "terror state." They use terror as a weapon to try to control us.

AC: It reminds me of Daw Suu's comment, "We'll certainly get to our destination if we join hands." You're advising people to not believe fear, and to join hands?

MMM: Yes, for sure. But not only that. This fear-driven divisiveness in society is the deliberate tactic of an authoritarian ruler. It's one method to make people scared, and to make people ignorant. If you have enough food to eat, and you have enough of a salary from a good business, then, generally speaking, it's harder for you care about others. You will primarily work for your own family. Then you become somewhat ignorant of other peoples' needs. What I mean to say is that you can easily ignore others.

AC: I see; the regime coerces people into thinking of their own well-being and that of their family, while ignoring the context; not having compassion for others, your neighborhood, your country, all ethnicities? That's been a defining characteristic of Burma's dictatorships—creating ignorance and self-centeredness as well as fear and terror?

MMM: Yes, for sure. Because it's so easy for them. Make the country poor. It's so easy. Once you're in poverty you will have to find food for your own family, for yourself, and then you can't think any further. And the opposite is true as well, thus the manipulation of their so-called cronies. They too have been orchestrated but rather than through fear, they torture them with reward and comfort. Two forms of control, two sides of the same totalitarian coin.

AC: So, on the one hand, impoverish the people. Mentally starve them. Terrorize them with the fear of physical violence. And on the other hands, control the rest of them through either meager rewards, like enough to eat and get by, and control the big fish with big rewards. Sounds like the behavior of a mafia kingpin, a corrupt ruler and I may add, some American presidents. But more to the point: If you see these things, don't believe them? Do the opposite?

MMM: Yes. Do not allow yourself to be manipulated, coerced, or cower to fear.

AC: That's the advice?

MMM: Yes. And then they targeted one group who could make noise, who could create an uprising—the students. They singled out the student body and broke up all the universities and all places that students could gather. As you know, the university in Yangon is in quite a crowded place. They broke up the university, and put small versions of it everywhere, in different towns. By closing the universities and building smaller versions in the outskirts, they decentralized us and scattered the students everywhere. Our unity was a major threat to their power.

AC: Thus, the deliberate anti-democratic tactics of a totalitarian government?

MMM: Yes. I'm not sure of the number of new universities they built but it was a lot. They were everywhere, and far away. Before, we only had universities in the big cities like Yangon and Mandalay. Yangon was a good opportunity for us to meet different people from different parts of the country. And we made many friends. I had a Karen friend, a Kachin friend, and so on. We loved each other. We didn't have any sense of "divide and rule." We'd never heard about *'Burmanization'* before. I loved my Karen friends so much. I loved my Kachin friends, equally. They were so humble and honest. And they adored us. We had a deep bond together. Nor did they see us for even one minute like a 'Burmanizing' force taking everything out of their states. They never felt that. We were brothers and sisters. It was beautiful. These special friendships gave us a true sense of unity and a taste of what was possible for the whole of the country.

AC: You grew up in a country with every major religion, and many minority ones as well. Burma is a nation of 55 million people with numerous languages and dialects and ethnicities. Let us talk a bit about the crisis with the ethnic groups. It's fair to say that there's a full-scale war in Shan State? One in Kachin State? And a full-scale conflict in the Rakhine area? And, obviously, for the last 30 years, the entire country, your entire population—primarily Buddhists—have been under siege by the central government run by a succession of dictators. Please help me understand: What is going on in Shan State, and why? Why is there war there? And why isn't that war stopping under this present government, run by Daw Aung San Suu Kyi and the NLD?

MMM: For us, we don't know much about those civil wars in ethnic areas, because the state newspaper only refers to the rebel groups as bad people. And we know its propaganda. They might talk of the KNU (Karen), or the KIA (Kachin), or the SSA (Shan), but not exactly accusing Shan ethnic people, or Kachin ethnic people, just "the rebel groups." That is why I said we didn't have any problem with the other ethnic people. We felt like we were just civilians together, living together in this country.

AC: Why is Burma's 400,000-strong army, with jets and helicopter gunships, engaged in a full-scale war in Shan state? Why are they killing ethnic Shans?

MMM: The civilian government cannot control the army. The army wants to create their own image as well, as the most powerful armed organization in this country.

AC: What you are saying is that Daw Aung San Suu Kyi and the NLD government do not have any control whatsoever of the military?

MMM: Yes. That's right. None. She has no control of the military.

AC: So Senior General Min Aung Hlaing has absolute control? And Daw Aung San Suu Kyi and the government has no influence with him? He does what he wants when he wants?

MMM: She is trying to compromise with the military, but when the military attacks an ethnic area, they make their own decisions.

AC: Why doesn't she say, "Senior General, please have your men stop attacking the Shans. We're a government of national reconciliation. Let's heal the country together." Is she saying that and they're not listening? Or she hasn't said it because... what? A concern for a negative reaction? Possible detention, again?

MMM: We do not know what she is or is not saying, other than we believe in her abilities and her compassion for all people.

AC: So, she could very well be saying these things but they're not listening?

MMM: Yes. They're not listening.

AC: Why aren't they willing to listen? Is it resources at stake? Oil, timber? Rubies? Sapphires? Is it China's involvement? Or is it that General Min Aung Hlaing has no control of his Regional Commander? Or is it Than Shwe ordering everything from behind the scenes? Does no one know?

MMM: If you look at the Constitution, there are three ministries that the government cannot control, which are controlled directly by the military general—defense, border affairs and home affairs. Those are directly controlled by the military general.

AC: This is the 2008 Constitution that Daw Suu and everyone wanted to change, and they refused to change it? And it's the same constitution that's banned her from being president?

MMM: Of course. The same one.

AC: That leaves us with the question, that although they won a landslide victory, we have a military created constitution that's imprisoned them within a military government?

MMM: Yes, that's right.

AC: A *faux*-constitution that enshrines their control ad infinitum. She couldn't change it and they're still in power, and, obviously, they're not listening and they're killing the Shans, they're killing the Kachins, they're killing the Rakhine. And is it true that the pillage of land and land-grabbing by the military and people of power is still prevalent in this country?

MMM: Yes.

AC: I was just reading in the paper that around a hundred activists have been imprisoned in the last month and are standing trial for speaking out against the military. You're saying that although Daw Aung San Suu Kyi won the election, she has little power? Regardless, what is her strategy in moving the country forward?

MMM: You might have noticed that just after the NLD took power in the 2015 elections, the new government's first step was to continue the peace process. The new government knows very well that peace is the most important thing for our country to achieve. And, as a consequence of the military government, let's say from 1988, the previous government's strategy was inherited from the British divide and rule policy. They used it very well.

You might also know that in the 1990s there were a sequence of ceasefire agreements with the armed ethnic groups. Before 1988, we could count 10 big ethnic armed groups—Burma Communist Party, KNU, KIA, SSA. Those are the main major ethnic armed organizations before '88. But after the military coup of '88, General Khin Nyunt made a peace agreement with different ethnic armed groups, and then a lot of new armed groups came up. During that time in, let's say, 2010, when President Thein Sein started the peace process, there were more than 30 ethnic armed organizations, because of the divide and rule policy.

AC: Are describing a country at war with itself?

MMM: Yes, and how can one government stop all those ethnic armed groups? The strategy they use is the strategy from the king era—"might is right." So, when people have weapons, power, or wealth, they control the states. They're just trying to share power with the ethnic armed groups who are doing business in their own territory.

AC: You're saying that the country is a tapestry of warlords, a tapestry of different mafia?

MMM: Yes. That's correct.

AC: Is Burma still a dictatorship, with a different name?

MMM: We can't say it's fully a dictatorship. We have some external freedoms, some external civilian power, but we have not completely reached a democratic government. We are still under military rule, in part. What I can say is that in this country there are two governments. In other words, part of the military government is still active and alive.

AC: The military government is all pervasive. They control homeland security, the police department, all branches of the military, border control, state security, surveillance, and it's all constitutionally protected. This is reconstituted dictatorship.

MMM: Apart from that, they are economically rooted. There are giant corporations doing big business here. They are founded by the former military generals. They trade in oil, gas, petrol, gems, timber, food, and real estate, and it includes a share of the defense service.

AC: Not a pretty picture. Big brother goes international with military protection?

MMM: Yes. This is what's known as the 'cronyism' in our country. And most of the cronies are somehow related to the previous military government.

AC: So not only does the military still rule key ministries, but almost all of your resources, your oil, gas, etc., as you said, are under their control. I was told the other day that there's a massive pipeline from the Bay of Bengal off the coast of Rakhine that goes right into southern China. Is that correct?

MMM: Yes, that's true.

AC: Is that a crony-based military operation?

MMM: Yes, of course. That came to be before General Than Shwe left power. They had a series of different MOUs between the Chinese government and the Burmese government. I think that some Chinese state-owned firms reached an agreement with Myanmar to construct a multi-billion-dollar deep-water port and industrial area in a special economic zone at Kyaukpyu, along the coast of the Bay of Bengal. It includes a $1.5billion oil pipeline and parallel natural gas pipeline running from the Bay to Kunming in China's Yunnan Province.

AC: So, it's fair to say that much of the upheaval in Rakhine is oil related, along with China and cronyism and the military?

MMM: Yes. And look no further than your own country's invasion of Iraq and its ongoing relationship with Saudi Arabia and other places of oil interest as well. Oil. Money. Power. Militarism. Cronyism. Whatever it takes to keep the economy of greed and ignorance running. It's global.

*"People should be aware that Daw Suu
still doesn't have full power in this country."*

ALAN CLEMENTS: So much of what we're seeing in your country, in terms of struggle and conflict, is born from the unraveling of decades of dictatorship, with its unbridled corruption and violence. Only Daw Aung San Suu Kyi knows what she's saying and what's being said to her among the powers that be that run this country.

On another note, many in the media, along with some world leaders, are beginning to condemn Burma, primarily for the struggle in Rakhine State with the Rohingyas. And Daw Suu is the de facto president with the title of State Counsellor. She's also being criticized a lot in the international media. Her fellow Nobel Peace laureate, Desmond Tutu, along with 19 other Nobel Peace Laureates, recently signed a letter condemning her so called "silence" on these issues. I'm not saying that I agree but what I am saying is that these are highly respected people—and I'm sure it came from a lot of deliberation, and I wouldn't be surprised that those laureates had some back-channel conversations with Daw Suu before they chose to release that letter. You followed Daw Suu for four years and listened to her every speech. You know her as well as anyone. Your thoughts on the emerging controversy?

MON MON MYAT: I think people should be aware that Daw Suu still doesn't have full power in this country. She only has power from the people. She won the election because of people power. The 2015 election was just one of the last steps of the military government, according to the 2008 Constitution. The 2015 election was even conducted according to the 2008 Constitution. That is why even though the military government doesn't want to hand over power to the civilian government, they have to accept the civilian government because of their own constitution. They control those powerful ministries because they want to keep power in their hands to protect their well-being, and to protect their business interests. This is the power struggle between the civilian government and the military government.

AC: You're doing an official film biography covering the life story of Daw

Aung San Suu Kyi. You have interviewed her a number of times. You have many more interviews coming. You know her intimately well. What should we know about her thinking, feeling and psychology in relationship to post-election victory? Help us understand her relationship with the military, the military-drafted Constitution, the lack of control along the borders.

MMM: It's simple and complex at the same time. She is empowering our people. And, as a further step, she's trying to empower the military.

AC: National reconciliation in action?

MMM: Exactly. She's risked her popularity to build trust with the military, because she knew very well that this country won't change without the military taking part in the process. So she's taking the long *Dhamma*-based process of reconciliation for our people with the military and vice versa. Because, remember, the military was founded by her father—General Aung San—and she keeps telling the soldiers that she always felt like they are her brothers and sisters. Not only has she never hated the military, she shows love and respect for them. And she is trying very hard to elevate their way of being soldiers to that of what her father intended, disciplined and dignified, for the people, and not against them.

AC: Reconciliation of the oppressed and oppressors alike. She's building trust. And you said that she's unconcerned with popularity?

MMM: Yes. She's unconcerned with popularity, even from her fellow laureates. So, she is speaking out to heal the country. I'd like to give you a recent example. It's related to the perception of the international community, and the perception of the military mindset, and of extreme nationalist groups—she is between those two extremes. As you know, the international community always thinks about the rights of minority groups, protecting minority groups and human rights. This is one extreme. The other extreme: the majority Buddhists living in this country. They have a very nationalist attitude. Our country gained independence using this nationalism, so the way of thinking is very much nationalist. That is why, with nationalism and patriotism, once they suspect others of invading this country, they feel we must fight them. For example, they think of Bengali as an enemy—they think they're going to invade our country. That is why they don't want to accept them.

AC: "Bengali" is another name for the Rohingya?

MMM: Yes, because most people assume they are originally from Bangladesh.

So, then they are not indigenous. That is why they don't want to grant their ethnic identity as "Rohingya."

AC: You're saying this is a Buddhist-based problem, or a military-based problem, or both?

MMM: Both.

AC: Both; but, for most citizens, this not a problem? They look upon all people, the Kachins, the Shans, the Karens, the Rohingyas, equally as human beings entitled to human rights, of course. But some of the Buddhists and the military have prejudice?

MMM: Yes.

AC: Is this a conversation you have with friends, or that you hear from others on the radio, in the newspapers? It's pervasive in society?

MMM: Yes. It's common knowledge. I did some surveys for my article, and read articles written in local papers, and found they have a nationalist bias. Not the *Saṅgha* but primarily the media. The way they write is nationalist. Not all of them, but the majority.

AC: Are Burmese in general prejudiced against Muslims?

MMM: Normally not, but once you act as a kind of politician and arouse a sense of nationalism, then the people are easily led. It's easy to persuade them.

AC: I've talked to monks in this country over many years. I talked to Prime Minister U Nu when he was alive, and he said that the biggest threat to this country wasn't communism but Islam. I know that historically they often refer Muslims as ones who pillaged the monks and nuns at the time of the Buddha, ransacking, raping, murdering them. Essentially, as I understand it, Muslims where responsible for the annihilation of Buddhism in India and the same in Pakistan and Afghanistan, which were formerly Buddhist countries. Indonesia, Malaysia, and Bangladesh, as well. And now Burma is surrounded by the largest Muslim nations in the world—Indonesia and Bangladesh and I think India has over 200 million Muslims, second only to Indonesia. Does Burma fear being overwhelmed by Islam? Is Islam an existential threat to Burmese Buddhists?

MMM: Yes. It's Islamophobia, like in countries in Europe as well. This is happening across the whole world, in the same way a country like us only just learned about democratic practice. It can happen. It's not strange.

*'The international community,
and the international media,
don't see clearly.'*

ALAN CLEMENTS: I must say that my country has committed wholesale slaughter of innocent Muslims in Iraq, a false invasion based upon weapons of mass destruction that didn't exist. Look at the ongoing horror in Afghanistan. Look at my president in America today, wanting to ban most Muslims from coming into the US. There is a fear of Islam in America and you're right, all over the world. Terrorism is also alive in well in the world. And that includes not just Islamic terrorism but American terrorism as well. And Burma is not separate from that global context. Fear and terrorism are everywhere, as well as the fear of terrorism?

MON MON MYAT: Yes. The policy of Daw Aung San Suu Kyi is to try to give citizenship rights to the people who didn't get citizenship rights previously. Under the new government, they started issuing ID cards to those communities. But the biggest problem is that they don't want to accept the IDs without explicit reference to their Rohingya identity.

AC: You as a leader, as an active citizen promoting international human rights and human dignity at your festival, and with your own book and your film; if Daw Suu was here today, and asked, "Mon Mon Myat, please help me to understand what I do not see in myself, that if known, would better help me to help our people. Also, what's the best way, in your opinion, to respond to the crisis in Rakhine State? Is there more I can do?" What would you say?

MMM: I think that you should clearly see terrorism and human rights as different issues. It is true that people living in Rakhine didn't get their rights as citizens in this country. So, as a new government, we must give citizenship rights to the people living in that area. This is obviously providing security for those people. But, as a government, we must also protect our border area. And we must certainly protect people from terrorism. We have these two separate issues here, with a very thin line between them.

Overall, we must see clearly. The government has a responsibility to protect the border as well as to protect the civilians, including the Rakhine and the Rohingya, or Bengali. But at the same time, you can't mix up the terrorist attacks and the attacking of the Rohingya people. They're totally different. As I said, the government has a responsibility to protect people from terrorist attacks. And the government also has a responsibility to protect the minority Rohingya. So, we must see these two different issues clearly. The international community, and the international media, don't see clearly.

AC: Aren't they just reporting on the facts that they're hearing and seeing?

MMM: Not even the facts—sometimes they just make up news based on information they've received without even verifying that information. There are many examples of this. There's a lot of fake news. Even Al Jazeera TV admitted there's a lot of fake news coming through their own agency.

AC: And Daw Suu and the NLD government did appoint Kofi Annan, the former secretary general of the United Nations, to a special commission. I think—correct me if I'm wrong—Daw Suu and the NLD leaders also included the ASEAN foreign ministers, brought them together to witness and discover the truth. She's supporting aid from other Islamic countries, neighboring ASEAN counties, to be given to the people in Rakhine. She's done quite a lot. But what hasn't been done?

MMM: Yes, she has done quite a lot. But people in the media largely overlook these points you brought up. She's done something completely different to the previous military governments. Previously, they never released any information related to Rakhine State. They only issued one-sided news. Now, what Daw Suu's government is doing is trying to follow up on individual, single issues, like when rumors come up in the international media, they try to prove them as rumors.

The government today is responsive. They release immediate news about the Rakhine issue. They know it is a sensitive issue for the international community as well, so they release information quickly. They respond quickly to the international community and its accusations.

One thing that has not been done enough is that the international media needs to verify all the sources they gather related to this issue, and not just wield the bias of protecting minorities. In addition, they need to be aware of the whole background of this highly complex issue.

AC: When we met, you explained here in your office for the Human Rights and Human Dignity International Film Festival that you offer workshops to help understand human rights and human dignity. Are there any such workshops and programs being directed towards the *Saṅgha* and the military, for them to better understand the importance of universal human rights with respect for multi-ethnicity, and respect for multi-faith?

MMM: This film festival is based not only in Yangon. We run a travelling film festival across the country. Over the last four years we've taken it to more than 90 places, including numerous university campuses. Also, we delivered a copy of the Universal Declaration of Human Rights to every person who came to a festival. So that they can read it, keep it, and know their rights. It's in Burmese.

Then we made a quiz and asked the article number that was relevant to students, about rights to education, the right for healthcare, the right for social security, trying to get them to read the UDHR. In many villages they would gather and read it. And we would stand up and ask, "What is the number of the article on the right to education, what is the number of the article on freedom of expression," something like that, just so they'd read it. Previously, for delivering this small leaflet you'd be imprisoned. And a long imprisonment at that.

AC: As discussed, we were both outside of Daw Aung San Suu Kyi's front gate on University Avenue back in '95 and '96, listening to her speeches on freedom, nonviolent activism and democracy. I had an American passport—the worst that could happen, I thought, was being detained and deported—but everyone there, including you, risked losing your home, your job, your family, your freedom; torture; possibly rape. When I met Daw Suu for the first time, I asked her, "What was the essence of your country's nonviolent struggle for freedom that you call a *revolution of the spirit*?" She replied, "Courage; the courage to care about things larger than your own self-interest. And if enough of our people do that our revolution will be successful." That was 23 years ago.

MMM: The freedom we have today is because of the many people who dedicated their lives to standing up for freedom, and in so doing, suffered, were tortured, and served long-term imprisonment. Not only Daw Suu, but leaders like U Win Tin, U Tin Oo, U Kyi Maung, U Win Htein, Min Ko Naing, Ko Ko Gyi, and so many others. Some people even died in prison. I remember one remarkable documentary at the first film festival, submitted by a young man who made a film about political prisoners, a testimony of the human rights abuses in prisons here in Burma. So, this one activist was in prison for 12 years, and he's talking about how he was tortured, how he was moved from one place to another, how he suffered, and how he tried to survive in prison. The title of the film is *Survival in Prison*. This film was included in the travelling film festival, and we brought both the filmmaker and the political prisoner along. At one screening, a woman stood up and told the former political prisoner and the filmmaker, "I never knew this; if I were your mother, this would be really painful." She was crying. The former political prisoner was crying as well. So, through the film festival we can tell people how people suffered under the military dictatorship. It's part of empowering people. We were trying to push the boundaries of the government, testing how much freedom they are giving, how much space we have to tell the truth to the people.

AC: You're consciously pressing the boundaries even now?

MMM: Trying to—every day, a little bit more.

AC: "How free are we, really?" And expanding that freedom as far and wide as possible?

MMM: Yes, over the last five years we've tried to push those boundaries. It's quite hard. It didn't come easily.

AC: I so appreciate your candor, your compassion, your patience, your articulation of such complex feelings; a huge gift.

When I first met Daw Suu and U Tin Oo, and U Kyi Maung, U Win Htein, and more recently U Win Tin—these are among my closest intimates—and my *Dhamma* teachers, the late Venerable Mahasi Sayadaw and his successor Sayadaw U Pandita, I was repeatedly told by Sayadaw U Pandita especially, as well as Daw Suu, U Tin Oo and U Kyi Maung, that in the process of challenging authoritarianism do not vilify anyone. Do not demonize the so-called enemy. We are activists with *mettā* (loving-kindness), and *karunā* (compassion). And today, we are in a world that needs healing. We need to stop the divide, the demonization, the fear, and learn to hold hands and embody a future to believe in. By way of saying, your country has empowered national reconciliation as its main desire as a government. My question: How do you look into the eyes of the oppressor, into the eyes of those people who've made so much money on the backs of your people, who still today luxuriate in wealth, and empower reconciliation? What are the requisites of reconciliation? What is the wisdom at the core of this process? What does it look like, week to week, as a living experience?

MMM: Forgiveness. Forgiveness is the heart of the matter. We cannot forget the cruelties that have happened in the past, but we can forgive those who did them, those who supported them, and those who ordered them. Forgiveness is the only quality that can cure the suffering in our hearts, as well as suffering in the hearts of the oppressors, as buried as that suffering may be. They are also insecure in their life, because they know that they oppressed many, many families in our country. They have done many bad things to many people and for a long time. So, they are also insecure, and guilty and scared too. They will be feeling very unsettled for their wrongdoings. I'm sure of it. They will also be suffering because of their *karma* (actions). One way or the other their gross misdeeds will haunt them. This is the natural *Dhamma* law of *kamma* (cause) and *vipāka* (effect). If we show forgiveness to them, it will make it much easier for reconciliation.

Nor can we just exclude them from the community—they are a part of the community.

Most of all, to build up the country we must work together. This is also what Daw Suu has said—"I can't work alone to get democracy for this country. We must work together." And we work at what we can. This is supportive of her way of nonviolence. This is our responsibility.

AC: Sadhu, sadhu, sadhu. Thank you for your beautiful words, your inspiration, your courage. I hope millions will read your words. With all the faults in the world, with the struggles in Burma, you have ushered in democracy with a firm commitment to Gandhi's principle of nonviolence, the Buddha's principle of nonviolence, and to the primordial beauty of *ahimsa* (harmlessness). You did it without resorting to violence. That, to me, is profound, and encouraging. And here you are, today, continuing to do that. May your beloved country be a beacon of hope and light around the world. May Daw Suu and all of her boys and girls, may the former dictator, may all the cronies, come together in reconciliation. Thank you from my heart for your life and your inspiration.

MMM: Thank you for interviewing me as well. It's been a pleasure. Just one last comment: We don't wish to exclude anyone. We want to include everyone. That is also why we showed the film about the suffering of a political prisoner. And the other filmmakers we train, they also try to talk about the suffering of the veteran soldiers, and how they suffered. Those films will also air on our MR TV, so the whole country can see it. We do not want to leave anyone out of our embrace of reconciliation, whether it be soldiers, the Tatmadaw, torturers, killers, members of any religions, or ethnic groups. No one is excluded from our quest for national reconciliation.

AC: May it be so. May everyone in the world hear your words. May they embody the activism of love. May there be global healing. May our children's children have a future. I really thank you from my heart. And let me encourage the whole world to read your book and to see your film, *A Long Way Panglong*.

Conversation with Mon Mon Myat, January 2020

ALAN CLEMENTS: In a recent article of yours for the Irrawaddy I read the line, "It is now part of the world's politically correct orthodoxy to blame Daw Aung San Suu Kyi for the Rohingya refugee crisis and to condemn her for defending Myanmar against the genocide case brought by The Gambia before the International Court of Justice (ICJ)."

For those unfamiliar with the situation, The Gambia is one of the 57 member countries representing the Organization for Islamic Cooperation (OIC). It is accusing Myanmar of genocide against the Rohingya in the case brought before the ICJ.

Rather than me asking many questions, you being so versed in the subject, would you please elaborate on the key points so that anyone in the world, whether they have or have not been following the crisis in Rakhine, would be both up to date and aware of the facts, as you have investigated them as one of the world's foremost authorities on the topic? And before you comment, would you please include as much as you wish on informing our readers on the Muslim terrorist group, the Arakan Rohingya Salvation Army (ARSA), and their role in the crisis, especially "the mass killings, forced relocations and sexual violence that occurred before the Myanmar army ran its clearance operations," as you state in your article. And, details of the former UN secretary general Kofi Annan fact finding mission to Rakhine, as well as the most salient details of Daw Aung San Suu Kyi's statements a few days ago before the ICJ in The Hague?

MON MON MYAT: In September 2016, following a request from Myanmar's State Counsellor Daw Aung San Suu Kyi, the Kofi Annan Foundation and the Office of the State Counsellor established an Advisory Commission on Rakhine State. The Advisory Commission on Rakhine State was widely rejected by both ethnic Arakanese and Muslim Rohingya. Although the mandate of the commission was to find "lasting solutions to the complex and delicate issues in Rakhine state," many, including Arakanese politicians and Rohingya militant groups, immediately turned a blind eye to the commission appointed to find solutions.

It's very interesting for me to find the origin of the Arakan Rohingya Salvation Army (ARSA). I have doubted that there must be a conspiracy issue behind the ARSA which was formed in 2013 after 2012 communal violence in Rakhine. ARSA uses two ways: underground guerrilla warfare to recruit and train villagers in Rohingya community along the Bangladesh border, and media advocacy through international news agencies to rage war against Myanmar government.

ARSA's first violent attacks on border guard police in northern Rakhine State was in October 2016—just one month after the Annan commission was established. ARSA claimed the second violent attacks on border guard police in 25 August 2017, just one day after the Annan Commission's final report was released. It is very clear that ARSA's intention is not to find any solution but to fight against Myanmar to claim ethnic identity and then to territory. Suspicious video footage of ARSA was released a few days after attacks on police outposts. In the footage,

ARSA Commander Ata Ullah said loud and clear: "Arakan belongs to Rohingya."

In one of the AFP reports, it was mentioned that some Rohingya accused the rebels of provoking the army into revenge attacks and inviting nothing but misery upon the long-persecuted minority. AFP quoted a prominent Rohingya at a Bangladeshi camp as saying: "These regular farmers-turned-fighters with few weapons will bring nothing but more woe to Rohingya Muslims." Without any capacity to protect their people, ARSA made things worse and created a situation whereby almost 700,000 refugees have fled to Bangladesh soil. ARSA leaders also said in an interview with Reuters, "The attacks were aimed to invoke a response." Bertil Lintner also pointed out "the timing of ARSA." He said in an interview that "the attacks completely killed the report. It was by no means a coincidence. They want a more militarized space. So, on one hand, while people are blaming them for provoking the Army, on the other, a lot of angry young men have turned to them as they had hoped."

It is very interesting to look at how ARSA came to social media and who are listed among its online network. ARSA established a Twitter account on March 31 in 2017. ARSA posted its first tweet linking to an exclusive interview of its leader—Ata Ullah, who was born in Pakistan and raised in Saudi Arabia—with Reuters news agency: "Exclusive: Rohingya rebel leader challenges Myanmar's Suu Kyi, vows to fight on." He said, "If we don't get our rights, if one million, 1.5 million, all Rohingya need to die, we will die." He said this in the Reuters interview. It is an awkward thing to see a Pakistan native leading Rohingya, and then commanding whether more than one million people live or die.

ARSA's twitter account follows Rohingya activists Tun Khin, Maung Zar Ni and Ro Nay San Lwin who are based in the UK and Europe. The account also follows major rights groups such as Amnesty International, Human Rights Watch, Fortify Rights and the UN humanitarian aid agency and a few activist journalists such as Adil Sakhawat who wrote the exclusive *Journey into Rakhine* for the Dhaka Tribune in which he travelled into ARSA-occupied territory.

Just after the violence broke out in Myanmar's western part in August 2017, tragic tales of Hindu women ran on several news sites as major wire news agencies such as Reuters, AFP and other local newspapers, the Dhaka Tribune and the Daily New Age based in Bangladesh, reported about those women.

In the first report covered by Reuters in early September 2017, the witnesses told that "Myanmar forces and ethnic Rakhine Buddhists" attacked them and killed eight Hindu men. The story quoted a Hindu woman, Anika Bala, 15, and she said, "They asked my husband to join them to kill Rohingya but he refused, so they killed him." She said Muslims helped her get to Bangladesh.

But later on, the story was changed, that the attackers were "Muslim militants." The women were abducted by Muslim militants to the camps in Bangladesh and forced to convert to Islam. And they are forced to tell untrue stories.

An example of how this newer narrative is emerging is found in a report written by a journalist from The New York Times: "Yet I have seen Rohingya people quoted in the foreign news media telling stories that I know are not true. Their accounts, in some cases, are too compelling, like a perfect storm of suffering."

As I mentioned ARSA's two tactics earlier, the group has built their image through the act of terror on one hand and media advocacy on the other hand. Finally, violence invites more violence—the Myanmar government promptly declared ARSA a terrorist group and immediately responded with anti-terrorism security operations. Today, the Myanmar military's "clearance operations" are being highlighted as genocidal intent in the case submitted by The Gambia against Myanmar before the International Court of Justice (ICJ).

AC: How could the international press have handled the situation differently/more constructively?

MMM: I think both international and local press could have handled the situation constructively and professionally regardless of nationalist or internationalist sentiments. If they are really concerned for the rights of innocent people effected by armed conflict between Myanmar military and ARSA, the press should handle it carefully about the delicate and complex Rakhine issue.

AC: Is ARSA still a threat in Burma?

MMM: I consider ARSA as a paper tiger created by a powerful group from behind. As long as ARSA is backed by that particular group, it will be a threat to Burma.

AC: I read recently that "more than nine years after it was formed by 26 Arakanese (Rakhine) youths, the Arakan Army (AA) today is a 7000-member strong army which is gaining progress in its bid to establish a stronghold in its homeland, Rakhine State." The piece went on to state, "hundreds of AA troops launched a coordinated attack on four border guard police outposts in Buthidaung Township on Friday December 6, 2019. Only after the Tatmadaw (Myanmar Army) sent reinforcements and attacked from the air, the AA troops retreated. Thirteen police were killed in the attack during which the AA abducted 18 police and their family members..." Would you please explain who the AA is and their relationship to ARSA and why is AA fighting the Burmese military?

MMM: The Rakhine Commission finds "a sense of lawlessness along the border with Bangladesh." The Bangladesh-Myanmar border area has seen illegal trafficking in humans and drugs for many years. Uneducated and jobless young men, unprotected children and young girls living in refugee camps along the border become prey of human traffickers.

In a graphic by the BBC, Bangladeshi and Rohingya trafficking routes are shown to originate in Cox's Bazaar—home to Rohingya refugee camps on the Bangladesh side of the border.

A report released by UN High Commission for Refugees in 2015 showed about 25,000 people, including women and children, were trafficked in the three months from January to March 2015—double the number in the same period in 2014.

A US Department of State's 2017 report said transnational drug trafficking organizations operate within Bangladesh with underground operations stretching from Myanmar to India. There have been numerous reports in local media of vast hauls of illegal narcotics in Rakhine State.

The Rakhine Advisory Commission's final report highlights that "drug smuggling is reportedly funding the activities of non-state armed groups, such as the Arakan Army (AA) and the Arakan Rohingya Salvation Army (ARSA)." The illegal drug trade is the delicate reality of Rakhine and has remained unsolved for decades.

The Annan commission recommends the Myanmar government to establish a joint commission with Bangladesh to discuss bilateral relations including "combating human trafficking and drug smuggling, and security cooperation to combat violent extremism."

ARSA is using terror to claim Rakhine territory and using the lives of several hundred civilians as their shields.

"ARSA's violent actions inevitably will harm, not help it, despite its claims to be fighting the Myanmar state—and not Rakhine civilians—for the Rohingya cause," International Crisis Group pointed out in its report.

AC: I also learned that the AA has Barrett MRAD sniper rifles which have a unit price "of over $10,000 on the black market at the Thailand-Myanmar border." The sniper rifle is often used by the border guard forces of Israel and armed forces in Norway and the Netherlands. How does the 7,000 person AA army get their weapons and where is the money coming from?

MMM: I'm afraid that I do not have enough knowledge to answer this question.

AC: What do you make of the opinion that the threat of terrorism is moving away from the Middle East towards South East Asia? And is it true that funding for ARSA has been traced to Karachi, Pakistan and from there to Afghanistan with ties with people formerly connected to Osama Bin Laden?

MMM: In this case, Bertil Lintner is more knowledgeable. I learned from his report. Please do a search for "Bertil Lintner, Rohingya refugee crisis is not Muslims versus Buddhists." He's thoroughly researched this issue.

AC: If there's no hope of reconciliation without economic development in Rakhine State, can we expect to see more conflict before there's a solution?

MMM: Economic development is one of the key factors to build national reconciliation not only in Rakhine State but in the whole nation because abject poverty for many decades caused a lot of problems. To "learn to liberate their own minds from apathy and fear," as Daw Suu once wrote, is more important than economic development to build reconciliation. We can't build reconciliation without freedom from apathy and fear among people. We have been seeing more conflict in Rakhine State in 2018 until now because of AA's attempt to get a military stronghold in Rakhine State.

We can see growing distrust and fear among the different communities in Rakhine State. Wherever there is conflict, the process of economic development would be delayed. Then a vicious cycle of conflict will continue in that particular area.

AC: Is there a conflict between Eastern (China, Russia) and Western (USA, Europe) economic and political interests in how the situation is resolved?

MMM: Geopolitics plays an important role in Myanmar's political context, as Myanmar is a strategic place located between the most populous democratic nation, India and the world's most populous authoritarian country, China. Under the military government, Myanmar had to depend largely on China and Russia as Western governments imposed various sanctions on her. Once U Thein Sein took power, he tried to make alliances with Western countries under the title of "Peace Building" in order to escape from China's enormous influence but he wasn't able to take the office for the next presidency term. Unfortunately, the ruling NLD government has faced a new wave of communal violence in Rakhine State since they've taken power. The NLD government is trying hard to resist economic pressure from China (as a heritage of military rule for more than two decades) and political pressure (for democracy and human rights) from the Western countries. Despite Western pressure on the Rohingya human rights issue, Daw Suu has made an effort to expand diplomatic and economic ties with Japan, South Korea, India and ASEAN countries in order to reduce dependency on China. However, China still plays a critical role in Myanmar's peace process as they have influence on the Northern Alliance composed of four ethnic insurgent groups: the Arakan Army (AA), the Kachin Independence Army (KIA), the Myanmar National Democratic Alliance Army (MNDAA) and the Ta'ang National Liberation Army (TNLA).

Myanmar is torn between staying with the East for authoritarian rule and going with the West for liberal democracy, but she is still in the middle of nowhere. Too much pressure of the international community on Myanmar and her immature democracy will result in nothing other than the possibility of pushing Myanmar back into authoritarian rule or driving our country toward anarchy.

AC: Do you think the government is being sincere in its repatriation efforts?

MMM: The government's attempt to accept returnees is obvious. In the news report published in the Irrawaddy, it is stated that "So far, a total of 397 Rohingya have voluntarily returned independently of bilateral agreement procedures established between the Myanmar and Bangladeshi governments. The refugees have returned both by boat and on foot across the border, according to the Maungdaw District General Administration Department." The same article states that "for returnees under the official bilateral agreement between Myanmar and Bangladesh, the Myanmar government opened two reception centers in early 2018: one in Taungpyo Letwei, for those returning over the land border, and one in Nga Khura for those returning by boat. However, no one has officially returned under the bilateral agreement."

In my opinion, the main concern of the government is the return of suspected members of the ARSA. Government officials have been checking all the voluntary returnees against the data that authorities have on the suspects, in accordance with the law and regulations, according to the Irrawaddy report.

I cannot make a judgment on how much the government is sincere because I have limited knowledge about this, but no matter whether the government is sincere or not, they must accept the returnees. Thousands of returnees were accepted in 1978 and 1992 under the Ne Win government and military government. Myanmar government and Rohingya population often plays cat-and-mouse game over times.

According to my research data, we can find exodus history of foreign race in Myanmar as follow:

1963-64: Massive exodus of Indian and Chinese (Approx. 500,000 to 800,000) after the first military coup

1978: Dragon King Operation (citizen registration project and illegal immigrant crack down) - 200,000 (Refugee returnees 187,197)

1991-1992: Pyi Thaya Operation (illegal immigrants crack down after 1991 Deadliest Bangladesh Cyclone) - 250,000 (Refugee returnees 236,000)

2012-2013: 120,000 (Religious Conflict)

2017: 500,000 (After Militant Attacks), more than 400 militants killed

AC: Is there anything else you would care to share about the crisis in Rakhine as well as anything else about the transition to democracy in your country?

MMM: Media plays a difficult role in the Rakhine crisis. Because of restrictions on media in both Myanmar and Bangladesh, the news can be different depending on whom we listen to. For those interested in the truth this crisis, we must look deeply into the issues, and the news sources. It is highly complex.

On a closing note: if the real intention of ARSA is to save its own people—the Rohingya—and fight for their rights, it should not be using terrorist tactics. Rather than taking care with commission's recommendations, ARSA rushed in to claim territory in Rakhine State and encroach on Myanmar's sovereignty. The world has no place for terrorism. It is the wrong approach, everywhere. And it is the wrong approach in Myanmar. ARSA should cease their activities permanently.

In addition, as ARSA doesn't really represent the Rohingya in Rakhine State, the Myanmar military doesn't represent the people of Myanmar. Because of ARSA's terrorist actions to the Myanmar military and the brutal clearance operation that followed by the military, tens of thousands of Rohingya are torn between Myanmar and Bangladesh. Both the Myanmar military and ARSA have become a threat to the Rohingya people. If both sides continue using violence as a way to solve the problem, this vicious cycle of conflict in Rakhine State will never end.

AC: May it end soon. Thank you very much for your detailed analysis.

MMM: Thank you, Alan.

Discipline in Myanmar in the Time of Global Pandemic

MON MON MYAT March 31, 2020

As military representatives recently opposed charter amendment in Myanmar's Parliament during a global pandemic, it brought to mind the words of German sociologist Max Weber, who described the nature of military discipline: "They are trained to shoot and stop shooting on command. …. individual thought or contemplation is never tolerated in a disciplined force."

But are they trained to protect the lives of citizens? Why didn't Weber say this in his essay?

Military lawmakers in Parliament are trained to safeguard the Constitution at the command of their higher-ups, not to follow their individual consciences. Their votes count towards a collective cause, under a "one race, one voice, one command" system. Individual thought is not tolerated in any military's chain of command, including that of the Tatmadaw, as the Myanmar military is known.

The charter was drafted under the State Law and Order Restoration Council military government, with the aim to "establish a political structure that could create a civilian government in line with the Tatmadaw's idea of nation building," as Ye Htut mentions in his book about Myanmar's political transition. The most important characteristic of military culture, "discipline", is even included as a basic principle of Myanmar's charter: the "flourishing of a genuine, disciplined multi-party democratic system."

Weber observed discipline has "one commonality." Ancient Egypt's rulers, the pharaohs, used discipline to manage thousands of slaves while building giant pyramids. Mine owners in the late Middle Age controlled miners with such discipline. Discipline enforced among enslaved Africans on sugarcane plantations during the Americas' colonial period and among modern factory workers is the same, according to Weber.

Note too that discipline is not democratic—and it is often anti-democratic. Nearly automatic discipline is something that every army imbues in 16 and 17-year-old boys through the rigors of basic military training. This is where young boys learn to march, exercise and kill on command, without reference to anyone except their commanding officer. This is of course the discipline that the military officers bring to Myanmar's Parliament, where disciplined military officers habitually obey their commanders, and not the people, or their own consciences.

It is unsurprising that the recent attempt by the National League for Democracy (NLD) government to amend the charter has failed because the Constitution was designed only for the disciplined force of the army and for a government in line with the army, but not for majority rule or rule by a charismatic figure like Daw Aung San Suu Kyi.

Two main obstacles in the 2008 Constitution—the Tatmadaw's control of three key ministries (Defense Services, Home Affairs and Border Affairs) and its ability to hamper constitutional amendment—are the brainchild of former senior general Than Shwe, as Ye Htut observes.

With one single phrase in Article 436 (a), the charter is locked up: "it shall be amended with the prior approval of more than seventy-five percent of all the representatives." This simply means that the charter cannot be amended without the consent of at least one military lawmaker.

In the process of disciplining the army or the modern factory, "the human being is adjusted to the functions demanded from him. The human being is stripped of his personal biological rhythm, and then is reprogrammed into the new rhythm according to the prerequisites of the task", according to Max Weber.

If we look at how military lawmakers in Parliament responded to charter amendment, we see that all they did was keep the green book of the Constitution as the army adopted it in 2008, irrespective of democratic norms or elections. Almost all of the NLD's proposals to amend the charter were denied, mainly by military lawmakers and their allies in the Union Solidarity and Development Party.

The military parliamentarians acted like robots, preprogrammed to safeguard the Constitution, or like the Sphinx statues that guard tyrants' tombs in Egypt. Army discipline became "blind obedience" to military command, rather than to the sovereign people.

In his essay about discipline, Weber explained how mastery of the technical details of a legal system becomes the center of power in the modern state. That illustrates why the former senior general installed robots with "blind obedience" to safeguard the Constitution: the center of power is placed in the green book.

The UN's Fact-Finding Mission (FFM) on Myanmar also observes "impunity is deeply entrenched in Myanmar's political and legal system, effectively placing the Tatmadaw above the law." Its report highlights that "the Constitution and other laws provide for immunities and place the Tatmadaw beyond civilian oversight."

Modern-day conflicts and disasters, however, blur the line between civilian and soldier, especially in the time of the coronavirus pandemic today. This is what democracy really means: the capacity to overcome programmed, unthinking military discipline.

In the time of a global pandemic, it becomes clearer that the army is not the only disciplined force to protect the sovereign power, as we see the role that doctors and nurses, health workers and media professionals play on the frontlines to protect the lives of citizens. They become frontline troops to prevent against, fight and control COVID-19, because the virus does not spare anyone, regardless of their might.

"Blind obedience" of disciplined soldiers at the tomb of the tyrant won't last long, because the tomb has no life. Although the center of power is placed in the green book, it is no use during a disaster that comes out of the blue. The power of each individual has become crucial today to stop the global pandemic—because no one wants to be the last man in this world.

CHAPTER 35

CONVERSATIONS *with* TIM AYE-HARDY

January 2018 through January 2020

- "Change depends on how fast we can transform our own selves."
- "The way the army controls and runs the country is not so different from extremist groups."
- "The international media... try to make things sexy and restricted by simplifying the crisis."
- "Two critical things are needed from the leadership to move this transition forward."
- "We don't have anybody building or could build a bigger boat at this transition period. The NLD has the biggest boat right now that everyone can ride on to the other side."
- "In order for us to build trust with our enemies... we need to go beyond our selves."

Tim Aye-Hardy was a prominent student voice during the 1988 uprising, speaking to crowds of thousands on human rights and freedom and narrowly avoiding multiple arrests. Expelled from the Rangoon Art and Science University (RASU) for his involvement in the protests, he later immigrated to the United States, where he lived for 25 years, before returning to Burma in 2014 to witness the country's ongoing transition. Tim is both an inaugural Carl Wilkins Fellow with the Genocide Intervention Network, Equity Initiative Fellow, and Sr. Atlantic Fellow with The Atlantic Institute based in Oxford University. He is also Chairperson of the International Forum Planning Committee with the UNESCO Chair & Institute of Comparative Human Rights. In addition, he has worked closely with refugees for many years. In these detailed interviews from 2018 and 2020 he explores Burma's shifting political and social landscape, the challenges the country faces as it strives to meet both domestic and international expectations, the role of the international media in perpetuating misconceptions and the realities of progress under a parallel government. The conversations conclude with an insightful discussion of the *Dhamma* of democratic transition and the continued relevance of the NLD (National League for Democracy).

*"Change depends on how fast we can transform
or transition our own selves."*

ALAN CLEMENTS: You're a prominent voice and long-time activist for your people's nonviolent struggle for freedom. Let's start here: Would you outline some of the obstacles or challenges that your people are facing here in Burma in the transition from dictatorship to democracy?

TIM HARDY: Well, there are a lot of challenges, as we all know. When I try to understand life in Myanmar as I've lived it for the last five years, continuously, especially right after the NLD (National League for Democracy) government came into power, there are two layers to what's happening. One is the 2008 military-crafted Constitution, and the transition in which the military still has significant power and control. While the direction has been set, the pace of the transition is pretty much dictated and controlled by that constitution. It was terribly smart of the military to come up with that constitution; that part is something that will take a long time to change.

AC: A constitution only in name, engineered, as it were, with the mindset of dictatorship that essentially enshrines quasi-dictatorial-military rule, and freedom from persecution, ad infinitum, correct?

TH: Yes, you could say that. However, I think things will gradually change and improve as we move forward. But the pace of the transition depends on two things. One factor concerns those military officials and authorities in control—how much are they willing to let go; how secure will they feel in releasing their grip on power?

AC: How comfortable they are in releasing themselves from fear?

TH: Power is everything to them. It's rooted in their concern for the safety and protection of themselves and their family members—their fear of prosecution of past crimes and wrongdoings, and in protecting their illicitly accumulated assets and wealth, as well as their ongoing continued hold on their elite status, while continuing to exploit our country's resources and economy.

AC: As the Buddha said, like hungry ghosts—greed feeds on itself in a never-ending cycle of perpetual hunger. He called this *Saṃsāra*, circular existence.

TH: Yes, we must break this authoritarian chain, once and for all. That depends on how much we can we bring out in the people of this country the radical will to rise up—rising up in terms of political consciousness and social and economic consciousness. And not like in the past—not rising up with demonstrations on the streets. We need a change in consciousness. And to me, right now, we are at a critical point where the entire country needs to rise up—rise up for the new dawn of societal transformation.

AC: A new revolution of consciousness; the transformation of the old to the new?

TH: Yes. And that change, that transformation, will depend on how fast we can learn, reflect, and transform our own inner selves.

The other component is based on the military: their perception of how comfortable they feel to also make the necessary changes to move our country forward into a genuine regard for rule of law, fairness, and universal human rights.

Those two things will determine how fast we'll get to the final destination of a truly democratic society.

AC: A democratic nation as a union, inclusive of all ethnicities?

TH: Indeed. But currently, it's not pretty. It's not good in the sense that the NLD government, when they came to power, they were ill prepared, which makes sense since they'd been living under harsh authoritarian rule for decades.

Of course, no one thought that all it would take is a landslide election victory and then we'd have full control of Parliament. That point is obvious when you look back and see that right after the elections The Lady (Daw Aung San Suu Kyi) herself needed to take on four ministerial positions because somehow negotiations or decisions were not made in time. If they were planned properly, we would not see such challenges. But these challenges are not just ordinary challenges, they're impacting the transition as well as their personal performance as well as the expectations of the people who voted for the NLD.

On the other side, Myanmar needs to effectively improve the economy and the overall well-being of the citizens in order to have a successful political transition. Although the NLD government claims to be moving into a market economy and trying their best to attract more FDI (Foreign Direct Investment) in Myanmar, simultaneously, the economy is sustained primarily by a group of military-and-crony-owned companies. The vast majority of these companies are closely related to the military era and military families, both former and current.

Even more concerning is the fact that these military-crony-owned companies are being solidified at this very moment. Thus, becoming even more resistant to change. This, in turn, is making it increasingly more difficult for the civilian government to create a level playing field in order to allow independent investors and companies, both foreign and domestic, to come into the country to create more competition and choices for the citizens.

AC: A capitalistic-military-crony-driven-economy?

TH: Precisely. Such examples of military and crony owned industry are everywhere. You can see it in the banking sector, airline industry, retail sectors, the garment industry, gems, timber, oil and gas, labor, construction, and much more.

This outmoded authoritarian hurdle is not only impacting the country's economic growth, it's affecting the day-to-day lives of ordinary people in Myanmar. The people are forced to pay higher prices on everything, especially transportation and consumer products and services, while their incomes have not increased, and inflation goes up and up. Meanwhile, jobs are increasingly scarce, particularly high-paying ones.

AC: What is the average family wage for the Myanmar citizen?

TH: Most families earn $2 to $3 a day by everyone in the family who are working, which includes under-aged children. This amount doesn't even cover their basic needs for the day.

Of course, this is a fragile and unsustainable situation that could easily and quickly lead to a severe crisis or breaking point and in the near time, that is, if we do nothing about it.

Also, corruption and the informal economy (that part of an economy that is neither taxed nor monitored by government) is substantial in Myanmar. In fact, it's one of the largest informal economies in the world, where billions of dollars are moved through the system every day with drug trafficking, smuggling of goods and equipment, jade and precious stones, illegal migrations, and many more moving across all our borders with Thailand, China, India and Bangladesh.

If I am not mistaken, Myanmar ranks 136th out of 176th countries in the Transparency International Corruption Index.

And corruption remains one of the most challenging issues for the NLD government to tackle. It's widespread and pervasive across almost every sector.

AC: A challenging situation for leadership.

TH: Yes. Right now, what we're seeing is that if The Lady, or whoever has control of this NLD government, is unable to make significant and appropriate changes within the leadership structure, we could face grave conditions. Those challenges may not surface as political right away, but they'll gradually unfold as a socio-economic crisis. And as that crisis unfolds, ordinary citizens will have no other choice but to take out their disappointments and anger on the streets, on social media and other public displays. Invariably, this will trigger greater political unrest and social instability across the entire country. And no doubt, military forces will be used to restore order and stability, at least for the short time.

AC: Not a pretty picture.

TH: But that could easily be the future of Myanmar, that is, if significant leadership changes are not made in time and the transition failed to provide and fulfil the basic needs and aspirations for ordinary citizens.

In light of that potentiality, perhaps the NLD could start by learning from the previous organizational culture of the military regime, where the top-down hierarchical authority was maintained to achieve overall stability, while democratization of power and decentralization of authority are tolerated at each level. To achieve this, the country needs transformational leadership that can bring about real and sustainable change for all the people of Myanmar.

Essentially, democratization of leadership and decentralization of power are needed in Myanmar more than ever, since the root causes we're facing are all interrelated yet unspecified. To achieve that, current leaders need to become adaptable to the changes that are required during the transition as well as capable of creating an environment with systems that allow such adaptation, transformation and cooperation with various the stakeholders.

AC: Business as usual is not sufficient during this historic transition time?

TH: Outdated and dysfunctional government structures, environments and policies need to be changed during these early phases of the transition in order to avoid unnecessary obstacles and delays. Again, for this to happen, we need visionary leadership to carry out this critical transition in Myanmar.

AC: Where to start?

TH: By changing the organizational culture within the NLD party. As is, they use a hierarchical decision-making structure. If this continues, gradually the government and civil service culture will therefore change. Change requires simultaneous changes in leadership, environment-systems, and overall capacity of the people. Not an easy task. But it must be done and done soon to capitalize on this unrepresented political dividend from the 2015 elections.

AC: It all comes back to leadership?

TH: It all comes back to leadership. We can't emphasize that enough. To achieve our goals in a peaceful, inclusive and sustainable means, we need mindful leaders and courageous reformers, women and men, who are capable of understanding the real concerns, fears and losses that will be endured by those who have greatly benefited from the old authoritarian system. Meanwhile, we need a sound strategy to create a new or transformed environment where a new generation of reformers and those who transitioned from the old system could join together to journey towards a peaceful, inclusive, sustainable and prosperous Myanmar. Only this type of adaptive leader can understand how to guide us through the historic transition that we're currently experiencing here in Myanmar.

AC: A key skill you are looking for in leadership?

TH: One of the main skills for adaptive leaders is self-awareness. They must be comfortable mindfully dancing along the edge or the thin line between old and new systems. They must know when to turn up or turn down the heat in order to bring the best out of everyone throughout the process.

Also, as you know, self-awareness is not a skill that one can acquire by reading books and listening to lectures. Instead, one must consistently practice being mindful of one's own mind—intelligently aware of one's strengths, weaknesses, and emotional states. So, self-awareness or mindful intelligence, as you call it, is one of the most fundamental and essential skills that is needed for Myanmar's transitional and adaptive leaders

AC: Going back to the 2008 Constitution, which was essentially conceived by the former dictator, U Than Shwe, and his closest military associates—it enshrines, as I said earlier, the military. That enshrinement means they make all decisions concerning the armed forces; all decisions concerning law enforcement; the police; border control; surveillance; weapons procurement and use; and of course, defence matters. All key positions of power are constrained by the 2008 military-crafted Constitution and run by the military elites. Essentially, Myanmar is a military run country with a powerless civilian majority government? Is that a wrong assessment? How would you piece up the power pie in Burma?

TH: You could say we have a parallel government—two governments managing the same country.

There are those three key ministries, those positions with ministers appointed by the military chief-of-staff (currently Senior General Min Aung Hlaing) and then you have other parts of the government run by the NLD elected government.

Not only that, the military appoints 25 percent of the seats in Parliament (both union and state/regional levels) to their own active military officers, and they can be replaced or removed by the military chief-of-staff anytime without providing any reasons or explanations.

It's a smart, carefully planned and executed military-crafted constitution.

On the other hand, any significant amendments to the Constitution require not only over 75 percent of the vote in Parliament, they also need a nationwide referendum with two thirds of the eligible voters voting for the amendments. In other words, it's impossible to change the Constitution without military approval.

AC: Thus, perpetual control by the military.

TH: Further, Myanmar's democratization process is infinitely fragile since most people understand and internalize democracy quite differently. At the same time, the level of trust in political institutions is extremely low; most people think democracy is directly linked with personal freedom, liberty, and prosperity. The lack of understanding on collective freedom, which is based upon mutual respect and rule of law, is quite evident in their daily lives.

This challenge alone is nearly impossible for the NLD to overcome since it requires them to provide quality civic education to many millions of people who grew up under a military-mindset of authoritarian rule. Meanwhile, the NLD government must continue to try to construct democratic institutions while doing everything possible to amend the military-drafted 2008 Constitution.

A formidable set of tasks, no doubt.

AC: So, a parallel government is the best way to describe life in Naypyidaw today?

TH: I believe so. Two separate groups with different interests, perspectives and agendas are serving in the government. Of course, this is not a good thing. And it's impossible to move forward without causing significant frictions and disagreements.

An additional challenge is that one side of the parallel government doesn't have authority over or even access to the other side's financials and activities. For example, there's no military oversight committee in Parliament. As far as I know, even the existing Budget or Finance & Planning committees cannot question or ask for an account of military spending and its missions and operations.

AC: It's assumed that the military holds the power within the "parallel government" structure as you described it?

TH: Well, it's not clear which side has majority or minority. But we can say that significant power is being given to the military according to the 2008

Constitution. As discussed, in this situation, the military holds critical permissions and opportunities to manage and control almost everything of significance. And that control is disproportionately more than the NLD's civilian government's position.

For instance, take the peace process—the military is right in the middle of it. The military dictates how fast, how soon, and with which ethnic groups they want to engage, and which ethnic groups they want to side-line, and so on. These things are more or less controlled and facilitated by the military.

Right now, we're seeing communal violence clashes in Northern Rakhine between the military and ARSA (the Arakan Rohingya Salvation Army) that caused an international outcry that resulted in enormous pressure placed on the NLD civilian government to take actions on the perpetrators from the Myanmar military side.

Even the recent incident in Mrauk-U with the Rakhine nationalist protest—the police shot at the crowd and killed a protester. I believe this could also be a part of the intentional design flaws of the Constitution, so as to make sure that the elected government won't gain full control and therefore make effective decisions that benefit the will of the people.

Overall, the authority of the military is evident everywhere in Myanmar, especially with the numerous armed conflicts taking place throughout the country. Almost one-third of the entire country is in conflict-affected zones. Some wars have even turned into grave humanitarian emergencies.

It'll be impossible to reduce the authority of the military as long as such conflicts are taking place, especially in the ethnic regions where valuable natural resources are substantial. As you know, Myanmar in abundant in oil, gas, timber, jade, sapphires, rubies, and so much more, and, of course, unthinkably cheap labor. Because of all these interrelated hypercomplex issues, Myanmar is currently in the red category of high-risk countries according to the 2017 Fragile States Index.

These issues and many others are the major underlying causes for the NLD government to be so destabilized and therefore unable to govern the country effectively.

AC: And from here?

TH: Overall, our democracy process has serious risks and is fundamentally flawed and fragile by definition, since most people, as I said earlier, understand and internalize democracy very differently. In addition, the level of trust in our political institutions is extremely low, as most people think democracy is directly linked with personal freedom, liberty and prosperity.

It seems like democracy for most of our citizens, especially in low-income and uneducated communities, is to organize and influence majority opinions or consensus on any issues or needs that they need to overcome or fulfil and act upon the results without others, particularly on minority and opposition concerns, rights and aspirations.

Lack of understanding on collective freedom and liberty, which is based upon mutual respect and rule of law, is painfully evident in their daily lives in Myanmar. Combine this with the lack of enforcement and protection of basic rights for everyone and lack of proper education, our society could soon be driving itself towards much greater conflicts, widespread chaos and potentially catastrophic instability. I pray this is not so.

AC: Would you explain, in a nutshell, the complex tapestry of violence in Myanmar today—where are the most active military engagements throughout the country?

TH: I'm not closely following the recent military engagements, but as far as I know, sporadic fighting is taking place between north Shan State and the south of Kachin State. That's the hot zone right now. Other fighting is taking place between KIA (Kachin Independence Army)/TNLA (Ta'ang National Liberation Army)/AA (Arakan Army, with 20,000 uniformed soldiers) and Myanmar Military in North Eastern Shan State and Rakhine State and some are in Southern Chin State.

AC: What's going on in Shan State?

TH: In the Shan State there are several armed groups (PNLA, SSA-N, SSA-S, UWSA, etc.). There are other ethnic groups also in Northern Shan State. For example, the Wa, Ko Kant, and the Arakan Army, and the KIA are all there, and then the TNLA is there as well. Some have signed the NCA (Nationwide Ceasefire Agreement) and some have not. Currently, I believe 11 armed groups out of 21 have signed the NCA with the government. Overall, so much is going on in Shan State, not only the fight for self-determination but also the extraction of natural resources.

I think you know that Myanmar is the 2nd largest producer of opium in the world behind Afghanistan, and it's believed to be the world's largest manufacturer of methamphetamines, more commonly known as crystal meth and ice. This massive and lucrative international drug trafficking is coming out of Shan State, neighboring southern China.

AC: I read an article sometime back in which the International Crisis Group (ICG) pointed to Shan State as the Meth Capital of the World, the world's largest producers of the drug. When you think of the horrors and costs faced by those addicted to it, one wonders how an entire region a few hundred miles from here has managed to find its way probably into every major city. One wonders how a 400,000-man, well-equipped military here in Myanmar cannot put an end to this scourge.

It makes me wonder who the beneficiaries are from this continued operation.

I also wonder how much money is at play here and the politics involved?

Oh well, another time.

Will you say a few words about the Kachin war?

TH: The Kachin war is the world's longest continuing armed conflict since 1948 for their right to self-govern and control natural resources. Fighting is taking place particularly in the north along the border with China, and other areas where KIA-controlled gold and amber mining are located.

Recently, it's interesting how these armed groups are coming together in the north to resist the Myanmar army. The Arakan Army was not in Kachin State before. This is a new addition and founded in 2009. Interestingly, you could question why the Arakan Army was not very active (almost non-existent) or operating in Arakan State before they started to move into Rakhine State around 2018.

AC: In a way you could say they're unifying?

TH: They're coming together in military operations. But, on the other hand, there's another larger ethnic grouping, a group of ethnic armed groups banding together in advocating and negotiating with the government in the political transition.

So, there are two different groups. You'll see that the same groups are also involved in these two separate larger groups.

AC: Regarding the riot in Arakan yesterday, based upon this author who advocated armed resistance to the military, can you say a few words about the shootings at Mrauk with Dr. U Aye Maung?

TH: Well, U Aye Maung is a Rakhine nationalist and was also an MP. He's a strong advocate for the independence of Arakan State. He participated at the event in January 2018 to commemorate the 233rd anniversary of the fall of the Arakan Kingdom to the Myanmar king in 1785. At that time, he gave a speech urging Arakaneses to march towards the goal of independence. A lot of Arakanese people feel similar sentiments because they were sacked by the Burmese king back in the day—that's how the riot started, with the anniversary of losing their king and country.

AC: It's embedded in ancient history?

TH: Yes, and they also blame the Burmese for the atrocities that are taking place in their state. They say it's because there is a lack of support from the Myanmar government.

I don't know what percentage, but many Arakanese I spoke with, deep down they feel like their state is going through turmoil because of the Burmese conquering them, and then the British coming in, and bringing in a lot of Indians with them. I'm not blaming Indians, but a lot of foreigners came in with them, many as forced labor.

Many of the Arakanese feel they have no control, no protection; losing their land; losing their livelihoods; losing their sisters and daughters to those foreigners. Because of that, you start seeing other religions and ethnicities becoming stronger, and then the Arakanese become less significant and unable to protect themselves. Further, jobs are not there. There are many problems they were forced to face since the 17th century.

AC: You've been living here in your own country for some years. You've returned after living in the states for 25 years, having left Myanmar in '89. You know democracy, you know human rights; you've lived in a country with freedom of speech and so on. My question: How would describe the psychology, the mindset, of Burma's army? Who are these people? And before you answer, please allow me to be frank, speaking as a father with a daughter:

From an outside point of view, the military displays all the characteristics of an institution without conscience. Recently the international media and many world leaders have condemned them for what they are claiming is ethnic cleansing. Some are even calling it genocide. Regardless, hundreds of thousands of Bengalis or Rohingya have fled the country in terror, many recalling rape, with the vast majority saying, 'It happened based upon the terror and torture and murder of the Burmese army.'

You know it firsthand; you fled this army's violence during the '88 uprising.

How many of your peace-loving brothers and sisters were killed?

How many others were tortured in interrogation centers and in prison?

How many others lost their minds and their futures subsisting in the jungles?

We know the horrors in Karen State.

We know the horrors in the Shan State, and Kachin area.

The world stood in horror as they slaughtered their own Buddhist monks.

And who wants to compare degrees of evil? Dark is dark here in Burma. Who are these men?

And they wrote a constitution in their own image that eternally enshrines—if I can say it—themselves, a uniformed killing machine seemingly without conscience.

Allow me to conclude with this. During the war in Yugoslavia there was a lot of gallows humor. One such joke stood out: If you murdered one person, you would normally get life in prison or capital punishment. If you murdered four or more over a week or two you were a serial killer, and if you had a good lawyer, you'd be deemed criminal insane and would likely spend your days in a prison psych-ward. But if you committed genocide you are invited by world leaders to talk peace, you're wined and dined and celebrated if you sign a peace accord, ending the bloodbath.

Why does everyone tiptoe around Big Brother?

Is this a case of a collective Stockholm Syndrome?

Your thoughts?

TH: Let me address the situation here. Based on my experiences and the current circumstances, with what we endured with the military's massacres in '88 and in 2007 with Saffron, and even going further, back in 1962, the manner in which the army controls and runs the country is not different from atrocious self-interested extremist group. They empower and enrich themselves, especially high-ranking members, and they do so without any significant ideology or principle.

AC: Going deeper?

TH: When you look at Burmese Army, we see two layers. The bottom layer is pretty much ordinary soldiers struggling with their daily lives, just to get by. They are without proper education, without critical thinking skills, without moral discipline, without the basic needs of day to day life. That's one layer that exists within the army, and that layer is controlled, manipulated, and ordered by another layer—an extremely small group of individuals at the very top. In this structure, folks from the bottom layer are always trying to get to an upper layer. Climbing the ladder, so to speak, is the only promising future that's permissible throughout the military structure. And all significant rewards and punishments are based solely on one's personal relationship with a higher authority than one's self.

Those folks in the upper layer have everything that you could imagine—power, control, money, mansions, influence, consumer goods, anything and everything is at their disposal.

In short, there are multiple layers created within the military structure which allows different levels or echelons of power to control, or influence or exert authority at each layer below one's own level. The way the elites control the military is through these layers, where the authority and power at each layer is not questioned by a higher level nor is it required to have any meaningful explanation or significant justification if something goes wrong.

These are the multiple layers of institutionalized totalitarian dictatorship. In this authoritarian structure the mindset of the military is impossible to break up due to a particular cause, ideology, movement, or social change. It's a self-replicating feedback loop that gathers momentum as it regenerates person to person.

AC: In other words, dictatorship is a bad app. Is it worse now than in the past?

TH: In the past it was far worse. For instance, the commander of a particular division or command pretty much was a king within his division. The commander had full control of his region and could do whatever he wished or needed without opposition.

Further, the commander-in-chief of the country, of the army, did not question much, or do nothing significant to intervene, unless the local commander was becoming a threat to the power and stability within the military structure.

It seems that the reason they set up this kind of structure and how they've been able to maintain it for such a long time is because the central authority in the military doesn't provide sufficient resources or supplies to maintain regional commands. They are unable to even provide needed weapons by the central command. Therefore, each commander must figure out their own way to maintain and stay alive and in control. Because of the need for survival, so to speak, they could break rules and protocols and commit all kinds of crimes and atrocities in order to maintain their power, position, and command.

That's where you see the disconnect between the layers that created the environment and culture of impunity for the near endless crimes and injustices against the local population, especially on ethnic and minority groups.

That's how it's been structured and ruled for many decades in Myanmar. It's a structure of domination and corruption based on fear, uncertainty, and impunity without the rule of law.

At the top you have this dictatorial mentality we have a bleeding into the lower ranks. Lack of education prevents these individual ordinary soldiers from understanding what's exactly going on, or who is benefiting out of all this. The majority of these young soldiers have not even finished primary and then they're brought into the military, trained, brainwashed, and given arms to kill and follow the order. Most of them believe they're doing the right thing, because they don't have any other way of connecting the dots and understanding the bigger picture.

Lack of critical thinking leads to brainwashing and full mind control.

During the 2007 Saffron Revolution, the military leaders at the top brought in soldiers from different ethnic groups and different religions. They were told denigrating erroneous stories about the monks and other peaceful demonstrators. So, these brain-dead soldiers had no problem whatsoever shooting or beating up our Buddhist monks and other innocent peacefully abiding protestors.

AC: In some cases, while they chanted the Buddha's *Mettā Sutta* on loving kindness?

TH: Yes. The tragedy. The horror. The shamelessness. That's how we need to understand the authoritarian military structure. As I said, it is not much different from other self-serving extremist groups, when it comes to serving its own interests and prosperity. It's pretty much the same fundamental.

When you are deprived of basic needs, economic prosperities and education, people will believe untruthful fabricated stories, because, as I said, they're unable to connect the dots by themselves, unable to think critically, unable to see other alternatives to escape their deprived lives and struggling conditions.

AC: You have a dictatorship that's morphed its dictatorial mindset into regional commanders and they in turn, control through fear, intimidation, violence, and reward. And so, in a way, the military enshrining itself in its military-crafted Constitution enshrined its power perpetuity? How genius. Right out of the play book for Orwell's *1984*.

TH: Pretty much, that's it.

AC: They act with impunity, and there's no retribution from the top, there's no rule of law to hold them accountable?

TH: Pretty much. That's why they're saying, "Hey, we don't have any known or published policy when it comes to intimidation and violence," but the policy is indirectly given out by these layers of control and reinforcement is done discreetly. Also, there's no retribution from the top, since each layer is operating within its own sets of "rule of law" where each individual commander sets his own rules and policies that will mostly benefit themselves. Of course, at the same time, they are the ones who enforce and judge those rules or laws.

We talk about corruption, within the military. But corruption is also entrenched throughout the system, due to extreme greed—a fetish for money, wealth, power, and narcissistic-control, along with the intended disengagement between the psychology structural layers of domination and subservience.

This is also the very same structure that existed outside the military that lasted for over five decades. The system and structures were created intentionally and in such a way that the authoritarian regime could thrive and prosper from one top layer to the next top layer, generation after generation. In this way, successive dictatorships controlled and dictated how the people of Myanmar should think and behave.

AC: Big Brother needs to speak with the Buddha in between sessions with an existential psychotherapist. Talk about a complex tapestry to unravel and reweave. In other words, corruption is generational and ubiquitous throughout the country?

TH: Big time. If you want to get promoted, if you want to be assigned to those cherished areas where you can pretty much collect money and fees on just about everything and, furthermore, do whatever you want when you want it, and on your own terms, without any documentation, nor obeying any law, and without anybody questioning you, if you want to get those positions, you've got to pay a hell of lot of money to your own high commander or authority.

Even if you want to get a higher position, there's a certain level of training you have to go through, certificates you need. Even to get into those trainings you have to bribe through commanders and authorities. As *dāna* (generosity) is ubiquities throughout Myanmar's monasteries, bribery may well be as pervasive throughout society. Although, I'm not really sure how much of this stuff is still taking place within the military these days. But there is still some significant level of corruption and abuse of power being carried out in the country.

You can easily witness the behind-the-scenes-power-manipulations by mindfully observing the outcomes and consequences all around us. For example, you'll see people, especially relatives of high ranking officers and former military officials, starting multi-million dollar businesses, building shopping malls, private hospitals and other construction projects, such as roads and bridges, along with export/import companies, telecommunication companies, and the like, within days or a few weeks, without any prior experience or investment. These activities and behaviours were quite obvious right before the military officially stepped aside in 2011, and somewhat less obvious in early 2016 after the NLD won the landslide elections in late 2015. Regardless, you see them happening all the time.

AC: So, the idea of national reconciliation in this country that Daw Suu and the government put forth, even if there was constitutional law that gave the civilian government control of the military, it sounds like there's too many heads of the dragon to control. Asking the obvious here: dictatorship has gone national—the military mindset is everywhere?

TH: Well, yes and no. Due to the transition, what I described earlier in terms of how the military controls and runs the country is gradually changing, I think. Now you see regional commanders with less authority, and a lot of trade between borders has become more visible and legalised. So, they have less room to exercise their unchecked authority.

AC: That's a positive change that you are seeing in Myanmar?

TH: Yes. I think we'll gradually see a new generation coming into the military who will realise, "Ok, we have nothing. Things are opening up. We have not much to benefit from the old ways, so we must focus on the new way—that of professionalising our lives in the military and doing what a dignified army set out to do under Bogyoke Aung San (the founder of Burma's Army and Aung San Suu Kyi's father), that of protecting the country and the people and not attacking innocent people and looting the country," that sort of thing. I think that long awaited attitude will develop as this transition keeps moving forward.

AC: And do we know the relationship between Snr. Gen. Min Aung Hlaing and the regional commander in Rakhine State who is responsible for the so-called ethnic cleansing?

TH: I think the military is not structured and setup to take actions and conduct inquiries by themselves effectively, or on their own, due to the multi-layer top-down organizational structure I mentioned earlier. So, even if those atrocities had taken place in western Rakhine State, the commander is pretty much fully in charge of the region with very little or no direct supervision, reporting or direction from the higher authority or command.

Even if you managed to realize or discover the underneath layers, in this case, in the upward layers, it would be challenging to find hard evidence or concrete links to the higher authority and command.

When I spoke of military corruption, you're not going to find evidence that these commanders are involved. But people who deal with these bribes and corruptions are directly linked with them. It could be their family members—sons, daughters, wives, close relatives and friends; and be sure of it, military wives are very powerful in Myanmar and play significant role in coordinating and executing these kind of deals and arrangements to benefit themselves and their close circle of family members and cronies.

AC: The corruption before wasn't nearly as bad as it is under Than Shwe?

TH: Exactly. Much worse and quite obvious during the military time when the entire country was locked up and disconnected from the international community. That's when Sr. Gen. Than Shwe's wife was pretty much one of the most powerful people in Burma, back in the day. She still has a lot of influence, especially over the cronies that they've manufactured during their military reign.

These same people and cronies who benefited enormously back in the military time are still dominating and manipulating today significant parts of the economy and socio-economic prospects in Myanmar. They still own and manage multi-sector businesses and companies in Myanmar, and somehow managed to influence the NLD government not to open up major economic sectors, especially the ones that they've been involved, to outside competitions. Particularly in banking, oil and gas, airlines, energy, gems, and import/export sectors. That's where they're most active. Since a hand-full of cronies and their close circle of connected people are dominating the market, it's convenient to coordinate the flow of goods, prices, and services in the country. Which in turn affects the quality of services and products along with pricing, since there's no significant competition or available choices. So, at the end of a day, the ordinary people of Myanmar ended up paying higher prices for low-quality consumer goods, foods, and services. All the while, jobs and wages are extremely low.

As I said earlier, prices are so high compared to the wages that ordinary people have to spend their entire daily earnings on foods and essential goods in order to just get by.

In this situation, people become more vulnerable and willing to take on risky activities to get through the day, since the majority are already living on an edge.

This situation will easily turn into chaos and instability in society that could further hinder or even derail our historic transition in Myanmar. So, corruption is not only bad for short-term prospects, it could completely alter the country's future, that is, if we let it go unchecked.

AC: You painted earlier a vivid picture of how Myanmar is controlled primarily by the military and how they have carefully cultivated a culture of reward and corruption, as way of controlling regional commanders and their subordinates. But, now, corruption runs through the family system—through the wife, children, and relatives—and further into big business and the cronies, the elite few who own the resources, oil and gas, the gems, the trees, the highways, the banks and so on. Enshrining the military is enshrining the economy—goods and services and the money supply—as well as the army and their weapons, and therefore enshrining the use of surveillance and violence and the courts and judges on their terms; the whole of Burma is controlled and manipulated by the military.

Am I accurate?

TH: That's pretty much what's happening right now. Resources and assets acquired through cronyism and corruption are solidly in the hands of family members and relatives that protect and preserve those assets and privileges by any means necessary, and for as long as they can.

AC: In addition, we have a parallel government to the military and their cronies called the NLD government, led by the president and State Counsellor, Daw Aung San Suu Kyi. This 'elected by the people civilian government' has minimal power but it's far better than what it was when she was under house arrest and her colleagues in prison. And they're making incremental, miniature changes, correct? In other words, that's where we are to find hope in this historic transformation from dictatorship to the first light of democracy?

TH: Yes. You're right. We are far better off right now than we were a few years ago under the military regime. However, there are times when I wonder what would have happened if Daw Suu and the NLD had decided not to cooperate with the military, and continued to fight for their initial demands (the so-called Shwe-Gone-Daing Demands) and compelled the military regime to honour the 1990 election results. Perhaps violent clashes and bloodshed would occur for a short period, until we will have achieved total regime change.

But now, this historic transition—chock full of uncertainties, scepticisms, risks, and challenges, along with the military's unwillingness to completely let go of the power—could go on for a long, long time.

But hope is still alive.

Incremental small changes are all we have at the moment.

On that note, I sincerely hope this transition yields a peaceful and prosperous federal democratic system for everyone in Myanmar, including the military and their cronies. Moreover, we owe it to the children and their children to work as hard as we can towards unity among all people in Myanmar.

AC: May it be so, and without violence.

TH: But you know, even with these incremental changes—we are facing significant resistance these days. Any changes to policies and laws that alter the existing social and economic ownership hierarchy are instantly faced with a brick wall.

Why? High ranking officials, both current and former ones, and their family members, along with their close relatives, continue to be deeply involved in many sectors of the economy. No changes seem possible, even small ones.

Frankly speaking, we're not sure if the NLD government has the wisdom and courage to overcome these obstacles at this point. Time will tell. I guess this will be the only measure for us to assess how long this transition toward a democratic society will go on. It could go on for decades and even so, we wonder if it will be genuine democracy.

AC: A basic question: How do you define the meaning of a crony here in Burma?

TH: Cronies are individuals who get special permissions and opportunities to exploit, control, and sell off the country's resources or to establish companies and businesses to import/export restricted goods and services through their close relationships with high-ranking military officials and authorities for mutual benefits.

Back in the day, our country was locked up and isolated. Perhaps the most restricted or closed country in the world. During this time, cronies became rich by, for example, importing cars from outside the country, which is not allowed without an official permit. So, if you're a wealthy person, you want to buy a nice car, you need to have that essential piece of paper to import/buy the car that you want. To get this document, you'd need a signature of the minister or high-ranking official who is in charge of the import/export sector, and most of the time who was also a member of the military.

So, what do you do? You negotiate or pay his sons or daughters or whoever is close to them, to get that signature/permit. That permit to import a car could be worth $100,000 or more, depending on what kind of vehicle you want to import. So you pay that sum to those who're close to the official or a crony to get the paper.

Think about it. You've just given $100,000 to your son or daughter or close friend or crony, just by signing a piece of paper. That piece of paper is sold to those cronies or individuals, and they turn around and import the car or cars with that document. They then sell it back to those who want to buy it or keep it for themselves. It normally costs $40,000 to $50,000 USD for a new Land Cruiser or SUV—a four-wheel drive that will set you back around $300,000 USD in Myanmar.

So you can imagine how rich they became in a flash. This is the life of the privileged in Myanmar. The life of a crony. And this is small money compared to the cronies in oil and gas, construction, banking, telecommunications, weapons, and so on.

At present, the core group of cronies are in the process of legalizing all this black money and assets that they've illegitimately acquired during the military time through their current multi-sector businesses and companies. They have also figured out ways to avoid paying taxes along the process.

I guess you could also argue this is the way it works all over the world.

AC: Yes, and ten million times more lucrative in most places in the West.

Chinese President Xi Jinping is presently in Myanmar for a two-day state visit. As you know, he's the first Chinese president to visit Burma, their southern neighbor, in nearly two decades. Apparently, the two countries will sign several MOUs (memorandums of understanding) on key projects under the China-Myanmar Economic Corridor (CMEC), which is part of the Belt and Road Initiative (BRI), Beijing's massive infrastructure plan for the region.

Before I ask my question, I found out that President Xi and his delegation will stay at the Horizon Lakeview Hotel in Naypyitaw. What I discovered is that the Lakeview Resorts consortium is owned by Myanmar-based Asia World Company (AWC).

Digging deeper, and no doubt you know all this, AWC is the largest corporate conglomerate in Myanmar, responsible for the new international airports in Yangon and the capital, along with most major roads and highways, in addition to deep sea ports, power plants, gas and oil concessions, and telecommunication, the likes of which is a near total monopoly on big business in Burma.

Of course, one instantly thinks "crony," and favoritism from the military.

Searching deeper I found was that AWC's chairman was Htun Myint Naing.

Still further, I found out that Htun Myint Naing is a pseudonym for Tun Myint Nain and that's a second tier pseudonym for the third tier pseudonym, Lo Ping Zhong, who is actually Steven Law, the son of Lo Hsing Han, and the most notorious drug trafficker in Burma, along with a worldwide drug trafficking syndication that rivals the Taliban's global opium and heroin trade. It's no wonder that Mr Law—the owner of the Lakeview Hotel where China's President will stay—is considered to be the wealthiest person in Myanmar.

In this final part of my introduction to my question, I further discovered that Steven Law's father, Lo Hsing Han, started his opium-trafficking career as chief of a local militia in Burma called Ka Kwe Ye (KKY), which was established with the encouragement of Burma's former dictator Ne Win to fight the Communists. By the early 1970s it's said that he was one of the most important figures in the Asian drug trade. When the Kokang and

Wa insurgent troops in Myanmar mutinied and toppled the Communist leadership in 1989, Burma's notorious chief of military intelligence, Khin Nyunt, found in Lo Hsing Han a useful intermediary to insurgent groups and bestowed upon him lucrative business opportunities, and with it, unofficial permission to run drugs with impunity.

In June 1992, Lo Hsing Han founded the Asia World Company, allegedly as a front for his drug operations. His son, Steven Law (aka Htun Myint Naing & Tun Myint Naing), now runs the company. Among its projects is the Sino-Burma oil and gas pipeline project running into China from the Bay of Bengal off the coast of Rakhine State, along with a deep sea port at nearby Kyaukpyu, as well as the massive Myitsone hydro-power plant and the Tasang hydro-power plant. All companies that the Chinese government have investments in.

My point: Clearly Mr. Lo and his son, Steven Law, were two of the military dictatorship's most important business partners, with their primary source of wealth coming from drug trafficking. Let that point speak for itself, but my question: Is it possible that much of the Muslim/Burma military crisis in Rakhine, that Aung San Suu Kyi has taken much of the fall for, was intentionally created to obscure the deeper issue, that of securing oil and gas income for Burma's military and their cronies with China's endless need for consumption? In addition, is it not likely that Burma will become the second Tibet, not officially, but unofficially?

Would you please shed as much light on these issues as you wish?

TH: Well, I believe China's interest in Myanmar goes way back to the cold war, with the country becoming a much more strategic neighbor in recent years due to its unique location with access to both the Indian Ocean and South Each Asia market. In addition, China undoubtedly has a major interest in our rich natural resources, particularly oil and gas, as you mentioned.

Regarding this oil and gas sector: it has been extensively exploited throughout successive military regimes and benefited largely their relatives, close friends, and cronies, especially Mr. Steven Law and his AWC (Asia World Company). As you've mentioned, these military-connected-cronies and their cooperation with the military elite goes beyond our recent military regime, which was led by Sr. General Than Shwe. And they are the ones that have been pretty much selling off the country's natural resources for their own benefit and doing it for decades.

Meanwhile, the recent Rakhine crisis is causing some uncertainty for China's initiatives in Myanmar due to the local and international community closely monitoring the crisis as well as development in the state, especially in the northern part of Rakhine.

Overall, the extreme pressure on Myanmar of recent time by the international community to resolve the Rohingya issue in Rakhine State is making Myanmar form a much closer alliance with China, which of course benefits both countries. In this instance, China will most likely come out as the big winner, sooner or later.

China's interest in Myanmar is a long-term ambition, with construction of the deep seaport in Kitakyushu town which is located in the southern part of Rakhine state. In addition, China's building of oil & gas pipelines and a rail track from Kitakyushu to Kunming in southern China, along with development of the Special Economic Zone in Rakhine State (SEZ), are both part of President Xi's large scale Belt and Road Initiative (BRI) that involves about 70 countries around the world. It's a mega-vision and Myanmar plays a significant role in its realization.

Essentially, both the deep seaport and SEZ projects provide China with direct access to the Indian Ocean where imported oil from the Middle East and gas from Myanmar will be sent to China without going through the Strait of Malacca and the security-heavy (with its large US Navy presence and military activity) South China Sea.

So, it seems that the oil and gas sector will continue to expand in Myanmar and major money, wealth, and power will continue to be realized for those stake holders who already have controlled the sector, particularly for the elite cronies and those close to the former military regime.

As for Burma becoming the next Tibet: with Mandalay nearly 80 percent Chinese and growing, and with this direct long distance oil and gas pipeline into China along with sharing a long porous border with the country, well, of the 33 divisions and provinces in China, the top ten are as large as Myanmar and some of them are nearly double the population of our 55,000,000 people. With that said, I guess, will Burma become the next Tibet? Well, anything is possible. Meanwhile, let's call Myanmar a big gas and oil supplier of China, a bit like Saudi Arabia is to the US. Something like that.

AC: A more noble topic: Say you had Daw Aung San Suu Kyi sitting here, and you also had the chief ministers of her democratic government sitting here with her. They want to hear from you. They want your honesty. They want to know what you felt were the grievances of the people, as well as your own perceptions of their shortcomings. Of course, this is not an exercise in venting. Rather, it's for the purpose of assessing your feedback—taking what's true and right and implementing those changes to the best of their ability. What would you share?

TH: Let me answer this way: When you're talking about people, there are two layers coming out of this transition. You have the majority group, ordinary people or struggling class. Then there's another group or minority of individuals benefiting from the transition. You see this minority group's spending power increasing: they are going to nice restaurants, buying nice homes, clothes, and cars, et cetera. You see this even though it's a miniscule percentage of people who can afford such things. Those folks are the one's prospering from the transition.

If I could speak not for them, but for the majority, especially those people who voted NLD—those poor, underprivileged, uneducated people—I would say that when they voted NLD and for Daw Suu, they didn't know much about the political system; they didn't know much about the Constitution; nor did they know much of anything.

All they knew was that they trusted Daw Suu and the NLD.

They believed that Daw Suu would do the right thing. They had faith that she would bring them out misery and poverty and all such sufferings. That's the only reason they voted for the NLD and Daw Suu.

They didn't know much more than that. Again, they didn't know much about the Constitution or how the government works, or what sort of challenges they would be faced with politically. That was far, far away from them.

Now, what I've seen and what they've seen, is that inflation is going up and up. They have also seen the trade deficit going up and up. The prices of basic goods and foods going up and up. And equally, the people cannot find jobs.

In addition, the education system is still in a dysfunctional state and unable to provide a favourable outcome for people to make a living out of their education. The healthcare system is also dysfunctional. When you put these realities together, it's not a pretty picture.

These same people who voted for the NLD and Daw Suu could easily turn around and come out onto the streets and start demanding these basic things from the same government they voted for. That could very likely be one of the possible scenarios if we continue down this current path. As I said, when you put these harsh realities together, it's not pretty.

These are serious issues that we should be thinking about.

When you talk about Daw Suu and Ministers sitting here with us, I think for The Lady and the government, for them to take this country and these people to where they hope and where they need to be, it's not an easy task.

Firstly, you need to have the right people. That means not only people with experience and education but people who can connect to these ordinary people, understand the struggles and the challenges they're facing daily. I believe these people need to have not only compassion but a lot more... how to say it? I don't want to bring in religion and Buddhism here, but I wonder how to incorporate these people, how to bridge with the other side, which is the military and those folks who are out there. That is going to be the most significant challenge. Without being able to build trust with them, without being able to make them feel safe and secure—those are the very qualities that will determine how fast we reach a full democratic society.

Without that, no question—we will not get there, because they're the ones holding a big chunk of the power in this country. We must honour and support them.

AC: To heed your vision, what is needed?

TH: There are two parts the government should consider. One is to build their own capacity and make the best out of the ministries—the part of government they have control over. For example, education, healthcare, transportation, communications, and trade. These areas need people with skills and experience. They must also have commitment and good intentions. That part, we have those people. The first step is that needs to be changed—I'm not saying that none of them have these skills. Some of them may have them but most, as far as I know, don't have the skills required to run their own division or even their own sector. That's the first step that must take place and it needs to take place immediately, or as soon as possible.

The second step is more critical, because you need to move beyond your technical skills and experiences. You need to connect and make the other side feel safe—that they are family. As in, if we go along together, it's going to be ok.

To do that, they themselves need to be content. They themselves need to see beyond their own ego and self-interests. This requires going beyond themselves. They need to empower caring as a way of being.

If I had an open opportunity to speak to Daw Suu and the Ministers, I would advocate those two things.

On top of that, within their time in government, things are not going to be completed. We need to bring up and train the next generation of leaders to take over. This must happen soon. We only have a little over three years left. If the NLD government gets re-elected in 2020 elections, then we will have a little bit longer to train our next generation leaders.

I'm not sure to what extent the training of future leaders is taking place. But, as far as we can tell, we are not seeing much of it. Rather, we're seeing the same old-minded people with closed minds. Seeing that tells us that the next generation of leaders is not be taking place as much as it should be.

Those three things must happen.

The first thing is to get the right people in the right places, because even if you get the right people in the right places they're still going to face many challenges due to the military mind set from the last five decades of dictatorship still in place. The leaders of those regions and ministries have to be on top of not only their own technical skills, they need a serious understanding of how to transition people already in the system, because we cannot leave them behind. We cannot just change the entire ministry or department. These folks were born into the system, grew up in it, always waiting for someone to tell them what to do. There's no accountability. There's no responsibility taking place.

AC: How do you create an environment so that people will be accountable for their own actions, for their own duties and responsibilities, and also be rewarded and provide positive reinforcement according to those contributions and skills and also their accomplishments?

TH: That is another underlying system that every ministry and every regional government needs to work on. So, changing the leadership, and then leadership also needs to understand how to change those who are already within the system. These are competing priorities.

At the same time, you need to connect with the people and be able to provide their basic needs—education, health, and that sort of thing. Not only that, you must stay close with those under your department or ministry. You must bring them together. You must care and be skilful.

You also need technical skills when working with the internationals and other partners, including ministries and other supporters.

You also need to be aware of the other side of the government, the other parallel government.

These are some of the competing challenges that the NLD government faces.

Alarmingly, I don't think they are aware of them nor understand how all these issues and challenges are interconnected. I don't think even The Lady herself thought this through. I'm not questioning her ability, because if she did, we would probably see a different environment in the government and outcomes.

AC: Myanmar is in the international news, in part, based on the Kofi Annan Commission's report, when, shortly after its release, 30 military checkpoints and police stations were simultaneously attacked by ARSA (the Arakan Rohingya Salvation Army). Oddly, the media focused not on ARSA's terrorist attacks, but on the so-called disproportional response by Burma's military forces, that led the United Nations to condemn what they perceived as "ethnic cleansing." Of course, the region saw a massive exodus of Bengali/Rohingyas into neighboring Bangladesh, with many of the traumatized speaking of rape and other such horrors.

Meanwhile, throughout these months, certain people have condemned Daw Suu—one of them being Desmond Tutu, her fellow Nobel Laureate, and even the Dalai Lama weighed in. Then we have Bob Geldof who referred to her as a "handmaiden of genocide." Bono of U2, once a die-hard supporter, called on her in a *Rolling Stone* magazine interview to resign.

Essentially, she's being vilified for having failed, as they see it, in her role as a being of moral conscience who was awarded the highest human rights awards for her courageous nonviolent activism. They feel she should have used her power and position as Myanmar's Sate Counsellor to speak up about the atrocities committed by Burma's army to the Rohingyas.

I'm putting this out so that an international reader unfamiliar with the crisis can understand the framing of the question.

You're on the ground here in Burma, and you're living in the capital city most of the time. You know many of the principle players in government. You are also a long-time friend of Daw Aung San Suu Kyi and have attended meetings with her. You're influential and connected.

Please help us understand the appropriate response to this criticism.

Could Daw Suu have done more?

And if so, what could she have done that she didn't do?

What should we understand?

And how does your answer configure with her slow and arduous approach to national reconciliation, her primary stated aim for the country?

TH: I don't think the picture is as clear or black and white. The crisis has many narratives and many causes and many layers. That's the first challenge.

The international media is not going to dissect and present the complexity of intersecting issues to the international community.

Overall, the international media is sensationalised. They try to make things sexy by oversimplifying the issues. This is pretty much standard for anywhere, not just in Burma with the Rakhine crisis.

If you look at the crisis in Africa or crisis situations in other countries, that's what they do, especially because they're targeting Westerners who are far removed and disconnected. Those readers don't even have enough time or interest to understand what the true causes are, or what's really happening. For them it's just, "Ok, people are killing people, people are dying, who has a gun, who doesn't have a gun, who is innocent?" That's it. "Ok, donate some money or read some more stories," sympathize and move on with their capitalist world life. That's what I witnessed in the US for the 25 years I lived there. Right?

You come home and you only get an hour or two to watch TV, two hours before you go to sleep, wake up the next day, do the same thing, right? So, the international community, the international media, that's what they're feeding people.

I'm not concerned about what they write and what they miss.

I think Daw Suu feels the same way.

That's why she doesn't pay much attention to the media, especially the international ones.

These individuals, even Nobel laureates and other celebrities reacting to those bits and pieces of news coming out of Myanmar, either look deeper and learn the facts or keep their heads buried. The same with all the so called well respected international news channels and even some NGOs and dot orgs. So much political correctness, misinformation, uncorroborated allegations, and, no doubt, driven by a hunger for ad and donor dollars. They're unprofessional. If they were doctors, we would call it malpractice.

Take the piece by Reverend Desmond Tutu. I read his article. He's obviously disconnected and has no real understanding of what's going on. He even accused The Lady of being hungry for power and the highest position, which really shows he's clueless and rude as well. She's the one holding the highest position in this country, in terms of the civilian side. The president is a figurehead of the state. Even the former dictator knows that. But Tutu didn't. So, when you read these articles and news you can see clearly how little they understand the situation inside Myanmar.

I don't think we should waste time trying to understand what these people are saying. They're just reacting. They're public figures. If the majority of the public feels this is what's happening, and they are somehow drawn into that same reaction, well, so be it. But I have no sympathy for shallowness. That's my take on that side.

By the way, you may know this, when Bono of U2 wrote the song "Walk On" about Daw Aung San Suu Kyi, it won the Grammy Award for Record of the Year in 2000. At the awards ceremony, Bono never even mentioned her name, although she was under house arrest at the time and the prisons were filled with political prisoners. Did he use her name for profit? If so, maybe he should resign.

AC: If I may, what's your take on the accusation of "ethnic cleansing"?

TH: Clearly, when you see 750,000 people coming out of a country or region, you don't have to ask a fortune teller what the hell is happening. Something serious is going down. Otherwise, why would these people flee without anything, right? So, what's happening within is no question. And that 'something' must be stopped and prevented from happening. Whether they are Rohingya or Bengali, whatever they believe in, whatever the colour of their skin, that's something that we need to deal with immediately and effectively. They must be protected.

AC: The situation reflects a catastrophic failure of government.

TH: But, when you say "government," which government? We talked about it earlier, who is in control, who is causing the mass exodus of these people? How much of the civilian government has control of those regions? Clearly, they don't have much control, as far as we know.

But, we knew that nationalist groups, even some nationalist monks, were involved. We know the military is involved in region clearance operations. We knew that.

But these accusations are evidence based, right?

That part is the responsibility of the government.

But, you have the chief minister of the region—in the beginning, even the minister couldn't travel to these regions. The military wouldn't allow them due to security reasons. The military is not able to prove any security, not even providing transportation.

It's a horrible mess.

AC: And the reason for that?

TH: They said it's not safe to go there. The civilian government had to sit and wait until the military said, "Ok, we'll take you there."

These are things the international community didn't know or understand.

Even with the distribution of food—it's not possible for the civilian government.

AC: And regarding Daw Suu?

TH: I think she could have done more. Because she could just come out and speak on behalf of basic human rights and basic protection without causing trouble or accusations or bringing an even harder edge from the other side.

She could have said, "Look people, these are our fellow human beings, regardless of whether they crossed the border or were brought in by the British, or were born here. They have been with us for generations. They live in our country. Let's embrace them. Protect them. Shelter them. Feed them. Care for them. Above all, let no harm come to them."

I was expecting that sort of message from The Lady.

AC: Previously you painted a clear picture—correct me if I'm wrong—that regional or divisional commanders don't report to their seniors or even let their intentions be known.

Maybe Daw Suu had no real idea what was going on, right? Or maybe she was being told misinformation by the military. Or nothing at all. U Win Htein told me they're never informed about anything from the military about the military. A complete black out. Or maybe her only source of "news," right or wrong, is from the international media—the New York Times, Guardian, CNN, the BBC, etc. And even so, it's given to her in briefings, as she's unthinkably busy.

I'm not trying to make excuses for her. I'm just trying to piece this complex puzzle together as well as provide a definitive historical record for generations to come. And yes, I stand by Aung San Suu Kyi. All three of us—you and her and me—share the same *Dhamma* teacher. As you know, Sayadaw U Pandita was a moral giant with a radical courage and a depth of mindful intelligence. She's a highly ethical being. She's mindful to a fault.

TH: I agree. She's highly ethical, courageous, and disciplined, and in a complicated position. And you're right: in a way she's being kept in the dark by the military, because, as U Win Htein told you, there's no internal reporting or briefings taking place.

The truth is, Daw Suu has spoken out repeatedly about the crimes and atrocities, not only in Rakhine but nationwide. But the international community expected to hear more and wants her to take significant actions against the perpetrator, which is impossible at this stage.

As you know, everyone close to her over the decades spent many years as political prisoner and many of them were severely tortured. You also know, her very own legal advisor working with her in the capital—the Muslim lawyer from Rakhine, U Ko Ni—was recently assassinated at the Yangon International Airport in a plot said to involve ex-military officers. In other words, she knows the meaning of crimes against humanity. She knows full well the meaning of human rights abuses.

But the media, especially the international media, only picked up on what they wanted in Rakhine and only that that which supports their claim and storyline. The media's job is to make it simple and sexy—sensationalizing and simplifying these decades-long conflicts is what they do best.

Look at other areas of crisis—Sudan, Rwanda, Syria, the Middle East, Yemin, etc. Most people in the West have no idea where these places are located on a map, much less their histories, politics, and causes of crisis.

Outside of the few, they have no interest to understand the layers of the issue, since these crises have very little or no impact on their comfortable and predictable lives in these well protected countries.

I do not mean to be critical but many people in the world and especially in the West are not only ignorant of the world but misinformed based on the prevailing mainstream propaganda. They see a few seconds or perhaps a minute or so of an atrocity taking place on their TV screen, and then the media provides their own story and bias on who's right and who's wrong, who's good and who's bad, so that folks back in the West don't have to think too much about it.

Then, if moved, make a few quick and easy actions (call your senator, make a donation through a click, sign-up for online petition, post a rave on Facebook, etc.) to feel better about all these killings and atrocities. This will give a green light for politicians to make noise and speak out about it, mainly through the same media that created these sexy and sensationalized stories in the first place. Which is mainly to fulfil their voters' bias, or uninformed and unchecked wishes or wills. Then, the actions and consequences that come out of all this digital monkey business will turn into some kind of foreign policy changes, aid redistribution, withholding support and assistance, etc., and who gets weapons and trade favours and who doesn't.

AC: People seem to think she was in collusion with the military, with Senior General Min Aung Hlaing. Some called her a "puppet of the military."

TH: That's a false assumption. It's not accurate.

AC: Would you explain why that's not so?

TH: Because those events taking place on the ground are not even directly connected or orchestrated by the regional level, even at the union level. As far as we know the union level is not giving direct commands to the commander in charge of the region.

AC: It goes back to the psychology of how power is structured in the military?

TH: Yes. They won't question. They won't say, "Kill them or get them out." No. These are localised decisions and actions that got out of control.

AC: Sub-units that are not held accountable to higher authorities?

TH: Yeah. They just have to handle any incident based on their own convictions, understanding, and capacity, their own personal biases, and, of course, protecting self-interests as well. That's how it happened in Rakhine, and the crisis quickly got out of control. By the time it reached the international community and even to the highest authority in Myanmar, it was too late. They can't just come in and take action—even for them to take action it's going to be very challenging to gather and collect sufficient evidence and conduct interviews.

Also, the military doesn't have an independent and authorized investigative system or culture. Top command gets incident/fight reports compiled and edited by local commanders.

As I explained earlier, all roads lead back to the layered-matrix military-driven authoritarian structure. So, there is little or no room to hold anyone accountable for committing atrocities. And there will be no significant actions taken by the higher commands or authorities. If they do, it'll end up destroying the structure and everyone will end up in a bad situation. So they'll never let this happen, not in their life time.

That's why no one will say anything damaging nor tell the truth. I believe this is exactly what happened at Eindin village with the killing of 10 Rohingyas or Bengalis by the military sub-unit (about 10 or 15 soldiers and one captain).

Remember, things happened quickly on the ground. You had 4- to 5,000 Rohingyas wielding machetes with many other home-made weapons surround a village and government school. Inside were 200 local Rakhine people and Buddhist monks holding out without weapons or any means to defend themselves. So, the local army commander made a decision to execute the 10 captured Rohingya militants in order to free up the soldiers guarding the captives. This way the soldiers could get out to disperse the angry mob outside the village and drive them away.

The incident immediately escalated right up to the local command and that was it as far as they concerned. Of course, that is, until the international media got hold of the photographs of the killing.

Of course, it's tragically sad this happened in Rakhine. That changed everything. These people once lived side-by-side and their children studied at the same schools. Teachers taught safely to everyone regardless of who they were and where they were from.

Things are different now, sadly.

AC: A tapestry of violence, without a clear starting point; *Saṃsāra*.

In political terms, from your own insider's point of view—all sides are to be blamed? All sides are responsible? All could have done more to de-escalate the madness? Meanwhile, innocent people are uprooted and traumatized, all based on ignorance, greed and violence.

TH: You could say that. But I don't think they have acceptable accountability or a sufficient record of hard evidence of whom came and on what day, or who did what.

What we do know is that Muslim militants—ARSA—staged a coordinated attack on 30 police posts and an army base in Rakhine, and at least 59 of the insurgents and 12 members of the security forces were killed. We also know that the head of ARSA said more attacks would be forthcoming. No free country in the world would tolerate such terrorism.

With that said, as explained earlier, it's a complex situation.

Regardless, I'm sure soldiers at a local level or sub-unit level knew exactly what happened in Rakhine and how it happened, and who did what. On the other hand, it'll be challenging or perhaps even impossible to identify the perpetrators who were torching villages, killing innocent people, burning them, and doing all these atrocities during the crisis, when they were not wearing any uniform or identifiable clothing.

AC: And all these multiple reports on the Burmese/Bangladesh border of women who talk of being raped and gang-raped—can you imagine that happening with Burmese soldiers?

TH: Well, according to various UN and other rights reports, they have done it before, in other states and in other ethnic areas—in Shan and Karen areas.

AC: These Burmese Buddhist boys gang-rape a girl on the ground of her hut or in an open field?

TH: Not all military personnel, especially soldiers, are Buddhist.

Also, the military shoots and kills anyone that they wish to shoot and kill.

As you know, they've killed our Buddhist monks and students in the past.

I'm not sure how these things took place, but it's got to be some sort of ignorance and pressure placed on them. They could be ordered by their own group, whoever's in charge of the group or division says, "Ok, let's just do this," and that was it.

That individual in charge of the group or division may or may not have a direct command, and the instruction may not come from his bosses—it could be his own personal decision or personal conviction, or personal anger or ignorance—but when it comes down to the lowest level of the military they may not have any other choice.

They probably don't even want to commit these crimes or atrocities. Most likely, I think, they are forced or pressured to do this, forced by their superiors and by their own ignorance or even by the rapidly intense and dangerous situation on the ground.

Perhaps some of them might even believe that "these are the people that we must drive out, because they are invading our land, they're destroying our religion and traditions, they're destroying our people."

AC: They would be indoctrinated with supremacist propaganda?

TH: They've got to be, otherwise normal human nature won't do this. They've got to have some sort of serious influences in their practise.

Also, keep in mind that Myanmar is a poor country with an inadequate education system, so most people lack critical thinking skills and exposure to the outside world. In this environment, indoctrination and propaganda are common and easy to seed.

AC: Apparently, ARSA has roots to Pakistan and links to foreign extremist groups. But before I get into my next questions about Islamic terrorism in Myanmar, I brought a copy of Bertil Linter's recent article in Asia Times that I'd like to read for the record, so readers of this book get a thorough look into the role of ARSA, by Bertil, one of the finest investigative journalists in the world, titled, "The truth behind Myanmar's Rohingya insurgency." He writes, "While Myanmar's emergent Arakan Rohingya Salvation Army (ARSA) claims it's like other ethnic armed groups fighting for self-determination across the country and should not be branded as a terrorist organization, the realities on the ground tell a different tale.

"ARSA represents an entirely new type of insurgency, one which the Myanmar military has demonstrated it is wholly ill-equipped to combat. Other ethnic resistance armies in Myanmar, such as those from the Kachin, Shan, Karen or Mon, dress in military uniforms with the names of their respective groups prominently displayed and badges showing their ranks.

"ARSA's Muslim fighters, by contrast, mingle with villagers and wear civilian clothes. After their low-grade attacks on security force targets, ARSA insurgents are known to retreat across the border to neighboring Bangladesh, where people speak the same language and adhere to the same religious beliefs. In that sense, ARSA's tactics more resemble the Muslim insurgents in southernmost Thailand, adjacent to Malaysia, than Myanmar's other ethnic armies.

"Without sharing the ideological doctrines of Nepal's and India's Maoists, ARSA appears to have aped their fighting techniques. Rather than facing Myanmar's army in battles and ambushes, ARSA, like Nepalese Maoist insurgents did when they were active and the Indian Naxalites do today, prefers to mobilize hundreds of unarmed villagers to attack state positions in the middle of the night.

"Defenders of the targeted state outpost, usually small and isolated, get the impression that they are being surrounded by a much bigger fighting force. The relatively small attacking party then moves in, kills the intimidated soldiers or police and escapes with their weapons. It's a style of attack familiar in South Asia but altogether foreign until now in Myanmar.

"While ARSA's military capacities are limited—with the total number of active trained combatants likely not exceeding 500—its propaganda machine is wide-reaching, with statements issued on Twitter and other social media platforms in surprisingly fluent English and in a language that aims to make the insurgent group appear moderate and reasonable.

"In one of its first announcements on September 9, ARSA declared a month-long unilateral ceasefire to enable aid groups to reach Rohingya refugees and avert a full-blown humanitarian crisis. Aid groups have estimated over 400,000 Rohingya have fled Myanmar for Bangladesh since ARSA's August 25 attacks and the military's brutal counteractions.

"It was a bold declaration for a lightly armed group that is by no means a proper organized army. Many of the group's attacks have been launched with machetes. At the same time, ARSA has failed to explain how attacks by their few and poorly equipped cadres facing the might of the Myanmar army could be seen as acts taken to "protect the Rohingya."

"If reports from the area received by Asia Times are accurate, local people are furious with ARSA for giving the Myanmar military an excuse to "ethnically cleanse" the area of Rohingya and other minority groups.

"On September 14th, ARSA said it wanted to "make it clear" that it had no "links to Al Qaeda, the Islamic State in Iraq and Syria, Lashkar-e-Taiba or any transnational terrorist group." ARSA also wanted "it to be known by all states that it is prepared to work with security agencies to intercept and prevent terrorists from entering [Rakhine] and making a bad situation worse."

"Security analysts and terrorism experts are not convinced considering the group's clear links to foreign extremist groups, including in Pakistan. ARSA's leader, Ataullah abu Ammar Junjuni, also known as Hafiz Tohar, was born in Karachi and received madrassa education in Saudi Arabia.

"There are hundreds of thousands of first, second and third generation Rohingya living in Orangi, Korangi, Landhi and other impoverished suburbs of Karachi. Nearly all of them are stateless, although they have lived in Pakistan for years and most by now were born there. The areas where they live are long-time hotbeds of extremist activity, with some known to have been recruited to fight in the wars in Afghanistan.

"ARSA was initially known as Harakah al-Yaqin, or "the faith movement." The moniker had clear religious connotations and notably did not contain the words Rohingya or Arakan (Rakhine). It was only last year it started to use the more ethnically oriented name ARSA, perhaps in an attempt to distance itself from the radical milieu in which the movement was born.

"According to intelligence analysts, its mentor is Abdus Qadoos

Burmi, another Pakistani of Rohingya descent. Likewise based in Karachi, he has appeared in videos spread on social media calling for 'jihad' in Myanmar.

"Abdus Qadoos has well-documented links to Lashkar-e-Taiba, or the Army of the Righteous, one of South Asia's largest Islamic terrorist organizations that operates mainly from Pakistan. The group was founded in 1987 in Afghanistan with funding from now deceased Al Qaeda founder Osama bin Laden. Abdus Qadoos has even appeared in meetings together with Lashkar-e-Taiba supremo Hafiz Mohammed Syed.

"ARSA's second-ranking leader is a shadowy man known only as "Sharif" who comes from Chittagong in southwestern Bangladesh and does not appear in any of the group's propaganda videos. He reportedly speaks with an Urdu language accent, the official language of Pakistan.

"ARSA itself may have been able to recruit angry and desperate young men among the Rohingya in Rakhine state and refugee camps in Bangladesh, but, according to security analysts, there are also 150-odd foreigners among their rank.

"Most of them are from Bangladesh, eight to ten come from Pakistan with smaller groups from Indonesia, Malaysia and southern Thailand. Two are reportedly from Uzbekistan. Trainings held in the Myanmar-Bangladesh border areas have been carried out in part by older veterans of the Afghan wars, the security analysts say.

"It is now clear that the simultaneous attacks on August 25th required meticulous planning. In the months before the attacks, as many as 50 people, Muslims as well as Buddhists suspected of serving as government informants, had their throats slit or were hacked to death in order to deprive the Myanmar military of intelligence in the area.

"The timing of the attacks was hardly a coincidence. On August 24th, the Advisory Commission on Rakhine state, chaired by former UN secretary general Kofi Annan and commissioned by the Myanmar government, released its report suggesting peaceful means to end the conflict in the area.

"Under the current chaotic and violent situation, it will be difficult to revive its proposals, leaving the road open for more destabilizing militant activities.

"Videos released by Islamist groups in Indonesia show groups of young men undergoing military training in Aceh, northern Sumatra, in preparation for a jihad in Rakhine state. Massive demonstrations in support of the Rohingya have been held throughout Bangladesh, where the influx of refugees has quickly become a domestic political issue pitting the ruling Awami League against a fundamentalist-backed opposition.

"Given the Myanmar military's ferocious reaction to ARSA's first clash with security forces last October 9th, an exchange and subsequent "clearance operation" which forced as many as 70,000 refugees into Bangladesh, analysts consider it inconceivable that the group did not anticipate an even stronger response to the more widespread attacks of August 25th.

"If the group's goal was to "protect the Rohingyas," as ARSA has claimed, its attacks backfired horribly. But the militants must have calculated the wider benefits that could be derived from the blowback. The international publicity surrounding the Rohingya's plight has been unprecedented, promising new and potentially lucrative support from the Arab and Muslim worlds and more angry young men to recruit.

"But the victims of this cynical game are the hundreds of thousands of Rohingya and others who have been forced from their destroyed homes and now languish in squalid camps in Bangladesh or the inhospitable no man's land along the two countries' increasingly hellish border."

My question, Tim: Talk to me, if you would, about Islamic terrorism in Myanmar. Is it a fear among the people? Is it inevitable? Do you fear jihad throughout Myanmar? What's the feeling in Naypyidaw today?

TH: From what you read, and I also know based on other facts, documents and evidence, ARSA has connections with other Islamic terrorist groups, and the influence of Islamist extremists is there.

In the past, they were unable to rise up because of the military's full control of the country, and you see the Arakan issue started right after the transition started, in 2011. The first incident of the woman raped and killed, when all this started—before that the word "Rohingya" was hardly used and even the Muslim population didn't identify themselves as Rohingyas.

But, all this changed dramatically after the first communal conflicts between ethnic Rakhines and Muslim Bengalis/Rohingyas, and got out of control when, as you just read, ARSA simultaneously attacked 30 border checkpoints on August 25th, 2017.

As we know, this was the day before Kofi Annan's report was announced, and in which they knew ahead that the word "Rohingya" was not going to be included. It seems that pretty much everything was planned out since the early days to reach this stage where we're facing many challenges and pressures from outside.

If you look at the northern part of Arakan, the crisis area, 90-95 percent of the population are Muslims or Bengalis. That is something the international community is responsible for and also why these extremist terrorist groups are very much active. Al Qaeda and other groups are very much interested. Some of those leaders, as you stated, trained in

Afghanistan and other Islamic countries. Of course, we have ample evidence of these things. They are the ones who pretty much recruit and then plan and attack, because now is a good time. The transition from military to civilian government, Myanmar's current situation, is the best time to do these sorts of things. This is the worst and weakest time of any country, especially with a parallel government.

This parallel government is also not really collaborating and or supporting each other. If your brothers and sisters are fighting against each other, it's much easier for the outsider to come and take advantage of it.

Yes, Islamic terrorism is a real threat in Myanmar.

It has already started, and look where we are now.

Oddly, no one reported it, other than a few investigative journalists, including Bertil and yourself.

AC: Myanmar is vulnerable to outside threats?

TH: It is. When you look at it before and ask why ARSA didn't stage [these attacks] before, why they didn't do extremist campaigns before, it's because they couldn't. The military was running the country. They knew they could be killed or arrested, and the international community would have nothing to say about it. They would have even celebrated it. Now, the media has opened up. This was smart of ARSA and clearly a carefully planned move.

AC: Why is the term "Rohingya" unacceptable to Arakanese and Burmans?

TH: The Burmans—the Burmese people—and Arakanese people are not accepting the word "Rohingya" because it's binary language. If you translate that word into Burmese, it simply means "Arakan people." So you have an ethnic group that already existed in this region called Rakhine, and at the same time another group with a different origin, different customs and traditions, a different appearance and different religion, also claiming the same ethnicity. When that happens, the existing group will fight for their identity and are not going to take people challenging it. It's like accepting it will wipe out their own existence, their own ethnicity.

This is the same as, let's say, how Caucasian is an ethnicity. If either Indians or Arabs come in with their own words in their own language saying, "Hey, *we* are Caucasian," what are you going to do if you're a Caucasian?

You're like, "No! You're not!" Right?

That's why the word Rohingya is not accepted.

I don't think it ever will be accepted, in this country.

That is something the international media has no idea of—what that means, what that translates as, or transpires to.

Sure, you could argue, every group has a right to call themselves whatever they want to call themselves. But if what they want to call themselves is something that's already there, then you're going to have some problems with existing groups or individuals.

That's no different in Western society or any other society. That's why we have patent laws in the Western world. If someone has already claimed their rights and properties, you can't then have another group come along and claim the same thing. Then we'd have a problem. This is what's happening, so there are many layers involved.

AC: Easy enough to understand, if explained properly. Although I do wonder if there are Rohingya who do not identity with being called Rohingya and would prefer the term 'Bengali.' Live and let live, right? A solution to misinformation?

TH: Regarding the international media and the international community: What I would like is for this NLD government to have a weekly or monthly briefing and or press conference to start sharing up-to-date on-the-ground issues, and explaining a bit of the history. We need to be much more transparent, skilful, and pro-active in dealing with this kind of significant issue. We must learn from the mistakes to improve communication, given what's happening with the international community and the media.

There's a clear lack of understanding of how public diplomacy is lacking in this government. They don't even have people who can speak English effectively. So, hire those who can. Provide them with talking points and clear guideline to communicate, especially with the international community.

These are the things we expected the NLD government to do, at the least, even though they don't have control over it. "Look, here is the situation, here is what we know, here is why we cannot accept these conditions and terms and names, here are the problems." And then break that up into layers, narratives and causes.

Yes, we have Muslims living there for generations—my great, great grandfather was a Muslim man. He came from the region that back in the day was Persia. He was a Muslim and converted to Bahai faith, then he married a lady from Thailand captured by the Burmese king in Mandalay. That's my part of the family. We know Muslims were there from the 5th or 6th century. But they were not called Rohingya. They were just Muslims. But they were Arakanese, living there, right?

Then you also have a migration problem, because I knew my uncle and aunt were immigration officers in charge of the region, back in 1970-something. We knew these people were given money and in return provided with National Identity Cards, because I knew who was there. That group needs to be dealt with separately.

Then you have an existing group brought in by the British.

So, we need to really lay out this strategy and plan, with sound evidence and solutions for each group. We can't lump them together and say, "let's deal with one solution." There's no magic solution to deal with the whole. You need to understand these different causes, layers, and narratives, and then formulate correct solutions for each. That's the only way we can do it.

To do that, the government of Myanmar, the NLD government, must have a strategy with experts, breaking up the people according to what is actually taking place, according to what happened in the past, and what needs to be done for the solution. Then, we must communicate that to the international community, the United Nations, everybody.

That would educate people willing to be educated.

It would also quiet the pressures.

"Two things are needed from the leadership to move this transition forward."

ALAN CLEMENTS: You mentioned the necessity of cultivating youth leaders for the future of democracy. How do you envision empowering new voices of freedom, new voices of democracy, and new political parties that emerge that further the foundation provided by the NLD and evolve into a more full and secure expression of democracy?

TIM HARDY: A while back I was having a one-to-one conversation with the education minister about reform, and he asked me what I would do if I had a chance to manage the education system. I told him that if I had a choice to do anything I wish, I want all your people to go away for six months to a year, letting them take educational-vacation—the entire ministry. Let them go learn English and technical skills, and as much as possible about democracy. Don't get involved in anything other than an education-vacation, to enhance the knowledge and skillset of the entire ministry. During that time, rebuild and restructure the entire ministry, then bring everyone back in, gradually.

If I had a chance, that's what I feel is most needed for the NLD or any ministry or institution in this country.

AC: At the root of this suggestion, why?

TH: At the moment, we have two problems: a structure problem and a culture problem. For the transition to succeed, we need to overcome those two problems. The structure problem is a bit easier to fix. Just develop new policies and strategies, and modify the existing ones to change the structure, bring in new people, bring in experts and consultants and implement it. Done. That's what corporations and companies do, when they have a structure or management problem. They bring in experts and new management.

You don't have employees and people with outmoded traits and traditions in the new culture. Right now, we have mixture of both. Even if you bring in new leaders, new ministers, and a new chief minister, you still have this group of people with old beliefs and practices who are closed and fixed-minded in their ways of thinking.

Further, they do not take responsibility or ownership for their mistakes.

Of course, such changes don't happen overnight. They were conditioned, trained, and pressured to become that type of unmindful person.

Human beings are smart and adaptable, right? We can be put into pretty much any environment, under any condition, and find a way to survive. We must find a way to survive. This is what the old school did, adapt to survive.

If I were born into this authoritarian society and had to survive, I'd adapt to this controlled and oppressive environment. I'd need to stop thinking. I'd stop creating new ideas, other than survival. I'd stop thinking about what is best to do to make society a better place because the pressure is too great under totalitarian rule to think for oneself. If you do, you suffer, or you are imprisoned, or both.

AC: As Orwell said, "2 and 2 equals 5." Think like I tell you or else.

TH: Exactly. Authoritarianism demands that you shut up, listen, believe lies, and do as you are told. Otherwise, as I said, you'll be killed, jailed or tortured or forced to flee in exile.

If you stay and survive and work under the iron fist for 10 to 20 or 30 years, you're done. Even if you are subjugated like that for a year, you could be done. You're done as a free thinking, rational minded human being. Your brain, your family structure, your society, your everything becomes forcibly conditioned to survive.

AC: Unless you are a freedom fighter and decide not to cower, like you and so many other courageous activists in your country...

TH: Indeed, but I'm speaking about the multitudes who did not have the inner clarity or resolve to stand up. But right now, more people are beginning to understand their rights and duties as citizens under a new more liberated society.

We're seeing that the collective will of the people and the transition we are in slowly changing the external environment. Physical or external structures are actually changing, slowly. Government structure is changing. Military structure is changing. The civilian role is becoming more confident, slowly.

But these individuals who were brought up in the previous system, their internal structure, their internal transition, has not yet started. Frankly, I don't believe it will ever happen for most of them. They're already 50 and 60 years old. This is all they've known; their conditioning is all they have. This is who they are—it's become carved into their being, it's their identity. You, as a leader, to change that is virtually impossible.

Those two things are currently taking place: structural and cultural changes.

AC: Will everybody come along in this transition?

TH: No. I don't think we can bring everybody along. Nor will everybody want to come along. But we must try to bring along as many people as we can, because we can't leave them. Even if only 20 percent adapt to the new environment and practices, that's better for us. Even the ministers, the chief ministers, if they have this understanding, motivation, and forward thinking, which I believe the current minister of education has, that's a great thing.

That's one of the reasons I stick close to him, sharing and working with him; I see that; he has good intention, good understanding, he reads a lot, he understands that the current structure needs to change—and he doesn't have sufficient exposure, capacity and resources and experience to change this problem.

Even the structure problem is not easy for him to change.

That's what we see right now in every ministry.

AC: Regarding leadership, what's needed?

TH: As I understand it, two things are needed from the leadership to move this transition forward: they need to understand, and they need to be able to step back.

"Step back" means not telling people what to do every single step; allow these individuals to think for a while, formulate their own solutions. Allow them to share these ideas within themselves, right? Make them feel like they're part of this change, part of the process. To do that, these leaders need to step back a little. Even if they have a perfect solution, even if they know what the next step should be, they need to hold their horses and allow others to create this environment. Why? Because they need to feel empowered, they need to feel the ownership.

To recognize these sorts of changes, these leaders must have good practice—I'm not saying just meditation, but good practice in understanding themselves. This is beyond technical skills. This is transformational skills. If they're just telling them "Do this: after you learn to read, next step: 1 plus 1 equals 2." No—just hold it for a while. Allow them to come out with what it should be, 1 plus 1. It may not be a perfect answer but at least the process would allow them to come together, build confidence, feel like their voices are heard.

That sort of environment needs to be created by these leaders. But the problem is, I don't think it's taking place. Nor do I think it's taking place from a very high level.

For instance, if you go a cabinet level meeting, you listen to the one who is always talking, always telling the ministers what to do. If you go to the ministry level meetings, who is the one instructing? If you go to a departmental meeting: that structure is the same as a military or authoritarian structure, one person at the top position is always instructing and directing without any meaningful dialogue or engagement. To change that, leaders must step back. Stay quiet for a few minutes. Listen. Maybe even be humble and skillful enough to pretend that you don't know the solution. Pretend like you are with them in formulating this correct new solution. Only then will you get support and collaboration and from there evolve a creative team.

Overall, there's two things I think they feel: fear and uncertainty. Fear of losing their comfort zone. By comfort zone, I mean the mindset they've been surviving in for the past 20 or 30 years; waiting for someone to tell them what to do. In that environment, you don't go to trainings to learn new things. You don't have to learn new skills. You just sit ready to serve, right? That's what allows you to get promotions, salary increases, and other benefits: you make sure you fulfill everything your boss desires. That's fear. What will happen? They don't know. They're afraid of losing that environment, they fear letting go of their current structure and comfort zone. Because this is also connected with their family, their friends, and relatives—everybody is tied into this environment of fear. They're so worried about losing their comfort zone, they choose fear over creative engagement. That's one thing.

The second thing is uncertainty: they don't know what's out there. Where is their initiative and imagination? If they simply started to change the way they think, the way they act, taking ownership, taking initiative, speaking out, starting to share their ideas and opinions—it's a brand-new world out there. A world where everything positive could happen.

In the past, creative thinking was squashed. All these things that define a free-thinking mind were killed; and if you defied Big Brother you'd get sacked or whacked or end up in prison, or even tortured until you learned to shut up and so as you are told, right? So now they're not sure—"Should we say something, should we not, should I share?" Even if they know that their boss or the minister thinks it's right, they're not sure. Uncertainty is pervasive.

AC: Totalitarian trauma.

TH: We need the mindful courage to challenge the habit of blind obedience and dare to have our voices heard. We must step up. We must encourage each other to exercise our freedom—our freedom of thought, our freedom of speech, our freedom of creative expression and have "the courage to care for things large than one's own self-interest," as Daw Suu encouraged us to do in your book of conversations together, *The Voice of Hope*.

Our leaders must make others feel that it's good and right to care for one another and to speak out. That this is good and right to share. That it is necessary to have open lively discussions for freedom of thought and democracy to take root and thrive.

To do that we all need to come down and be part of our own people.

I'd call it a return to caring.

Or love and compassion in action, as Daw Suu calls it.

> *"We don't have anybody building a bigger boat.*
> *The NLD has the biggest boat right now."*

ALAN CLEMENTS: The elections are near; a new generation is eligible to vote—call it the youth vote. You have a chance to speak to the youth of your country. The question: "Why should we care?"

What's in it for us?

Why should I vote?

Why should I become involved in politics?

And if I do become involved, what should I understand?

How will it affect me and my family, or my future family?

Help me understand why I should belong to this emerging culture of democracy through my participation in social, spiritual and political life here in Burma.

Before you answer, if you can also please speak to the taxi driver driving 12 hours a day to put rice and curry on the table for his newborn, and also to the hundreds of thousands of boys and girls forced into working in cafes, in some ways slave labor, to give money to their parents in some other distant location, along with the radically impoverished in the countryside, those many hundreds of thousands that live under plastic. And equally, speak to the youth, if you would, of the uber-wealthy, many of whom are indoctrinated in hedonism, indulgence, and cronyism.

What do you want them to know, please?

TIM HARDY: I want to say is that it's challenging to understand the current situation, as well as the direction our country is going. For the youth of this time, they're enjoying their freedom and probably more engaged in their personal developments and accomplishments.

With that said, I feel like most of them are not seeing the bigger picture. Not seeing how they are intimately connected with others. And how important the elections are, and more importantly, how critical their participation in this democratic process is for themselves and everybody else as a whole.

So, a political consciousness needs to arise first. To do that, we need to start with political parties, especially the NLD. This is something that needs to take place as soon as possible. It's already late. That's the first thing that political parties need to be doing—informing and empowering the youth to awaken politically.

The second thing is the upcoming elections: how should we vote, who should we vote for, and what's the outcome? I look at it as us—"us" meaning the country or society as a whole—trying to cross a river to the other side. This side is a military dictatorship, the other is a free and democratic society. While we are crossing this river, the river has many dangers. We cannot have everybody building their own boat and going forward with their own votes, unable to understand the dangers that we face along the crossing, and then being unable to protect ourselves. Now is the time for us to band together with a huge boat where everyone can fit, and we trust the leader; we even support and encourage them to take us to the other side.

Now, everybody hopes the NLD and Daw Suu will do just that, but now we're barely starting to leave this shore and we're already facing problems. But when you look around, there's not many other choices that we have. No one is building a bigger or better boat; we don't have anybody doing that right now. The NLD has the biggest boat. Support them. Join them. Do everything you can to assist our journey to the other shore.

At the same time, if we're unable to get together and get on the one big boat to cross the river and leave dictatorship behind, then there'll be more attacks that will take place. This will make it easier for the USDP or military to overpower us, because we are somewhat scattered and separated. We would be easy to manipulate, even vulnerable in changing our mindset and direction.

For instance, you may be asked or told, "Why are you crossing to the other side? You're not going to make it! Look, your boat is leaking. Nor do you have a proper captain. Best to stay on this side." That's what a military dictatorship will want you to do.

So, everybody may start to think, "Ok, it makes sense; I only have 20 people. I don't have enough money and resources. Why am I joining this political party and fighting for democracy? I'll just stay here and figure out a way to survive."

That is the thinking, and that type of thinking is already taking place.

It must stop.

It undermines everything we want as a free and democratic society.

On the other hand, the big boat needed to cross the river is not fully functional at this time, but it's at least moving along. But those are the choices that we have.

To me, it's clear: let's stick to the big boat, even though the NLD is not fully functional and has many problems and challenges. And of course, Daw Suu is not perfect—she's facing serious issues and challenges as well. But let's stay with her and the NLD.

Let us remember that even though Daw Suu understands what needs to be done, she's just another human being. I know that. We all do. She's human. We all are. But, let's stick to the vision and cross the river, come what may, and leave this military dictatorship behind.

And more importantly, each of us should ask, "What can I do to help?"

We don't have to be on the captain's seat.

Even if we are in the back of the boat, that seat is important.

Let's make sure that the back is secure, and not leaking.

Most of all make sure we're not causing problems that will slow the boat down. This is not a time for negativity.

To the contrary, it's a time for all to be the best that we can be, emotionally, psychologically and spiritually. Each of us can contribute in our own ways in crossing the river.

It has been five decades of dictatorship and our country is in ruins from it. The wealth has been stolen. Lives have been lost and or broken.

Let's get this boat of democracy moving more quickly and cross the river.

That's what I would suggest to the youth of this country to do in preparation to 2020 elections. Let us all help to raise political consciousness among the youth. And be clear: now is not the time to build another boat. There are not sufficient resources or capacity to do so. None of us have that. Let us stay aligned with Daw Suu and the NLD and put dictatorship behind us. And hopefully the military comes along with us as well. Democracy is a far better, more secure, and creative environment to live in and bring up one's children. I know, I came of age in America. For its many flaws, it gave me freedom and a high regard for universal human rights.

AC: As Nelson Mandela once said, "Sometimes, it falls upon a generation to be great. You can be that great generation. Let your greatness blossom." May the youth of Myanmar hear your calling for greatness. My question: What are the more obscure or hidden obstacles that you see Daw Suu facing in crossing the river?

TH: To start with—and this is not a criticism of Daw Suu, it's constructive feedback—my way of building the biggest, most efficient boat to cross the river (the shared goal among the vast majority of us) is that, firstly, I'd like to invite her to recognize the necessity of expanding her leadership qualities to include, how should I say, *otherness*—the input and wisdom of others, as elevating and expanding of her own understanding.

On a practical level: listen more, talk less, question more, seek more input, empower unity through diversity, which is something she speaks of a lot. Open up the atmosphere in the cabinet meetings. Be more inclusive. Step back, a bit. Chill. Relax. Listen. Feel. All those kinds of things that create a much more relaxed, engaging, and creative environment.

And, people make mistakes. But she needs to understand what is critical, making right decisions or bringing these people along? She needs to do both. She can't move forward without bringing these people with her. And at the same time, she needs to make sure that these people make the right decisions and take the right steps.

Right now, I think she's pressured to take the right steps. To do that, when you're in that mode, it's easy to forget or neglect bringing the entire team on board. Yes, there is some sense of urgency and that time is short. Make a decision! Take action now! But, if you do that, who's going to implement those actions? Who's going to carry on with those actions?

If I had a chance to speak with her, that's what I would suggest, of course, politely and diplomatically. After all, we are in the boat together *(laughs)*.

AC: In a nutshell: listen more and be more inclusive?

TH: Yes. Listen more and understand that she needs to bring the rest of Myanmar with her, especially the ethnic minorities. She can't go it alone. I think that's the very first step she needs to really let in and understand. We are in this together.

AC: She's somewhat blind to this or is it a slightly shadowed compassion?

TH: Not so much blind but, yes, she's driven by her own desire and inspiration and commitment and compassion to help others, to bring the people to the other side. She has so much of that effort to *help*. Perhaps too much. As you said, it may be a "slightly shadowed compassion."

You know, as a long-time meditator, when you meditate intensively in retreat you must have a proper balance between effort and concentration. Otherwise, you become agitated, restless and miss your mark—not seeing the object clearly, and possibly even interpreting reality wrongly. Daw Suu seems to be forgetting or neglecting at times to concentrate or focus on empowering the people—the very people who will be rowing the boat with her to the other shore. Her job is only to make the decision—she can't row the boat by herself. She needs these people to row the boat. You cannot have one role without the other.

AC: Is she not aware of these things? Is she not being advised by those near to her about the reality of life among the people? Overwhelmed with duties? What is it?

TH: As far as I know she's been isolated for a very long time. That's one of her shortcomings, I believe. We all have them, and I clearly have tons of my own shortcomings. But setting the obvious aside and continuing in the spirit of democracy and moving the boat forward, in my humble opinion, she surrounds herself only with a very few trusted folks. I think two or three, at most. And the problem is that those two or three people may not have a comprehensive understanding or the experience she needs to run this challenging country and steward the boat away from military dictatorship.

The stakes are very high. Tyranny or freedom, cooperation or corruption. A creative and prosperous society at peace with itself or one ravaged by never-ending wars, cronyism and reconstituted military dictatorships. We are at a precipice and we must be smart. The stakes are high. She must be smart.

AC: Those few people near to her are afraid of telling her the truth?

TH: Afraid, or insecure, that they won't have all the information. If a leader acts on limited information, then decisions will be at times—or most of the time—incorrect and incomplete.

Even the president of the United States has 33 or more advisers, right? And, they can't just sift through everything every day. There are so many things happening around the world each day.

Even in this country the issues are many and complex. Daw Suu needs more advisors and the spirit of that group must be committed to radical honesty, diversity, and healthy disagreement.

AC: Daw Suu—17 years of isolation under house arrest and away from family and intimate company; such a complex psychology to integrate. Only to have her husband pass away and then many of her most intimate colleagues—U Win Tin, U Kyi Maung, the former general, Aung Shwe, and others also passed on. She's held the suffering of the people in her heart as her own suffering. I mean, we're dealing with a rogue military, and a violent dictatorship. Stating the obvious, they've imprisoned so many of their own people, murdered their own monks, raped their own women. And really what I'm trying to get to here is that she has spent the better part of her adult life in isolation. And even today, she's in a kind of nationwide arrest. She has no real power. She's hemmed in on all sides, and essentially powerless, other than the power of her own voice and conscience. And on top of it she's being universally vilified by the international media and abandoned by her fellow and sister Nobel laureates and many world leaders. And yet, she remains composed and forward moving without a hint of retaliation. Pretty amazing, to me.

In other words, are we not seeing her own slow and arduous education of the people of Myanmar—including the military—on the meaning of freedom, rule of law, dignity, and genuine democracy? And moreover, her stated aim of peace and national reconciliation?

TH: Right.

AC: Has all this been orchestrated? The military has enshrined itself, not just through the *faux*-constitution but now through global support; they've gone from international pariah to a somewhat barely tolerated institution that may even be a substitute for Aung San Suu Kyi herself? Is there such a negative sentiment building towards her, with a potential split in the vote that could lead to the NLD losing power in the upcoming election, and a ghost-like dictatorship is enshrined forever?

TH: If the NLD continues on the same path and strategy that they are on currently, to get majority votes will be a slim chance. And we know for a fact that the USDP is rebranding, splitting up into smaller parties and giving people money to join them. There are four or five parties already out there. People don't even know who the leaders of those parties are, but they have lots of money.

AC: The USDP is breaking up—creating proxy parties?

TH: Exactly, the dictum of dictatorship—divide and rule. Very cunning, very smart. People have told me, "Hey, do you know about this and that new party? They will give you 10 million Kyats to join." It's happening as we speak.

With the pace of transition and with the current criticism from the international community toward the NLD and the government, combined with the NLD government's inability to make things happen, and then also having these individuals in the party that are speaking out and saying things that are out of touch and without compassion, these are a cancer and the self-destruction of their own party.

Be sure of it, the military and General Than Shwe planned it this way.

We are seeing a self-fulfilling prophecy—like a snowball that keeps rolling.

If Aung San Suu Kyi and the NLD leadership are unable to stop and understand and re-strategize around what I mentioned earlier about those changes, they could face serious challenges in getting the majority vote. That means they will not be forming a government.

Remember, the USDP only needs 26 percent to form a government, as 25 percent is already in Parliament. So, for them to get 26 percent by rebranding themselves would be a significant challenge, and I would not be surprised if in the next year or two some of the former prominent democracy activists and 88 Generation leaders come together with those rebranded USDP or proxy parties. Even to get a few votes, the key is to split. When they vote in Parliament for the government, they can all vote together, because the military is already there. That's a strategy that we'll most likely to see materialized as we get closer to 2020 elections.

I'm not sure how much the NLD is aware of that happening. I'm not sure if they have any political strategists who are analyzing the current situation, forming a new strategy for the party or country. But that is what we're seeing right now from outside, and that will most likely happen if things continue unchanged.

Then you can't just ask the people for a second chance when 2020 is getting closer and you were unable to fulfill their expectations, desires and inspirations during the last four or five years.

Then, their livelihoods, their day-to-day survival is challenged, getting worse by the week. People said, "Ok, fine, we'll give you five years." Now: "We've lost everything. My kid has dropped out of school. They're now selling water at traffic lights. I have to sell my land to become a day laborer. The crops are not providing basic needs because the government fails to protect the border and then a lot of products are coming in from China that are cheaper, so domestic production is killed."

In addition, we used to produce lots of flowers in the north. It's now much more expensive coming from our own country than from China. So, they stopped growing flowers. They can't grow them to lose money.

It's the same with other products. Many people lost their jobs due to this China phenomena, which triggers high unemployment and less taxes coming in.

Then you have inflation going up, trade deficits going up.

The banking system is also in serious trouble, unable to circulate money effectively, and a lot of them are running negative.

There's still a lot of significant crises in the country that most likely will happen if things continue as usual. What we are seeing in Rakhine State is just one crisis. If current policies and strategies continue, we're going to face both economic and social related crises in the near future that are unable to fix overnight.

Nor is it an issue of changing leadership.

We must have policies and strategies implemented before economic prosperity can start. It's not just overnight that you sell whatever you have. Even if we were to produce more, we need investments. With investments, we don't have skilled labor. Investors are not going to come if they have to spend more on operational costs. They will go to other more stable developing countries where they get only four or five percent return. Here you can get 10 percent return, but your risk is high, your operational costs are higher due to lack of skilled labor, and insufficient legal protection for your business investments. That's why you don't see FDI's coming as much as we expected. Without FDI we can't develop and produce domestic products and productions, and on top of that we don't have enough skilled labor force.

We have millions of kids and young people throughout the country without skills. Even the Chinese and Vietnamese construction companies bring in their own general workers from their own countries. When I was returning from Vietnam on my last trip, Vietnamese day laborers were getting on the plane with helmets and jumpsuits to go to Myanmar to work on large construction projects.

I asked them, "What's happening, why are you flying to Myanmar?"

They said, "We get more money coming to Myanmar."

They only get paid $350 or $400 a month in Vietnam.

When they come here, they make up to $1000 a month.

Think about a company that's investing. If they get local labor, they could save a lot of money. Even the law says 20 percent of the labor must come from Myanmar, but you can't even find that 20 percent.

These are the conditions that are squeezing us in, so it will be challenging for us to see the NLD coming through again.

*"In order for us to build trust with our enemies...
we need to go beyond our selves."*

ALAN CLEMENTS: Without an NLD victory in the 2020 elections, what is the future of Daw Aung San Suu Kyi?

TIM HARDY: This is it. You can't rebrand. You can't rebuild. She'll be 75 when the election comes. Even if she wakes up and rebrands the NLD, there are no other leaders in her party that can bring people together like her. There's no second place for Daw Suu. No third place. Without her, the NLD will definitely split into two or three or more groups.

AC: Back to a core issue: How to handle the corruption in Burma?

TH: Corruption happens, not only because we choose it, but sometimes we just happen to be in the wrong place at the wrong time. From that place of complexity, we could easily assume some sort of illusion of leadership, or illusion of strength. We have a false view of reality and a false view of ourselves, and in an instant, if unmindful, a bribe occurs, corruption takes place. And then...

AC: It goes right back to what Sayadaw U Pandita often said, how effective leadership required a comprehensive training in mindful intelligence.

TH: Exactly. And, as you know, he often spoke of the need to cultivate an abiding regard for *hiri* (moral shame) and *ottapa* (moral regret). Also, a deep regard for *dāna* (generosity), *silā* (morality), and *bhavana* (the development of positive sates of mind). If you're going to reconcile something, he encouraged us to reconcile our own *moha*, our own ignorance.

AC: Yes, the *Dhamma* of reconciliation. He spoke at length about this in our book of conversations, *Wisdom for a World in Crisis and Mindful Advice for the People of My Country*.

TH: Meditation and mindfulness training is really missing at the top level of leadership. I'm not suggesting religion. Nor is this a Buddhist thing. It's self-transformation. It's a wisdom training. Mind development.

For us as human beings, in order to build trust with our enemies and in order for us to work together as a team, we need to go beyond our selves. We need to reflect and then question our own intentions and desires. We need to be mindful. As I was saying, to do these things our mind must be trained. Our mind must be in control of our own self. Without that, how are we going to get to the other shore? How are we going to understand and even listen before we say something?

Those are some of the things needed to challenge corruption and wrong views and to move steadily to the other shore.

AC: Actually, Sayadaw U Pandita and I had been speaking before he passed away of offering a secular *Dhamma* intelligence, *Dhamma*-immersion, or mindful intelligence training for leaders and former political prisoners here in Myanmar. I am sorry it never came to be. He was inspired by the vision.

But as you were saying, becoming mindfully conscious of one's own mind, so to speak, may be the only true hope we have for a nonviolent world, a world that respects our differences as vital to freedom and democracy, not just in Burma, but probably anywhere in the world.

TH: I agree fully.

AC: But right here in your country, the birthplace of *Dhamma* intelligence, perhaps it could start with a forum in Naypyidaw where Sayadaw's vision of mindful intelligence was put forth in a weekend training? Should it never happen, I brought with me his words on the virtues of a leader.

He said, "In order to understand what qualities a good leader needs to have in terms of the *Dhamma*, first of all, we have to look at the qualities of a good friend, a *kalyāṇa mitta*. There are six qualities this person should have:

"*Piya*—to have good personal behavior, not just pretending. When one has good personal behavior, one is loved by those around one. This is the first quality that needs to be mentioned.

"Not only does the person have good personal behavior, they have a good mental attitude and are able to help others. Due to this, the person receives the respect of others. There must also be this quality of being respected, called *garu*.

"These two qualities combined lead to *bhāvaniya*, which means to be the recipient of others' *mettā* (loving kindness).

"The next quality is *vattā*, which means when there is something to be said that is beneficial and true, the person can speak frankly.

"Further, when they receive criticism from others, they can accept it. This is called *vacanakkhama*.

"And the last quality is that they do not use those who depend on them inappropriately—*no c'aṭṭhāne niyujjako*. This means not urging people who depend on you to do things for your benefit that aren't good for them to do; not to use people for your own selfish means."

He concluded by saying, "A person who possesses these six qualities is a good friend, or *kalyāṇa mitta*. One has to start by understanding this. That is what the Buddha taught. If a person possesses these qualities, one could choose that person as a friend, mentor, or a teacher." He went onto reiterate that these same qualities were the mark of a good leader.

TH: Beautiful. And may the mindful intelligence training happen. Of course, count me in along with everyone I know.

AC: A final question: you're a voice of freedom. You left your country alone, with no English skills, trekking for weeks through malaria-infested jungles, living in remote border camps, nearly starving, living through hell. Soon thereafter you are in America, living in New York City, and you become highly educated with a Masters degree. You've done incredible work for your country, for the United Nations, for UNESCO, on boards; you are a man of integrity.

You've now been back in your country, and I ask you: What do you see for yourself in Burma? Are you looking at running for political office? Are you joining a particular political party? Do you have a vision potentially to become the minister of education? Do you see yourself one day becoming the president? What do you see for yourself?

TH: I'm going through some internal reflections and assessments in deciding what would be the most effective next step for me, because I've been reflecting on what I've achieved and been doing since I got back to Myanmar, questioning and assessing impacts and directions, where I want to be and where I should be next. Of course, getting into politics or running for public office is always in my mind, ever since I was a young boy. My great-grandfather, Thakin Thein Pe (Taing Chit, Mandalay) was a well-known politician during the colonial time. My grandmother was also involved in politics during her early years with Do-Ba-Mar Movement and Organization, which advocated for the Burma's independence from the British. And my father was also involved in various worker unions and movements during the socialist time and one of the co-founders of the Democracy Party in 1988, right after the 8888 nation-wide uprising. So, politics and working for the people runs deep in my family and I do hope to get involved in one day. But, I'm not joining any political party at this moment since I'm still assessing the situation on the ground and also still find many things to do for out-of-school kids and child laborers, along with supporting the education reform process in Myanmar.

Also, I'm learning much since I returned to Myanmar in 2014, especially learning and realizing the long-term impact by the decades of repression and authoritarian rule on the people's aspiration, behaviour and attitude.

As you mentioned, I feel like I've been through a lot since the 1988 student movement and that, personally, I feel like I'm ready to take on any challenges right now. But, on the other hand, it's a bit challenging to decide since there are a few competing choices out there, and also some of the choices and opportunities are unclear in terms of potential impacts and consequences.

Of course, my aspiration is to always contribute and assist the people of Myanmar to experience their full potential and realize more peaceful and prosperous society for everyone.

Right now, I'm just enduring this historic transition while assisting and supporting both the minister and Ministry of Education to the best of my ability and coordinating between various stakeholders on the education reform process.

I'm definitely gaining insights on overall education system, and also barriers and challenges that are preventing individuals from achieving their full potential.

Hopefully, sooner or later, I'll be able to get involved in a much more meaningful and impactful way with or without any political position.

AC: Well, I personally hope that you continue to use your voice, your mind, and your actions for the betterment of your people, and I'm here to provide as much support as possible for your highest vision.

I am inspired by your words and your courage to be the best that you can be. Thank you for taking the time to share your innermost thoughts with your people as well as for all freedom loving people, worldwide.

TH: Thank you, Alan. It's also been a great opportunity for me to share all these thoughts and experiences with you. And thank you for your own long-standing dedication in compassionately supporting the freedom of our people.

AC: Allow me to close with one of Sayadaw U Pandita's most cherished Burmese sayings. He would say, "There is a worldly saying, not a Pali one. It goes like this, 'If he's not part of it, it can't be done. But he alone can't do it. If you aren't part of it, it can't be done, but you alone can't do it. Without me, it can't be done. But I alone can't do it. Only when he, you, and I are part of it can everything be done.' This is a Burmese saying."

TH: Sadhu, sadhu, sadhu.

AC: Sadhu, sadhu, sadhu.

CHAPTER 36

CONVERSATION *with* AN ANONYMOUS ACTIVIST

2020

- "The new Myanmar is full of hatred."
- "It was never about human rights. It was about Burmese rights."
- "The ethnic minorities now hate her... Nobody trusts her anymore."

Anonymous is a human rights activist and writer from Shan State in Myanmar. He speaks candidly about the changes in the socio-political landscape of Myanmar, and the challenges and limitations of the new government.

"The new Myanmar is full of hatred"

ALAN CLEMENTS: How would you describe the "new Myanmar?"

ANON: The new Myanmar is full of hatred, nationalism, and patriotism. It's all mixed together in our country in a recipe of Burmese supremacy. It's shocking how the military regained voluntary support from the whole population of the very people they oppressed for more than 50 years. So many people now support them for viciously cracking down on the Rohingya.

AC: A national Stockholm Syndrome? Make excuses for and support your oppressor?

ANON: Frankly, I'm speechless about Myanmar. Look at the two Reuters journalists, Wa Lone and Kyaw Soe Oo, were set up and arrested and jailed.

AC: What was the reason to do this? Sending a message to the international media?

ANON: They are sending a message to international journalists—you. And right before their arrest—the last week of November—the government had been restricting visas on foreign journalists. Now, it's almost impossible to get a journalist visa.

AC: Why do you think Daw Aung San Suu Kyi would either allow this or be knowledgeable of it and not speak out? And why not change the laws, not fight for these journalists, not fight for freedom of speech and freedom of press?

ANON: I think you might have a better answer because you are the only person who's spoken to her in depth and for that long in history.

AC: I have written to her recently, and I'm going to Naypyidaw soon, and although I have a love for her—and remain close to several people close to her—I am not on the ground like you are. But, I am confident in asking direct questions, mainly because our mutual teacher, the Venerable Sayadaw U Pandita, the former Buddhist monk who passed away recently at 95, trained me in this way: ask direct and honest questions for the purpose of knowing the truth, and not to collude with anyone. She knows this, and she made it clear to me: ask anything that you want and let me answer anyway that I want. And we both honored that process. I found her to be radically real and honest. So, yes, I will ask her that question if the opportunity presents itself.

ANON: I don't think she'll have an answer.

AC: Please say more ... why?

ANON: Well, I don't blame her on some things. Okay, we all understand that she does not have any control over the military. We don't know for how long this will keep happening, but we know she doesn't have any control over the veto power to change any situation on the ground. Because on the ground, the ones who commit human rights abuses are not her people. These atrocities are done by the military. We understand that and accept the fact that she's not responsible.

AC: There's no doubt what happened in Rakhine was the result of the Burmese military?

ANON: Yes, no doubt whatsoever. I have zero doubt. No one of any intelligence does.

AC: But she doesn't come out and say it as such?

ANON: No. She missed a chance to tell the world that this is not her. She missed the chance many times. Like when, let's say, the first satellite images came out in September last year from Human Rights Watch showing the near total destruction of 214 villages—she could have easily said to the world that "We will investigate these matters," because satellite pictures don't lie. Instead, the next day, her spokesman had a press conference, simply lying: "These satellite images are wrong."

She missed the opportunity, so many times, to exercise her moral authority and speak out against human rights abuses. The entire world was waiting for her to speak up and she utterly failed in her commitment to protecting global human rights.

AC: If you were to set aside everything that you consider true and right—not an easy thing to ask you—and try to understand what could be going on Daw Suu's mind, why do you think she has acted in the way she has?

ANON: Well then, I have to ask you a return question: have you ever seen her, during all the years of revolutionary struggle, represent any minority group? Further, have you ever seen her speak up for any minority group her whole life?

AC: What about her initiation of the 21st Century Panglong process? She has clearly made peace and national reconciliation between Myanmar's ethnic armed groups and government forces a priority of her civilian government. No?

ANON: *(Scoffs)* She doesn't know how to talk with ethnic minority groups. She gives them orders rather than sitting down with them, having tea, talking openly. She's clueless about the differences in our country. And I think she's getting information from people close to her, and not getting information from people on the ground in those ethnic areas who really know the lay of the land, so to speak, and the mindset of the people.

AC: You're saying Daw Aung San Suu Kyi is racist?

ANON: Yes.

AC: An ultra-nationalist as well? Burmans are the superior ethnicity in Burma?

ANON: I don't know if I would say it that way, but she does think of herself as superior to others. I think that is partly due to her being brought up to lead, because everybody was sympathetic to her and her family. Because she was so young, everybody was always giving the best to her. She was always flattered.

AC: Let me be clear: The criticism you have with what's happening in Rakhine is that Daw Suu missed an opportunity to use her iconic international respect as a defender of global human rights—right up there with Nelson Mandela—and she failed? She had a near total lapse of conscience and compassion? She remained silent at a time when she needed to speak up? Is that the main criticism?

ANON: Yes. That's right.

AC: What about the argument that she is instituting a policy of national reconciliation? Her chief adviser, U Ko Ni, who was assassinated. When I met with one of her principle advisors recently, he told me directly: "Word on the street is that she's next. Do you really think we don't know what's happening here?"

I dare ask: Do you think the military would assassinate her if they felt their future was more secure without her?

ANON: I don't think so. The military is way smarter than the NLD, because they have ruled the country for so long, and they know exactly how their propaganda works. Nor do I think they have ever had a plan to assassinate Suu Kyi.

AC: They need her?

ANON: Yeah, they need her for a monkey show.

AC: She's a pawn on Than Shwe's stage unknowingly acting out a script he's written?

ANON: Absolutely. But some things are in her control. That's why I'm upset with her. Some regressive laws—those disdainful colonial era laws—are under her direct control and can be abolished immediately, because she holds majority seats in Parliament. But no—they do nothing. Nothing at all! To not change a heinous law in over two years? It's unconscionable. What is she thinking? There is simply no excuse for such neglect.

AC: It begs the question, why? She's smart, ethical, and mindful. And yes, a times short tempered. And so am I. That was the Daw Suu that I came to know during our conversations at her home. And again, speaking with her in San Francisco in 2012, I instantly felt the same way. But the question remains: Why? Why is she not changing repressive laws that she could easily change them? And why is she not challenging the military and General Min Aung Hlaing by speaking out?

ANON: Yes. Exactly. And please do ask her these questions when you see her. We all want to know. As for me, I have no idea what she's thinking, what's going through her mind, but to us it's inexcusably wrong.

AC: It could change.

ANON: It must change. Under her administration there is one very repressive military law that has been used by the NLD themselves against journalists as well as the public. There are more than 90 legal cases against journalists for so-called insulting Daw Aung San Suu Kyi. Okay, if she thinks that this is a repressive law, and if she were truly a freedom fighter, if she were truly a genuine human rights activist, she would have dropped them right away. The case against her is far more than the military. This ludicrous law has been used more by the NLD than the military. Can you believe it? A democracy icon is more repressive than a dictator. There's something seriously wrong here. Way, way off.

> *"It was never about human rights.*
> *It was about Burmese rights."*

ALAN CLEMENTS: Please let me take my time with this observation. What I'm hearing is that there's an ethical gap between the Daw Aung San Suu Kyi the world knew and loved as a nonviolent freedom fighter challenging military dictatorship and Daw Suu the tactical politician seeking reconciliation with that same military, while trying to restore honor to an institution founded by her father. In other words, there's a credibility gap here, right?

Perhaps underneath it all there's a psychological issue that's not being addressed? I found it interesting that when Daw Suu was awarded the Vaclav Havel Award for Creative Dissent in 2013 in San Francisco, they gave away a book, titled, *Psychopolitics*, by the renowned neuropsychiatrist and psychologist Jean-Michel Oughourlian. In short, it's an analysis of mimetic desire in individuals and how it plays out in nation states, through rivalry and at times violence. I found it interesting as a way of exploring the deeper psychological roots of the crisis here in Burma. On the one hand, we've seen decades of nonviolent feminine inspired activism, and on the other hand, we have this patriarchal 'might is right' group of military men (and their wives and cronies) who have all the power, and all the resources. Then suddenly, within a short period of time, Daw Suu's 30 years of nonviolent revolution that captured the hearts of millions around the world collapses, nearly overnight. She's goes from global icon to international villain. From peace activist to colluding with ethnic cleansing. Or worse, what Bob Geldof called her, a "handmaiden of genocide."

Clearly, she's been psychologically and emotionally impacted by 17 years of incarceration, the assassination of her father, the death of her brother as a young girl, the loss of her husband, separation from her children, the torture of her people; how could this not impact her? Is she a victim of Stockholm Syndrome? Where she's in collusion with the perpetrators of violence? In other words, setting aside right and wrong for a moment, I'm asking, "why?" Why is she doing what she is?

ANON: It could very well be Stockholm Syndrome. It could be unrecognized trauma. But the thing is, when she and the NLD started the election campaigns, they had so much support from the people, and she promised that she would work with the entire nation to amend the Constitution. But when she found out, when U Ko Ni found out, how she can be the de-facto leader of the country, she forgot about it all. She ceased caring about amending the Constitution. Why? Another question I ask you to ask her.

AC: But she tried hard to have the Constitution changed, right?

ANON: Before the election, yes. Right after they won, she's been completely silent about it.

AC: She knows something that we don't? Regardless, what we assume she knows and doesn't know, doesn't work for you? She's failed her role as leader?

ANON: Yes. She has also failed her own moral responsibility and authority to the people.

AC: Is this a majority opinion throughout the country?

ANON: No. We're the minority.

AC: Daw Suu has huge popular support in the country, that I have seen.

ANON: Yes, she does. But I would call it blind support. And ironically, she does have more popularity now than before, because people feel like if you talk against Daw Suu you're talking against "the heart of my mother."

AC: Okay, let's look at it from another angle. Why are we seeing this "blind" allegiance to Daw Suu knowing that the military are people who have committed grave human rights atrocities? Why are these incredibly courageous people of your country colluding in this way with the "mother"? Why are they not going into the streets as they did in '88 and in 2007 with Saffron?

ANON: Because it was never about human rights in Burma. It was about Burmese rights. In their history, this is what they had been fighting for.

AC: Please explain.

ANON: It was never about minority rights. It was never about human rights. It's a particularly Burmese and Buddhistic form of rights. But not about human rights. Take for example the anniversary of U Ko Ni's assassination, coming up on January 29th--

AC: Sorry to interrupt, but could you explain who he is for those who do not know?

ANON: U Ko Ni joined the NLD in 2013, after being a legal advisor for Suu Kyi for many years. He was credited with finding loopholes in the 2008 Constitution and, in particular, with creating the office of State Counsellor, which enabled Suu Kyi to become the de facto head of government in 2016. He also advocated constitutional change in Myanmar, believing that the Constitution, which of course was drafted by the military, should be replaced and not merely amended. As I understand it, he wrote six books on human rights issues and democratic elections and was also actively involved in the interfaith movement. And it is also important to note that he spoke out against the Myanmar nationality law that stripped the Rohingya of Burmese citizenship.

AC: Thank you. And as you were saying?

ANON: As you know, U Ko Ni was assassinated in broad day light at the Yangon International airport while holding his young granddaughter in his arms, no less. After devoting so much of his life to Suu Kyi, she should have that very day, that very evening, gone to U Ko Ni's family and consoled them. But she did nothing. Nothing at all. She didn't even send flowers. What does that tell you about her character? Her priorities? It's unconscionable, truly.

Further, he went to Jakarta solely at her request. Let that in, that this man went there at *her* request. And, moreover, he was tirelessly working for her night and day as the only prominent Muslim that was in any position as adviser to her, doing a job of unthinkable importance in looking, as I said, at how to reform and possible replace the 2008 Constitution. Could there be a greater role of greater importance for anyone in this country? He held the legal keys to ending military dictatorship, for good. She trusted him. He was in her innermost inner circle. And he's assassinated on your watch, working for you, and you didn't show up for the family? You abandoned them at their greatest moment of need. Forget about being State Counsellor. And you call yourself a Buddhist? Sorry, this is not a friend. This is not a person of conscience. You should have gone to the family the very minute you heard he was murdered! And I have heard through the grape vine that what I am saying is also felt U Ko Ni's family.

AC: Can you say more about what you know?

ANON: Yes, they were devastated beyond belief. One could easily argue that she didn't care about him all along and simply used him. How else can you understand it? Stockholm Syndrome? I ask you to ask her that question directly: Why did you not go immediately to U Ko Ni's family at their greatest time of need? Ask her on behalf of all our people.

AC: If the opportunity presents itself, I will, for sure.

ANON: There's one story I haven't told you about U Ko Ni. I heard that Suu Kyi not only didn't go to the funeral, didn't contact the family, didn't send flowers, in fact nobody showed up. So, a friend of mine went to U Ko Ni's house. There my friend was on the street, but he didn't want to intrude on the family, because they were grieving. Of course, as a journalist he said, it would be bad manners to disturb those who are grieving. So he waited outside and let their community and Muslim leader know if his oldest daughter, ever wanted to talk about how the family felt, they were downstairs. Well, as it turns out, after the family talked to all the diplomats and their guests, they invited him in. But just as they were entering the building, one NLD guy came and put a small paper with a plastic over it, maybe 1 cent plastic bag—how do you call it? Not congratulations, but...?

AC: Condolences?

ANON: Not condolences. It's like an award of some type. Very strange. And that NLD guy, somebody who they didn't even know he said, tapes this small wrapped-in-plastic paper acknowledgment-of-some-sort on the door. Whatever it was, was so insulting and inappropriate that the Muslim community that had gathered to pay their respects to U Ko Ni's grieving family were outraged. There they were—the entire community of people who had gathered were now downstairs and on the street. They were in disbelief and angry. And apart from that, the NLD person who brought the paper started looking at them as my friend told us, and started shouting at the whole Muslim community there on the street: "Who told you to let these journalists in? The NLD has already made it clear that you do not talk to the media."

The Muslim community explained to the NLD guy that U Ko Ni's family wanted to talk to them, and further, it was none of his business. Could it have gotten worse? This NLD guy started physically threatening the Muslim man who answered him, right there in front of them. And then they had this intense argument. If my friend had not seen this with his own eyes, you would probably think it was true. But there it was. At first, he didn't want to get involved, because he said to the Muslim community leaders that if it was too difficult then he could just leave. But the community leaders said, "No, it's fine, please stay."

U Ko Ni was the only NLD party member. The rest of the family were not part of the NLD. My point: It is not the business of the NLD if U Ko Ni's family wants to speak with the media. Obviously, it's up to the family whether to talk to the media or not. And so, the family asked him to please wait. And then they had a huge fight with this NLD guy who dared come to the home of this grieving family, a traumatized family grieving the loss of Suu Kyi's most important colleague, who tapes up a plastic-wrapped award paper for this hero of human rights who gave his life for his country and Suu Kyi. It's beyond disgraceful. And my friend concluded that his Burmese colleague who was with him that day who witnessed the event, was also outraged at the NLD and Suu Kyi. How do you say it? It was the straw that broke the camel's back for him. And not just him, for many, many others as well, he said.

Later on, this story leaked out internationally about how the family felt about Suu Kyi not showing up, not offering flowers, no phone calls, no condolence letter, nothing. A truly tragic day in Burma's history.

AC: I am truly sorry to hear of this. I will wait and ask her about this event, if I see her in Naypidaw.

ANON: She won't answer. What can she say? No matter what she says or does not say, it's too late.

AC: Regarding national reconciliation: Daw Aung San Suu Kyi has made it clear that in this challenging process of forming a peaceful union—attempting to close the divide between the oppressed and oppressors, and heal the decades of wounds—she does not want to condemn one side or the other. A very Buddhist thing—the wisdom of the middle way. In other words, by not condemning anyone one side or any one person, she avoids inflaming tensions, or triggering guilt and fear and regression—a return to oppressive and violent behaviors. After all, Burma could explode at any time, removing all chances of democracy ever coming to this country. What are your thoughts on Daw Suu's vision of reconciliation?

ANON: I think her idea of reconciliation is between herself and the military.

AC: Isn't it not possible that she's thinking for the long term in Burma, say in ten, twenty, thirty years from now, with the formation of a harmonious Union of Burma, that includes a lasting peace with all ethnic groups? In other words, perhaps she's walking the slow road to reconciliation?

ANON: I simply don't believe so.

AC: She should be speaking out against this disproportionate military violence?

ANON: We are not asking her to condemn anybody, just simply say sorry, or, you know, "this is so sad." Be human. That's all.

AC: Have you been arrested or imprisoned?

ANON: No. But I know many who have been both arrested and imprisoned, and tortured for that matter. Others who died in prison.

AC: Do you think that the long-term incarceration and torture of most of the NLD leadership in government has negatively impacted them psychological and emotionally? The wounding from such trauma influences their decisions and actions?

ANON: That could be possible. But under the military government, since I was not imprisoned nor studied the impact of trauma from torture on political prisoners, I cannot answer that with any certainty.

AC: Is it true that the NLD disqualified all Muslim candidates from running in the last elections?

ANON: Yes, the NLD leadership intentionally excluded over a dozen or so Muslims from its candidate list—to so called placate Buddhist hardliners.

AC: So, what you're alluding to here is that most of the senior NLD came of age, so to speak, under General Ne Win's xenophobic dictatorship, and tacitly agree with hard-line Buddhist groups in Myanmar heavily driven by anti-Muslim sentiments?

ANON: Yes, that's precisely right. Why did they not select Muslim candidates? Under Thein Sein's government, we even had a Rohingya lawmaker in the central Parliament. But not today under the NLD.

AC: You're putting the NLD in the same category as the Buddhist monk, U Wirathu—staunch Buddhist's who thoroughly look down on Muslims? Is that your message?

ANON: All I can say is the NLD's behavior speaks for itself, and to me, it speaks of hate and discrimination.

AC: Have you experienced war?

ANON: Yes, unfortunately. I was born and grew up in Shan State under a near constant barrage of bullets. As you know, a big part of the region is a war zone. What you probably don't know is the living hell of growing up in everyday war.

AC: Would you say what you're saying to me to Daw Suu herself?

ANON: If she let me speak with her, yes, of course.

AC: We're all together sitting at a table, you'd speak your mind, just as you are?

ANON: Definitely. Completely.

AC: Well, let it be said, because your words, as you know—this interview—will be included in our forthcoming four volume set of books, *Burma's Voices of Freedom*. Very likely, Daw Suu will read your words.

ANON: May it be so. But let me add, I do not want my name used in this interview as it is not safe to speak your mind as I am doing in Myanmar today. As I said, people are going to prison for freedom of speech. That is so sad. That we are not safe to speak our minds freely and openly is a great tragedy. So I request you to not include my name in this interview but let it be known, that my views are shared by many. The views themselves are far more important than the person who said them. And I will also say this, I would say them to her directly if she would meet me. And if we did meet, I would be respectful and formal in approaching her. But more importantly, I want her to know how most of the ethnic people in our country live; what their physical surroundings are like; what their day-to-day existence is like; what it's like to grow up in a war zone; what it's like to know nothing in your life but conflict, violence and betrayal.

AC: You really don't think she knows any of that, especially after having had so many colleagues and friends who suffered in prison and under the cruelest forms of punishment and torture?

ANON: No, I don't think she knows. She doesn't understand that. She doesn't understand the severity of the circumstances. Rakhine is only the most recent crisis in a long history of multiple crises in Burma. But she's never experienced it. Experiential knowledge counts for a lot.

AC: She's removed from reality and the day to day life of the minorities, the traumatized and impoverished?

ANON: Maybe if she really wanted to know all the people of our country she could go on an exposure tour and spend a week in northern Shan State, and in Kachin, and a week in an IDP camp outside of Sittwe and experience the traumatized, the maimed, the raped and broken, the hungry infants. She needs those experiences to wake up. She needs a major interruption to break her heart open and feel the pain of others as her own. It's not there at the moment.

AC: She's that out of touch? After all these years of being in her own country, with people parading through her house—I've witnessed people coming to her from all walks of life who've lost members of their family, who've had daughters raped, people who've been tortured, they're hurting, and she's there with them, consoling them. Why do you not see this, know this? Why do they call her "the great mother"? As I said, I have witnessed her compassion many times.

ANON: People who went to her house were mostly not minorities.

AC: I see, you come back to the minorities a lot, essentially, saying she doesn't have an awareness of what's happening in Shan State, Kachin State, Karen State, with the Rohingya in Rakhine. And, as you've alluded to, she's prejudiced, if not racist. Is that really what you think?

ANON: I don't think she's racist, at heart. It's the experiential knowledge that she doesn't have.

AC: She's suffered without food at times during her house arrest, forced to sell her furniture, the house leaked, it was cold, she had no--

ANON: That's nothing. That's not like being in the jungle when you are under heavy artillery fire with jets and helicopter gunships. Nor is it accurate that she didn't have food during her house arrest, because they in fact did allow her food. She even had her own chef. She was allowed to have what she needed at those times. Remember, the prisons were filled in Burma, with people loyal to her and to the struggle for freedom, who were routinely tortured. She lived in a mansion on the lake with access to books and radio and the comfort of a bed and furniture and plenty of food. Yes, she has done a lot for Burma, but the fact remains that she has done almost nothing for the minorities. And frankly, she threw the 700,000 traumatized Rohingya even further under the bus.

AC: Let me just jump around here. Until this project is done, I will pursue a meeting with her and give her a chance, as I've always done, to "speak to the world," freely and openly. And if she wants to do that, she can. And if she doesn't, that's her choice.

Since you and I are here right now, what would you want me to ask her? What are some of the most intimate, difficult, complex, pointed questions that I could ask her? Please, I invite you ask her right now, through the written words on this page.

ANON: We want to know what she's thinking. And I have already posed a number of important questions that I would like her to answer, from U Ko Ni to the neglect of the minorities, to the collusion with the military, to the silence on the Rohingyas crisis, and so on. The truth is, we're so out of touch with her these days, or I should say, she's so out of touch with us, that we don't know any more about what she's doing, what she's thinking, who she is, really. How is she leading the country? In what way? How deeply does she understand the whole country? I really want to know: who are you inside?

AC: Why not ask her for a personal meeting?

ANON: Well, for one, so many of us over the years have repeatedly asked her for meetings and up until now, nothing. We have never been given a chance to meet. Not even a response from her office. Never. In fact, she's thoroughly abandoned many people loyal to her, both people from inside the country and foreigners as well.

AC: Why no interviews with the media?

ANON: You'll find out soon enough. And if you do see her, ask her to reconsider allowing her party members to speak with the media. How can you be a member of a democratic government that's representational of a people, but not allowed to give media interviews? That's a complete disconnect.

I'm sorry to go on this way, but so many of us have had it with her. She controls everything. She's authoritarian. She's arrogant. She's mimicking the ways of her oppressors. And ironically, the fear of being controlled has backfired against her, and now she's acting out the very thing she fought so hard to overcome. So, I would say to her: "Daw Suu, trust." Come back to your heart. Come back to the woman we knew in 1988. Come back to your voice of hope, your loving-kindness, and compassion and caring.

AC: What do you think she fears?

ANON: I don't know. But please ask her, what do you fear? Why so much control? Why are you shutting good people out—good people who are committed more than ever to further helping you and our people? Why? And moreover, please find a way to put yourself in check and change these things. Be mindful of this. This is our country and we may only have one opportunity to put dictatorship behind us.

AC: Has she lost a lot of supporters?

ANON: No, I don't think so. But she has certainly lost many in the press core, many international activists, and many intellectuals. In other words, she has lost a lot of good, smart, and caring people who could help both her and our people achieve our shared goal of democracy.

AC: Her voices to the world?

ANON: Yes. Yet another squandered opportunity of many of the most important people. And not too dissimilar to the way U Ko Ni's family was treated. And this is precisely what I've seen happen repeatedly over the past 10 years with the NLD, and pretty much with the entire '88 Generation. They were all freedom fighters for the very same freedom as Suu Kyi and the NLD for thirty years, but, when things were freer, they were discarded or neglected or both, however you want to see it.

When the '88 Generation was able to work openly and freely in society, they didn't want anything from the government, they were not interested in power, they didn't want to be part of the political system—all they wanted was to assist the thousands and thousands of farmers who are raising legal cases against the military; a military that stole their land and ordered them to get off it. The '88 Generation was the only organization willing to help the farmers. They also tirelessly helped all our people at the grass roots level, people who were in serious trouble, barely getting by. It was not the NLD's interest to help them. In the last six or seven years, I haven't seen anything from the NLD to help marginalized people. The '88 Generation were the ones, because I went to every event. I didn't see any NLD, ever. The only thing the NLD was doing was political matters, how to gain power, how to gain seats and all that. Another question for you to ask Suu Kyi: Why have you abandoned the farmers who suffered under the military? Why have you abandoned the marginalized? Why? And please do not say that you have helped them. Just explain why you have not helped them.

"The ethnic minorities now hate her… Nobody trusts her anymore."

ALAN CLEMENTS: What do you see on the horizon up until the elections?

ANON: If Suu Kyi keeps going the way that she is right now, the one good thing is there will be much more ethnic representations in the next parliament after the elections, because the ethnic minorities at present hate her. They don't want her. They don't like her leadership. They trusted her and put all their faith in her for national reconciliation. And a few months after that, the victims of the airstrike bombings in the ethnic areas of northern Shan and Kachin State no longer trust her. Nobody trusts her in the ethnic regions anymore. How can they? She lets the military bomb our ethnic people.

Of course, she will still get most votes from the Burmese majority. But at the same time, the USDP and military backed party, will also get more seats than in 2015, because in a lot of areas, the NLD was so stupid. For instance, in Mon State they were arguing about how to name a bridge. Can't you just allow a Mon name on a Mon State bridge? They actually voted in Parliament, to name it after Suu Kyi's father. As a result of this arrogance and stupidity, the Mon people voted for the USDP in the by-elections. So, the USDP won. This is also happening in so many areas that the NLD will lose many seats, when it comes to the election.

There was also this other ridiculous event: a comment was made from the NLD Mon State Chief Minister U Aye Zan, about the food shortage, when he told residents to "eat only one dish of curry" at mealtimes in order to bring down food prices. It's totally absurd and yet, another indication of how out of touch these NLD people are with reality. It's somewhat surreal really. People were asking what the government's plans were on making the price of food lower, because inflation is high so high market price is also high, and the Mon minister told the public, "Our country is poor. We should only eat a dish of curry. If we don't go to tea shops and only eat a dish of curry in our homes, won't the food prices decline?" He went as far as telling the people that another way of bringing down prices is to stop donating food to the monasteries. He then urged everyone to take the example of England and Russia, which rationed food during the world wars, then our country's economy will be good. These folks are simply too incompetent to run the country.

AC: Burmans really don't know what it's like to be a non-Burman in Burma? There's a complete cultural difference in the way they speak to one another and treat one another?

ANON: Yes. But I don't blame them, because this is how the military kept people apart. The more you see the differences, the bigger problem this will create amongst societies. That's what they wanted for more than 50 years, and they were really successful about it.

Overall, the majority of Burmans have no idea what it's like to be a minority. For instance, when I first moved to Yangon, I was so upset that I didn't want to live there anymore, because when I had a phone call on a bus, speaking my ethnic language, everybody sitting near me stared at me. Like a zoo, like a monkey. I got so upset.

AC: They looked at you with disdain?

ANON: They stared. People simply do not know what diversity means in this country.

AC: Understandable after 50 years of tyrannical propaganda-driven totalitarianism?

ANON: Yes.

AC: Wars, occupation by the British, decades of dictatorship, torture and rape and so much more… You need nation-state psychiatric training, within a global culture of violence, to lead and heal this country.

My *Dhamma* teacher, the late Venerable Sayadaw U Pandita, and Daw Suu's meditation teacher as well, advocated for leadership training in *mettā* (loving-kindness) and *karunā* (compassion) and what he called "spiritual intelligence," or *Dhamma* intelligence, something I changed to "mindful intelligence"—a wisdom training, as he put it—in how to know the right course of action from the wrong one. Essentially, it's the experiential study of mind states and their respective functions through thought speech and actions, both on self and others.

ANON: May the world hear this.

AC: Speaking on a practical note, is there anyone from the military who you think would speak with me—and go on record—as a voice of freedom in our books? By the way, these books are meant to support Daw Aung San Suu Kyi's call for national reconciliation.

ANON: Of course. It's important to talk to the military, if not directly, through the books themselves. But yes, try to speak to some of the key people in the military.

AC: Do you think there's a chance of talking to the former dictator, U Than Shwe?

ANON: No one's ever had access to him. None.

AC: I would say to him, "Please, sir, may I invite you to say anything you wish to your people to support the transition to democracy and national reconciliation. We will print your words verbatim. And, may I encourage you, sir, in your statement to consider the wisdom of apologizing to your people on national television for the mistakes made by the military over the last 30 years."

ANON: That would certainly go a long way towards the peace and stability of our country.

AC: And what about the Senior General Min Aung Hlaing, would he meet with me?

ANON: No idea, really.

AC: My plan is to go to Naypyidaw and stay for several months. Stay low-key, put out invitations and keep my *Dhamma* motivation high and active.

ANON: Great idea. That's the way to do it, because it takes them time to answer, and you have to ask repeatedly... But what will you do in Naypyidaw while you are waiting? It could be months.

AC: Show my good will by being patient. Meditate a lot.

ANON: Actually, Naypyidaw is a good meditation center, because it's quiet.

AC: I'd want to make it as easy as possible for General Min Aung Hlaing to say, please visit me today and ask anything, openly. And I ask, "What would you, sir, like to share with your people and leaders of the world about your country's transition to democracy and your feelings on achieving national reconciliation?" That's all. That's everything.

ANON: That's a great idea, Alan. May these men see the wisdom in speaking with you and may the same be true for Daw Suu.

AC: Thank you. May Burma become a peaceful union. And may all people work towards a harmonious future.

ANON: May it be so.

CHAPTER 37

CONVERSATION *with* AN ANONYMOUS SUPPORTER *of* DEMOCRACY

2018

- "The majority of the Burmese people are not anti-Muslim."
- "The main problem is not with the army but with the narrow-mindedness of some Rakhine people."
- "The army thinks The Lady is trying to overpower them."
- "The only safe place, if the vote splits, is another strong democratic party."
- "It was Than Shwe's Plan A to let Aung San Suu Kyi take power and let her fail."

"The majority of the Burmese people are not anti-Muslim."

ALAN CLEMENTS: Thank you for taking the time to speak with me today, and as a high-profile, long-term activist, under the conditions with numerous activists being jailed for speaking out, I fully respect and honor your desire for anonymity. How about we start with you sharing whatever it is that interests you the most, please.

ANONYMOUS: Let's start with the Rakhine crisis: I don't see any substantial evidence that genocide is occurring, as we are being accused. How many bodies have they found? How credible are the witnesses? Most are unreliable—that's what we have experienced, here inside the country. Despite the many stories, when we fact check, there's no hard evidence for genocide. Stories are being fabricated. That's what we've found. Now, we are not defending the army. They are a poor-quality force. Nor are they strong Buddhists. Further, they're somewhat nationalist. They may not like Indians. And usually what happens, for example, back in 1988 when these young soldiers were brought into Yangon to quell the uprising, they were told by commanders—and we know this for a fact—"these young people are insurgents fighting the government." Our soldiers were totally misinformed and brainwashed, and so the way they reacted was terrible; unacceptable; unspeakable; tragic. But when we asked the soldiers, they had been misinformed, and on top of that, indoctrinated and doped. The worst combination. So, they lost it. They killed so many people. They killed our own people. But there's no point in defending them. They are a miserably poor army. And it's their commanders who are at fault. Along with the senior generals and, of course, Saw Maung. But the vast majority of our Burmese people are not racist nor anti-Muslim.

AC: Being the devil's advocate here, isn't there a clear and present danger that Islam will likely take over Burma? Almost everyone I have spoken with, including some senior monks, feel that if economic, ethical and spiritual corruption continues in Burma, at the level it is—unabated—and jihad takes roots with selective terrorist attacks in the country, for example, at the airport, the Shwedagon Pagoda, a Buddhist monastery, a five-star hotel, etc., then in 10, 20, 30, or so years, the country will become yet another domino in the Islamic takeover of South East Asia. Your thoughts?

ANON: Yes, it's possible. History has shown that to be true. And Islam is rapidly growing in Burma. And yes, there are well established groups here who are strongly against Islam, unreasonably strong. In fact, I have friends willing to fight them by all means. But there is no substantial evidence that Muslims are doing bad things to us. But you are right, there are many in Burma who think Muslims will take over our country. But at that moment, that's misinformation. There is a lot of Islamophobia in the world today and Burma is not exempt.

In Scandinavian countries, for instance, the way that many people think about the "Islamic threat" is very different from reality. And it's much worse here. In some states in the furthermost part of the country, the authorities themselves have said the majority of our population has now become Islamic. That's simply not true. I have travelled to some of these places to see for myself and it is not as they say it is. Yes, there are many Muslim villages along the border with Bangladesh. In some areas this is true, but among the whole population in Burma Muslims are a minority, less than five percent. But people think they've become a majority.

AC: So you're saying the threat is an exaggeration?

ANON: Yes. We don't need to worry. And yes, the population of Muslims in the country is increasing. But Burma will not become an Islamic country in the next 50 years. That won't happen. The greater issue to be concerned about is our economic position. We are an impoverished nation, teetering on collapse. People don't dare say it, but we are. And the core issue—why the country is vulnerable—is the radical decline of Buddhism quantitatively and qualitatively. The population of Buddhist monks has decreased by almost a third in one decade. That's a rapid decline. In some states it's dropped by 50 percent. And the quality of one's Buddhist understanding, that of the *Dhamma*, has also declined. Overall, Burma is in decline. Maybe even more rapidly than anyone thinks.

AC: Why such a radical decline in monastic Buddhism?

ANON: It all began in 1990 after SPDC refused to recognize the election result. Then a thousand monks commemorate the 8888 uprising in Mandalay, and they were brutally suppressed. To boycott against the military government according to Buddhist rules, Pathanikuzana ritual was performed widely across the country. Hundreds of monks, including most revered senior monks and their monasteries, were brutally smashed and hundreds were sent to jail. Afterward, the generals tried to appease the monks again, by offering big perks to the Sangha Mahanayakas who accepted them. From that time, senior monks became corrupted with big monasteries, big cars and ample donations. At the same time, these monks lost the general public's faith. That is when they started to point out the danger of Islamization, to frighten their devotees. Young militant monks believe in their indoctrination and started to attack Islam in every way they can. There was an illegal exodus of many northern Rakhine Muslims to Mon state, who settled there en-bloc and also alarmed the local populace.

As I said, we are impoverished. We are an extremely poor country. More and more of our people are forced to work like slaves to survive. We have close to five million people that go illegally to Thailand and Malaysia, who work in unforgiving conditions as migrant workers and send most of their money back to their families. Without that money they would likely starve.

You have been out to the most destitute areas of Yangon. Hundreds of thousands of people living in squalor—conditions so bad you cannot describe them. Even the police refuse the patrol the areas, they have become so lawless. In such a situation, Buddhism is not helpful for them.

AC: What are the defining features of Burma's army? What are they trained to do?

ANON: The army is low quality and brutal. They have a sadistic attitude of "Take no prisoners. Kill all." That's what has been going on for the last half century. Whatever happens, they are ordered to "kill everyone in the field." If you check the casualty list, everyone has been killed. No arrests. No wounded. "Take no prisoners." Brutality, sadism, and indoctrination define our army. It pains me to say it, but it is true.

Another slogan, "bring water by all means" also makes the situation worse. Soldiers believe that ends justify the means. Fabricated reports were made later to cover up their brutal actions everywhere.

AC: This of course, is what we are seeing in Rakhine? Unspeakable atrocities.

ANON: Yes. This is our Burmese Army. But it is not racism. It's brutality.

AC: They're indoctrinated? Take no prisoners, kill everyone, regardless of race or religion? They killed Buddhist monks during the Saffron Revolution. They massacred the Karens; I wrote about it in *Burma: The Next Killing Fields*, back in 1990. And the same with the Shans and Kachins, and now the Rohingya?

ANON: Christians, Hindus, Buddhists, Muslims, monks, nuns, kids, it doesn't matter. In some cases, army officers brought some prisoners in from the field, and it caused problems. Because these prisoners become witnesses to all that happened. So the best way is to kill everyone. And that's what our army does.

AC: So, in Rakhine, the exodus of nearly a million Rohingyas into Bangladesh is classic Burmese Army brutality? History has shown, from insiders like yourself, that "take no prisoners" is the signature style of a military clearance operation here in Burma?

ANON: Of course. You witnessed it yourself in Karen State. Nothing is different today except they are more equipped, more deeply indoctrinated and better at killing. And it will continue—they will do it in the future as well. Let them invade Bangladesh, everyone will run away. Although Bangladesh has a superior army and superior weapons, the Burmese Army, once they invade, will kill indiscriminately, every civilian. I'm telling you, central command says, "take no prisoners," and that is what they do in the field—a disciplined orgy of murder.

AC: I'm sorry to press you so intensely but no one has ever spoken with me so bluntly about the army. What you're sharing, is well known among you and your friends?

ANON: Yes, very well known. This is Burma. We live here. It's a small country. People talk. People listen. We have wars going on all over the country. We ourselves have been attacked by our own army. Most everyone I know has suffered in prison. Most have been tortured. Our military forces are brutal. Out in the field, there's no discrimination, whether people are soldiers or civilians the army kills everyone. That's their way of fighting on the frontline. It's the way that armies fight. That's war. Look at your country in Iraq, Afghanistan. Merciless. And the most sophisticated planes on earth with precious guided bombs and missiles and still, how many innocent people are murdered? "Take no prisoners" is what psychopaths preach.

"The main problem is not with the army but with the Rakhine people."

ALAN CLEMENTS: The allegations of Rohingya women being raped and gang-raped, this is also typical of the Burmese Army?

ANON: Rape, yes. But they won't gang rape, that's not usual. That is not in the rules. But, on the frontline, it happens when the situation is preferable for them to do such things. Rape, for young soldiers, is a tendency since they are not a disciplined army. They will rape when they have a chance, but it's not policy. It is not agreed by the majority of the army, but it happens. Because the quality of the soldiers is so low, that can happen, but it is not due to the government or the Burmese people, and it's not against the Muslims. Even if they were Burmese Buddhist girls, if they happen to be on the frontline, they will be raped.

AC: Disgusting. Sexual violence as a tactic of war? This is the norm for the Burmese army?

ANON: Totally.

AC: Horrible.

ANON: Horrible.

AC: So, Senior General Min Aung Hlaing is lying when denies that the army is committing such atrocities?

ANON: Of course, he's lying. He is a skilled manipulator. That's why he's a Senior General appointed by Than Shwe, who was trained in psychological war tactics. The report you get from will be rosy. That is also typical of the army. Whenever there is fighting, they report there is fighting, how many people have run away, how many bullets were used—all these things are completely fabricated, made up. They do one thing and say another.

AC: So, the regional commander and other senior officers in the field in Rakhine will simply lie to General Min Aung Hlaing? And they both know it's a lie, and that's the way business is done in the Burmese army?

ANON: Yes. Step by step lies. Sealed by collusion. Not even the divisional commanders know the truth. The more lies there are the less chance of the truth being known. But everyone knows the policies expected of them. Of course, they know these horrible things happen because this is how they were trained, and they all came up the ranks from lower levels. Again, the main concern is to win the battle by all means and "take no prisoners."

AC: To win, with no prisoners and report lies back to central command?

ANON: That's it. And there are some additional rules but not many. But the situation has become complicated with Rohingya campaign. There are maybe 100 rape cases, but it will be exaggerated to 1,000, to 3,000 or even 5,000 cases. And in this way, there is more pressure from the outside world to do something. There is a better chance for the Rohingya outside of the country, as it is not safe for them inside. So, the more they exaggerate the more likely they can stay outside the country.

For instance, the area in Maungdaw in Rakhine is not safe for locals to move around. There is no security. Only when there are armed forces present are they somewhat protected. Otherwise, the locals are unprotected. And the Rakhine Buddhists are afraid of the Rohingya Muslims. There is a huge hatred now between the Rakhine and Rohingyas. There is no chance of reconciliation, and the administrative structure has also collapsed. Most of the Rakhines in the Rohingya hotbed are now resettling away from northern Rakhine.

AC: No chance of improvement?

ANON: We must try to improve the area for everyone. That's what we're doing now, according to the recommendation of the Kofi Annan Commission report. Only if the area were more civilized and peaceful will there be reconciliation. They have a lot of things to do. They must be much better than the other areas around the country. Only then will the Rakhines and Rohingyas coexist. And the main problem today is not with the army but with the Rakhine people. The Rakhine are not accepting the Rohingya, because of ARSA, the Islamic terrorist group, attacking 30 military and police outposts.

AC: Why did ARSA do this?

ANON: Why does any terrorist group commit terrorism? To further their agenda of funding, the spread of radical Islam, to secure Rohingya sanctuary, hatred of 'other,' economic reasons, the perception of oppression, all of these and more. And now, rumors are going around among the Rakhine people about how horrible these Rohingyas people are. And, for Rohingya people, they have no one to protect them. ARSA may be winning the PR battle but the Rohingya are suffering more now than ever before. The situation is not good and getting worse.

AC: What is your response when someone asks you, "Why didn't Daw Aung San Suu Kyi speak up during these atrocities to the Rohingya people?"

ANON: For me, The Lady does not understand the situation. She didn't have enough information about the battlefield, what actually happened on the ground. During those days, she was uninformed because these were military matters. She didn't even believe, at that time, that 100,000 people fled the country. She said, "Oh, that's impossible; many people are still living there; why do they run away?" She didn't think they were afraid.

Also, there was a threat from the Rohingya ARSA group, that if they didn't run away, they would be considered accomplices of the army.

AC: ARSA was willing to sacrifice the Rohingyas?

ANON: For the sake of the Rohingya country, they are even ready to sacrifice their own lives. But they are not a well-trained army; ARSA is just a group of terrorist-bandits.

AC: Is there a fear that jihad will spread throughout Burma?

ANON: Real jihad can come from the outside world, but not from ARSA.

AC: From where? Pakistan? Saudi Arabia? Funding for ARSA has been traced to Pakistan. Isn't Burma fertile for jihad?

ANON: It could come from anywhere with the inciting of more hatred. The hatred is pretty high at the moment. Where it could go is anyone's guess. Look at 9/11 in your country. Look at the roots of al-Qaeda. They formed in Pakistan. As you said, funding and logistics for ARSA have been traced to Pakistan. Burma cannot be fertile for jihad under military supremacy. Burma army is more brutal than ARSA.

AC: But still, there must be some fear of jihad? Some people talk that way now in Burma?

ANON: Yes, we have information that the Islamic Group, ISIS, infiltrated the country last month along the borders. Some of them were arrested.

"The army think she is trying to contain them or overpower them."

ALAN CLEMENTS: Back to Daw Aung San Suu Kyi; essentially what you are saying is that she is uninformed, isolated, and has no access to information from the army?

ANON: Yes, because the military keeps her ill-informed. And further, the relation between them is not good. The army thinks she's trying to overpower them. She was close with Shwe Mann, and he's considered a real traitor by the army. They openly declared him to be a traitor.

AC: A psychological war in Naypyidaw?

ANON: Yes. Shwe Mann and his group of 20 have become a special commission appointed by The Lady to take care of religious issues, above the Parliament. There were 21 expelled from the USDP, sent away. The USDP CEC, all the top people, the whole group, were expelled. It was during the party congress that the army took over, took them all away, and the newcomers filled the CEC posts.

AC: Essentially, you're saying the military doesn't like or trust Daw Aung San Suu Kyi?

ANON: The army and the USDP on one side, and The Lady and Shwe Mann on the other side. All Shwe Mann's group are ex-USDP.

AC: You're saying Daw Suu is isolated?

ANON: Yes. But the problem is that she doesn't know she's isolated. She thinks of herself as well informed because she keeps all of her trusted people around her. And they all tell her everything is ok. They report only the good things.

AC: So, they're not truth tellers? They are afraid of her reaction if they speak the truth?

ANON: Most people who are around her know that if they tell the truth they cannot stay close to her anymore. That has happened many times in the past. The people who speak the truth are not accepted. There are arguments and they're quickly expelled.

AC: She has every right not to align with someone's so called truth, correct?

ANON: Of course, but your truth and another truth may not always be aligned. She's not looking for dialogue about an issue. She's looking for alignment, agreement.

AC: Where do you align and where do you not align with her thinking?

ANON: One thing is that the way she thinks is not Burmese. I'll explain. When you think about our country, you have to think the way Burmese people think. The way people respond is not the same as the way she would like them to respond, so it's difficult for her as the leader.

To put it bluntly: she doesn't speak our language. She's a worldly person, so she can relate with international leaders. But when it comes to our local Burmese people, we have to agree with her. That's the only way to approach her. Otherwise you cannot approach her or be close to her.

AC: What do the "Burmese people" you know want to say to her that she's not willing to hear or listen to? What is she not aware of that you would like her to be aware of?

ANON: The people want to change the country as she does, but the political system is not right; the economic policies are not right; the people she's chosen are not right; her choices are not correct; and she trusts you only if you agree with her. These are not the marks of a good leader, to me.

AC: You're saying she's autocratic? Or that she knows what she wants and doesn't want?

ANON: What I'm saying is that she's not a leader, full stop. She's charismatic. People love her; although many people don't like her, they still love her. She got the top leadership position even before she formed a party, even before she decided to get involved in Burmese politics. Her first meeting at Shwedagon Pagoda back in 1989, with 500,000 people listening, was the largest in our country. That was the first time people had ever seen her or heard from her, but even at that time the whole country was behind her.

AC: Because of her father, General Aung San?

ANON: No. Not because of her father. It was because of her style. And from her side, when the NLD was formed, there were three portions. One is from U Aung Gyi, a kind of economic group. Another was an army group, and then her side was called the intellectual group. The army group became a richer party, the U Aung Gyi group became the UNDP party, but her group never became a party. They were intellectuals, lawyers and even artists, but no politicians. Nor does she even like politicians. To lead the country, not as a politician, is very awkward. It's not a good thing.

AC: But look at what she has accomplished: most political prisoners have been released; there's some form of dialogue going on with the military; there's some semblance of democracy after decades of dictatorship; tourists are coming into the country, international businesses are coming in as well, human rights are being talked about, openly; and she has, as a leader, achieved all that and more. So, what you are saying is that what's required to move the country forward is a much greater leader than Daw Aung San Suu Kyi?

ANON: From the very beginning, I didn't consider her a political leader. She learned politics in Oxford, but she didn't become a politician. I have had the same feeling all along.

"The only safe place, if the vote splits,
is another strong democratic party."

ALAN CLEMENTS: And the people of your country still unanimously stand behind Daw Suu?

ANON: The situation here is that people are afraid the army will come back, or the USDP will come back. The only safe place, if the vote splits, is another strong democratic party like the 88 Generation group. If the vote splits, the USDP can come back. That happened in the last by-election—the people lost confidence in the NLD, and many NLD people stayed away and did not vote. There, when in the first place it was a strong NLD constituency, a third of those NLD voters do not show up. The USDP won.

AC: What motivates Daw Aung San Suu Kyi to do what she does every day?

ANON: From my point of view, she simplifies everything. Whatever information she has, she thinks the whole country is behind her, and that she is doing the right thing. These simple principles she is following are quite enough to lead the country for its betterment *if* the army agrees to it, *if* the USDP people do not cling to their power, and *if* the outside world understands us more. Then it is not her weakness. If she knew she had some weakness, she would be ready to change it, whatever it is. She has very strong good will, but she is now in the trap of the army. She has little power to move outside that trap. According to some people, it was Than Shwe's "Plan A" to let her take power and let her fail. Let her fail badly, so that she will never return.

AC: Can you say more?

ANON: From the beginning, people were saying the army gave her power with that plan. It was said since they handed over power, and it came true.

AC: So there really is no democracy here? It's all an orchestrated totalitarian facade?

ANON: Democracy, from our point of view, has to be practiced even with the Constitution limited, as it is. In many administrative structures there are many things we want to do which we cannot do because of constitutional constraints. But with democracy, if we practice it well, even in the party, it can get better. Democracy is for change, to exchange views and change small things all the time. But the way she is ruling the country does not allow people to change. And for this, she blames the Constitution, or the army, which does not let us change. That is the only answer she knows.

AC: That the army is preventing us from moving forward?

ANON: Yes.

AC: But she doesn't see it as an obstacle in the long run, does she? She's taking the long road. Although the Constitution was written to enshrine the military, it could very well change in 10 to 20 years, correct? That's her attitude, "In the long term we will have a democratic Burma"?

ANON: No. She actually thought she could change the country in the first five years. She thinks she can change a lot because she doesn't understand the real situation. In reality, she cannot do much, because her party is weak and ill-informed.

AC: So, from your point of view, the future of democracy in Burma is with people like Ko Ko Gyi forming a new party that is aligned with the youth, and gaining more and more popularity over time, to do the job that she wanted to do in five years but couldn't?

ANON: What's happening now, after two years of this new government, is that people are starting to realise the obstacles, the weakness of the government and the party and The Lady. Now they realise what's happening, so they are trying to change. That's why the five regional ministers all quit during the last few days, and one chief minister also quit.

AC: Many people close to her are defecting, they're leaving?

ANON: Some were forced to leave, and some left for their own reasons. It will continue within the next month. Even at the national level we are expecting five national ministers to be replaced, within the next two or three days. Things are starting to change.

AC: These are good changes?

ANON: Good but overdue changes. People are starting to think about real change. At first, they thought they could continue, but they can't. If changing things is good, more changes will come, and better people will come to power in one of two years' time. The NLD can continue, if they dare to change. What happened was they did not change because they feared for their reputation—"Oh, this government is changing too much, they are not good people"—but that is not working. The way they procrastinated is not working. Now The Lady knows the situation.

AC: She knows what?

ANON: That change needs to occur. But she only knows some of it. Not all. She even said, two days ago, that the economic situation is not that bad. But for businesspeople, the situation is unacceptable. They cannot continue. Only now, very recently, all kinds of complaints were made, putting pressure on the government to change. So, if it starts to change, it is not like the previous government. In the previous government, it was centralized on principle. This time it is centralized on a personal basis, not on principle. It can be changed.

AC: And Than Shwe is still in power on some level?

ANON: Than Shwe is watching. If he thinks he needs to interfere, he will do it. He has the power to interfere, at any time.

AC: Thank you for taking the time to share your views.

CHAPTER 38

A CONVERSATION *with*
KO YE WAI PHYO
January 16th, 2020

- "Freedom of expression is the most important issue we face in Myanmar today."
- "Daw Aung San Suu Kyi is behaving in the very same way as some of the generals before her."

"Freedom of expression is the most important issue we face in Myanmar today."

ALAN CLEMENTS: Let's start with what Athan does as an organization here in Myanmar, and if you would, a little about your own background in activism.

KO YE WAI PHYO: When I was a student, I was a member of the Student Union at Yangon University. At that time, I was involved in student activism, such as campaigning to reform the National Education Law and to release all imprisoned students. Essentially, we wanted academic freedom, student rights and the immediate release of our prisoners of conscience. Then, two years ago, I met with Maung Kaungkha, Aung Khant and we founded the Athan organisation, as a way to focus on freedom of expression, because we feel freedom of expression is the most important issue we face in Myanmar today. Because of its importance, our country needs as many activists as possible for this universal human right. In fact, we feel that everyone in the country should speak up—freely. Why? Because the majority of court cases against the people are based on the government and the military attempting to deny our freedom of expression.

What we do as an organization? In Athan, we have three branches: research, training, and advocacy. In research, we investigate what we deem as violations of freedom of expression. We make legal analysis and then document cases of violation and the lawsuits. In addition, we publish reports and statements.

In trainings, we explain the meaning of freedom of expression, primarily to community leaders, student unions, and activists. For instance, today, two of my colleagues are going to Meiktila to give a freedom of expression training. We have many such trainings and we plan to do many more.

The third branch is advocacy. We often go to the capital, Naypyidaw, and meet with government officials, the parliamentarians, and sometimes we go overseas to do international advocacy. The reason we do international work is that we believe that sometimes just doing internal advocacy (just dealing with local government) cannot be successful, because members of Parliament, or the government, or ministers, or the military, do not much care about the local human rights defender. What they do care about is the international pressure. That is why we go to the United Nations and other international organisations to explain the crisis we are facing with freedom of expression here in Myanmar.

At other times, we pressure the government directly. Take the case of Wa Lone and Kyaw Soe Oo, the Reuters journalists who were detained on December 12, 2017. At the time of their arrests, they were investigating the murder of 10 Rohingya Muslim men and boys in Inn Din, a village in Rakhine state.

When these two journalists were arrested, Athan made a major campaign to raise awareness of their situation. Even so, the government charged and sentenced them to 7 years' imprisonment. We were outraged by this atrocity. So, we protested and took the campaign worldwide. As a result, many international organisations and international media joined in the campaign. The BBC, RFA, and CNN came on board. Even the UN and a number of other international parties pressured the Myanmar government. Because of that, the civilian government released Wa Lone and Kyaw Soe Oo on May 7, 2019 after more than 500 days in prison.

Now we are making other campaigns. Recently, we made the Blue Shirt Campaign. The blue shirts represent the political prisoners, because in Myanmar the uniform of the prisoners is blue. So, in the Blue Shirt Campaign, rather than protesting, we go into the Myanmar courtroom when a defendant is sued or charged by the military and make our presence known. This includes cases such as the Peacock Generation [a performance troupe sentenced to six months hard labor], the Min Htin Ko Ko Gyi case, and other such cases brought about by the military. So, we go into the courtroom and stand there. From a legal point of view, no one has the right to protest inside the courtroom. So, we just stand silently, wearing our blue shirts with "Respect Freedom of Expression" written on them.

Of course, we strongly condemn these lawsuits by the military. The lawsuits themselves are criminal and our presence in the courtroom makes that point loud and clear, despite not saying a word.

We also have another campaign similar to that. I think you will already have heard that the government shut down the internet in the nine townships between the Rakhine and Chin states. We condemn that government action. So, we made a campaign to condemn shutting down the internet, because it's a violation of our human rights. Since no journalists are allowed to enter the conflict zone, information is essential. We do not know the truth of what's going on and we want to know. The government needs to be held accountable. Without the internet, everyone is blind. As I said, when there is no accountability it is much easier to act with impunity. Privacy promotes atrocities.

Our campaigns are meant to support freedom for all, including the military and the government. In fact, Athan would have likely been the first to instigate an international campaign to highlight Daw Aung San Suu Kyi's illegal incarceration back in 1989, should we have been around. And the same with the other 10,000 or so political prisoners over the years. But here we are doing all we can at the start of 2020.

AC: If you would, please take us back into the courtroom.

KYWP: There's usually three of us in the courtroom, and maybe 20 or 30 outside the courtroom. But the group outside are still within the court compound and everyone is also wearing the blue shirt with "Freedom of Expression" on it. It is also important for everyone to stand up and remain silent. We are not there to interrupt the judiciary system. We are only there to show the judge and others who are accusing the defendants that your wrongful actions are known and will be shared with the world. We are also providing moral support for the accused.

AC: It's rare for the outside world to get a window of direct experience inside a Burmese courtroom, where so many people over the decades have gone before judges and these *faux*-trials, from U Tin Oo to U Kyi Maung, to Daw Aung San Suu Kyi, to U Win Tin and U Win Htein, and U Aye Maung, Ko Ko Gyi, Min Ko Naing, Nilar Thein—thousands of people have gone there to be sentenced for being nonviolent activists, for using freedom of expression to peacefully challenge the machinations of institutionalized dictatorship. But so few have really seen inside the courtroom. What happened in the case of the Peacock Generation performers?

KYWP: Let me say this: There is great pressure in the courtroom, and it starts from the judge. The judge is under enormous pressure, as are the police in the courtroom—the ones who arrested the performers. All of them are under the weight of doing as they are told by their superiors. This blind obedience is a direct carry over from authoritarian dictatorship. This is fear-induced coercion from Burma's Big Brother. 'Do as we say, or else.' They're all afraid.

AC: They've abandoned their integrity, their self-worth, their dignity?

KYWP: Yes, that's it. And their fear is tangible—it can be easily seen and felt. See, the judge and the police are afraid of their superiors. Meanwhile, they oppress the lower level. The lower level are the defendants, the activists from the Peacock Generation and so on.

In the courtroom, anybody has the right to attend a hearing. But the judge does not allow it. His only reason to prevent people from entering is that it is small. But that too is a violation and not a reason to restrict freedom of expression or human rights.

There are so many other examples of this kind of behaviour. Like the police—according to their protocol, the police car must stop far away from the court and bring the defendants to the courtroom on foot. Regardless, the car parks are inside the court compound, but still the defendants are handcuffed. And that's wrong according to the law. Nor is it necessary but they do it anyway.

The police treat activists, performers, artists, and journalists like criminals. They're not criminals. They're political prisoners. They are in handcuffs for their beliefs and freedom of expression and their caring for the rights of others. That's wrong and our job is to point out that's wrong for the welfare of the many and the future of our country's prosperity.

We need to overcome being seen as a dictatorship and transition into a democracy that respects universal human rights, and of course, rule of law, not military law or civilian dictatorship law, but genuine constitutional law. Real constitutional democratic law and not the phony one we have. But that's another matter.

AC: So, the judge is not free to make a decision based upon integrity; they're pressured from above. Who are those people? Who pressures them?

KYWP: It depends on the situation. In Myanmar, the judge decides based not on the cases but on the power behind them. In the case of the Peacock Generation, the power is the military. In the Min Htin Ko Ko Gyi case, the power is the military. In the case of Wa Lone and Kyaw Saw Oo, the two journalists, the power was from the government. So, it depends on the situation. But the sure thing is the judges; they're just making decisions based upon power. They see who the defendants are, and who are the complainants. If the complainants are a high power, maybe MPs or high-ranking generals, or maybe someone special from a government organisation, there's pressure for the judges to do what the complainant wants.

AC: If the military decides to charge someone, the military always wins?

KYWP: That's right. If the government charges someone, the government always wins, in 99 percent of the cases. If the military charges someone, the military always wins, in 99 percent of the cases. Verdicts are known in advance of the trial, in 99 percent of the cases.

AC: In the case of the Peacock Generation, they're a performing spoken word theatre group of young people, and they were charged for defaming the military? They received six months in prison with hard labor?

KYWP: Yes. And that is just a single case. Actually, the Peacock Generation was sued under eight lawsuits. Five lawsuits are still ongoing in Botahtaung, and in four townships in the Ayerwaddy Region. In Mayangone and Botahtaung, there were two lawsuits from each township. One is with 66(d) of the Telecommunications Law, and another with Section 505(A) of Penal Code. In total there were eight lawsuits form different townships. One year with hard labor is just one lawsuit, in 505(A). Another lawsuit is another one year. They also got six months imprisonment in the 66(d) lawsuits. So, they may be in prison for a very long time. It's far from complete.

AC: What did they do exactly?

KYWP: They are my friends. They are brave. Essentially, the five group members got one-year prison terms under a law that bans information that endangers or demoralises the military. What they were doing was theatrically and satirically pushing through their performance to amend our military-created undemocratic Constitution. And I was there when they were tried and sentenced.

The last time they went to court the police viciously pushed my friends into the police car, and one of them said back, "And we must push to amend the Constitution. The Constitution is not right."

In other words, we young people will never stop our activism, and we will never stop our freedom of expression. We will keep going. They kept saying exactly what they believed to be right, true, and democratic. That is why I say they are brave.

AC: So that the world understands, this is a famous spoken word performing theatre group and they're on stage—what did they do exactly or what did they say on stage to warrant being imprisoned with hard labor?

KYWP: Several things were seen as dangerous. The first was pushing for amending the undemocratic, military-created, military-enshrined Constitution. Politically speaking, amending the Constitution is a very sensitive issue—the military are very reactive over their undemocratic constitution. We can easily see the fear in their faces and in their body language in the way they behave in Parliament. So, the performers pushed these things. Another thing was about the ICJ (The International Court of Justice).

AC: But they're just joking—so what? They are artists, satirists, comedic activists. What's the problem? Why not laugh with them? This is nothing. The military has been taken to the International Court of Justice for accusations of genocide, and here they are imprisoning young boys and girls for suggesting that the Constitution be changed.

KYWP: At the root of it, the military are terrified of activists. From Ne Win's military coup in 1962 and on to Than Shwe and then Thein Sein, so many of the military guys are afraid of activists and our activism. Because activism can bring them down.

AC: So, the root psychology is the fear of losing power?

KYWP: Yes. They are driven by fear. They are frightened human beings. That's why they are vicious to their own people. Why else would you harm someone? Why else would you imprison someone for their love of activist art?

AC: And so, activists are much more important to repress than international opinion, because activists, like in '88 or in the Saffron Revolution of 2007, or what you're doing with being in the courtroom as activists, threatens their hold on power?

KYWP: Sure. They fear losing power, and they also fear damaging their reputation. They also want to hold onto their property. They have become very wealthy over the decades through many illegal means. In addition, you can see in the 2008 Constitution that they wrote it in such a way to actually defend themselves—they, the ex-military guys, like Than Shwe. The Constitution defends him so that no one can sue him. He and the old guard have absolute immunity from prosecution.

AC: And so, if I'm Burmese and I'm saying that the 2008 Constitution is undemocratic and that it should be changed, that could be seen as a cause for defamation? Could I be imprisoned for saying that?

KYWP: Yes. All defamation cases are criminal cases, not civil ones. That's the problem.

AC: But don't Than Shwe, Min Aung Haling, the Tatmadaw, the court, the judges, don't they know it's a lie? The colonels, the generals, the dictators, the judges, they must know that their children think "this is totalitarianism, not democracy." I mean, "Dad, I love music, I love dance, I like to sing, I like poetry, I like theatre, I like comedy"—what is going on in the lives of these leaders where they are so terrified of freedom?

KYWP: It's simple: they know they've done wrong. So, they repress the people out of fear of prosecution. If they don't repress the people, the people will speak out and protest and accuse the government. It's because they are not right—if they were right, the people would support them.

They know they've done wrong, so they're repressing anyone who is perceived as a threat to their power.

AC: Is it only fear or do they have some sense of *hiri* and *ottapa*—some sense of conscience, some sense of moral shame and moral regret?

KYWP: I think it is more about fear than anything rooted in conscience. Remember, they have had a long, long history of killing our people, even the monks in 2007. As you know well, the prisons were filled with political prisoners. They torture. They rape. They force hard labor upon people. They do not value life. In true democracies, a person kills 5, 10, 20 people over a period of a year or two or so, they are called a serial killer and deemed criminally insane and given life imprisonment or a death sentence. Under dictatorship in Myanmar, you can kill many thousands over many decades, and you live like kings and queens. And now they created a constitution that enshrines their hold on power and protects them from prosecution. Now, you tell me what criminal insanity means? And you tell me what activism would mean to you, if you lived under such an insane situation?

AC: I can tell you this, it is an honor to speak with you as a courageous voice of freedom in your country. And may your words soften the hearts of all those who read them. My question: You truly think that they know they've done wrong? And a follow up question: How to turn their fear into an awakening of conscience?

KYWP: Yes, they know they have done wrong, absolutely. As I said, that's why they made the 2008 Constitution as it is, to protect them and their families. In reality, in democracy, if they were right, people would support them. They would keep power officially. It's because they knew they were in the wrong that they made the 2008 Constitution and, in addition, made so many repressive laws, like 55(a), 55(b), and also the criminal defamation law.

AC: A challenging question, perhaps. You are a leading activist in your country for freedom of speech. People cherish this right worldwide. I don't see how democracy can exist as a democracy without being able to say pretty much whatever you want, when you want, to whom you want, especially in the papers, on stage and in poetry and music and theatre and film, and at home with your wife and your children. On the other hand, the military and former military leaders take their position seriously—they're afraid. They're putting boys and girls younger than their own children in prison here and punishing them with hard labor. They're sending a very clear message: you mess with us, we've killed our own Buddhist monks in

2007, chanting the Mettā Sutta, no less, and we'll take you off the stage and make you really fear ever using your voice again.

Now, my question: If former general Than Shwe were in this room with us and he said to you, "I admire your work at Athan but the truth is, you are right, I'm afraid," how would you advise him on turning that fear into an awakening of conscience? What would you say to U Than Shwe?

KYWP: What I would say is this, and I would say it with as much *mettā* or loving-kindness as I could ever imagine saying anything: "Sir, you have done wrong and you know it. Release your fear. You have fear because you know you did many wrong actions. It is good that you know that killing people, imprisoning people, having them tortured and raped was bad. You know that allowing your generals and cronies to steal the land of our farmers and our people was wrong. You know it was wrong in the same way you know it would be wrong if someone ordered you and your wife and family out of your home and onto the street in Naypyidaw. Imagine if that happened, sir? And there you were out on the street with nothing other than the clothes on your body? You are a Buddhist. I invite you, sir, to reflect in this way. Your fear means that you have a respect for *sīla* (ethical intelligence). It means that you are a practicing Buddhist. If you release your fear, your regrets and remorse will begin to be released as well. If you release your fear, you can begin to free your mind. Because you're older now, this is the only way you can live in peace. If you keep doing these types of bad actions, you will never find true joy, or true peace. Your fear will haunt you until you die. Your fear will carry over into your next existence. You will likely be reborn in a hell realm. As a Buddhist you respect the law of *kamma*. As our Buddha said, "Our life is shaped by our mind; we become what we think. Suffering follows an evil thought as the wheels of a cart follow the oxen that draws it. Our life is shaped by our mind; we become what we think. Joy follows a pure thought like a shadow that never leaves." Please, sir, for the betterment of our country and the future of peace, admit your mistakes and seek amends with the people." That is what I would say to Than Shwe.

AC: I'm U Than Shwe, and here's my response: "Yes, you are right, I have fear. But my greater fear is for my wife, my children, and my grandchildren, and I also fear for my former generals, as well as for Senior General Min Aung Hlaing, and his family. In fact, there's a lot of people in my life that I'm concerned with, because if I admit my wrongdoings, what are you going to do with me? What will the people want to do with me? What will the civilian government want to do with me? Are you going to send me to The Hague and have me tried as a war criminal? Are you going to put me in solitary confinement in Insein Prison? Are you going take all of our wealth and property and privileges? I fear in this way. The fear of my future outweighs the courage I would need to admit my wrongdoing and face the consequences." How would you respond to him?

KYWP: If reflecting as I just suggested did not work, I would advise him to visit any number of the IDP (Internally Displaced People) camps in our country. There are well over 200,000 displaced people in IDP camps having fled his violence in Kachin, Kayin, Shan and Rakhine states. In these camps, there are many families who have lost everything. Their lives were stolen, though they did nothing wrong. And now, they live as prisoners of Myanmar military violence in IDP camps. Please, sir, "look into the eyes of these people. Look into the eyes of the children. They did nothing wrong. They are suffering many bad things every day because of you. You must have compassion for them. And you must have remorse for your own actions. Think of these people as your family and not only your own immediate family. Imagine if they were in fact your family. What would you do?"

AC: But you're asking me to acknowledge my fear, and I'm afraid you're going to put me in prison.

KYWP: That's justice. No one will harm you. You can stay in prison in The Hague. Say they sentence him and these other military guys; they should go to prison for 30 years or 50 years or their whole lifetime. So what? Ultimately, you are not going to be killed, even though you've killed so many people—in 1988 and in 2007, so many times. And in present times, we don't know really what's happening in Rakhine or Kachin states. We do know that many people die daily. Babies, children, women are hurting, hungry, frightened, and dying. Even pregnant women. They die every day. And no one hears much about it. Media cannot go there. The Internet and phone services are shut down. What we are told are lies. So, ultimately, sir, you would not be killed—you will just be imprisoned. And even then, it's an international prison, not a Burmese prison. Burmese prisons, as you know, are among the most terrible on the planet. Nor will you be tortured. Only your fear will torture you if you do not address it as you should, like the good Buddhist you profess yourself to be.

AC: So, you're advocating that there be justice served to the oppressors and to those whom they ordered to carry out the oppression? You don't want a truth and reconciliation council like they did in South Africa or Chile, you want justice?

KYWP: Yes, that is exactly what I mean. It is hard to say and hard to represent what the people want, but the truth is that now, what Daw Aung

San Suu Kyi is doing is not what the people want. She's always talking about national reconciliation, but it's only reconciliation between her and the military. It is not reconciliation between the people and the military, and not between the ethnic people and the military. She's just attempting reconciliation between herself and the military. So, when we talk about reconciliation, what is it? What is the real process? We just close our eyes and just ignore the past? Just say that we forgive them and can live peacefully now? That doesn't make sense politically. If they are allowed to stay like that, ok, eventually they will release power, so that's good politically. But where is the justice? We can get democracy and they can peacefully live out their lives with their families, but where is justice? So many people have died. As I mentioned, in the IDP camps—over 200,000 people are living in hellish conditions. The Rohingya—it was genocide. Call it like it is. So many Rohingya have died—not even just the Rohingya, but other minority groups, like Kachin, Karenni, Shan, and many others, all the minority groups have been discriminated against, have been killed. When we forgive the generals, where is justice? So, reconciliation is a fantasy and, ultimately, not what this country needs for a better future. If we let the horrors of the past be forgotten so easily, it is a sure invitation to some other group or some other wannabe dictator to rise up and do the same. After all, if it doesn't work out, create a fake constitution that enshrines self-protection, guarantees their wealth, and let them have their free and fair multi-party elections while I read books on Orwell in Burma in my mansion in Naypyidaw. What point is there to democracy if there is no respect for justice and rule of law? It seems like a libertarian fantasy and nothing to do with reality.

What if you were in an IDP camp, what would you want? What if the authorities took your home and dumped you and your family in parched swamp land? What if your daughter were raped? I ask you as you ask me, what is right? Not what you think is right, but what is truly right for the future of democracy?

AC: I hear you. I pray that the stakeholders in your country hear you as well.

> *"Daw Aung San Suu Kyi is behaving in the very same way as some of the generals before her."*

ALAN CLEMENTS: If I can go a bit further, to be clear: You said that Daw Aung San Suu Kyi represents the government, and that she's putting forth a vision of national reconciliation based upon her own preference and that of those close to her, and that she's seeking reconciliation between herself and the military elite—but she doesn't represent the people or the ethnic groups. Is that correct?

KYWP: Yes, that is what I am saying.

AC: Can you elaborate?

KYWP: It is not only my opinion. And we have so much proof. In 2015, so many ethnic organisations voted for Daw Aung San Suu Kyi and the NLD to win the election. But before the election, so many ethnic organisations requested Daw Aung San Suu Kyi to meet with them. Just a single meeting, very simple. Nothing more. She could have done it very easily. But she chose not to.

After she won the election, the ethnic organisations kept requesting to meet with her. She denied them, again. But after her election victory, who did she meet with? She chose to meet with Than Shwe, and she choose to meet with General Min Aung Hlaing. The people in all ethnic organisations were surprised, but they were patient and kept supporting her, saying, "Ok, we will just wait and keep watching."

In April 2016, when the new government officially took power and they formed a parliament, at that time, the ethnic organisations renewed their requests that she meet with them. But what did she do? She not only denied their request yet again, she's continued to deny it up to this very moment. This is a complete betrayal of her promise. She prides herself on integrity yet when caring and commitment are required most—for her to honor her most basic values—she fails. She betrayed the ethnic groups and their leaders, and she betrayed herself and her own party leaders.

Frankly, Daw Aung San Suu Kyi is behaving in the very same way as some of the generals before her. She keeps playing the people for her own need for power. That's how I feel now. Again, I am not alone in this feeling. I wish I were, but I am not. Listen, in 2015 I supported her fully—all of my friends supported her. We did everything we could to support her in winning the election.. But when her government took power, they began to sue us, and charge us, and imprison us—so many civilians, so many activists, so many politicians have suffered under her for simply practicing active democracy, for using our freedom of expression that had been repressed for so long. She asked us to believe in her. To believe in democracy. She asked us to embody our love of universal human rights. And when we did, her government, filed lawsuits, sued us, and imprisoned good people, people who voted for her.

I can go through a list of such people and tell you every detail of their cases. That is what we do here at Athan. Dr. Aye Maung and the writer Wai Hin Aung, they have both been imprisoned for 21 years for making a single speech in Arakan State, on the Arakan Day Celebration. They got 21 years in prison for freedom of expression. They got 21 years in prison for voting for Aung San Suu Kyi and the NLD. They got 21 years in prison for voting to end the nightmare of totalitarianism.

For the Bamar, Independence Day is very important, Union Day is very important, Thingyan is very important—and if someone criticized the Bamar, "Oh, your Independence Day should be called 'Imprison Anyone Who Doesn't Agree With You Day,'" or something like that, the Bamar may be angry.

But in the Rakhine, the Rakhine people, the Arakan ethnics, they have the right to celebrate Arakan Day, and the politician Dr. Aye Maung, made a single speech on Arakan Day, and on that day so many soldiers came into the field and dispersed the people. They all ran away in fear.

But some people did not run. Instead, they stood up. So, the soldiers shot them. Over 10 Rakhine died on Arakan Day. And Dr. Aye Maung and Wai Hin Aung were detained and imprisoned for 21 years. For what? For making a single speech at Arakan Day for the Arakan people and for the Arakan ethnics. So what is wrong? They didn't do anything wrong. And they were sentenced to 21 years imprisonment for doing nothing wrong. It's bullshit.

So, how can we believe Daw Aung San Suu Kyi and this government any longer? It is just like the old times, a dictatorship in female form. It's hard for us to keep believing. In fact, we have given up on her.

I am only 25 years old and my generation wants something beyond dictatorship and beyond what Aung San Suu Kyi thinks she's doing. She did what she did to get us to this point but it's no longer working. We need a new vision of leadership.

AC: I appreciate your honesty and passion. Especially in the context in which we're speaking. You're saying things that come under the heading in my country as a human right, that of freedom of expression. In fact, I brought with me a copy of the Universal Declaration of Human Rights (UDHR), and would like to read the following: Article 19 of the UDHR states that "everyone shall have the right to hold opinions without interference," and, "everyone shall have the right to freedom of expression; this right shall include freedom to seek, receive and impart information and ideas of all kinds, regardless of frontiers, either orally, in writing or in print, in the form of art, or through any other media of his (and her) choice."

So, although what you are saying may been heard as provocative, it is none other than "your opinion." Which brings me to my question: Say you have an audience with Daw Aung San Suu Kyi, and she says to you, "Your work, and that of your colleagues at Athan, is really important to the democratic process in Myanmar. Without freedom of expression there is no democracy. With that said, it's a highly sensitive period. I can't tell you all that I know, day to day, being the State Counsellor, dealing with all the complexities of foreign dignitaries, military generals, MPs, the upcoming elections and so on—it's complex. But, I'm aware, as a human, that I am also challenged at times by *lobha, dosa, moha* (greed, anger and delusion); In other words, I have my areas of blindness. But I'm asking you—I'm remarkably impressed by your work, by your courage, and what you do, and I'm asking you—please share with me in the most direct and compassionate way possible what you want me to know that I don't see about myself. What should I see that you see, and how can I change those ways of being, and why?" What would you say to her?

KYWP: Well, I just spoke my mind pretty freely, but I will go further and answer your question. After all, this may very well be the most direct way in speaking with Daw Aung San Suu Kyi. This is what I want to say: What the people want is good politics, a good system, a good country and a real democracy. They don't want only a good leader anymore. At present, the people have no hope for good politics, a good system, and real democracy. So, please change. It's that simple: Daw Aung San Suu Kyi, please change your way of thinking.

The way so many of us see it, is that her thinking is based on her—the person—on changing 59(f) [that bars her from the presidency]. Ok, I agree with that, because 59(f) is not right. It's a restriction on human rights. Ok, I agree. But she's sacrificed a lot of things in an attempt to change 59(f) in the Constitution. She's made a deal with the military. But in the final results, the military got what they wanted, and Daw Aung San Suu Kyi didn't get anything. Furthermore, we, the people, want to see Daw Aung San Suu Kyi as she was in the old times, not in the present time. In the old time, Daw Aung San Suu Kyi was brave and a strong leader. So many politicians in Myanmar, when they go through an election campaign make promises—"Ok, we will build a road, we will build a bridge and so on." But Daw Aung San Suu Kyi didn't say anything like that. She guaranteed respect for human rights and a good political system. She never talked of fancy things, like building roads or building bridges. She just said, "I will guarantee human rights. I will guarantee a good political system. If we have a government, we will not be corrupt."

But after she was elected, her promises vanished into thin air. And further, this very government is corrupt. We know that. And they don't stick to democratic principles. They're charging and punishing people who criticize them. That is not democracy. Are we supposed to overlook that? Are we supposed to ignore that contradiction in her speech and actions? No! She asked us to participate in building democracy with her and when we exercise freedom of expression in any way that she considers negative, she acts like the very dictators who incarcerated her. That's not democracy. That's like the fake Constitution. That's fake democracy. Fake human rights. That's not freedom of expression. That's called, 'speak in the way I define as free and cross the line and I'll punish you severely.' As I said earlier, these friends of mine are not only being imprisoned but given hard labor.

My main point is this: The people I know and work with all want Daw Aung San Suu Kyi to be how she used to be—the true voice of freedom and not the compromised, somewhat power-driven version of it. We want the old Daw Aung San Suu Kyi. "Where are you?" That's what I would really like to say to her. I want to ask her one question. "Who are you? How come you are no longer yourself?" And before she answered, I would say one more thing: "Please answer this question on national television to the whole of the people." Because I am not alone in this feeling. I am only 25 years old and the youth are soon to inherent her legacy. We want true freedom and democracy and not just Aung San Suu Kyi alone.

AC: Why do you think she has changed from the Daw Aung San Suu Kyi that you remember to how you see her today? What has gone on for her?

KYWP: I think it's very simple: it's about power. In a Burmese proverb—I think you are familiar with it—we say that if some property is easy to steal, the billionaire will want to steal it. Of course, the billionaire already has plenty of money, but they see that they can steal something easily, so they do it. Power is like that. When people see power, they can't think rightly. It blinds you. I think Daw Aung San Suu Kyi is like that. When she was faced with a power struggle, because the 2008 Constitution restricted her from being president, she did what the military did. I mean, ok, what does it matter? The position of president is not the problem. If the NLD can nominate a president and put ministers in parliamentary seats, Daw Aung San Suu Kyi will still play behind the scenes with all the people, and the people will know that Daw Suu is the real leader. It's not necessary to be a president, but she just wants to be a president. Finally, it didn't happen, so she became the state counsellor, but as state counsellor she just negotiated with the military, not with the ethnics. Our country needs nation building, state building.

In nation building, a very fundamental concept is negotiation between the ethnicities, the diversities. So many ethnic people hate the Bamar. I am Bamar, but I am not angry towards them. I have sympathy for them. In fact, sometimes I hate Bamar—not the people, not the person, but the system, the Burmanization, the privilege. Sometimes there is a clash between the diversities. In the whole country, Bamar is the majority, and they have privilege and power, because the military are all Bamar Buddhists. And they hire low ranking soldiers, maybe Hindu, maybe Islamic, or ethnic people, but in the higher ranks they never appoint ethnicities or Christians or Muslims. They just appoint Bamar Buddhists. And when you go to the bank, you will just see a Bamar, maybe sometimes a Christian, but not Hindu or Islamic, because we don't see Islamic culture in the banks. I mean Bamar is privileged in the whole country, and so other ethnic people hate them.

There are so many wrong things in our country. We should make negotiations, and the government is responsible for that. It is nation building. She's not doing that. She's not negotiating with the diversities and the people and is not building these kinds of fundamental things. She's just building elite power, the power between the military and the NLD, between the government and the military. That's all.

Let me remind her of something she once said, "It is not power that corrupts but fear. Fear of losing power corrupts those who wield it and fear of the scourge of power corrupts those who are subject to it."

We want her to come back to the Daw Suu she once was, before she got seduced by power.

AC: Why do you do the work that you do? What motivates your activism?

KYWP: Since I was young, I felt something was wrong. For instance, our education is not based on critical study, just memorisation. In the exams, I must take the exam with the same word, if I change some things in an essay, like the curriculum books says the father is U Ba but my father is not U Ba, so in the exam if I put my real father's name they will not give me a mark. I will fail the exam. So, I felt wrong all the time growing up. Then, when I got older, I started looking around at the environment, at my neighbours, and I could see that it was also wrong for them.

Another example is when I was young, my father and I watched foreign movies almost every day—and those foreign movies were not official; the government banned all such Hollywood movies. They only showed Chinese and Korean movies. But my father borrowed foreign movies from his friends, and we watched them, and we saw that in foreign countries the situation was very different. I began to see that everything was wrong here in Myanmar. And I wanted everything to be right. So, I became an activist. I started with the most basic right: freedom of expression is the most basic right in a democracy.

Now, I am talking with you in this way because of my passion for freedom of expression. I am openly expressing my feelings and my experiences without any desire or intention to harm anyone. I am doing what I was encouraged to do—speak freely to help transition the country from dictatorship to democracy. So, I am expressing my fundamental human right. We at Athan believe that freedom of expression is essential for everyone to come out of the horror of self-censorship for fear of being jailed.

AC: You represent a new generation. The majority of people in your country are young. What do you want them to know that you know, that would be helpful for them to actively participate in democracy? Also, how to stop making themselves wrong, in the way that you saw yourself being made wrong, when you were young? And I invite you to include the youth in all 135 ethnicities throughout Myanmar.

KYWP: For the young people like me, I want to remind them of three things: justice, humanity, and bravery. If the young people, or someone else, remembers these three things every day, he or she cannot go wrong. Justice, humanity, and bravery.

For example, on the bus, if there are old people or a pregnant woman, it's no problem for us young people to stand up and offer a seat. We can move for the pregnant woman or disabled people. This is justice. This is humanity. It is the right thing, and the right thing is justice.

And sympathy; sympathy is humanity. Standing up is brave. Some young people, they're ashamed of doing something right. In this kind of situation, someone who stands up for those people is brave.

I believe justice, humanity, and bravery are everything. If someone remembers these three things every day, those people cannot go wrong.

AC: Burma is in many ways the newest child of democracy in modern times, coming out as it is, from decades of totalitarian violence. Your people have dealt with harsh realities. They continue to deal with them. But there is your voice, there's the voice of activism, there's the Peacock Generation. There are people every day, right now, saying they want a different society.

My question: many people will read your words, both in Myanmar and around the world. And I wouldn't be surprised if many world leaders read your words. Representatives in the United Nations will also read your words. Daw Aung San Suu Kyi will read them. Perhaps General Min Aung Hlaing will also read them, as well as U Than Shwe. Young activists; Greta Thunberg, the 17-year-old from Sweden, who's calling on everyone to come out of their addiction to denial and address the environmental apocalypse that we're in—people are even talking about near-term extinction.

I would like to invite you to speak to the world, in any way you want. Speak to the world leaders, speak to Greta, speak to the people of your country, the activists on the streets, in the schools, in the prisons around the world, on how best to support your country's freedom and transition to democracy.

KYWP: I think now the world is changing, like a change from the stone age to the iron age. Now, the world is changing, moving into a new age. In this new age, we respect and value humanity, the animals, the environment, the oceans the young people's activism, democracy, and freedom. And liberation, because some groups need liberation. This is the new world we are becoming. But world leaders, including our Myanmar leaders, are conservatives. They are conservatives not because of the ideology but because they are not brave enough to face reality—to deal with these humanitarian and environmental emergencies. By and large, these issues are being faced by young people's activism.

So, leaders worldwide, including Myanmar leaders, need bravery to face the new age with its unprecedented complexities. As the world changes, we the people overcome our faults and do everything we can to not only improve the situation, but to avert disaster. The only way forward is to respect freedom, liberation, and democracy and face head on the catastrophic environmental issues, that are entirely human created. It is a time for global activism and pray it is not too late. That is why at Athan we are acting with extreme urgency. The time for playing it safe is over. It is a time for radical bravery. Nonviolent bravery. A revolution of the spirit, as Daw Aung San Suu Kyi once called for. If I may interject with something I have brought with me in anticipation of our interview. I know you were a former Buddhist monk in my country and that you co-authored *The Voice of Hope*—the book of conversations with Daw Aung San Suu Kyi.

Please allow me to read this passage of hers.

"Within a system which denies the existence of basic human rights, fear tends to be the order of the day. Fear of imprisonment, fear of torture, fear of death, fear of losing friends, family, property or means of livelihood, fear of poverty, fear of isolation, fear of failure." She then says, instead of "a revolution which aims at changing official policies and institutions," she calls for a "revolution of the spirit," without which "the forces which produced the iniquities of the old order would continue to be operative, posing a constant threat to the process of reform and regeneration."

She goes onto say, "It is not enough merely to call for freedom, democracy and human rights. There has to be a united determination to persevere in the struggle, to make sacrifices in the name of enduring truths, to resist the corrupting influences of desire, ill will, ignorance, and fear."

I want all my people to reflect on the wisdom of her words and recommit to them in action and speech. May it be that we have no need for Athan in Myanmar because all our people enjoy freedom of expression.

AC: Thank you. May it be so.

KYWP: Thank you for the chance to contribute, for myself and for Athan, in your work. I also thank you.

CHAPTER 39

CONVERSATIONS *with* DAW THAN THAN NU

January 2020

- "They said, 'Sorry Sayama, sorry madam, sorry sister, it's because of your father we had to take up arms.'"
- "We don't have the authority in Burma, we don't have statesmanship."
- "They decided to do something from the outside. It became revolutionary."
- "The problem is pride. At present, we have two governments."

Than Than Nu was born in 1947, one year before Burma's independence. She is the fourth child of Prime Minister U Nu and Daw Mya Yi. She studied Planning and Development at the Institute of Economics in Rangoon. In 1969, she followed her parents into exile, first for six years in Thailand, and then to India, where she settled and worked until 2003. She worked with her husband for twenty years at the Burmese language service of All-India Radio in New Delhi, before retiring and returning to Yangon. Than Than Nu is currently the Secretary General of the Democratic Party (Myanmar) and Founder and Chairperson of the U Nu Daw Mya Yi Foundation, which carries out charitable work in the domains of education, disaster relief and healthcare.

"They said, 'Sorry Sayama, sorry madam,
sorry sister, it's because of your father
we had to take up arms.'"

ALAN CLEMENTS: Thank you for taking time to speak with me. You're one of five children, two sons and three daughters, and your father, U Nu, was the first prime minister of Burma. I'm honored to speak with you.

DAW THAN THAN NU: Thank you very much. It is a pleasure to speak with you.

AC: If I may, allow me to provide a brief context: I first came to your country in 1977, and in 1979 I ordained in Yangon as a Buddhist monk under the Venerable Mahasi Sayadaw. I practiced meditation at the monastery that Sir U Thwin and your father founded—the Mahasi Thathana Yeiktha—and, of all places within the 20-acre compound, I was given a room that was built for your father. And so, I had this special relationship with your father, living in meditative silence in his room at the monastery he cofounded. And further, your father was the one, I was told, who found—after a nationwide search in 1947—my preceptor and teacher, Mahasi Sayādaw, and brought him to Yangon to teach at the Yeiktha. In addition, back in 1980, I was blessed to meet your father at his house next door. I remember having a lively discussion with him at that time about the role of *Dhamma* and politics. Of course, as Burma's first Prime Minister, and a devout *Dhamma* practitioner and meditator, he was passionate about the subject. Sadly, I never saw him again, as he went into exile in India and passed away in 1995. All by way of saying, again, what an honor to speak with you today, and there are many questions I'd like to ask you; from *Dhamma* issues to democratic politics, to General Ne Win's military coup d'état against your father's government in 1962 and his subsequent incarceration, and of course, your views on the present moment, with this tenuous transition from dictatorship to democracy. And notwithstanding, your views on the crisis in Rakhine State, as well as the ongoing wars with the ethnic groups around the country. Along with anything you'd like to discuss, of course. Again, thank you for taking the time to speak with me.

DTTN: Again, it is a pleasure. Please ask anything you wish, openly.

AC: Your father was a democracy hero, an icon of freedom and human rights, both in Burma and worldwide. But, oddly, few people know of him, and here I am doing these books—*Burma's Voices of Freedom*—in four volumes, and I thought we must not finish them without including something about your father. I've interviewed many people over the eight years since starting this project, and I'm thinking the only person missing is someone related to Burma's first prime minister, U Nu. And here I am blessed at the very end of this project to meet you.

As someone who knows your father perhaps better than anyone alive (other than perhaps your brothers and sisters), please share with me, and our readers, the most interesting points, decisions and accomplishments that you know about your father that would be important for the people of Burma, and the wider world, to know.

DTTN: I hope you have read my father's autobiography?

AC: I'm reading it now, after having by chance met your nephew the other day when I was walking down a back road, and by chance seeing the small blue sign hanging on a gate—U Nu Museum—which led me to you.

DTTN: Funnily enough, so much of what I know about my father is only through his autobiography, *Saturday's Son*. And I tell you that quite frankly, because I was young at that time when he first became prime minister, and even at the time of Ne Win's coup d'état in 1962—I was only 15. Also, my father was highly secretive about his political activities, or I should say, impeccably private. He didn't reveal much, even to my mother. I think he wanted to keep home life somewhat monastic-like, but he was also a private person.

My father was also a very determined man. Once he decided to do something, he did it bravely, unwaveringly, without giving up. He stayed with something until the end. This was my father's most prominent characteristic: determination.

To give you one instance about his secrecy in his political activities, I will tell you briefly about something mentioned in one of his books—the name of the book is *Burma under the Japanese*, and in Burmese, the title means five years of Burma's struggle under the Japanese. (It was translated into English also.) In that book, at the end, at the point when the Japanese were withdrawing from Burma, he said he travelled south together with Dr Ba Maw, who had gone along with the Japanese as something of a hostage. So, my father had decided to go along with Dr Ba Maw, travelling together with his wife—my mother—and although the Japanese were withdrawing, this wasn't well known and there was still some uncertainty. Nobody knew exactly what was happening. But, when they'd reached that point, my father turned and whispered something to my mother. She was so delighted and so happy, and my father wrote in his book that it wasn't because the Japanese were withdrawing, but because this was the first time that he'd revealed a political secret to her [the secret being that the Japanese were withdrawing from Burma].

In general, he didn't want to share his activities with his family, because sometimes during those days they had to work in secret. He didn't even tell my mother these things. As I said, this was one of his characteristics. And with his colleagues, among them, General Aung San was one of the best comrades.

AC: Do you remember anything about General Aung San? Perhaps something your father or mother told you?

DTTN: I was born after General Aung San's death. He was assassinated on July 19th, 1947, and I was born on October 31st, 1948. Although I never met him, I heard many wonderful things about him from others, especially from my mother. She was very close to General Aung San, as was my father. He would come to my parents' home, many, many times for meetings with my father, and to have meals. He liked my mother's cooking very much, she said. They were like brothers and sisters, very close.

AC: I understand that your father was the president of the Rangoon University Student Union, and Aung San was the editor, and publicity director. This was back in 1936. I didn't know that their friendship and colleagueship went so far back.

DTTN: Yes, they were very, very close from way back. But nobody knows that my father was the president of that student union—people only know that General Aung San was the student union president. My father's name is generally not mentioned. The public, the Burmese people, know only that General Aung San was the university student union president. But at that time, there was a president elected every year. The president's post was for only one year, for each person. With no extension. So, my father became the second president, and after that General Aung San became the next student union president.

But another thing is that General Aung San was still very popular among the Burmese people because of the work of my father and their colleagues. After General Aung San was assassinated, sometimes it happens that one person, whether he was a martyr or hero, after a few months or even a few years, their memory fades from public interest. But for General Aung San, my father and his colleagues, their teamwork was so... how should I say it? They worked hard to keep General Aung San's memory alive, by making the people understand the importance of General Aung San's work, and his tireless courage. Each and every time my father had the opportunity to talk about General Aung San he did. Because of that the public had a heightened awareness of General Aung San.

AC: So, your father was an activist for democracy and freedom, and anti-colonialism, early in his life, as far back as age 28, as a student at Rangoon University. And he was outspoken too. I read an article that he co-wrote with Aung San. In it they wickedly criticise the university rector, saying among other things, they hoped he would suffer "eternal damnation for treachery." And they were both instantly expelled from university because of this?

DTTN: Yes. My father very much disliked the university rector, but not because he was British. My father didn't hate the British. Of course, at that time Burma was under British rule, but all they wanted was make the country free, liberate our people from British rule. They were not anti-British. They were anti-slavery, anti-oppression. What they wanted was freedom. They wanted independence.

AC: Britain ruled Burma for 134 years, from 1824 to 1948. There were three Anglo-Burmese wars, and your country gained independence from Britain on January 4th, 1948. But General Aung San was assassinated on July 19, 1947, along with six cabinet members, before independence. Would you please explain where your father was during the formation of this cabinet with General Aung San? I understand your father actually went to London and signed the Independence Accord with the British

Prime Minster Clement Atlee, and that was in 1948. So how did that happen, and where was your father at the time of the formation of the first government?

DTTN: One thing is that first, General Aung San went to London, to help with this agreement with Mr Clement Atlee. But that accord was not fulfilled, because of a difficulty primarily with the Shan people—they didn't understand much about General Aung San's trip to London. So some people talked against the accord. Thus, the accord was not fulfilled at that time, and General Aung San returned to Burma.

Another thing was that they asked whether he had the signatories of his people, especially the Shan. But Aung San didn't take signatories from any of the ethnic groups. This was also a problem and one that he did not anticipate. All he was thinking about was Burma's independence, and that's why he went to London. He didn't consider taking an agreement from the ethnic people, so it was delayed for some time. That was in '47. And as a result, they protested in Burma.

Also, while General Aung San was in London, protests broke out about signing the agreement. That was because U Saw, a conservative rival, who masterminded the assassination, organized the protests. He was against General Aung San. As was much of the British administration who sought to try Aung San and other members of the Burma Independence Army (BIA) for treason and collaboration with the Japanese during the earlier part of the war. General Aung San had many rivals. Like my father he was radical and outspoken.

AC: How was it that your father, after General Aung San's assassination, was chosen, or was it decided that he go to London, to sign Burma's historic independence Nu-Atlee agreement?

DTTN: He was chosen by the new cabinet that was formed after General Aung San's assassination and that of his cabinet members.

AC: And how did that cabinet come into formation?

DTTN: Actually, my father didn't want to be in politics at all. Every time they asked him, he said no, that he would go back to his hometown and do his writing. He was only interested in writing books. And, at that time, he had become a very pious Buddhist, because when he was young, he was notorious for bad behaviour.

AC: That's why he called his memoirs *Naughty Saturday Born*?

DTTN: *Saturday's Son*. But in Burmese it means far worse than 'naughty.'

AC: So he had strong *akusala* (unwholesome actions)?

DTTN: Yes *(laughs)*.

AC: What kind of things would he do?

DTTN: It's in my father's autobiography—he did all sorts of things. He lied, cheated, drank—he was a heavy drinker, and at a very young age made his own liquor. As I said, when he decided to do something, he did it bravely, unwaveringly *(laughs)*. Even when making his own brew *(laughs)*.

AC: You used the word pious, meaning "Buddhist," in that your father had become taken in with the *Dhamma*? And this was to counter his bad behaviour?

DTTN: Yes, that's right. And my father had fought with many people from his home village also. Some people older than him even wanted to kill him. For instance, one person took him to a nearby river, and pushed him in, thinking he would drown.

AC: So, it's fair to say that your father was a man redeemed by the *Dhamma*? He overcame his misguided behaviours through the power of meditation and mindful reflection on the rights and wrongs of thought, speech and action?

DTTN: Yes, that's right. It changed his way of thinking, speaking and acting. See, his father—my grandfather—sat him down and talked to him, slowly and patiently, about the *Dhamma*. It was my grandfather who provided the *Dhamma* influence on my father. In particular, he taught the importance of following the Five Precepts—they form the very basis of proper and righteous human conduct, and I believe that people in positions of power should always keep them in mind.

AC: Now, digressing a bit: Do you know many of the details of how your father was involved in the formation of the Mahasi Thathana Yeiktha Meditation Centre here in Yangon? And I may add, and perhaps you know this, it has over 600 branch centres throughout the country today, all of them offering unlimited time and space freely as *dāna*, for meditators to practice long term intensive mindfulness (*Vipassanā*) meditation.

DTTN: Yes, *dāna* and *Dhamma* in our country go hand in hand. But to answer your question: At that time, in Rangoon, we didn't have many meditation centres. Meditation was not popular at all. But my father heard about this Mahasi Sayadaw in Seikkhun, in central Burma. He heard about this young monk through Sir U Thwin, a famous businessman in our country. He and my father were very close friends because of their affiliation with religious affairs. And as you likely know, Sir U Thwin donated the original five acres of land for the Mahasi Yeiktha. Together, they invited Mahasi Sayadaw to come and stay in Rangoon.

AC: Do you know how he heard of Mahasi Sayadaw?

DTTN: Only very little, because Mahasi Sayadaw, at that time, lived in his native village Seikkhun. Word started to spread that he was a very talented speaker, preaching and giving *Dhamma* sermons.

AC: He was well known in the country at the time?

DTTN: Yes, to a degree. But not much, because Seikkhun is a relatively small place, and tiny compared to Rangoon, nor is it very well known. But going a bit further, this is what happened, as I understand it: After Mahasi learned meditation in the south, at Thaton, from the Venerable U Nārada, also known as Mingun Jetavan Sayādaw, he returned upcountry. And, sometime after the Japanese invasion in World War II, the authorities gave evacuation orders to those living near the monastery where Mahasi Sayādaw resided. But it was close to an airfield and hence exposed to air attacks. Mahasi Sayādaw then returned to his native village and took residence at a monastery and devoted himself to meditation and at the same time wrote his great work, *The Manual of Vipasssanā Meditation*, a comprehensive treatise expounding both the doctrinal and the practical aspects of the *Satipaṭṭhanā* method of meditation. During this time, the people of the neighboring town of Shwebo suffered almost daily air attacks. And during this time, Mahasi Sayādaw's reputation spread as a skilled teacher of *Vipassanā* meditation. After Sir U Thwin heard Mahasi Sayadaw speak, he and my father invited the Venerable Sayadaw here to Rangoon, and when Sir U Thwin donated land, they conducted the first mindfulness retreat with 25 yogis. Only after that did my father start preparing for the Sixth Buddhist Council or the Chaṭṭha Saṅgāyanā.

AC: As a result of your father's actions and those of Sir U Thwin, the Mahasi Sasana Yeiktha became the birthplace of the worldwide mass lay meditation movement. Mindfulness, which, as you know, is the essence of Buddhist meditation, has gained worldwide popularity today. And it came from your father having a vision with his friend Sir U Thwin to bring meditation to Rangoon. What a compelling accomplishment.

DTTN: My father loved meditation. Meditation and the *Dhamma* changed his life. It has also changed my own life.

AC: It has totally changed my life as well. Sadhu, sadhu, sadhu. Now, back to politics, if we can. How was it that your father became the first democratic prime minister of Burma?

DTTN: He was chosen by his colleagues, just after independence. As soon as we got independence there were rebels of many ethnic people, and from our own Burmese also, and then the communists too—red communists, white communists—and then from the very army that General Aung San started as well. They took all the guns and ammunition and as a rebel group went into hiding. It was a chaotic time in our country. You could call it the great unravelling. The country came apart and was severely divided. Burma as we had known it became so small it was called the Yangon Government.

AC: Because the government could only control Yangon? Not even Insein, only 20 miles from downtown?

DTTN: That's right. Insein Township was dominated by Karens. It was very strange that Saw Ba U Gyi, the first President of the Karen National Union, was very close to my father.

AC: Yes, I understand that the Karens and Burmese have had a long and tumultuous history together. As you know, the Burmese have been brutal towards the Karen people. I witnessed it first-hand some 40 years after this period and wrote about it in my book, *Burma: The Next Killing Fields.*

May I ask, how was it that Saw Ba U Gyi and your father become friends? I thought the Karen National Union (KNU) declared war on the Burmese government in 1949.

DTTN: One incident that I can recall perfectly illustrates how they two men honoured and respected each other even though they were technically at war. It was a time when the KNU even controlled parts of Rangoon (as far as Insein), and the Burmese government was called the "Rangoon Government" because of the very limited territory it controlled. Saw Ba U Gyi asked my father through an intermediary whether he would like to lunch with him, and even offered to come pick him up at his house. My mother felt that this could be a trap and begged my father not to go. Nevertheless, he went along when Saw Ba U Gyi came to the house in a car to pick him up. He had lunch with his old friend and was safely brought back home.

My father went throughout the country, to so many places, making friends with all the ethnic people. But now, it's a sad thing that there are still so many ethnic problems all over the country. And whenever there is a meeting with the ethnic people, when I am among them, they say, "Sorry, sister," or sometimes they say, "Sorry, Sayama," "We have to tell you something; we had to take up arms because of your father." This is what they tell me. The Kachin. The Chin. Even the Mon people speak with me this way. Wherever I met them at conferences or meetings, they said, "Sorry Sayama, sorry madam, sorry sister, it's because of your father we had to take up arms." My father was blamed, scapegoated.

AC: What was the reason? Was he a Burmese supremacist? A nationalist? Denial of their rights?

DTTN: I suppose one reason is that he has passed away, and can no longer defend himself, and another thing was that he was very religious. But he was not like Ne Win or the present generals. Even at this moment, nobody points their finger at General Ne Win. They forgot him. They also forgot General Than Shwe. They only remember my father, and they don't remember him in a good sense, only in a very bad way. "Because of him," "Because of him," always blaming him for the ills of the country.

AC: If I may, what do they remember? What are they referring to as "bad" enough to take up arms against the Burmese government?

DTTN: Those ugly things. The Kachin will say that it was because my father, in 1961, just before the army coup, declared Buddhism the state religion. The Kachin will say that because of this they had to take up arms. But these Kachin, they took up arms a long time before the country became a Buddhist country. But even then, according to law, in Parliament, even though Buddhism became the state religion, all other religions must have their own equal rights. This is written, but they forgot about that also.

AC: They didn't honor that, but your father intended that?

DTTN: Yes.

AC: But they said it was a mistake to make Burma a Buddhist country?

DTTN: Yes.

AC: And so today, the night before 2020, still the Kachin, the Shan, the Karen, and others, blame your father for the ethnic problems?

DTTN: Yes.

AC: Because of the Buddhist issue. And also, you're saying that when General Aung San went to London to sign the independence treaty, there were protests in Rangoon, because they felt left out of this agreement. You're also saying that even in 1948 when your father signed the independence accord in London, Burma was pretty much confined to the city of Rangoon, and still that was owned and controlled by the Karens. So essentially, Burma was a micro geographical area, compared to the Burma we know today? That's Burma post-independence. So, your country came apart after independence?

DTTN: Yes, you could say that. But another thing is that my father and his colleagues worked as a team to make Burma one country. Because of that, after 1950, Burma became one of the richest countries in South East Asia, in education, in economics and in healthcare. Rangoon University was very popular and was considered the most advanced university in all of South East Asia.

> *"We don't have the authority in Burma, we don't have statesmanship."*

ALAN CLEMENTS: I'd like to go into some more contemporary issues and then come back to some more historical insights. In regard to these books, I've been talking now for eight years with many leaders in your country—that is, since I was allowed back in after being banned for 17 years—and almost every conversation goes directly towards the ethnic problem. So, I'd like to explore that issue with you.

We've got long-term war in Kachin State; long-term wars, multiple wars, in Shan State—multiple armies; 20, 30, 40 or even more different armed militias in Burma today, I'm told, with many hundreds of skirmishes monthly. More recently, the AA (the Arakan Army)—a 10,000-man uniformed and very well-equipped army, with the most modern weapons, used in the Netherlands and Israel; two years ago: 20 soldiers. Today, I hear there's many thousands of them also in Kachin State, with at least 10,000 in Rakhine. They're even demanding taxes from the people and big businesses in the region; they're very well formed and skilled at fighting, and they're fighting face to face with the Burmese military. What is the core problem with your country as it relates to the ethnic people? And how come no one has been able to solve it post-Independence?

DAW THAN THAN NU: Because just before Ne Win's 1962 coup d'état, they were demanding federalism, so my father also started thinking of federalism. And then, he also wanted to have this federal democratic country of Burma. However, Ne Win came to know about this, and because of that his coup d'état happened.

On the night of the 1st of March 1962, at midnight, they were having a meeting with the Shans and other ethnic people as well, at the broadcasting station on Pyay Road. At the same time, General Ne Win was at a concert.

So, my father also returned home, and whenever he returned home late, and because he was not staying in this house at that time—it had now turned into a museum—and because whatever he needed he asked my mother for, because he also didn't have money (and he didn't take the prime ministers salary), he retired to a small building at the back of the compound. Sometime previously he'd asked my mother, "Why don't you build a small house, smaller than this one, only two rooms and toilet"—one room for his bedroom and another for his writing, his study. And this was because here everyone knew him, and every now and then people came and met him. Because of those kinds of disturbances, he said he wanted to move to a small house, a small compound behind the museum. My mother had asked the landowners and they agreed, and she built a small house for my father. So, when he came in, he had to pass my mother's bedroom, and would tell her that he'd come back.

So, as I was saying, at midnight he went to that small building, and after an hour or so, my mother heard gunshots from nearby. So, she knew something had happened, because she'd also had those kinds of experiences over the years in political life. She then woke us up and said something serious had happened, said that we must be alert, not asleep. So, we all got up and were wondering what had happened. And then, within an hour, tanks came to our compound, came right inside the compound. Of course, my mother knew immediately that it was a coup d'état, because similar things had happened in 1957, when U Ne Win was preparing for a coup d'état with Colonel Aung Gyi.

Back in 1957, my father had spoken to General Ne Win about such a scenario. "If a coup d'état happens," he said, "it is not good for the country and the people, so you can take power for one year and I will discuss it in Parliament, and then I will do my own business doing this organizational work in my own party. But after one year you must prepare for an election." So, General Ne Win agreed.

Ne Win agreed but didn't follow through with his promise after one year. No election. Nothing. He kept power. So my father then reminded him that it had been over one year, and that he'd promised to prepare an election. After a year and a half, Ne Win was still in power. And then, strangely, people also blamed my father for that—"It is because of you that Ne Win has become power hungry."

AC: Because he appointed General Ne Win?

DTTN: Yes, he gave him power and asked Ne Win to rule the country for one year.

AC: And your father should have said no? That's what the people said?

DTTN: Yes, that he had to be much tighter in his control of the government, that he was too flexible. But people can say whatever they like.

AC: Of course, always, when you look back, hindsight is 20/20. But it's very difficult in the moment.

DTTN: Exactly.

AC: You were 15 years old at this time of the coup. You remember the people coming, the tanks, the gunshots?

DTTN: Yes, I remember it well. Although it was the prime minister's residence, only two or three soldiers were posted there. My father didn't like keeping many soldiers, many security guards, so we were very free. Whoever wanted to see my father, they just came in. They would just walk into the compound and knock on the door. Because this is a wooden house raised slightly above the ground, if you wanted to come inside, you had to open three doors and only then you are inside the house. That night the soldiers banged on the door and my mother said, "Coming, coming." But my elder brother, he'd just returned from Japan, where he was studying. He'd returned for a short visit, and couldn't find which key was for which door, because he hadn't stayed with us for quite some time. He couldn't find the key and so these soldiers who'd come into the compound were furious—they shouted, "Quickly, quickly, open the door quickly or we will shoot you!" But my mother said to them, "No, don't, he's my son." We were all in the sitting room, waiting.

AC: Did you know what was happening?

DTTN: Yes. I knew because my mother would sometimes talk about an army coup d'état, just wanting to let me know that anything could happen. My father wouldn't speak in detail but sometimes he'd tell me this kind of thing could happen.

AC: And had you met General Ne Win?

DTTN: Yes. I'd met him at functions. But I didn't have much of an idea about him, because I was quite young. When the coup took place, I was just 15 years old, and when I met General Ne Win, at that time I was not politically inclined, so I wasn't too serious about it.

AC: But his soldiers on his orders threatened to kill your brother?

DTTN: Yes. And they had already killed the Shan president's son. They killed him because of the same thing, because he opened the door too slowly.

AC: Did you feel hatred towards Ne Win?

DTTN: At that time, yes. But today, no.

AC: How do you feel towards this man who did so much to your father?

DTTN: Not only to my father, to the whole country. He and those close to him did so many ugly things, but I don't have hatred towards them. At the time, though, for some time, whenever I met the soldiers on the street, something happened to me; I had some animosity towards them. But now, those feelings have long passed.

AC: They blamed your father for the many problems; blame is a strong word, so allow me to ask you directly: Who do you blame for the problems in Burma?

DTTN: The present problems?

AC: From 1947, to '62, from '62 to 2020. It's much easier to look back and find what didn't work out, what went wrong, and who was responsible. If your father was scapegoated, then who would you blame for the problems from 1962 to today? Why is Burma in such a mess, politically?

DTTN: There are two blocks—from '62 to 2010 is one period, full stop. And then from 2010 until now. Two blocks. Because '62 to 2010 was such a mess that people became poorer and poorer—but poorer in the sense that if you see Burma you can't actually find the poor people, because Burmese people are always happy go lucky people, and they are always smiling. Foreigners also are quite sympathetic and very friendly with Burmese people, but education wise it has fallen off a cliff.

AC: But I'm asking why. From 1962 to 2010--

DTTN: Because of the coup d'état? Because of the Tatmadaw? I can't say because of Tatmadaw. I say that because General Ne Win was the main person who made all these mistakes.

AC: Why did he close the country and take Burma down a road of ruin?

DTTN: Because he wanted to be the one and only one in power. Ultimately, I don't know the real reason. He was the only person who had the exact answer. But for me, he wanted to be a dictator. And a strong dictator at that. Because whatever he thought, whatever he fantasized about, he wanted it to become reality. So, to be clear, from '62 to 2010, General Ne Win started this mess and continued it, moving it forward from one general to another general. And then the '88 tragedy. And the U Thant protests before that. But sometimes these generals, they are very clever. They start the problems. Like the '88 uprising—they started it.

AC: You're saying Ne Win and the military instigated the '88 uprising?

DTTN: Yes.

AC: Could you say more about why you think that is true? What are your reasons for saying that?

DTTN: Because there was some difficulty in the military. They wanted to create the problem, so they themselves started it. We have so many instances that they started. Like when we had lots of killings towards the Chinese because of that little red book—because Chairman Mao's *Little Red Book* was found in a nearby school. General Ne Win also started that.

AC: Let me be clear: Ne Win instigated the so-called nonviolent revolution in '88?

DTTN: He wanted to change people's minds and thoughts, so he did something. And then sometimes he did this, and sometimes he did that.

AC: But you don't want to say more?

DTTN: I don't want to say more. Because we need to build and maintain friendly international relations, not only neighbouring countries but other countries also. And it was in the past. But still now there are also some instances, so it is better not to say anything, because in our *Dhamma*, in the teachings of the Lord Buddha, it's said that it's very important that if you know something, don't go very far—don't take your mind very far with it. Don't decide yourself that this happened because of this or that. Don't say it like this. If something happens, best just to keep quiet. If you are in politics it is different, but in general, don't take this mind very far. If you see something, like in meditation, just observe "I see this," don't take it too far.

AC: And you see this as a good thing for your people, a good characteristic?

DTTN: Yes.

AC: But your country's at war with itself—embroiled in many wars with itself. You've been accused of genocide--

DTTN: But this is not war—this is fighting between our own people. We can't say "war." War means from outside.

AC: Well, maybe it's just a figure of speech, but "genocide" is a very strong word to describe something worse than war from the outside: killing your own people. I guess what I'm pointing to is that I'm here as a journalist, a historian, a lover of Burma, and I want to know, and the people that I know in Burma would like to know, not just "why," but also the solution. And in order to find solutions we need to know what the problem is, and I'm trying to really gain through my interviews with people clarity on some of the issues that normally don't get spoken about. One of the big ones is the ethnic issue.

Allow me to reframe the question this way: If I were the Kachins, after so many years of bombardment—rocket attacks, military killings, helicopter gunships, broken promises and so much more—why would I want to be a part of Burma? If I were the Shans, or the Karens, after so much merciless killing in these areas of your country, why would I ever want to be part of Burma? And in Rakhine State, after what's happened there in the last 20 or 30 years, and more recently in the last 3 years, with hundreds-of-thousands of people leaving based upon what seems to be unmitigated evidence that the Burmese military committed grave atrocities—it's not exactly clear how many, but even Daw Aung San Suu Kyi has admitted that there are some, and they're investigating them. More to the point: Why would I want to be part of Burma? Why does the Burmese government in Naypyidaw keep demanding that the ethnic groups remain in a union? Why not let Burma become like Yugoslavia and develop independent states? Why not have a Kachin State with their own constitution? A Shan State with their own constitution? A Karen State and Rakhine State with their own constitutions? And why not take care of business solely within Burma proper and give peace, rule of law, and reconciliation a chance? Why not inspire through example, in other words?

DTTN: Is this the way that outsiders want to see the country?

AC: I was in Yugoslavia during the breakup and the final year of the savagery. I never understood why it took mass slaughter when a republic wanted independence. All I am saying is that when war doesn't work, why not seek peace through peaceful means? But to answer your question, I've never heard anyone say it like this, and I'm saying it for the first time myself. But the more that I've spoken to your people, the more I can see why, after so many years of a Burmese army mercilessly killing for land, rubies, sapphires, oil, pure hatred of the ethnicities. I ask you, why not let each ethnicity in Burma decide their own destiny?

DTTN: So, I also want to ask you: Do you think that those kinds of merciless killings and sufferings were only suffered by the ethnics and not Burmese? We are also suffering, and we are also one of the ethnicities.

AC: But the Burmese are 80 percent of the country and you are also deciding the rules of conduct for each ethnic group. I'm not part of the peace process but I wonder how much easier it would be to simply withdraw all Burmese troops and weapons from Kachin and Shan States to start with, and experiment with a new way. Send supplies and services to those beleaguered regions and help heal through giving and stop killing. War stops by refusing to wage war. Someone has to take the high ground first. Why not the majority show good will here?

DTTN: But we are also suffering.

AC: What you're saying is that a lot of the ethnic groups also aggressively fight Burma?

DTTN: I can't say it like that, "aggressively." If they fight aggressively, it's because the other side has fought with them aggressively, so they retaliate. We have to see both sides. We can't say the Kachins are fighting aggressively. We can't say the military is fighting aggressively. We have to look at both sides, at why this military fights in such a way, and then why the Kachins also retaliate like that. But the main thing is that we don't have the authority in Burma, we don't have statesmanship.

AC: So, leadership is lacking?

DTTN: Yes, it's lacking, very much so.

AC: Within the Burmese military, the Burmese government, all leaders of all ethnicities, statesmanship is lacking?

DTTN: You could also say that right now the Burmese military is acting on its own. The government is acting on its own. The government cannot control the military—why?

AC: Why?

DTTN: Because there is no statesmanship. They should talk, the leaders—the military leaders and the government leaders. They should talk to each other. They are not talking to each other. Now, this Rakhine problem is a very serious problem, but they haven't sat down together and talked it over, not even once.

AC: Help me understand; what you're saying is that the real issue is the lack of statesmanship. And that the soul of that, so to speak, is the inability to know how to sit down and to talk, ask questions and to listen, argue and resolve this for the betterment of the people?

DTTN: Yes. During my father's time we were also facing lots of problems in this country, and then I even told you that we called it a Rangoon Government, not a Burmese government. Still, one thing was that my father was very good at teamwork, and they always worked in a very harmonious way. That's why in politics also they had this party, the AFPFL (Anti-Fascist People's Freedom League) and it had become a break-away party, but even then they could talk together and solve problems together, until the last moment, in '62 with Ne Win's coup d'état. From then until now, there's been no dialogue, and the military is ruling the country in a hopeless way. And then after 2010, they opened up and started a so-called multi-party system, a way to democratise this country. But it's not been fulfilled, even now.

AC: It's very interesting to me, because you're speaking as a woman—as a stateswoman; secretary of the democratic party, with a long history of democratic values—and what you're saying is that the easiest way to resolve all differences is "let's talk," let's have a dialogue?

DTTN: Yes.

AC: Why is something so simple so difficult? Imagine that you had all stakeholders gathered together, Daw Aung San Suu Kyi was here, Than Shwe was in that chair, Senior General Min Aung Hlaing was sitting over there, and all the ethnic leaders and armed groups from Kachin, Karen, Mon, Chin, Arakan, Shan states, all of them, and you're advising them, "Please listen, let's talk together, openly," and they're telling you, "We don't know how to speak with adversaries; please help us understand." What would you say to them?

DTTN: One thing (I have to interrupt your question): Before, when 2010 came and the generals opened up the country and they said, "Ok, you can form your own political parties," at that time until the 2010 election, when Aung San Suu Kyi was released from house arrest, at that time, the ethnic people—I know all the ethnic groups very well—they looked to Aung San Suu Kyi in a very esteemed manner. They thought that if Aung San Suu Kyi came to power then their problems would be solved. They had very high hopes for her. But before that, the NLD party was there, but she didn't get herself involved. But later on, U Thein Sein invited her to his president's residence in Naypyidaw and they had a good talk. And then he advised her to get back to politics, so she agreed, and became president of the NLD party.

After that, the 2012 by-elections—she participated in those elections and won. And then the rest of the places they won, from her own party. And then after that their party became stronger and stronger, advancing to a very good position. So the ethnic people, they're still hoping. I know this because I'm very close to some of the ethnic groups. I'm very friendly with them and listen to whatever they say. Because I never keep those things in my mind—all these things are in the past. Whatever they say I just smile and listen.

But they had very, very high hopes for Aung San Suu Kyi. And then, with the 2015 election, still they thought very highly of Aung San Suu Kyi. And after 2015, the people continued to have very high hopes for her. We can't say it was a landslide victory—she got many seats, but compared to our population it wasn't a landslide, but a majority.

And then the NLD started making mistakes. For instance, in Rakhine and in Shan States they have their own parties. And in Rakhine, the Rakhine party was neck and neck with the NLD, and then in the end the Rakhine party got the majority. The NLD's response? The NLD formed an NLD government in Rakhine. Did you know that? They formed an NLD government. Those are the mistakes. They shouldn't have formed an NLD government, but the chief minister of Rakhine State was NLD. In fact, someone from the Rakhine party should have become the chief minister. In Shan State they did the same thing. That's why the party headed by U Khun Htun Oo in Shan State has already deserted the NLD. They have their own party, but they deserted, because it was the same as in Rakhine—neck to neck, and then getting a majority, and then being sidelined. They formed their own NLD government in Shan State and pushed out U Khun Htun Oo's people. So many of these kinds of things have happened all over the country.

AC: So Daw Suu has abandoned the ethnic groups? Turned her back?

DTTN: Yes. But now she's started campaigning and is after those very same people, because the elections will come very soon.

AC: So what you are saying is that she abandoned them, and now, for political reasons, she's trying to get them back?

DTTN: Yes. But those people also are organizing themselves. For instance, in Chin State they have three groups, but now they've become one group. In Shan State also they had three or four groups, but U Khun Htun Oo's 'Tiger Head' party and the other parties, they have become united for the 2020 elections. In some other places also.

AC: In the ethnic regions, the ethnic people that you're close to, how do they feel about Daw Aung San Suu Kyi today?

DTTN: They mistrust her. I ran into a number of ethnic leaders at a conference, and I was surprised to learn that they had been systematically recording Daw Aung San Suu Kyi's speeches. They even played me a couple of recordings. They would routinely analyse the contents of the speeches, paying attention to the promises made by Daw Aung San Suu Kyi, and they would find large discrepancies between what was said and what was actually done.

AC: This was during a conference with the ethnic groups?

DTTN: Not all—about nine or ten groups. And then, I think I was the only person from a Burmese political party. So, they said that "In the coming 2020 election, we have to fight so that we win the election. We are going to fight for that, and then we will abandon her." I said, "You can't do that," so they asked me why, and I said because of what my father said to me. My father told it to me like this: "She is not a roadside girl." He called Aung San Suu Kyi "Suu Suu." "She is not an ordinary girl—she is the daughter of Aung San, my very close friend and our hero." He had very high regard for General Aung San, so, "Suu Suu is not an ordinary girl." Then I asked my father, "But in politics I sometimes have to say something critical, if something's wrong—if something's wrong I have to point it out," and my father said, "No, don't say like that; if you want to say something about Suu Suu, just tell me—don't tell other people." That's how much he loved General Aung San, and Suu Suu also. So, I told those ethnic people also, "No, you can't abandon her when we have to rebuild the country—Aung San Suu Kyi must also take part."

AC: So, you're encouraging them to stay with her?

DTTN: Yes. And not only them—we all have to unify to rebuild the country.

AC: Let me ask you directly: When someone has betrayed you—as General Ne Win betrayed both your father and the people of your country—and they're coming back and saying, "Please trust me," and people are pointing out contradictions, how do you trust that person? When they've abandoned you and betrayed you in the past, how do you regain trust? How would you encourage Daw Aung San Suu Kyi to make good on her failure of these people?

DTTN: I'm just talking about Daw Aung San Suu Kyi. I'm not talking about General Ne Win. General Ne Win is a different case.

AC: Ok, let's stay with Daw Aung San Suu Kyi then—would you encourage her to apologize to the ethnic groups, admit she made mistakes, and let's move forward together?

DTTN: I want to, yes. But another thing is that after she came to power, and now has become State Counsellor, she abandoned all the political parties, not just ethnic groups. She didn't recognise us. She said with the peace process going on, whichever political parties want to join the peace process must have at least one candidate in Parliament. Because she knows that the result of 2015 means that it's only her party and the USDP party—NLD majority and USDP in second position.

It was a very tough game in 2015 and we got only one person elected, from Mandalay. So, we are lucky to be in this peace process. But every politician, every political party, wants to be involved in the peace process, because they are countrymen and countrywomen who share that desire.

But she said no. So now, out of more than 90 political parties, only 22 parties are in this peace process. So, our party's chairman, he's involved, and then he has to go all over the country to meet the people and to listen to their feelings.

AC: So, let me get this correct: Aung San Suu Kyi has, from what you're sharing, betrayed her good will and her promise to the ethnic groups. She's abandoned even many of the democratic followers from other parties, who supported her and the people for years to overcome military dictatorship. Yet, she is the daughter of General Aung San; your father encouraged you to still support her, even back in '88, '89, '90. You still carry that belief in your heart today. You also communicate *Dhamma* as your guide; you are moderate even when you criticize. You're restrained. But you're in a position where someone has to tell the truth, because all roads lead back to the NLD and Daw Aung San Suu Kyi, to challenge this decades-long, continuous dictatorship.

I come back to the question: What would you advise her to move forward here? Because you could go forward and right slip back into dictatorship again, although there's a possibility of transitioning into democracy. And you have wisdom in what you're saying, and I beg of you, in conversation and in dialogue, how would you advise Daw Aung San Suu Kyi, at this point, for the betterment of your country?

DTTN: I don't have much to say except that she should talk with the political parties. It's ironic that in every speech she's said that if we want to work for the betterment of the country and for the peace process, we have to work hand in hand with all the people. You can't work alone. This is what she's said in each and every speech. But in practical terms, I can't say anything further.

AC: I read these same words that you're speaking pretty every day in the paper—the importance of harmony and working together. Unity through diversity. All the key words and phrases. But there hasn't been a history of that, as you see it. What can be done right now in this country to not make the same mistakes as have been made over the last five years, the last ten years? How to unify the people, truly? What's required at this point? Do we need statesmanship, stateswomanship? Do we need an outsider to come in and talk about how to talk? What's needed? The elections are coming up in a matter of months, and it sounds to me that the vote could be split. The next thing we know we have a civilian dictatorship.

DTTN: We have a civilian dictatorship right now.

AC: I'm asking you again, openly. These books will be shared with all your people, in your language. What would you say to all the people of Burma before they vote, to not have this dictatorship root even deeper?

DTTN: In 2010, the Burmese people—the whole country—they were not aware of the elections and didn't understand the meaning of democratisation. Especially, they didn't know what to do in the elections, because the methods are quite strange for them. They made many mistakes. And then, the military were still threatening also—I stood from Mandalay, and there were lots of threats from the military, who were still very strong at that time. So many threats, and even the people of Mandalay, when we went out campaigning, they dared not talk to us, they dared not take our pamphlets. They just took them and tore them up. And we have lots of small coffee stalls, and even if I went there to distribute my pamphlets and to talk to them, the same thing. I met one person, and when I approached him, he just wrote something on a piece of paper, and he showed me: "Please get out of here quickly." Not because he hated me, but because he said it was dangerous. Later, after I'd been to other places and returned to where I was staying, at a friend's residence, this man got the number of the place, phoned me and he said, "I didn't mean I didn't like you, but there's a real danger, that's why I told you to leave." I said, "Thank you very much," that's all, and the next day I carried with my campaigning. That was in 2010.

Then the so-called civilian government was formed, and I should say that U Thein Sein, though he was an ex-army man, he was good at politics. Every now and then he met the different political parties. At that time, we had about 108 or so parties. He called some of them group by group to Naypyidaw. The first group was our group—not only our party but ten parties altogether. He took us there by plane, and then he met us, and asked us one party at a time whatever we had to say—"Please talk to me openly otherwise I will not know what's happening in our country. You should say what the problems are frankly." And then he didn't only ask one person from each party, but several. So, we spoke very openly and directly. And then another point is that he wrote down everything by himself. He had his secretaries also, and his PAs, but he wrote everything down himself. Then he said, "I've noted it down and I will try my best to sort these problems."

The first time, I told him about our people who are still living in other countries. They very much wanted to come back, but they couldn't. Some were given visas, but when they reached the Yangon airport they were threatened and told they had to go back to the US or England or wherever it was. "Your visa is cancelled." These kinds of things happened. I helped one person at the time—he was at the airport for about six hours and his relatives were really worried. Fortunately, he called me from the airport, and I contacted someone, and he helped us out—the man left the airport after seven or eight hours. So, I told this problem to U Thein Sein also.

U Thein Sein wanted to build up the country in a prosperous way, and those people abroad wanted to come back and help the new government to become a prosperous country. He wrote that down, and after the meeting he said, "Daw Than Than Nu, I wrote it down very precisely, and don't worry, I will solve this problem within a few months," and he did.

Some other problems he also solved. And then sometimes he came to Rangoon and at the Rangoon Division government office he called all the political parties and did the same thing. Whenever we met, he asked people what kind of problems they were facing. But the current situation is very different.

AC: The reason for this is?

DTTN: Only she will know. I can't say.

AC: Do people of your social network talk about it, ask each other why? Do you have conversations about why she's acting this way?

DTTN: Social networking in Burma is also very complicated. I don't follow social media much.

AC: It's not so open?

DTTN: No, no—it's very much open, and for that reason I don't like it, because, some people, they don't understand what's going on in Myanmar. For instance, this thing with the ICJ (International Court of Justice at The Hague), the genocide problem—they don't know why The Gambia has accused Burma. So what will happen? Nobody knows. Nobody follows.

AC: Why don't they follow it? But her popularity in Burma has soared in the country and I see large billboards around the city with "We Stand with Daw Aung San Suu Kyi" on them.

DTTN: They don't really know what's going on. But on their social media they will say, "Our mother Daw Aung San Suu Kyi, we are with you, we are very proud of you," so much praise. Like the billboards.

AC: I'm aware that I'm taking a lot of your time, but I want to ask you this; what you're sharing, although I find it very interesting (I love Burma, I love the people), are things that I think people will really want to hear in this country. I know that people around the world will want to hear what you're saying, without a doubt. I've been following your country's politics from the day I arrived here and asked Mahasi Sayadaw if I could become a monk, and he said, "You can't because we're under dictatorship."

I had no idea! And from that point on, when I finally did get my visa from the government, a big procession comes into the Mahasi Thathana Yeitha and, of all people, it's Bogyoke U Tin Oo, the General under Ne Win who he imprisoned and was released after six years of solitary. Slowly over the two years he lived at Mahasi's center, he talked to me a lot about politics. I eventually met your father when he came back to the country in 1980 from India. Since that time, I have spoken to many thousands of people in public talks and many more on national and international media around the world. I say this because it has been my experience that many, many people sympathize with Burma. They believe in your country's ongoing struggle for freedom. They want to know the truth of this country; they want to know how to help the people of your country—I genuinely believe that. And at this point, I don't know that people really know what to think and how to help. And so, in my humble way, because I'm deeply committed to *Dhamma* and nonviolence, I feel that my motivation in speaking with you and bringing these voices of freedom to the people and to the world is based on *Dhamma*. Because I grew up in your country; I'm a son of *Dhamma* because of your father bringing Mahasi Sayadaw here. Together with Sayadaw U Pandita, they trained me on how to talk. In a monastery you learn to confess your faults openly. U Pandita would say you're a better man the more you talk about what you did wrong. You become stronger. It took me many years to understand that, and I'm still quite a child in that, but I feel stronger when I make a wrong and I make it right by at least acknowledging it in myself, and talk with contemporaries about my failings, and equally about my strengths. It made me a better person.

Yes—I feel that when people hear how they can help, how people in your country can learn to talk more openly to one another, it will be one of the greatest gifts in the world for all countries, because your people said "No" to 134 years of colonialism—your father signed the independence accord—they said "No" to war, they said "No" to military dictatorship, and they said "Yes" to changing things in a nonviolent way. That's rare. Your father met Gandhi. Your father is rooted in *Dhamma*; he's my father in *Dhamma*; he was instrumental in bringing *Dhamma* and meditation to your people and I was a benefactor of that.

Coming back to the central issue, all of us in the world want to know how to talk with one another, openly, more peacefully, and solve our troubles without violence, persecution and denigration. So, yes, I think the people in the world not only want to help but they want to hear this message that you're bringing, which is the power of overcoming our problems through open, compassionate, *mettā*-infused conversation. "Let's be open with each other and come together," as your father would, I can imagine, say. And let's heal the past and let's move forward.

So, I'm thoroughly committed to what I just said; I feel it in my soul. I feel it in this room with you. I feel it in this country among the people. I would like to believe that Daw Aung San Suu Kyi, the other members of Parliament, even General Min Aung Hlaing and Than Shwe and others want what's best for the people. I would like to believe that. And so, I'm going to end the book with our conversations, and so I would like to come back again and continue, if I may?

DTTN: Please do. It is my honor to speak with you and to our people as well through your books.

AC: Thank you.

"They decided to do something from the outside.
It became revolutionary."

ALAN CLEMENTS: So, thank you for taking the time again today, a continuation from yesterday. If I can, I would like to know more about you. I would like to know more about you and your background, some of the key moments of your life. I know you have a long history of supporting democracy and human rights, and for the overall prosperity of your people. Where did you spend the majority of your life? Was it both here in Burma and also in India? And where did you grow up as a young girl?

DAW THAN THAN NU: I grew up here in Rangoon. I was born here, at the Gymkhana Hospital; that's what it used to be called because it was built in the British days. Now it is still there, but we call it the Yangon Central Women's Hospital. I also went to grade school here and attended university here as well. I attended the Institute of Economics, starting in 1964, and graduated in 1968, during U Ne Win's regime. Before it was called the Social Science Building in Yangon University. The funny thing is I don't know anything about economics *(laughs)*.

AC: Why do you say that?

DTTN: Because I really don't know much about economics, but I studied economics after passing class 10. See, we had a group of very close friends, and only one of them passed with flying colours. So, she said she was going to study medicine. Medicine and engineering were very popular here in Burma, even up to now, that is, if you get very good marks. If you got the grades, you either went into medicine or engineering. But these days the competition has become much more difficult; in those days if you got 75+ it was much easier.

Another thing is that, because of the student demonstrations, the authorities decided to bring in students from other regions of the country, and at the same time disperse those from Yangon to other places. Now, Yangon university is much more crowded. Before, if you wanted to study here, there were students mostly from other states, like Mandalay or Bago and so on.

AC: And when did you begin taking an interest in politics?

DTTN: I have had an inclination for politics for some time now. But when I was young, I preferred going to university and mixing with friends. Even though I thought about politics occasionally at that time, my father as prime minister being hauled away and placed in detention, I had more of a human reaction to those things, rather than a serious interest in politics, as it were.

So, when I graduated, all my friends went on to employment, apart from me. I graduated September of 1968, and in April '69 we left for India, via Calcutta, with my parents and one of my brothers. And, I didn't know that my father left Burma for India to do revolutionary work.

AC: Your father was prime minister from 1948 to 1956, 1957 to 1958, and 1960 to '62. You were a young woman at this time, and then went to college, growing up in the first democratic family in Burma. What was that like, growing up in such a revolutionary family, coming out of colonial domination, and the war years?

DTTN: I don't know whether you will believe it or not, because during my childhood and then growing up, in Burma, in the Burmese way, we don't feel the way people do in your country or in European countries. In your country, at 18 you become a grown up person, but for us, if you are 20 or 25 and you stay with your parents and if you are not married, you are still a good child, you know? Because parents also look up to us, and we also stay with them, and we never decide things on our own. We asked our parents about every decision, but for us our father could not give that kind of attention, because he was a very busy person. So, whatever I had to tell, I had to tell my mother.

AC: The walls are covered here in your home with photographs of your father with famous people. He's with Nehru and Mahatma Gandhi, Mao Tse-tung, Khrushchev, Eisenhower, Ben-Gurion of Israel and so many others. And there's a framed Time magazine cover story with your father. When was that from and did you meet many dignitaries growing up?

DTTN: That was from August 1954. I was only 7 at the time. So, no, not at all. I hardly met any famous people other, than Mrs Indira Gandhi and a few others. My sister, on the other hand, met many such people, in the good old days, when she was already grown up. There's a 16-year age gap between me and my sister, so she met many people during the pre-independence times, because there was a lot of political activity. Although she was not interested in politics, she met and knew many politicians, and many activists and celebrities too. But I didn't.

AC: And your true interest in politics began—do you remember when and why?

DTTN: It started when I was in India. Rather, after the '88 uprising—that was when I started. First, we left for India, spending time in Calcutta, and then we went to Mumbai, Bombay, in the late sixties. My father left Burma for a medical check-up—he didn't want to go for the check-up, but Mrs. Indira Gandhi insisted. See, she came to Burma in 1968, about two years after he'd been released from confinement, and mentioned that he looked quite tired. Before she came, she'd asked General Ne Win that when she arrived in Yangon, she would like to meet U Nu, and Ne Win said no, this wasn't possible. Mrs. Indira Gandhi was their guest, and they said "no," because U Nu was nothing at that time. Because of that, Mrs. Indira Gandhi said, "Then I will cancel my visit."

AC: A woman of integrity.

DTTN: Yes. Because of her refusal they allowed her to meet with my father, and she came to know that he was not healthy because of his time in the army prison camp. He had a small wooden house built for him in the camp, where we were occasionally allowed to visit him. Maybe once every six months or so. Initially he was kept in an old two storey house, one built in the British time. We had to pass through Mingaldon and then there's this very old house, surrounded by the army camp. We first met him there, where he was kept separate from the rest of his cabinet members, who had been also been placed under detention but who were kept across the road in another building. So, my father was alone, along with one army captain, a Karen, who was always present in his building, around the clock. Ironically, that person has now become a friend of mine. Well, I didn't know him at the time, but not too long ago, during U Thein Sein's time, at a dinner function, he came to me and said, "Do you know me?" and I said, "No, I don't know you." He then explained that at that army prison camp he had to stay with my father. "Your father was kept upstairs, and I stayed downstairs, every day, 24 hours a day, for nearly two years." And surrounded by other soldiers as well. But he also said that he had always respected U Nu and had even climbed up a tree to listen to one of his sermons because there wasn't any room in the audience.

AC: What period was this?

DTTN: From 1962, 2nd of March, at the time of Ne Win's coup d'état to October '66.

AC: And so, Ne Win sent his soldiers to incarcerate your father. He took your father from you. How did Ne Win's betrayal of your father impact you? And how did it affect you to have your father stolen from you and your family?

DTTN: Well, yesterday I told you that at that time I had very strong feelings against them. But now it is totally gone. No animosity. Gone. Totally gone. Not only now, but for a long time now.

AC: And how did your classmates and friends relate to you, with your father being incarcerated.

DTTN: You may not believe it, but I didn't have very high-class friends at the time. My friends were ordinary people. Although my friends were not so high-class, I also knew the daughter of the president at that time, U Win Maung, but we were not close. And Aung San Suu Kyi also—I knew her from a very young age, but again, we were not close. It was just because my mother had to visit their house at least once a week to meet Daw Khin Kyi, to see to her well-being, on the instruction of my father. Whenever she went, she took me along with her, so I was at their house, but The Lady never talked to me. She said, "Come to my room," so she took me up to her room, and then "You sit here," and I sat there, and because she didn't talk to me, I didn't talk to her. When I was young, I didn't talk much either. But we knew each other very well—she even knew my pet name—but we were not friendly. And other friends, also—I have many friends, but not from wealthy and powerful families.

AC: So, you were going to Aung San Suu Kyi's house with your mother to go and visit her mother. Can you share more of this time in your life?

DTTN: Yes. We were in the same school also, but she was two years older than me, in a senior class.

AC: And when Mrs Indira Gandhi came, she insisted on visiting or she would cancel her whole trip, and then all of you went to India? How did that happen?

DTTN: Yes. Mrs. Indira Gandhi invited my father, because she said he looked tired and not too healthy after he'd been released from prison. In India, in Mumbai, there's a very good hospital, quite famous—the Breach Candy Hospital. I remember it well. So, my father agreed, because he also wanted to get out of the country, at that time, to do his revolutionary work.

We stayed for three months in Mumbai because we had to wait for other close associates of my father to come out.

AC: What was your life like in India? What did you do?

DTTN: Before that I want to tell you one thing, about what my father's arrest was like and how it affected me. On the 2nd of March 1962, when my father was taken into custody in the early morning, they said on their walkie-talkies, communicating with HQ, that "The maggot has been captured."

AC: That was their codename for him?

DTTN: Yes, their password. He was taken, and in the morning a few people came and visited my mother, because they had heard the news. But the majority, they dared not even come to the surrounding area. The first person to visit was my uncle, my father's younger brother. And then later on, my mother's elder brother, followed by her elder sister—she stayed close by, so she visited. Later, people who were close and in politics came, but there were very few people in general. Even our relatives, they disappeared. They were very much afraid of coming to our place.

So, my mother told me, "Don't go to school for at least four or five days," because she was worried about us also. And then my brother, the one who went with us to India, was also in high school. I think he was in Saint Paul's school, the boys' school, and she told both of us not to go to classes. After four or five days, my mother said, "Ok, re-start your routine," and I went back to school.

When the car dropped me at the school, before classes started at the girls' school, suddenly everyone from my circle of friends disappeared—they rushed inside the building when they saw my car. So, I also went inside, and I didn't look for anyone, I just went straight to my classroom. When I walked in, suddenly the classroom went silent. Nothing could be heard. Normally we'd all hang out and chat before school, but everyone fell silent. I didn't talk to anyone, just sat at my desk. They were afraid. I don't know what they were afraid of, but then the class teacher came in, and she was also a little changed. But I didn't mind. We just started the lesson, and then after that there was a recess for food, the lunch break, but nobody left the classroom, they just sat there quietly. Because I didn't get up, they didn't get up. Then I wrote a very short letter to my very close friends in the class—just on a piece of paper, where I said, "Are you coming with me to the canteen?" and I handed it to one person who was next to me. She was so happy she jumped out of her chair and called to the others, "Come, come, we must go to the canteen and have lunch break," and they all surrounded me and we went out of class.

AC: How beautiful. Now, you're in India; now what?

DTTN: In India, in Bombay, we stayed with Lalji Mehrothra, an Indian who was very rich, and a former diplomat. He was the ambassador in Yangon when my father was prime minister. My father was very close to all the diplomats, without formality—he was very informal with everyone. So, he knew that we were arriving in India, and I think the government also told him that U Nu would come for a medical check-up, so he invited my father and the whole family to stay at his home.

AC: Now, let me ask you: What do you mean by revolutionary work, specifically?

DTTN: It was because my father had tried so many times with his colleagues inside Burma to change the military government and it hadn't worked. And he talked with General Ne Win also. Not only himself; General Ne Win invited 33 politicians, and they talked, but my father didn't ask anything, except that "You have to organize an election." But, as we know, he didn't accept it.

AC: Not his style.

DTTN: No, not his style. So, later on, in the final stages, they decided to do something from the outside. It became revolutionary--

AC: Did your father advocate armed struggle against Ne Win?

DTTN: Yes. I have to say yes.

AC: I see; so, when you say revolutionary work, he advocated an armed resistance?

DTTN: Yes.

AC: An overtaking of Ne Win's military?

DTTN: Yes, but Ne Win's army was the regular army.

AC: But your father knew them very well, right? And thought they might defect and come to his side?

DTTN: Yes. He knew them very well, but if he decided upon something, he had to see it through. He always had to follow through on his decisions, whether it was good or bad.

AC: And then?

DTTN: And then he was treated in Breach Candy Hospital and after that we went to Kashmir—the Indian government organized it for us. And from there, after some time, we returned to Calcutta, and from Calcutta we reached Thailand.

AC: Now, how long were you in India, altogether?

DTTN: Only four months, initially, and then we went to Thailand. We reached Thailand in July '69, and then from July '69 we stayed until March '74—coincidentally, we came back to India on March 2nd '74. My father stayed in India from '74 until '80—six years. Then he came back here.

AC: And you came back with him?

DTTN: No, we were left behind. My father and mother returned, but my mother insisted we must be left behind. My father initially wanted all of us to return, but my mother said no.

AC: Too dangerous?

DTTN: Yes, she thought so.

AC: So, you left India after four months and went to Thailand, you, your brother, your mother, yourself and your father, and then your father stayed, and you went back to India?

DTTN: Yes, I returned to India with my parents—not only myself but also my brother, and my father's ex-security officer was with us. Actually, the officer went back to Burma, and later on his son married General Ne Win's daughter, while he was still doing revolutionary work *(laughs)*.

AC: Your father's top security guard's son married Ne Win's daughter?

DTTN: Yes.

AC: So very close family ties; you knew the son?

DTTN: Of course. They grew up in front of me.

AC: *(Laughs)* So this is really quite a family affair here in Burma, isn't it? Everyone, instead of just having an argument, you put each other in prison, you torture each other, take each other's money, exile each other, take up weapons.

DTTN: *(Laughs)* Isn't it so...

AC: And so how long were you in India in total.

DTTN: We went in '74 and my parent returned to Burma in '80, and we were left in India. We were in Bhopal. From there, after my parents left, we moved to New Delhi, to work with All-India Radio.

AC: And what did your work at All-India Radio entail?

DTTN: Well, this idea came to my father because even in Thailand we had a mobile radio station and we broadcast back to Burma. So, I was one of the broadcasters from this mobile radio. You could say it was an underground revolutionary radio station started by my father.

AC: And now you're enlisted in being a revolutionary speaking on the radio back to the people of Burma?

DTTN: *(Laughs)* Yes. But at that time nobody knew that I was Than Than Nu. Nobody knew, because we didn't use our names, we just broadcast.

AC: Did you use a pseudonym?

DTTN: No, nothing. Even my mother took part in a radio play, because my father wrote so many radio plays. So, my mother, myself, we took part in the radio plays also.

AC: What an unusually creative response to challenging dictatorship.

DTTN: See, before my father left, he said, "You are not new to broadcasting, so why not work with All-India Radio?" At that time, it was quite a popular radio station. So, I said, "Ok." And my father, before he left for Burma, met with Mrs. Indira Gandhi in New Delhi and requested that myself and my husband were given work. So Mrs. Indira Gandhi said, "This All-India Radio station is a very sensitive place, because it's a democratic country, so you can't just be appointed by higher ups."

AC: It had to be democratic?

DTTN: Precisely. There first had to have a vacancy, and then whoever wants to join must have an interview, and do written interviews, so my father agreed to do that.

AC: And you did this?

DTTN: We did this. So, they left. He had already spoken to Mrs. Indira Gandhi and then he left for Burma, and we were left behind. The government didn't ask us to come to New Delhi immediately, because in Bhopal we were given a huge house, with so many security people, and they gave us two cars, and then added two cars later on. The first two cars were imported cars, and then later on, because in India, for the VIPs and the cabinet ministers, they use their own India-made motorcars (Hindustan models made in Calcutta), they gave us another of these two cars with chauffeurs, and we had security men also. We had five or six servants.

AC: All provided for by the Indian government?

DTTN: Yes. So, they didn't say that we should immediately come to New Delhi. They said we should take our own time, but we wanted to move, because it was a huge house with just myself, my husband and two children, who were quite young. The older boy was already at St. Joseph college in the mountains in Northern India. But we said it was better we moved, even if we had to sit for interviews and everything, so we packed up and moved there. They gave us an apartment which was meant for government officials. It had small rooms but was nicely located. It had more than 500 plus rooms, all connected, from Block A to Block F. It was like a zigzag.

AC: What an unusually complex and compelling upbringing you had.

DTTN: As for the interviews, at that time there was only one vacancy, so I told my husband he should go, because he was the head of the house, but he said no, I should go. I said, "Why? I'm your wife, you go first!" But he said no, because this job was not created but given to us because of your father, so I had to honor him, as his daughter. "I am the son-in-law, you should go." I went there for the interview and written test and passed. Three years later my husband also got a job at the radio station.

AC: And what did you do at the radio station?

DTTN: Translator and announcer.

*The problem is pride. At present,
we have two governments.*

ALAN CLEMENTS: A two-part question, and please, interweave your answers if you wish. We talked yesterday of your father's deep turning toward *Dhamma*, and along with it, meditation and mindfulness. That means you grew up in a vibrant *Dhamma* atmosphere. What it is about this *Dhamma*, this Buddhist teaching, that your father was most moved by the most, and the same with yourself? What element of the *Dhamma* most nurtures you on a practical level, and the same with your father?

DAW THAN THAN NU: I can't say much about my father, but for me, starting from seven or eight years old, when we were so young, we were sent to the Mahasi Thathana Yeiktha every year, during the school holidays. We went whether we wanted to go or not. And then, after some time, when I was in the first year of university, the same—every year I went for 20 days to one month of intensive silent meditation practice. At that time, after one long retreat, my meditation teacher, Venerable Sayadaw U

Sujata, encouraged me to listen to Mahasi's Sayadaw talk on *nyanzin* and I understood everything he said.

AC: The progress of insight? The tape by Mahasi Sayadaw?

DTTN: Yes.

AC: A very rare honor to listen to that tape. Only yogis with exceptional insight are allowed to listen. Sadhu... Do you still go to the Mahasi Centre?

DTTN: Very rarely. And when I do go, I don't go for meditation, only for social gatherings, if invited. That's all.

AC: And you met Mahasi Sayadaw, no doubt?

DTTN: Oh yes, many times. Whenever my mother went there, I went with her. He had a remarkable stillness to him and was so very learned. You must know that my father organized the Sixth Great Buddhist Council here in Yangon and that Mahasi Sayadaw was the chief questioner at the council?

AC: Yes, what a remarkable vision. Sadhu, sadhu.

So, your whole family have practiced *Satipatthana*?

DTTN: Yes. All at the Mahasi Yeiktha.

AC: Well, we are all from the same *Dhamma* family. Sayadaw U Sujata and I were quite close. He was very good to me, as was Mahasi Sayadaw, always inviting me into their rooms for snacks, conversation, offering any form of assistance. The same with Sayadaw U Pandita, my second main teacher after Mahasi Sayadaw passed away in 1982.

DTTN: Were you at the monastery when Mahasi Sayadaw passed away?

AC: Yes. In fact, his long-time attendant, U Sobhana, who is now one of the two Head Teaching Monks at the center, came to Sayadaw U Pandita's cottage next door and told him first. He and I went directly to Sayadawgyi's bedside and then to the hospital with him where he passed away. I was also at his cremation a week later with tens of thousands of others gathered to pay their final respects to perhaps the greatest mindfulness meditation teacher in modern times.

DTTN: Why did you leave the monastic life?

AC: Ne Win's people came to the monastery and told me to leave the country on several occasions, and with no reason given. Only a 24-hour notice. After the third time, I said, enough and disrobed and carried on with my *Dhamma* life and work in the world leading meditation retreats in different countries. I assumed at the time that I was yet another victim of Ne Win's xenophobia, because I was one of the only foreigners at the monastery for a long time. Also, I think I told you that I became very close friends with former General U Tin Oo, who became a monk at the Mahasi centre after he was released from prison. Like with your father and so many others, Ne Win locked him away. And it was U Tin Oo who first introduced me to Daw Aung San Suu Kyi back in 1995 after her first release from house arrest.

DTTN: Yes, very much a family affair.

AC: A key question, with a preface; I am deeply inspired by your people. The collective moral courage is something I have never seen before. And from the horrors, most of your people want to forgive and achieve national reconciliation. Daw Aung San Suu Kyi has made reconciliation and unity the most important elements of government. I would think that she would want her legacy to be known as the one who inspired the people—all ethnicities and the military as well—to set aside differences and unify and make good on the vision of national reconciliation.

DTTN: And peace.

AC: Yes, peace too. And I'm expressing here a high degree of respect for the intentions of the stakeholders, such as Daw Aung San Suu Kyi, former General Than Shwe, Senior General Min Aung Hlaing, regional commanders, ethnic leaders, armed groups, all members of Parliament, the mayors, and ministers and leaders of all religions, everybody; respecting their best intention to be motivated by genuine goodwill.

DTTN: Yes.

AC: Which brings me to my question: What's required of your people and of your leaders to make good on national reconciliation?

DTTN: From the point of *Dhamma*, I think that the people you mentioned—everyone—should put pride aside. And then, as I expressed yesterday, everyone must be unified. Let me explain; during U Thein Sein's time, because he belonged to the army, and was appointed by General Than Shwe, and because General Min Aung Hlaing also belongs to the army, the government is from the army and belongs to the army. Today, the government is a people's government, with 25 percent army, and if the leaders of both sides put their pride aside, then it will lead to a more prosperous and peaceful way. The problem is pride. At present, we have two governments. So, the people's government, they cannot control the army. And the army cannot become friends with the government.

At the beginning it seemed like it would be work out, but, day by day, lots of problems surfaced. And then here and there fighting erupted. In my way of thinking, in *Dhamma* terms, the underlying issue is pride. This is an important point.

Now, in our country, it's a very sad thing that the *Saṅgha* (assembly of monks) are also divided. I don't know whether you feel that or not, but the *Saṅgha* is severely divided, between Ma Ba Tha and the rest (Ma Ba Tha is the Association for the Protection of Race and Religion in Myanmar). Ma Ba Tha are not just monks. They have many lay supporters as well.

On the other side, because I've been in discussions with the younger ladies, now there's a gender problem in the country. They're fighting for gender recognition and speaking out about it every chance they can. They want gender equality to be in the forefront of society and politics. When I speak with them, they say they are anti-Ma Ba Tha. But the way they speak shows they do not really understand the true or deeper motivation of Ma Ba Tha. And another thing is that nobody, not just the younger women, really wants to get to the bottom of the Ma Ba Tha issue and study it deeply.

AC: How did they come into existence and what would we discover if we did go into their beliefs more deeply?

DTTN: Because of this crisis in Rakhine, Ma Ba Tha came into the forefront. Ma Ba Tha monks thought that many Muslim men, not only in Rakhine but throughout the country, were desirous of marrying our Buddhist girls, and after, if they divorce, which is not uncommon at all, the ladies cannot inherit anything, nothing at all. This is their Muslim law and it runs contrary to everything we know within the *Dhamma* to be moral and right. On the other hand, if they were Muslim girls marrying Muslim men, they are, by law, entitled to some form of divorce settlement. But for whatever reason many Muslim men want to marry Buddhist girls.

AC: This is fascist and violent, downright stone-age. It begs the question of why those more intelligent Muslims, who do not subscribe to this expression of religious criminality, don't come together and ban the practice and make it unlawful?

DTTN: Well, a good point. Another noteworthy point is that for Buddhist girls, once they marry a Muslim, they must immediately convert to Islam. Whoever marries a Muslim male must convert to Islam.

AC: Isn't that a form of ethnic cleansing?

DTTN: Marrying and forced conversion is not the real problem—the problem is that the girls, if they do not give birth to boys, then divorce crops up very, very easily, and not only do they not inherit anything, they're often kicked out of the house. Based on these issues, this is the main reason why Ma Ba Tha has come into national prominence. Our young Buddhist ladies must study this situation, carefully. Everyone should study it carefully, including Muslims.

AC: You know, I want to say I am sorry for having such a visceral reaction to this information, but I consider it a mature response. I'm sickened by this. On a higher note, my late *Dhamma* teacher, the Venerable Sayadaw U Pandita, made the point to me throughout our 36-year-long relationship, that the key to peace in society was understanding the importance of caring for another in the same way you would like to be cared for. He would also say, you do not have to be a Buddhist or a Christian or a Muslim or a Hindu to understand that caring for others is the most basic condition for peace and harmony.

DTTN: We call it *mettā* and *karuṇā* in Pali, loving-kindness and compassion. We also say, there can never be enough of it in the world.

AC: And, coming back to national reconciliation: we know what the problem is—pride. How to transform that pride into courage and insight towards achieving reconciliation? What should the leaders do at this point?

DTTN: They should trust. Trust is important. But now, with the peace process which is still going on, Daw Aung San Suu Kyi, during U Thein Sein's time, when he started this peace process, she told the ethnic groups, "Don't come forward for the peace process, it's not the time. Only when we form a government will we start our own peace process." This, I think, was incorrect. So now, when they formed a government, they started a peace process, but there's much mistrust between each and every group.

AC: How to overcome the mistrust? How would you advise the leaders to set aside their pride and mistrust, set aside their own likes and dislikes, and find a higher way, a harmony of the whole?

DTTN: What I would say is that during U Thein Sein's time, for the peace process, he never came to the forefront of the process. He was smarter than the politicians. He was never in the foreground. He got his deputy, who was also the minster, to negotiate everything.

For trust, there must also be rapport. For instance, as I said, whenever invited, he went and discussed with them, and he would then invite them to Yangon. In this way, he discussed the issues with every group. At the Myanmar Peace Centre (now it's changed to NRCP—National Reconciliation Centre for Peace), every month during U Thein Sein's time, they had a meeting. I was one of the attendees. And they would ask everyone to speak out. If you speak out, you feel better than if you kept it all inside, without talking. And after the meeting, he invited all the ethnic groups, from top to bottom, and gave a dinner and spoke with everyone, openly. Sometimes there was songs and dancing. It meant that the people came closer together.

Now, nothing. And then, for the meetings also, Aung San Suu Kyi wanted to stay in the center. So, she was the head of this peace process, but she came to the conference, to the meetings, sat for 10 minutes and then left. She didn't listen at all. If she wants to be involved and make a difference, she should stay and listen. If she doesn't want to sit and listen, she should behave like U Thein Sein—don't come at all. Appoint someone as her deputy.

So now the deputy is her personal doctor. But that person can't say anything, because he's afraid of Aung San Suu Kyi, and he's also afraid because he's not a politician. He himself openly said, "I don't know anything about politics." So, when something is put to him by the ethnic groups, he says "I will ask Daw Aung San Suu Kyi." Whatever comes up, "I will ask Daw Aung San Suu Kyi." That's all. In addition, many other key politicians were not invited at all.

AC: Should there be an outside intermediary, a universally respected diplomat brought in to facilitate leaderships matters as well as the peace process?

DTTN: Oh, there are many! They are already here. When Kofi Annan was invited by Daw Suu, nobody liked it. Nobody.

AC: What to fault with the former Secretary General of the United Nations?

DTTN: Because we should go on with this peace process ourselves. Further, Kofi Annan didn't know anything about the Burmese way to peace. Nor did he know anything about Burma. And now also, some people from the Japanese government are involved in the peace process, and China also offered themselves. And many European countries; previously the EU was so active in this peace process, because of their financial assistance. Because of that the peace process has become more elaborate. Now the EU is still giving funding but they're not in any other way active.

AC: But peace has to happen.

DTTN: Yes, it must happen.

AC: And I ask the question as if I'm at the peace process. Here you are, with all the leaders, and you've asked them to set their pride aside, to set your own pride aside, and to set aside all misgivings. U Thein Sein set an example; let's openly discuss the issues, let's get with the peace process. Is there anything more that you would encourage the leaders to do in the spirit of your father, in the spirit of his dear friend, Aung San, to be more revolutionary in their approach to peace? What radical peaceful compassionate actions are required at this point, at this critical point in your country's transition towards democracy, to usher in trust, peace, and national reconciliation? It's been seventy years of multiple civil wars, and there must be a way to stop it.

DTTN: It's very difficult to say, because every month the stakeholders sit for closed meetings, and nothing happens.

AC: Stakeholders are...?

DTTN: From the military and ethnic groups, and from the political parties—they did not invite all the political parties, and this stakeholder meeting is not organized by the government. It's not private, but the organizer is involved with the government peace process, and he called this meeting with the funding of a few European countries, with their advice and their guidance. Stakeholder meetings are called every month, and you can say whatever you like. You can open your heart, but you can't tell anyone outside the process about what is said in the meetings.

AC: Now, I ask you in another way, a final time and with full respect; Daw Aung San Suu Kyi is the most prominent individual in Myanmar. She's seen as the mother of the future peace and prosperity for many millions of your people. You've also known each other since childhood. Your families are deeply intertwined—her father and your father were close friends. Your father, president of the Rangoon University Student Union; Aung San: Secretary. It's as close as close can be. You are family—the family of democracy, the family of freedom; Daw Suu is your sister. The people of your country are also your brothers and sisters.

If your father was here today and her father too, and your mother, and her mother, she and you (six people), and they're all looking at you and asking you, in a safe and appropriate environment, to please speak your mind; "Tell me the truth from the depth of your *Dhamma* being on what I need to see that you see that I don't see, to move this country forward"—Daw Suu's asking you that question—"I want to know the truth of what you think and feel"—what would you say to her?

DTTN: The same thing. To abandon her pride. This is the most appropriate thing. But like I told you yesterday, when I met with the ethnic groups, I told them, "No, you can't break with Aung San Suu Kyi, because we have to work together." But they said, "No, we don't like her attitude."

I told them that if they work together, she will change to the betterment of the country.

So then one person asked me, "Oh, you know about that fairy tale story, about the mice who are afraid of the cat, and so they discussed among themselves that one mouse should attach a bell to the cat, so that when the cat comes they could hear and they could run away instead of being eaten." I said, "So what?" And he said, "You are that person. You should go to her and put the bell on her neck."

AC: And will you do that?

DTTN: No.

AC: Why?

DTTN: It shouldn't be just one person's job. In any case, I have zero expectation that she would listen to me. It really has to be a united effort with many voices saying the same things.

AC: It's your country. You both love your country. You both have pride. We all have pride. You both love freedom and love democracy. You both love the future generations that will be born into a democracy and not a dictatorship, if you do. As your husband said to you about you taking the All-India Radio job first, because he deferred to your father, so too is the nation asking the same of you.

DTTN: I know, I know.

AC: It's bigger than you, it's bigger than Daw Suu. You know that. She knows that. This is the peace process.

Thank you for being so open and honest. Even if you're not friendly, you're both children of the Buddha, you're both sisters in *Dhamma*. We're all family in freedom. We breathe the same *Dhamma* air. She will read this book. This will be translated into your language—into multiple languages.

I'll ask you in another way: because she's not friendly to you, let it be; be bigger than her, be more friendly and courageous and compassionate with her and speak your mind. What would you say to her about setting her pride aside, and what next for reconciliation?

DTTN: So many people ask me the question, "Why don't you join Aung San Suu Kyi's party?" This is the question everyone asks. They ask me why I have my own party. I tell them this is not my own party. I'm just a member. It's not my party. As a political party, it's a team. I can't say it belongs to me, but I belong to it. But they said I should join Aung San Suu Kyi's NLD party. I said, "Listen, if you want to clap, you can't clap with only one hand."

I'll share a personal story with you. When Aung San Suu Kyi was released after the 2010 elections, we went to her office, the NLD office here in Yangon, to greet her and congratulate her—"we" meaning our chairman, myself and two other ladies, the under-secretary generals. And another male Central Executive Committee member. Altogether eight people went to her office. Her office people asked us to be there at 10:15 am. All of us were there before 10am, to be on time. She came at 10:30. We waited; she came in and we all stood up. Our chairman is very experienced person, and now he is 87, but still very active, a very seasoned politician, who worked closely with my father, and also worked with the then-deputy prime minister very closely. He knows the politics of Burma inside out. A very knowledgeable person, and Aung San Suu Kyi knew him as well. We all knew her, and she knew us very well, especially the two general secretary ladies and the chairman, because our chairman also worked with my father, and then formed his own party at that time, and was quite popular.

So, we sat there, and when she came in, we all rose up and greeted her. She told us to sit down and was not friendly. She didn't say, "Sorry for being late," nothing, just, "Sit down." And you know what she asked us to do? "Each and every one of you, please stand up and introduce yourself to me." I was shocked, because as I told you, I also knew her from a very young age. And she knew us all. But she said, "Stand up"—not even "please"—"Introduce yourself." So, the two ladies quickly stood up and were very happy, because the two ladies, whenever they met Aung San Suu Kyi at some function, they hug and then they kiss her. I never do things like that, because it's not my way—not only with Daw Aung San Suu Kyi but with everyone. I give full respect, but I don't hug in front of others to show I am very close to her. That's not my style. But they were happy, so they stood up and said, "I am so and so."

But at the very least, my chairman should not have had to stand up like a child like that, because she knew him very, very well and he is an elderly person. But even my chairman stood up, and she should have said, "No, no, not you, please sit down." Something like that. But he stood up and he said his name is U Thu Wei, "I am chairman of the Democratic Party Myanmar." I felt very hurt, you know?

Then came my turn. I didn't know what to do, but quickly thought I must follow suit, because everyone was doing it, so I stood up. I could see reflected in that inner mirror that I was not in a good mood. I stood up and said, "My name is Than Than Nu, I'm the secretary general of the Democratic Party Myanmar," and I sat down. For some other things I don't have this feeling, or the feeling comes and goes very quickly. I practice that way. I don't keep everything in my mind; very quickly I take it out. But this time, even now in telling you the story I feel very hurt.

Then we all talked, especially my chairman, and he said that we should all work together. She said, "Ok, on what kind of program would you like to work?" and my chairman said, "Anything. You can make suggestions also, and we can work together in any field."

So, she said, "We are strong in Tanintharyi, so why should we work there together?" My chairman said, "Ok, so in what way can we work together?" and she said, "First we should start working together with development work, because if we start with politics the government won't like it."

So, we said, "In development work, like going to the poor schools, we should give some donations for the children, something like that," in a very soft way, not in a strong manner.

She said, "Ok," and then she said, "So then I will write the blueprint for this plan." It meant that she didn't want to have discussion between the two groups. She wanted to become a boss. "I will draw up a blueprint."

So, my chairman said, "Ok, you can do whatever you like, but we will work together." And you know what? Up to now, nothing has come of it.

This is what the ethnic people are pointing out. Today she says something, and the next day it is gone into the air. We are waiting, because she said she was going to draw the blueprint. If she asked my chairman to draw the blueprint, he would have done it quickly.

AC: You know, I've met Daw Suu on a number of occasions; when we first met in 1995, soon after her first release from house arrest, she agreed to do a book of conversations together, that she titled, *The Voice of Hope*. We spent six months together—two or three times a week at her house, talking, taping, and transcribing the conversations. One of the very first questions I asked her: "Daw Suu, you call your country's nonviolent struggle for freedom "a revolution of the spirit," and my question is what is the essence of its meaning?"

She replied, "Courage." She went on to explain, "the courage to see the truth of a situation, the courage to feel the truth of what you see, and the courage to act on the truth of what it is you see and feel." And, ultimately, she concluded, "The courage to care for things larger than your own self-interest. If enough of our people do this, our revolution will be successful." In other words, putting the needs of others in front of one's own, making others feel like family.

I say this in support of what you're saying, because in my own life I've seen myself at times be driven by pride, by arrogance, by attachment to ego, and I've seen myself be hurt by it, and I've seen myself hurt other people by my own pride and arrogance. I say the obvious: it's easy to become corrupted by our own ignorance.

And as *Dhamma* brothers and sisters of freedom and democracy we need to bear in mind *hiri* and *ottapa* (moral shame and fear of doing wrong, the twin guardians of the peace). As Sayadaw U Pandita—my teacher after Mahasi Sayadaw passed away, Daw Suu's own *Dhamma* teacher—said, which was very new for me to understand at the time, we must understand the importance of *hiri* and *ottapa*. "You have to feel strengthened by admitting your faults, by fearing the consequences of wrong speech," etc. And we each need to use, as you referred to, the inner mirror towards ourselves and the mirroring for each other. We must have the mindful intelligence to own and honor our own shortcomings and turn them into strengths.

And so, I would like to leave our conversation in the spirit of this *Dhamma* mirroring of *hiri* and *ottappa* that I know Daw Aung San Suu Kyi is very well aware of because of her decades of involvement with *Dhamma* and with Sayadaw U Pandita.

And if Sayadaw U Pandita, who's in this book, if he were here in this room tonight and Daw Suu was here, and former general Than Shwe, and your father U Nu, and Aung San, your mother, and as if everyone in the country was watching us on television and he was asked the question, "What would you recommend, sir, for the healing of Burma, for the achievement of national reconciliation?" I can imagine him saying for each of us to give mindfulness to *hiri* and *ottappa*. To see that it's a strength to admit our weaknesses and faults, and to forgive one another, and where you've made wrong behaviour, wrong speech, openly admit this to the other. Come together and pray that national reconciliation is achieved by us all breathing the oxygen of this *Dhamma* that's bigger than Buddhism, that includes Islam, Christianity, the ethnicities, all of them. And I think that's the message that we need to hear, not just here but around the world today—set aside our differences, make apologies where we've made mistakes, and become more humble and work hand in hand together towards a peaceful future.

So, thank you from my heart for allowing me to speak with you, to hear about your family, your father, your life, your brothers, your country, your mother, and a chance for me to share my own views as well.

I thank you, I thank Burma, I thank U Ne Win for granting me my very first visa to be in this incredible country.

I thank U Nu for the vision of creating a mindfulness meditation center that has now gone viral *(laughs)*. What a gift to live in the Mahasi Centre and what a gift to experience the Venerable Sayadaw's *Dhamma* teachings.

I also thank U Thein Sein for unbanning me from Burma.

And I also thank U Than Shwe and General Min Aung Hlaing and everyone in government and the military for trusting that the motivation for these four volumes of conversations is one of *kusala*, wholesome actions, meant to bring people together, heal the wounds and move into peace *and* reconciliation.

If I have said anything out of line please forgive me, it was not my intention to harm or hurt the good institutions of this country.

And I pray that your message, Daw Than Than Nu, which is so very beautiful, such a humble message, is heard by the principle stakeholders, and that that message is taken deep into the heart and realised.

So, from my heart to yours, thank you for your *Dhamma*, your words, your wisdom, and may national reconciliation be achieved.

DTTN: Thank you for caring for our country and our people. I hope my words will add value to the peace and tranquillity of my country.

AC: Sadhu, sadhu, sadhu.

PHOTOGRAPHIC
SECTION

1996, Rangoon. Aung San Suu Kyi, flanked by (NLD Chairman) U Tin Oo (left) and (former Vice-Chairman) U Kyi Maung (right) speaking to the public gathering on the nature of freedom and universal human rights.

Credit: Burma Project USA Archives

1996, Rangoon. The National League for Democracy's (NLD) Executive Committee Members.

Credit: Burma Project USA Archives

Aung San Suu Kyi giving a talk in front of her home in Rangoon in 1995 with "students for a democratic Burma" lined in front of her.

Credit: Burma Project USA Archives

1940s. General Aung San – Aung San Suu Kyi's father – speaking to the people of his country. Many years later his daughter Aung San Suu Kyi, continues his work for democracy and a unified nation stating: "After all it was my father who founded the Burmese army and I do have a sense of warmth towards the Burmese army."

1988, Rangoon. U Tin Oo, Aung San Suu Kyi and Burma's first Prime Minister U Nu.
Credit: Burma Project USA Archives

1989, Rangoon. Aung San Suu Kyi tirelessly encouraged the people of her country to stand in solidarity and to never let their fears prevent them from doing what they know is right.
Credit: Burma Project USA Archives

Aung San and Daw Khin Kyi (Aung San Suu Kyi's parents) on their wedding day, 1942.
Credit: Burma Project USA Archives.

Aung San Suu Kyi addressing members of her NLD party at their Yangon office on Martyrs' Day July 19, 2011. Martyrs' Day is a national holiday to commemorate Gen. Aung San (Aung San Suu Kyi's father) and seven other leaders of the pre-independence interim government, and one bodyguard —Thakin Mya, Ba Cho, Abdul Razak, Ba Win, Mahn Ba Khaing, Sao San Tun, Ohn Maung and Ko Htwe—all of whom were assassinated July 19, 1947.
Credit: Burma Project USA Archives Courtesy National League for Democracy

1995. Aung San Suu Kyi, at her home in Rangoon, where she spent 15 years in detention due to nonviolently calling for an end to military dictatorship and the rise of democracy.

Credit: Burma Project USA Archives

Burma is an ancient land of 55 million people, with over 130 ethnicities and languages.

Credit: Burma Project USA Archives
Courtesy of Henri Cartier-Bresson

Aung San Suu Kyi offers food to a procession of young Burmese Buddhist nuns on traditional alms rounds in Yangon.

Credit: Burma Project USA Archives Courtesy National League for Democracy

Co-founders of the NLD, former General U Tin Oo and Aung San Suu Kyi, in Yangon.

Credit: Burma Project USA Archives Courtesy National League for Democracy

Aung San Suu Kyi offers dana – a morning meal – to her meditation teacher and Dhamma (spiritual) advisor the late Venerable Sayadaw U Pandita at her home in Yangon.

Credit: Burma Project USA Archives Courtesy National League for Democracy

Aung San Suu Kyi and Alan Clements in conversation over a six month period at her Rangoon home in 1995 and 1996, for the book they co-authored titled, *The Voice of Hope*.

Credit: Burma Project USA Archives

January 4, 1996. Union Day Celebration at Aung San Suu Kyi's Rangoon home, attended by hundred's of courageous democracy activists who defied the military dictatorship and risked imprisonment in order to honor freedom and nationwide democracy and respect for universal human rights.

Credit: Burma Project USA Archives

As the basis of democracy Aung San Suu Kyi reminds the people of her country: "My priority is for people to understand that they have the power to change things themselves."

*Credit: Burma Project USA Archives
Courtesy National League for
Democracy*

The NLD flag of the dancing peacock – the party symbol adopted from the Myanmar Student Union flag – displayed in the stairway of Aung San Suu Kyi's home in Rangoon during her years of detention.

Credit: Burma Project USA Archives

The National League for Democracy's Executive Committee Members on Union Day January 4, 1996 when members of all ethnic groups throughout the country celebrated unity and freedom at Aung San Suu Kyi's Rangoon home.

Credit: Burma Project USA Archives

Alan Clements at the front gate of Aung San Suu Kyi's Yangon home at 54 University Avenue.
Credit: Burma Project USA Archives

From behind Aung San Suu Kyi's residence overlooking Inya Lake and one of the many luxury hotels that were under construction at that time (in 1995), and remained vacant or closed for years due to the international boycott of travel to Burma in support of Aung San Suu Kyi and the peoples' desire for freedom and democracy.
Credit: Burma Project USA Archives

August 8, 1988, Rangoon. A non-violent uprising takes place nationwide, led by university students, seeking the end of totalitarian rule and the emergence of a multi-party democracy.

Credit: Burma Project USA Archives Courtesy of Steve Lehman

August 8, 1988. Prodemocracy demonstrations in front of the US Embassy in Rangoon, seeking support for the nonviolent struggle that quickly gathered momentum and spread nationwide.

Credit: Burma Project USA Archives Courtesy of Steve Lehman

Pro-democracy student demonstrators August 1988.
Credit: Burma Project USA Archives Courtesy of Steve Lehman

"Human beings the world over need freedom and security that they may be able to realize their full potential." Aung San Suu Kyi

Credit: Burma Project USA Archives Courtesy of Steve Lehman

Student demonstrators carry a poster of Aung San, Burma's national hero, and Aung San Suu Kyi's father.

Credit: Burma Project USA Archives Courtesy Alain Evrard

Freedom-loving students exhausted from growing up under the debilitating plague of military totalitarianism were at the forefront of the mass pro-democracy protests in August 1988.

Credit: Burma Project USA Archives Courtesy of Tom Lubin

PHOTOGRAPHIC SECTION

A student kissing the boot of a soldier blinded by his loyalty to the dictatorship during the prodemocracy demonstrations in Rangoon, August 1988.
*Credit: Burma Project USA Archives
Courtesy Ryo Takeda*

Soldiers loyal to the dictatorship poised to kill during the 8.8.88 uprising for democracy. Aung San Suu Kyi later states, "It is often in the name of cultural integrity as well as social stability and national security that democratic reforms based on human rights are [violently] resisted by authoritarian governments.

Credit: Burma Project USA Archives

Ne Win – Burma's maniacal dictator operating from behind the scenes – ordered his army to attack, and they did—ruthlessly shooting and bayoneting thousands of unarmed demonstrators over a two month period (August and September 1988).

Credit: Burma Project USA Archives Courtesy Alain Evrard

Aung San Suu Kyi speaking with the people shortly before her arrest and first six years of detention in 1989: "A revolution simply means great change, significant change, great change for the better, brought about through non-violent means.'

Credit: Burma Project USA Archives

PHOTOGRAPHIC SECTION

Students on hunger strike demanding freedom, democracy and an end to one party rule, city center, Rangoon. 1988

Credit: Burma Project USA Archives Courtesy of Zunetta Liddell

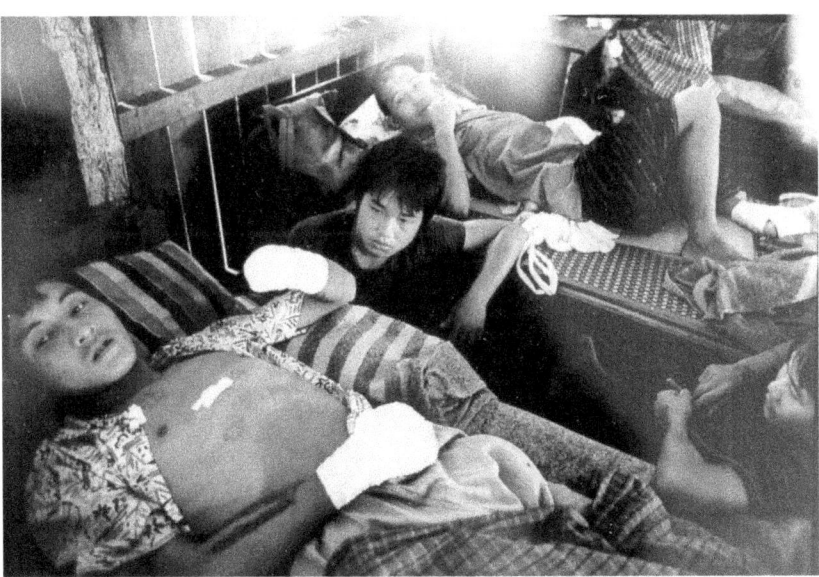

By mid-2008, nearly one million refugees had fled Burma into neighboring countries and makeshift camps along the Burmese border. During their journeys, refugees were often maimed by land mines, suffered and died from malaria and other diseases, and were enslaved by army soldier's loyal to the dictator.

Credit: Burma Project USA Archives

Aung San Suu Kyi was awarded the Nobel Peace Prize in 1991, while under house arrest, for her non-violent struggle for democracy and human rights. Her sons Alexander and Kim Aris and her husband Michael received the award on her behalf in Oslo.

Credit: Burma Project USA Archives Courtesy National League for Democracy

Aung San Suu Kyi, flanked by (NLD Chairman) U Tin Oo (left) and (former Vice-Chairman) U Kyi Maung (right) and Alan Clements (far left) on Union Day January 4, 1996 at Aung San Suu Kyi's home in Rangoon.

Credit: Burma Project USA Archives

1996, Rangoon. Alan Clements with Aung San Suu Kyi and U Tin Oo at her home during the making of their book of conversations, "The Voice of Hope." Every meeting was framed as "our first and potentially last," as she and colleagues were subject to rearrest at any moment. Aung San Suu Kyi states, "The only real prison is fear and the only real freedom is freedom from fear."

Credit: Burma Project USA Archives

The army ruthlessly attacked — killing thousands of unarmed demonstrators during August 1988.

Credit: Burma Project USA Archives Courtesy Alain Evrard

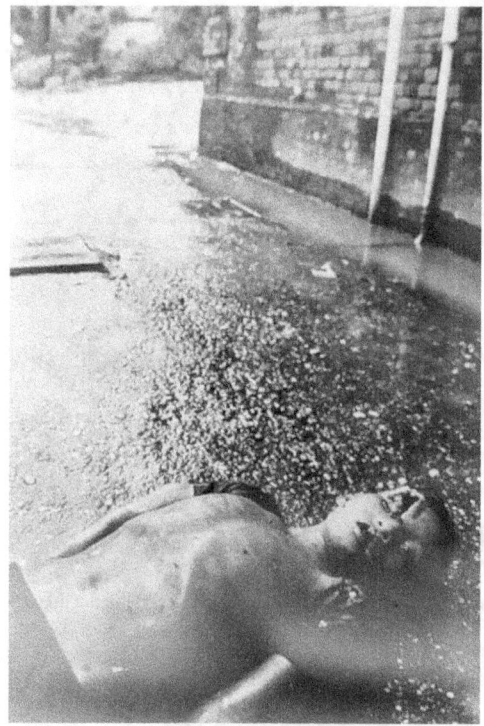

A victim of the street massacres in Rangoon August 1988. Thousands more were killed in the demonstrations, offering tragic wisdom to Aung San Suu Kyi's statement: "War is not the only arena where peace is done to death."

Credit: Burma Project USA Archives

Medics risked their own lives to rescue comrades dead and wounded in Rangoon during the '8.8.88' uprising.

Credit: Burma Project USA Archives

Aung San Suu Kyi spent 15 years under house arrest due to nonviolently calling for an end to dictatorship and the establishment of an open democratic society.

Credit: Burma Project USA Archives

Fleeing persecution by soldiers loyal to the dictatorship, Burmese students carry a wounded comrade across the Moei River into Thailand. 1988

Credit: Burma Project USA Archives Courtesy Bettman Library

Aung San Suu Kyi writes, "My attitude to peace is based on the Burmese definition of peace – meaning, removing all the negative factors that destroy peace in this world. So peace does not mean just putting an end to violence or to war, but to all other factors that threaten peace, such as discrimination, inequality, and poverty."

Credit: Burma Project USA Archives

Aung San Suu Kyi and her (late) husband, Dr. Michael Aris, in front of their Rangoon home, 1996

Credit: Burma Project USA Archives

One of the many scrolls Aung San Suu Kyi wrote and posted on the walls of her downstairs foyer during her first six year period of house arrest. The passage is a quotation from the writings of Jawaharlal Nehru, India's first Prime Minister.

Credit: Burma Project USA Archives

Any achievement that is based on widespread fear can hardly be a desirable one, and an 'order' that has for its basis the coercive apparatus of the State, and cannot exist without it, is more like a military occupation than civil rule... it was the duty of the...State to preserve...<u>dharma</u> and <u>abhaya</u> — righteousness and absence of fear. Law was something more than mere law, and order was the fear-

On 27 January 1947, General Aung San (Aung San Suu Kyi's father) and the British Prime Minister Clement Attlee signed an agreement in London guaranteeing Burma's independence within a year; Aung San had been responsible for its negotiation. At a press conference during a stopover in Delhi, he stated that the Burmese wanted "complete independence" and not dominion status, and that they had "no inhibitions of any kind" about "contemplating a violent or non-violent struggle or both" in order to achieve it. He concluded that he hoped for the best, but was prepared for the worst.

Credit: Burma Project USA Archives

Aung San Suu Kyi paying homage to her father's memorial in Yangon. On July 19, 1947, a gang of armed paramilitaries of former Prime Minister U Saw broke into the Secretariat Building in downtown Rangoon during a meeting of the Executive Council and assassinated Aung San and six of his cabinet ministers, including his elder brother Ba Win, along with a cabinet secretary and a bodyguard.

Credit: Burma Project USA Archives Courtesy National League for Democracy

For his independence struggle from the British and uniting the country as a single entity, General Aung San is revered as the architect of modern Burma and a national hero.

Credit: Burma Project USA Archives

Ne Win was a Burmese politician and military commander who served as Prime Minister of Burma from 1958 to 1960 and 1962 to 1974. Ne Win was also Burma's military dictator during the Socialist Burma period of 1962 to 1988. His maniacal rule was characterized by political violence, isolationism, cronyism, xenophobia, totalitarianism, economic collapse, and is credited with turning Burma into one of the poorest and least developed countries in the world. Ne Win resigned in July 1988 in response to the 8888 Uprising that overthrew his party and was replaced by the military junta of the State Law and Order Restoration Council (SLORC) and with it a succession of military dictators.

Credit: Burma Project USA Archives

Aung San Suu Kyi's father General Aung San – regarded as Myanmar's independence hero – was a personal friend of Jawaharlal Nehru (November 14, 1889 – May 27, 1964 – an Indian independence activist, and subsequently, the first Prime Minister of India). Aung San Suu Kyi has said that many of the challenges faced by Gandhi and Nehru along the path to India's independence were the ones her movement had been facing over the course of its struggle.

Credit: Burma Project USA Archives

Daw Khin Kyi, wife of General Aung San, who was assassinated when their daughter Aung San Suu Kyi was two years old, served as her political and cultural mentor. She was appointed Burmese ambassador to India and Nepal in 1960, and Aung San Suu Kyi followed her there. She studied in the Convent of Jesus and Mary School in New Delhi, and graduated from Lady Shri Ram College, a constituent college of the University of Delhi, with a degree in politics in 1964.

Credit: Burma Project USA Archives

A family photo in the 1940s of General Aung San and his wife Daw Khin Kyi – Aung San Suu Kyi's father and mother, along with her brothers, in Rangoon.

Credit: Burma Project USA Archives

PHOTOGRAPHIC SECTION

With her sons, Alexander (left) and Kim, May 1993—a rare photo of Aung San Suu Kyi while under house arrest.

Credit: Burma Project USA Archives

Aung San Suu Kyi, flanked by (NLD Chairman) U Tin Oo seated (left) and (former Vice-Chairman) U Kyi Maung (seated right). 1996

Credit: Burma Project USA Archive

On 19 September 1964 U Tin Oo became Commander of Central Regional Military Command. He was then promoted to the rank of Brigadier General and became Deputy Chief of Staff of the Tatmadaw (military) on April 20, 1972. On March 8, 1974 he was promoted to the rank of General and became Commander in Chief of the Tatmadaw. After his forced retirement in 1976, he was accused of high treason against the armed forces, the party (BSPP) and the state. He was subsequently arrested and tried for the alleged withholding of information concerning a failed coup-d'état against General Ne Win. On January 11, 1977, he was sentenced to his first 7 of 19 years imprisonment (and house arrest). He is co-founder of the NLD.

Credit: Burma Project USA Archive

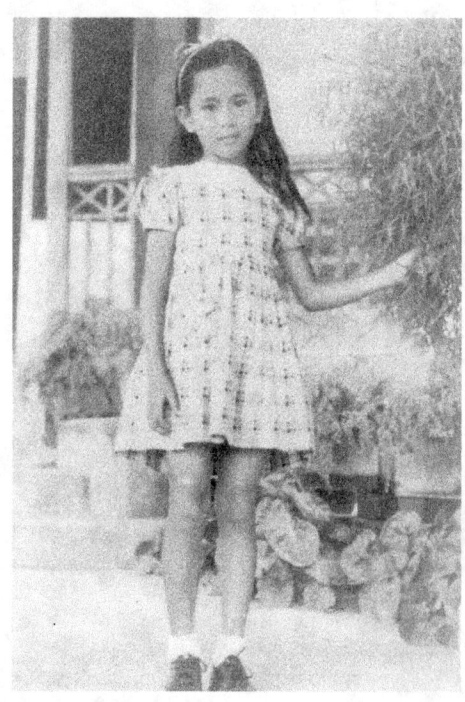

Aung San Suu Kyi, at about seven years of age.

Credit: Burma Project USA Archives

Burma's Tatmadaw on parade – a 400,000 strong army started by Aung San Suu Kyi's father, Aung San. "The democracy process provides for political and social change without violence," she states.

Credit: Burma Project USA Archives

Aung San Suu Kyi with the international media during a photo session at her residence a few days after her release from house arrest in July 1995.

Credit: Burma Project USA Archives Courtesy Yamamoto Munesuke

(former) Dictator (now retired) General Than Shwe and other generals. Aung San Suu Kyi states, "My opinion is the greatest reward that any government could get is the approval of the people. If the people are happy and the people are at peace and the government has done something for them, that's the greatest reward I think any government could hope for.

Credit: Burma Project USA

Chained "forced laborers" in Burma, estimated to be in the hundreds of thousands, used by the military regime to build bridges, roads, dams, and tourist attractions.

Credit: Burma Project USA Archives
Courtesy Peter Conrad

Former General and Dictator Than Shwe and his wife Daw Khaing Khaing paying their respects to a Buddhist shrine somewhere near their mansion in the capital, where they are protected by a round-the-clock contingent of armed guards.

Credit: Burma Project USA

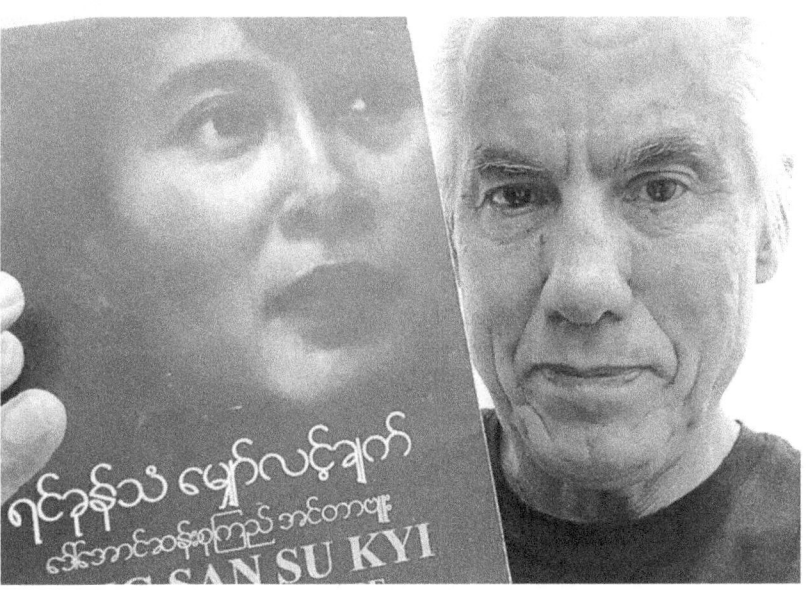

2012 Yangon. Alan Clements, co-author with Aung San Suu Kyi of the book, *The Voice of Hope*, with a Burmese copy of the book in a Yangon bookstore, that for the previous 15 years was an imprisonable crime to have in one's possession.

Credit: Burma Project USA

Aung San Suu Kyi outside her front gate on the day of her release from house arrest, July 10, 1995.

Credit: Burma Project USA Archives Courtesy Stuart Isett

Aung San Suu Kyi with U Kyi Maung at her Rangoon residence, 1995.

Credit: Burma Project USA Archives

PHOTOGRAPHIC SECTION

Aung San Suu Kyi in discussion with U Win Htein, one of her longest most respected friends and confidants during her decades in Burma, and one of the principle leaders of Burma's non-violent struggle for democracy.

Credit: Burma Project USA Archives

In 1995 and 1996, crowds defied the dictatorship's threat of imprisonment and gathered at Aung San Suu Kyi's gate on weekends to listen to her talks on democracy – to rise up in solidarity for the ongoing struggle for freedom.

Credit: Burma Project USA Archives

The pubic pro-democracy gatherings were stopped by Burma's military dictatorship in late 1996 and Aung San Suu Kyi was placed back under house arrest, and almost all of her NLD colleagues were re-imprisoned.

Credit: Burma Project USA Archives

1989 Rangoon. Aung San Suu Kyi with U Par Lay – Burma's preeminent spoken word satirist and comedian after his performance on Independence Day at Aung San Suu Kyi's compound. He was rearrested days later and sentenced to 7 years in prison with hard labor (in addition to the six years he had already spent in prison, also with hard labor, chained, pounding rocks 20 hours a day).

Credit: Burma Project USA Archives
Courtesy National League for Democracy

A police guard placed outside Aung San Suu Kyi's home at 54 University Avenue, Yangon, Myanmar.

Credit: Burma Project USA Archives

Rangoon University student leader at the time of the 8.8.88 Uprising Min Ko Naing, at a press conference for "88 Generation" in Yangon, April 2012. Having spent 19 years in prison, he is one of Burma's great revolutionary democracy dissidents and is the recipient of numerous human rights awards. The New York Times has described him as Burma's "most influential opposition figure after Daw Aung San Suu Kyi."

Credit: Burma Project USA Archives Courtesy of Kirsten Duell

Alan Clements interviewing Mon Mon Myat, a leading Burmese author, intellectual and dissident. She is cofounder of the prestigious International Human Rights and Human Dignity Film Festival.

Credit: Burma Project USA Archives

Alan Clements in conversation with U Win Htein discussing his 20 years as a prisoner of conscience, and on becoming an honorable member of parliament and a tireless voice for unity and national reconciliation.

Credit: Burma Project USA Archives

On September 23, 2008, U Win Tin (March 12, 1929 – April 21, 2014) is released after 19 years in prison in solitary confinement. As a prominent journalist and politician he co-founded the National League for Democracy (NLD). After his release from prison he refused to remove his blue prison-issued shirt as an act of conscience to remain in solidarity with the remaining political prisoners in Burma until they too were freed.

Credit: Burma Project USA Archive Courtesy National League for Democracy

November 13, 2010. Aung San Suu Kyi appears at her front gate after being released from house arrest by Burma's military dictator Than Shwe. She vowed to carry on the nonviolent struggle for democracy.

Credit: Burma Project USA Archives Courtesy National League for Democracy

U Thant was a Burmese diplomat and the third Secretary-General of the United Nations from 1961 to 1971. "As a devout Buddhist he said, "I was trained to be tolerant of everything except intolerance." He was the recipient of the Jawaharlal Nehru Award for International Understanding.

Credit: Burma Project USA Archives Courtesy U Thant org

Thakin Nu, a leading Burmese statesman and political figure who was the first Prime Minister of Burma under the provisions of the 1947 Constitution of the Union of Burma, from January 4, 1948 to June 12, 1956, again from February 28, 1957 to October 28, 1958, and finally from April 4, 1960 to March 2, 1962.

Daw Than Than Nu, daughter of Thakin Nu, She is the founder and director of the philanthropic organization – U Nu Daw Mya Ni Foundation (her beloved parents).

Credit: Burma Project USA Archives

NLD co-founder and Chairman U Tin Oo, honoring his beloved revolutionary colleague and friend, U Win Tin, also co-founder of the National League for Democracy, on the anniversary of his passing away April 21, 2014

Credit: Burma Project USA Archives Courtesy National League for Democracy

The second major crackdown came in September and October 2007, when Burma's army, under the dictator, General Than Shwe, brutally and mercilessly crushed the Buddhist monk-led pro-democracy Saffron Revolution.

Credit: Burma Project USA Archives

One of the regime's numerous "relocation camps," forced on people living in areas of strong support for Aung San Suu Kyi and the democracy movement. A New York Times article titled, "Burma: Horror Story of Mass Re locations," from March 20, 1990, stated "at least 500,000 Burmese are being forced to move from [most major] cities to new, ill-prepared outlying towns where malaria and hepatitis are rampant."

Credit: Burma Project USA Archives

Aung San Suu Kyi showing her respect (in a traditional Burmese Buddhist manner) to monks she invited to her home in 1996 to offer them a pre-noon meal.

Credit: Burma Project USA Archives

Dictator General Than Shwe on parade. Aung San Kyi and the government have consistently sought national reconciliation. In her words, "a regime is made up of people, so I do put faces to regimes and governments, [and in so doing] I feel that all human beings have the right to be given the benefit of the doubt, and they also have to be given the right to try to redeem themselves if they so wish.

Credit: Burma Project USA Archives

1995. Alan Clements with U Aung Ko, the male lead actor in John Boorman's celebrated feature film, Beyond Rangoon, depicting Burma's nonviolent struggle for freedom, based in part, on Alan's ground breaking book,"Burma: The Next Killing Fields?," with a foreword by the Dalai Lama. Alan was the script revisionist and principle advisor on the film.

Credit: Burma Project USA Archives

Chairman of the National League for Democracy (NLD), U Tin Oo, who has spent a total of eleven years in solitary confinement and five years under house arrest, with Alan Clements.

Credit: Burma Project USA Archives

Aung San Suu Kyi: "We want to empower our people; we want to strengthen them; we want to provide them with the kind of qualifications that will enable them to build up their own country themselves."

Credit: Burma Project USA Archives Courtesy National League for Democracy

Aung San Suu Kyi on the 25th anniversary of the nationwide democracy uprising of August 8, 1988, honoring the courageous leaders (Min Ko Naing, Ko Ko Gyi and so many others) along with the hundreds of thousands additional dissidents, as well as the 1000's killed by the unconscionable military crackdown that tried to end it.

Credit: Burma Project USA Archives Courtesy National League for Democracy

November 18, 2012. US President Obama and Secretary of State Hillary Clinton met with Aung San Suu Kyi at her home in Yangon, after being under house arrest for the better part of two decades, offering their dedicated support for her peoples unfinished non-violent struggle for democracy and human rights.

Credit: Burma Project USA Archives Courtesy National League for Democracy

Spiritual leader of Tibet and fellow Nobel Peace laureate, the Dalai Lama greets Aung San Suu Kyi, as reported in the Tibet Post International November 16, 2015.

Credit: Burma Project USA Archives Courtesy Tibet Post International

PHOTOGRAPHIC SECTION

March 2020. The once banned and criminalized Headquarters of the National League for Democracy (NLD) at 97B West Shwegondine Road, Bahan Township, Yangon, Myanmar.

Credit: Burma Project USA Archives

February 2020, Yangon. A policeman looks at Alan Clements' book of conversations with Aung San Suu Kyi (*The Voice of Hope*) previously banned in Burma since 1996 and an imprisonable crime if caught with a copy.

Credit: Burma Project USA Archives

Aung San Suu Kyi meeting Senior General Min Aung Hlaing, who has frequently stated in her speeches "that if you want to bring an end to long-standing conflict, you have to be prepared to compromise." This is the heart, so to speak, of her government's long standing desire of achieving national reconciliation.

*Credit: Burma Project USA Archives
Courtesy National League for Democracy*

The famed Shwedagon Pagoda in Yangon, over 300 feet high and nearly 2500 years old, is the unifying symbol of harmlessness and peace among Burmese Buddhists both inside Burma and worldwide.

Credit: Burma Project USA Archives

Aung San Suu Kyi states: "The struggle for democracy and human rights in Burma is a struggle for life and dignity. It is a struggle that encompasses our political, social and economic aspirations."

Credit: Burma Project USA Archives

Aung San Suu Kyi paying her respects to Buddhist monks on the anniversary of the August 8, 1988 Uprising.

Credit: Burma Project USA Archives Courtesy National League for Democracy

Aung San Suu Kyi paying her respects to her slain father at The Martyrs' Mausoleum in Yangon, located near the northern gate of Shwedagon Pagoda. The mausoleum is dedicated to Aung San and other leaders of the pre-independence interim government, all of whom were assassinated on July 19, 1947 and now designated as Martyrs' Day, a highly revered public holiday in Myanmar.

Credit: Burma Project USA Archives Courtesy National League for Democracy

2012. Alan Clements with his long time dear friend, and NLD parliament member, U Win Htein, in his office in Meiktila, central Burma.

Credit: Burma Project USA Archives

Aung San Suu Kyi states: "I think I should be active politically. Because I look upon myself as a politician. That's not a dirty work you know. Some people think that there are something wrong with politicians. Of course, something is wrong with some politicians."

Credit: Burma Project USA Archives Courtesy National League for Democracy

Venerable Sayadaw U Pandita and his long time attendant and translator, U Khin Hlaing in March 2016 during one of nine nights of conversations with Alan Clements (his long time student and friend). This was the Venerable Sayadaw's final Dhamma teachings for a world audience before he passed away a few weeks later.

Credit: Burma Project USA Archives

September 2012, San Francisco, CA. Aung San Suu Kyi is honored with the Vaclav Havel Award for Creative Dissent, with Alan Clements, his daughter Sahra Bella Clements Earl, and her Mother, Lorinda Earl. This was the first time Alan and Aung San Suu Kyi had spoken in 17 years, after he was banned from Burma in 1996 and she was placed back under detention.

Credit: Burma Project USA Archives

Deep in Karen State in 1990 where Burma's army had a scorched earth take no prisoner alive policy.

Credit: Burma Project USA Archives

The many thousands of Burmese students who fled the country's major cities after the 1988 uprisings were brutally crushed by the military regime, gathered in jungle enclaves along the Thai border where they formed the All Burma Students Democratic Front (ABSDF). The flag is the symbol of Burma's struggle for freedom.

Credit: Burma Project USA Archives

Alan Clements travelling the Moei River on the Thai Burma border after two months in Mannerplaw and surrounding areas in 1990, that resulted in the seminal book, Burma: The Next Killing Fields?

Credit: Burma Project USA Archives

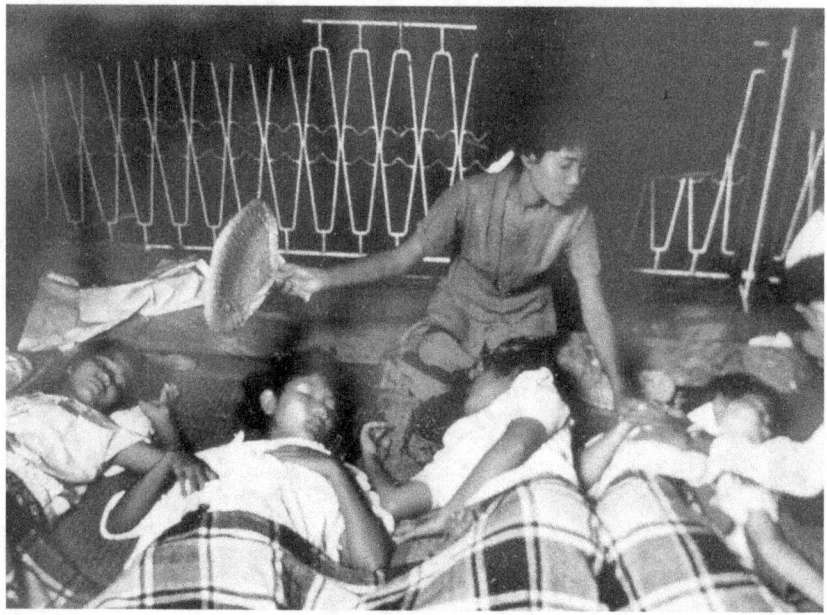

Burmese students suffering from typhoid and malaria in a refugee camp along the Thai border, 1990.

Credit: Burma Project USA Archives

Alan Clements with Tibet's spiritual leader, the Dalai Lama, who wrote a forward to his book, Burma: The Next Killing Fields? in 1990.

Credit: Burma Project USA Archives

Alan Clements – co-author of The Voice of Hope: Conversations with Aung San Suu Kyi – upon returning to Paris after meeting with Aung San Suu Kyi for six months in Burma, 1996.
Credit: Burma Project USA Archives

Mahāsī Sayādaw U Sobhana (July 29, 1904 – August 14, 1982) was a Burmese Theravada Buddhist monk and meditation master who is widely considered to be the father of the modern day mass lay mindfulness meditation movement that began at his Rangoon Mahasi Sasana Yeiktha Meditation Center (MSY) in 1947 under the invitation of Burma's first Prime Minister U Nu and Sir U Thwin. There are now 660 branch centers in Burma and over 100 more worldwide. Many leading politicians and government leaders over the decades have practiced meditation at MSY or with teachers trained at the center. Mahāsī Sayādaw was the chief questioner and final editor at the Sixth Great Buddhist Council in Yangon Burma in 1954.
Credit: Burma Project USA Archives

1979. Alan Clements, one of the first Westerners to ordain as a Buddhist monk under the guidance of the Venerable Mahasi Sayadaw at the Mahasi Sasana Yeiktha Meditation Center in Rangoon, Burma, where he lived and trained in vipassana (insight) meditation and Buddhist psychology for several years.

Credit: Burma Project USA Archives

Soon after the Venerable Mahasi Sayadaw passed away on August 14, 1982, Venerable Sayadaw U Pandita (on the right) became the Ovadacariya Nayaka (the Head Monk and main teacher) at the Mahasi Meditation Center Rangoon. Here he is seen paying his final respects to Mahasi Sayadaw, along with U Aggacitta (left) – Sayadaw U Pandita's student and main English translator at the time.

Credit: Burma Project USA Archives

At the Venerable Mahasi Sayadaw funeral procession in Rangoon, August 1982.

Credit: Burma Project USA Archives

After being expelled from Burma several times by the dictator Ne Win, Alan Clements disrobed as a Buddhist monk and left the monastic life in 1984 and remained under the guidance of Sayadaw U Pandita, who became his teacher after Mahasi Sayadaw passed away.

Credit: Burma Project USA Archives

Venerable Sayadaw U Pandita, Yangon. Aung San Suu Kyi writes, "My husband gave me a copy of Sayadaw U Pandita's book (while under house arrest), In this Very Life, the Liberation Teachings of the Buddha. "By studying this book carefully, I learned how to overcome difficulties of meditation and to realize its benefits...and how it increased mindfulness in every day life."

Credit: Burma Project USA Archives

December 2019. Denying that Myanmar had genocidal intent in its treatment of the Rohingya people, Aung San Suu Kyi urged the International Court of Justice in The Hague to let her country's justice system run its course. "Can there be genocidal intent on the part of a state that actively investigates, prosecutes and punishes soldiers and officers who are accused of wrongdoing?" she asked at the world court, while presenting her opening statement on the second day of public hearings related to Gambia's lawsuit alleging that Myanmar had breached the 1948 Convention on the Prevention and Punishment of the Crime of Genocide.

Credit: Burma Project USA Archives Courtesy National League for Democracy

PHOTOGRAPHIC SECTION

By late 2017, an estimated 650,000 Rohingya refugees from Rakhine, Myanmar, had crossed the border into Bangladesh, fleeing the persecution of Burma's army, in large part, provoked by ARSA – the Islamic terrorist group. According to Amnesty International May 22, 2018 "Myanmar: New evidence reveals Rohingya armed group massacred scores in Rakhine State" "[ARSA] A Rohingya armed group brandishing guns and swords is responsible for at least one, and potentially a second, massacre of up to 99 Hindu women, men, and children as well as additional unlawful killings and abductions of Hindu villagers in August 2017," Amnesty International revealed today after carrying out a detailed investigation inside Myanmar's Rakhine State. The plight of the Rohingya refugees is a humanitarian tragedy.

Credit: Burma Project USA Archives Courtesy National League for Democracy

In conjunction with the Buddha Sasana Nuggaha Organization (BSNO) of Myanmar, the Buddha Sasana Foundation of America, co-founded by Alan Clements and Dr Ingrid Jordt in 1984, and co-directed by Dr Jeannine Davies, organize an annual Wisdom of Mindfulness ten day meditation retreat at the Mahasi Sasana Yeiktha (MSY) meditation center for English speaking yogis worldwide to come to Myanmar to practice mindfulness at this renowned center and in context to the sacred country of Burma.

Credit: Burma Project USA Archives

Aung San Suu Kyi in Parliament in Naypyidaw – the capital of Myanmar – with long standing advisor U Win Htein (left) and Zeya Thaw (former hip hop singer in the band ACID and co-founder of the activist group Generation Wave) and NLD Parliament member and her assistant.

Credit: Burma Project USA Archives Courtesy National League for Democracy

March 2020. Burma's parliament rejects a constitutional amendment to reduce military political power. The NLD, headed by State Counsellor Aung San Suu Kyi, was unsuccessful in reducing the role of the military in Myanmar's parliament. The NLD proposed amendments to the 2008 (undemocratic) constitution, which requires more than 75% of members of parliament to pass constitutional amendments while giving the military 25 % of the seats under Article 436. This allows the military to veto any proposed constitutional amendments. Senior General Min Aung Hlaing of the military opposition claims that the military "has ... taken those seats as a measure to ensure national stability" while the country transitions into democracy.

Credit: Burma Project USA Archives Courtesy National League for Democracy

Senior General Min Aung Hlaing on Armed Forces Day. Aung San Suu Kyi has repeatedly called for dialogue and reconciliation. "I don't want to see the military failing. I want to see the military rising to dignified heights of professionalism and true patriotism."

Credit: Burma Project USA Archives

Aung San Suu Kyi with the late Venerable Sayadaw U Pandita at Panditarama – his monastery and meditation center in Bahan, Golden Valley, Yangon, shortly before his passing away in April 2016.

Credit: Burma Project USA Archives

Buddhist nuns paying homage to their Dhamma teacher the late Venerable Sayadaw U Pandita at Panditarama Meditation Center in Yangon. He was the meditation teacher to tens of thousands of yogis from numerous countries around the world, as well as spiritual advisor to Aung San Suu Kyi.

Credit: Burma Project USA Archives Courtesy of Panditarama Meditation Center Yangon Myanmar

NLD Chairman U Tin Oo, paying his final respects to his long time spiritual advisor and meditation teacher, Venerable Sayadaw U Pandita, days after the 95 year old Elder Buddhist monk passed away in Burma on April 16, 2016.

Credit: Burma Project USA Archives Courtesy of Panditarama Meditation Center Yangon Myanmar

March 2020, Yangon. Nayaka (senior most) Member of the NLD, Saya U Tin Oo, 93 years old, who, despite having had a stroke and unable to speak, understands fully everything that is said. He's one of the most respected revolutionary heroes in the history of modern Burma.

Credit: Burma Project USA Archives

AUTHOR PROFILES

About Alan Clements

Boston born Alan Clements, after dropping out of the University of Virginia in his second year, went to the East and become one of the first Westerners to ordain as a Buddhist monk in Myanmar (formerly known as Burma). He lived in Yangon (formerly Rangoon) at the Mahasi Sasana Yeiktha (MSY) Mindfulness Meditation Centre for nearly four years, training in both the practice and teaching of Satipatthana Vipassana (insight) meditation and Buddhist psychology (Abhidhamma), under the guidance of his preceptor the Venerable Mahasi Sayadaw, and his successor Sayadaw U Pandita.

In 1984, forced to leave the country by Burma's dictator Ne Win, with no reason given, Clements returned to the West and through invitation, lectured widely on the "wisdom of mindfulness," in addition to leading numerous mindfulness-based meditation retreats and trainings throughout the US, Australia, and Canada, including assisting a three month mindfulness teacher training with Sayadaw U Pandita, at the Insight Meditation Society (IMS), in Massachusetts.

In 1988, Alan integrated into his classical Buddhist training an awareness that included universal human rights, social injustices, environmental sanity, political activism, the study of propaganda and mind control in both democratic and totalitarian societies, and the preciousness of everyday freedom. His efforts working on behalf of oppressed peoples led a former director of Amnesty International to call Alan "one of the most important and compelling voices of our times."

As an investigative journalist Alan has lived in some of the most highly volatile areas of the world. In the jungles of Burma, in 1990, he was one of the first eye-witnesses to document the mass oppression of ethnic minorities by Burma's military, which resulted in his first book, "Burma: The Next Killing Fields?" (with a foreword by the Dalai Lama).

Shortly thereafter, Alan was invited to the former-Yugoslavia by a senior officer for the United Nations, where, based in Zagreb during the final year of the war, he wrote the film "Burning" while consulting with

NGO's and the United Nation's on the "vital role of consciousness in understanding human rights, freedom, and peace."

In 1995, a French publisher asked Alan to attempt reentering Burma for the purpose of meeting Aung San Suu Kyi, the leader of her country's pro-democracy movement and the recipient of the Nobel Peace Prize in 1991. Just released after six years of incarceration, Alan invited Aung San Suu Kyi to tell her courageous story to the world, thus illuminating the philosophical and spiritual underpinnings of Burma's nonviolent struggle for freedom, known as a "revolution of the spirit."

The transcripts of their five months of conversations were smuggled out of the country and became the book "The Voice of Hope." Translated into numerous languages, *The Voice of Hope* offers insight into the nature of totalitarianism, freedom and nonviolent revolution. Said the London Observer: "Clements is the perfect interlocutor....whatever the future of Burma, a possible future for politics itself is illuminated by these conversations."

Clements is also the co-author with (New York Times bestselling author) Leslie Kean and a contributing photographer to "Burma's Revolution of the Spirit" Aperture, NY) – a large format photographic tribute to Burma's nonviolent struggle for democracy, with a foreword by the Dalai Lama and essays by eight Nobel Peace laureates. In addition, Clements was the script revisionist and principal adviser for *Beyond Rangoon* (Castle Rock Entertainment), a feature film depicting Burma's struggle for freedom, directed by John Boorman.

In 1999, Alan founded World Dharma, a nonsectarian, trans-traditional organization of self-styled seekers, artists, rebels, writers, scholars, journalists, and activists dedicated to a trans-religious, independent approach to personal and planetary transformation through the integration of global human rights, meditation and the experiential study of consciousness, with one's life expression through the arts, media, activism, and service.

In 2002 Alan wrote "Instinct for Freedom – Finding Liberation Through Living" (New World Library & World Dharma Publications), a memoir about his years in Burma that chronicles his mindfulness meditation training and dharma-informed activism, while illuminating the framework of the World Dharma vision. In 2003 he co-founded with his colleague, Dr. Jeannine Davies, the World Dharma Online Institute (WDOI) that offers an evolving video master course based on his life's work.

Instinct for Freedom was nominated for the best spiritual teaching/memoir by the National Spiritual Booksellers Association in 2003 and has been translated into numerous languages.

Alan's two most recent books, "Wisdom the for the World –

The Requisites or Reconciliation: Alan Clements in Conversation with Venerable Sayadaw U Pandita of Burma," and "A Future to Believe In – 108 Reflections on the Art and Activism of Freedom," inspired by and dedicated to his daughter Sahra, has received distinguished praise from numerous leaders and activists, including Dr. Helen Caldicott, Joanna Macy, Dr. Vandana Shiva, Bill McKibben, Paul Hawkin, and Derrick Jensen (the environmental poet laureate) who wrote:

> "This culture is killing the planet. If we are to have any future at all, we must unlearn everything the culture has taught us and begin to listen to the planet, to listen to life – the core intelligence of nature and the human heart. This book not only helps us with the unlearning process – the greatest challenge humankind has ever faced – it provides the essential wisdom, the spiritual intelligence, to open ourselves to finally start to hear."

In addition, Alan has presented to such organizations as Mikhail Gorbachev's State of The World Forum, The Soros Foundation, United Nations Association of San Francisco, the universities of California, Toronto, Sydney, and many others, including a keynote address at the John Ford Theater for Amnesty International's 30th year anniversary. More recently, Alan was a presenter at the Tounché Global Consciousness Conference 2019 in Bali.

In conjunction with the Buddha Sasana Nuggaha Organization (BSNO) of Myanmar and the Center's Nayaka Sayadaws (Senior Meditation Teachers), Alan conducts with Dr Ingrid Jordt and Dr Jeannine Davies an annual Ten Day Wisdom of Mindfulness Retreat for English speaking participants at the Mahasi Sasana Yeiktha Yangon (MSY), Myanmar. For more information, please visit: AlanClements.com or WorldDharma.com

ALSO BY ALAN CLEMENTS

A Future to Believe In
108 Reflections on the Art and Activism of Freedom

"This book is the music of wisdom, a dance with the finest places of the human heart. It is also like a walk with your favorite friends, mentors and teachers as they point out the beauties of the journey. You will want to keep this timeless treasure within reach, so you can open it to any page, and let a paragraph or a line ignite you again to the truth of your own being."

—JOANNA MACY, AUTHOR OF *WORLD AS LOVER, WORLD AS SELF*

"Distilling the essence of world religions, cultures, politics, and spiritual traditions, Alan Clements' magnificent, timely book provides a courageous and intelligent compass personifying our aspirations for freedom and wisdom, and in so doing, offers insights on how to actively shape a future that gives life hope. With our planet in peril, it is imperative that we act now to provide a secure future for our children and future generations. Make this book your guide, mentor and friend."

—DR HELEN CALDICOTT, AUTHOR OF *NUCLEAR POWER IS NOT THE ANSWER* AND *IF YOU LOVE THIS PLANET*; FOUNDING PRESIDENT PHYSICIANS FOR SOCIAL RESPONSIBILITY

"In this radiant book is a new consciousness."

—LOWRY BURGESS, ARTIST, PROFESSOR, CREATOR OF THE FIRST OFFICIAL NON-SCIENTIFIC ART PAYLOAD TAKEN INTO OUTER SPACE BY NASA IN 1989

"*A Future to Believe In* is a treasure, not a mere book."

—PAUL HAWKEN, AUTHOR OF *BLESSED UNREST*

"This transformational treasure is more relevant now than ever before, and perhaps the most important book available to face the global crisis head on and transform our lives and the planet for the better. Please join the revolution, and share word of this masterpiece of 'mindful intelligence' and compassion with the world."

—MARCIA JACOBS - PSYCHOTHERAPIST SPECIALIZING IN WORK WITH VICTIMS OF WAR, RAPE AND TRAUMA. A SENIOR STAFF MEMBER OF THE UN AND OTHER HUMANITARIAN AGENCIES FROM 1993 - 2005, WORKING WITH REFUGEES AND OTHER WAR-TRAUMATIZED POPULATIONS

"At a time when the contemporary spiritual landscape has become dangerously gentrified and domesticated, Alan Clements restores us to our senses — wild and elemental. He summons the voices of those who, along side him, have not traded their souls for the market-driven need to be tame or acceptable, and points us to the wilderness of true, engaged, fiercely authentic awakening. This is why we are alive — to set freedom free, in ourselves and for others, in every aspect of our lives from the most mundane daily task, to the most profound political act."

—KELLY WENDORF, AUTHOR AND EDITOR *STORIES OF BELONGING*

"*A Future To Believe In* provides us with a standing wave of insight, a perpetually central pivot pertaining eminently to private and political spheres, inextricable, afterall. This book should be made mandatory world-wide for all heads of state."
—LISSA WOLSAK, AUTHOR OF *IN DEFENSE OF BEING, SQUEEZED LIGHT* AND *PEN CHANTS*

"We live in times that spread greed, violence, fear and hopelessness. We live in times when consumerism enslaves us while offering pseudo-freedom. Alan Clements labor of love, "A Future to Believe In: A Guide to Revolution, Environmental Sanity, and the Universal Right to Be Free," brings us reflections that inspire us to be free and fearless."
—DR. VANDANA SHIVA, AUTHOR OF, *EARTH DEMOCRACY; JUSTICE, SUSTAINABILITY, AND PEACE, SOIL, NOT OIL, AND STAYING ALIVE*

Instinct for Freedom: Finding Liberation Through

"During an era when a spate of shallow, narcissistic fiction has found a niche as 'sacred literature' Alan's work is a wonderful relief and reminder that the heart of spirituality still is, and will always be, compassion."
—BO LOZOFF, FOUNDER OF THE PRISON ASHRAM PROJECT AND HUMAN KINDNESS FOUNDATION AND AUTHOR OF *WE'RE ALL DOING TIME* AND *IT'S A MEANINGFUL LIFE*

"Rarely has a book touched me as deeply and personally as *Instinct for Freedom*. This profound work is a call to action, a spiritual force for change. May the beauty of Alan's writing and the power of his personal journey compel you to be true to your own heart so that we may all experience the gift of freedom in its purest form."
—CHERYL RICHARDSON, AUTHOR OF *STAND UP FOR YOUR LIFE*

"This superbly written, profound, and moving work addresses head-on the central question of our time: how to put meditation into action and so transform the real conditions of the real world. Its honesty and passion are liberating, and its message both timeless and acutely timely."
—ANDREW HARVEY, AUTHOR OF *THE DIRECT PATH* AND *SACRED ACTIVISM*

"Courageous and compelling, *Instinct for Freedom* is a vivid account of how one man's renunciation gave way to his own love and desire. This is a haunting and beautiful story, one full of teachings for seekers of all persuasions."
—MARK EPSTEIN, M.D., AUTHOR OF *GOING TO PIECES WITHOUT FALLING APART*

BURMA'S VOICE OF FREEDOM / VOLUME THREE

MEDIA AND SPEAKING INQUIRES FOR ALAN CLEMENTS

contact@**WorldDharma**.com

"How to describe Alan's presentations? A tall order. Love poems/riffs/odes/chants to the goddesses of compassion, deeply inscribed with the blood of Burmese slaves, soldiers in Iraq, Palestinian children, freedom fighters anywhere. A momentary entry into an internal tête-à-tête, ad infinitum; a glimpse at all that inner discursive dialog which marks us unequivocally as members of the human race. Just in case we get too spiritual, let's not forget that we are required to, by nature, include everything. To paraphrase the Vietnamese monk Thich Nhat Hahn's poem, "Please Call Me by My True Names," I am both the 12-year-old raped girl and the pirate who raped her. It is difficult to reconcile seeming opposites, and it takes the heart of a poet. Thich Nhat Hahn is a poet; Alan is one as well."

—MARCIA JACOBS, A PSYCHOTHERAPIST SPECIALIZING IN VICTIMS OF WAR, RAPE, AND TRAUMA; A SENIOR U.N. REPRESENTATIVE FOR REFUGEES IN BOSNIA AND CROATIA, 1993–1997; AND A FORMER OFFICER OF THE INTERNATIONAL WAR CRIMES TRIBUNAL

"Alan's life is material for a legend. An intellectual artist, freedom fighter, former Buddhist monk, he shares his insights and experience with a passion rarely seen and even more rarely lived. He'll make you think and feel in ways that challenge your entire way of being."

—CATHERINE INGRAM, *IN THE FOOTSTEPS OF GANDHI, PASSIONATE PRESENCE* AND *FACING EXTINCTION*

"I have known Alan for close to three decades. He is my first call when I seek insight and candor concerning personal and professional advice. As a speaker, his eloquence moves audiences to ask the questions behind questions about how we live, why we work, and how it fits together. Alan's presence—his remarkable ability to engage an audience, connect with their heart—stands alongside the best talent I have seen in the world."

—ROBERT CHARTOFF, PRODUCER OF ROCKY, THE RIGHT STUFF, AND RAGING BULL

"One of the most important and compelling voices of our times . . . Alan Clements is a riveting communicator — challenging and inspiring. He articulates the essentials of courage and leadership in a way that can stir people from all sectors of society into action; his voice is not only a great contribution during these changeful times, it is a needed one."

—JACK HEALY, FORMER DIRECTOR OF AMNESTY INTERNATIONAL, AND FOUNDER OF THE HUMAN RIGHTS ACTION CENTER

AUTHOR PROFILES

FERGUS HARLOW first "met" Alan Clements through Robert Anton Wilson's online Maybe Logic Academy in 2004, where Clements was conducting a course based on his book *"Instinct for Freedom"*. Harlow went on to become a key member of Clements' World Dharma Online Institute (WDOI) in 2007, and Clements has been a friend and mentor ever since.

From early 2013, Fergus has been Alan's personal assistant and colleague, working closely with him on producing all aspects of his World Dharma vision, including producing all aspects of these volumes; from initial fundraising efforts, to research, editing, and writing. Harlow compiled the Aung San Suu Kyi sections, as well as the latter part of the chronology, and transcribed and co-edited all of the interviews.

A keen student of yoga and the Dhamma, previous to this work he had been living and volunteering at various spiritual and retreat centres in the UK. He currently resides in Edinburgh, Scotland, where he is pursuing his own creative writing projects.